THE HEN HARRIER

Also by Donald Watson:

BIRDS OF MOOR AND MOUNTAIN

THE OXFORD BOOK OF BIRDS
(text by Bruce Campbell)

BIRDWATCHERS' YEAR
(contributor)

THE HEN HARRIER

By DONALD WATSON

T & A D POYSER

Berkhamsted

ISBN 0 85661 015 1

First published in 1977 by T. & A. D. Poyser Limited
281 High Street, Berkhamsted, Hertfordshire, England

Text set in 11/12 pt Photon Times, printed by photolithography
and bound in Great Britain at The Pitman Press, Bath

ERRATUM:

Page 200, 3rd line from foot of page
For 1971 read 1975

CONTENTS

Acknowledgements 9

Introduction 13

1 HARRIERS OF THE WORLD 19
General and specific characteristics 19
Origins and structural adaptations 34

2 IDENTIFICATION AND PLUMAGE 36
Comparison between Hen, Montagu's and Pallid Harriers 36
Albinism and melanism in Hen and Montagu's Harriers 41

PART ONE: THE HEN HARRIER

3 THE HISTORY OF THE HEN HARRIER
IN BRITAIN AND IRELAND 49
The decline 49
The recovery and present status 78

4 WHAT KIND OF PREDATOR? 86
Hunting methods 86
Hunting habitats 94
Food 95
Prey selection 105
Food consumption 107

5 THE BREEDING CYCLE: COURTSHIP
TO INCUBATION 109
Nesting habitats 109
Return to breeding grounds; pairing and courtship 112
The food pass and copulation 117
Nest building 119
The nest and nest sites 120
Social nesting 124
Polygyny 126
Neighbours 127
Laying and incubation 128

6 THE BREEDING CYCLE: HATCHING
   TO FLEDGING   130
   Hatching   130
   Feeding of chicks; hunting ranges and rhythms   131
   Development of chicks; mortality and cannibalism   134
   Other behaviour of chicks   137
   Breeding success and failure to breed   138
   Age of breeding birds   140
   Reactions to disturbance; predation on nests   141
   Moult of the adults   145
   The post-fledging period   147

7 MIGRATION AND WINTER DISTRIBUTION   149

8 THE HEN HARRIER AS AN ARTIST'S BIRD   158

   PART TWO: A STUDY OF THE HEN HARRIER
   IN SOUTH-WEST SCOTLAND
   Introductory note   167

9 THE BEGINNING: THE NINETEEN FIFTIES   170

10 WATCH IN THE HEATHER: THE FIRST NEST   172

11 MOORLAND NESTING: 1960–68   183

12 FOREST NESTING: 1965–75   196

13 WATCH FROM A HIDE   205

14 NEST SITES   218

15 BREEDING DATA   220

16 FOOD AND HUNTING GROUNDS IN THE
   BREEDING AREA   223

17 FOOD AND HUNTING GROUNDS IN WINTER   229

18 COMMUNAL ROOSTING IN WINTER   235

19 POSTSCRIPT: A CONTROVERSIAL BIRD   261

   Appendix 1: Local names of the Hen Harrier   267

   Appendix 2: Avian species mentioned in the text   269

   Appendix 3: Non-avian species mentioned in the text   271

   Appendix 4: Protection under the Acts of 1954 and 1967 272

   Bibliography   273

   Tables 1–30   281

   Index   301

COLOUR PLATES
(between pages 56–57)

1 Male and female Hen Harriers in forest breeding habitat

2 Nestling Hen Harriers

3 Female Hen Harrier brooding and feeding chicks

4 Hen Harriers over moorland breeding habitat
Marsh Hawks in typical habitat
Hen Harriers at winter roost

LIST OF FIGURES

1	Breeding ranges of harriers	22
2	Breeding ranges of Hen, Montagu's, Pallid and Pied Harriers	24
3	Winter and breeding ranges of Hen Harrier in Europe	25
4	Winter and breeding ranges of Marsh Hawk in North America	26
5	Breeding range of Montagu's Harrier in Europe	30
6	Winter and breeding ranges of Marsh Harrier in Europe	31
7	Status of Hen Harrier in Britain and Ireland c. 1825–1975	65–67
8	Recoveries of Hen Harrier in Scotland	153
9	Recoveries of Hen Harrier outside Scotland	154
10	Hen Harriers and nests in south-west Scotland	168
11	Hunting grounds in the breeding season in south-west Scotland	227
12	Sightings of Hen Harriers in four habitats, Sept–March	230–31
13	Numbers of Hen Harriers at Roost 1, Sept–March 1967–76	252–53
14	Aggregates of monthly peak counts of Hen Harriers at Roost 1	254
15	Aggregates of monthly peak counts of Hen Harriers at Roost 2	255

For Joan

ACKNOWLEDGEMENTS

This book is a blend of personal experience and wider study. Although more intensive work on some aspects of my subject may soon be published by others I hope that my book will interest the general reader as well as the more scientific ornithologist. Difficult as it is to strike a balance for differing tastes and degrees of knowledge I believe that there is a place for ornithological books which attempt this task.

I have received valuable help from a great many people. To mention them all individually would make a very long list. All those whose written communications have been referred to in the text will, I hope, find their names and the subjects in which they have particularly assisted, in the bibliography. I have received verbal information about Hen Harriers and related species from many others. To them all I express my warm thanks. There are, at the same time, a number of people without whose help the book could hardly have been written at all.

Eddie Balfour, the pioneer and acknowledged master of British Hen Harrier studies, not only gave me priceless information on his work but inspired me by his own monumental achievement in fieldwork and documentation of Orkney Hen Harriers. All those who knew him must have their own special memories of his quiet but dedicated enthusiasm which lasted for more than 40 years until his untimely death in 1974. Lately, James Cadbury has taken on the huge task of analysing Eddie's unique collection of data on Hen Harriers in Orkney and the full results of this will obviously be of great interest. Mrs Sunniva Green worked keenly with Eddie Balfour during his last few years and I am indebted to her for the loan of slides and for additional information, especially on harrier roosting in Orkney. I also owe a very special debt to Nick Picozzi who has recently researched extensively on Hen Harriers in Deeside and Orkney. He has somehow found time to read and comment on a large part of this book. His deep knowledge and professional approach have resulted in many improvements. The publication of his own work on Hen Harriers and their prey on a Kincardineshire moor is eagerly awaited.

I thank Bill Sinclair for kindly sending me tape recording of a lecture by Eddie Balfour on the Birds of Orkney.

I owe much to R. C. (Bert) Dickson who has studied Hen Harriers in

Galloway for many years and has sent me many communications on his findings, generously allowing me to make use of his data, especially on nests, food and roosting. Louis Urquhart has not only been a valued and expert companion on innumerable expeditions but has read and commented usefully on the text; he has frequently saved me from errors of detail. Chapter 17 owes much to the map on which he plotted over 250 winter sightings of Hen Harriers and he has freely shared with me his numerous personal observations. It is impossible to give adequate thanks to Dr Ken Brewster who has taken upon himself the role of intermediary with harrier students in many parts of the world, has lent me numerous important books and papers which I might never otherwise have seen and made many stimulating suggestions. I owe another very special debt to Desmond Nethersole-Thompson for allowing me to quote verbatim from his unique and colourful account of the old collectors, which he wrote specially for me. His personal knowledge of Hen Harriers in Orkney and in the Highlands has also been very valuable, while his son Bruin sent me his own interesting account of Hen Harrier nests in east Ross-shire.

Graham Williams gave me the benefit of his wide knowledge of Welsh Hen Harriers and even made a special visit to find out if harriers still featured on the inn sign at Llanuwchlyn, while he and Peter Schofield gave me a memorable introduction to the beautiful Welsh nesting grounds of the Hen Harrier. I am most grateful to Geoff Shaw for his help in several ways and for an account and map of the breeding areas in Central Scotland; and to Peter Strang for much valuable information on his 23 years in Hen Harrier country in Kintyre.

When I began this book, I knew little about the Hen Harrier in Ireland, although Major R. F. Ruttledge had kindly told me the basic details of the situation when I spoke to him some years earlier. From him I learned that Hen Harriers had never died out in Ireland. I had also met David Scott, the Secretary of the Irish Wildbird Conservancy, and discovered our common enthusiasm for Hen Harriers. When I wrote to him asking, hopefully, for a little information, I received almost daily letters, each crammed with news of Irish Hen Harriers, their history, distribution, nesting habitats and food. David Scott also sent me slides of a beautiful albino Hen Harrier. Much of this information came from his own fieldwork and researches but he supplemented it with contributions from harrier specialists in different parts of Ireland. I am extremely grateful to David Scott, but also to Ewart Jones, Ken Preston and Frank King for their willing help; the latter delighted me particularly with his news of an unusual Hen Harrier roost in County Kerry.

A young Dutch ornithologist, Jaap Rouwenhorst, who chanced to visit me in Scotland, has most kindly sent me useful information on harriers in Holland. Through him I was encouraged to approach W. Schipper, at the Ryks Instituut voor Natuurbeheer, who so helpfully sent me copies of his important papers on harriers and freely answered my questions. Dr E. Nieboer generously gave me one of the last remaining copies of his fascinating dissertation on 'Geographical and Ecological Differentiation in the Genus *Circus*'.

The late Ernest Blezard gave me the results of his expert analysis of pellets and remains; and more recently Ian Lyster, of the Royal Scottish Museum, has kindly done similar work for me. He has also allowed me to borrow numerous cabinet skins of harriers and given me every assistance on my visits to the museum. The Ringing and Migration Committee of the British Trust for Ornithology kindly allowed me the privilege of copying the recovery details of ringed Hen Harriers and I thank them; and particularly Bob Spencer and Chris Mead for making Chapter 7 possible. I also thank Chris Mead for giving me photocopies of his own maps which greatly helped in the preparation of mine. I am grateful to Tim Sharrock for sending me a pre-publication copy of the Hen Harrier map for the Atlas of Breeding Birds in Britain and Ireland and my thanks are due to the British Trust for Ornithology and the Irish Wildbird Conservancy for permission to use the Atlas map as a basis for my 1975 status map.

I much appreciate the facilities provided by John Davies, South Scotland Conservator, Forestry Commission, for studying harriers within the forests and also for smoothing my path on a visit to the forests of Kintyre. I also thank my many other friends among district officers, foresters and rangers in the Forestry Commission, for their assistance; John Corson, Alec Marshall, Mike Spernagel and Ian Watret have particularly helped by reporting sightings of Hen Harriers. Many other people have helped to make the South-west Scotland section of the book as complete as possible, notably K. W. W. Bartlett, Colin Campbell, Les Colley, Frank Dalziel, Sir Arthur Duncan, Dr and Mrs Kenneth Halliday, Raymond Hogg, David Irving, Richard Mearns, Mick Marquiss, the late Alan Mills, Dick Orton, Langley and Madelaine Roberts, Dick Roxburgh, Dr John Selwyn, Geoff Shaw, Brian Turner, Jeffrey Watson, David Whitaker, Jim Young and John Young. Both Will Dalziel and Jimmy Stewart, in the course of their shepherding work, became invaluable harrier watchers and gave me much friendly assistance. I thank Mrs E. Murray Usher, Mr A. Graham and Douglas Craig, as landowners and farmers, for their tolerance of my activities.

I have received useful information on harriers from many quarters and especially thank the following in addition to those already mentioned; D. J. Bates, Dr D. M. Bryant, Dr Bruce Campbell, the late Dr J. W. Campbell, David Clugston, Dr Peter Hopkins, Donnie Macdonald, John McKeand, Dr Ian Newton, Hugh Ouston, A. D. K. Ramsay, Dr Derek Ratcliffe, R. W. J. Smith, Bobby Smith, Alan Walker and Dr George Waterston. Tony Bell of the Institute of Terrestrial Ecology, Monkswood, willingly abstracted from his records all the data on analysis of harriers and their eggs.

Lars Svensson kindly sent me a copy of the Swedish journal, *Vår*

Fagelvärld, with his valuable paper on the identification problems of closely related harriers. Arthur Gilpin generously sent me prints of his fine photographs of a male Hen Harrier brooding chicks, and of a nest with a clutch of ten eggs. Harold Lowes also kindly gave me excellent photographs of Hen and Montagu's Harriers at the nest. Jim Young and Brian Turner allowed me to make full use of their photographic hide and I am especially grateful to the former for presenting me with a splendid selection of his Hen Harrier slides. My thanks are due, too, to Nick Picozzi, C. E. Palmar and Dr D. A. P. Cooke for making their excellent photographs available.

I thank Martin McColl and the Dumfries and Galloway Regional Library Service for going to the limit in providing me with books and for unfailing courtesy. I also thank the Librarian of the Edward Grey Institute for sending me an important paper. Trevor Poyser has been a most understanding publisher and shown great forbearance.

Finally I say thank you to my wife, Joan, for her prodigious work in typing the manuscript, for checking and often correcting my calculations and for her continuing encouragement and patience. All my family, too, have helped in various ways; Pamela by her constructive criticism of illustrations and Jeffrey by reading and improving much of the text as well as providing much help in the field; Katherine helped by abstracting the relevant passage in Turner's *Avium Praecipiuarum* from the Bodleian Library and Louise spent invaluable hours in sorting out the data on ringing recoveries and drawing maps.

Male Hen Harrier

INTRODUCTION

Before 1939, the disappearance of the Hen Harrier *Circus cyaneus* from most of the British Isles had the same apparent finality as that of the Osprey and the Sea Eagle. There was little chance of seeing a pair of Hen Harriers in the breeding season outside the Orkney islands and some of the Outer Hebrides or, possibly, in Ireland. When my family left the South of England and settled in Edinburgh in 1932, the horizon of my boyhood interest in birds was greatly broadened but did not extend to the haunts of harriers of any kind. I only once saw a Hen Harrier and this was a brown 'ringtail' in autumn. The colour plates of beautiful grey males by Thorburn and Lodge, which I had known since childhood, still represented an almost unattainable rarity. As a group, birds of prey attracted me no more than many others, but no young ornithologist could have failed to note that most of the larger predators, which figured prominently in the bird books, were sadly scarce. It did not require much reading to discover that this had not always been so and to learn that deliberate destruction by man and, in some instances, man's diminution of suitable habitat, were the principal explanations. In the first part of this book I have traced the history of the decline of the Hen Harrier and the recovery which has occurred since the 1939–45 war.

My first real encounter with any kind of harrier was with the Montagu's Harrier. In the first chapter, 'Harriers of the World', this and all other

Male Montagu's Harrier

species of the group are briefly discussed. In the summer of 1937 I went on a walking holiday in Western France with my friend Bernard Richardson. I found room in my large pack for a copy of Wardlaw Ramsay's *Birds of Europe and North Africa*, hardly an ideal field guide with its lack of illustrations, and with descriptions intended for collectors of specimens. Contrary to the prevailing view at home, that French birds were mainly to be found in cages, this expedition proved to be an ornithological revelation. There were Hoopoes, Woodchat Shrikes and Cirl Buntings in the public park of La Rochelle and, along the sun-baked coast, blue-grey cock Montagu's Harriers, elegant and graceful as big butterflies, were almost continually on view as they hunted low over the cut hayfields and marshy borders of creeks and ditches. As we climbed from the placid meadows and rich hardwoods of the Vienne valley to a wilderness of heath and birch in the foothills of the Auvergne, we were amazed at the abundance and variety of birds, including birds of prey. Once there were five kinds of raptor in view at the same time—a Sparrowhawk chasing a Goldfinch, several Kestrels and Buzzards, my first Red Kite, and two Hen Harriers which flew within thirty yards of us. Not far away we saw Goshawks and Hobbies too. At that time neither the landscape nor its birds could have changed much in the previous hundred years or more. The scene might almost have been in Perthshire before the era of game preservation had begun.

In those pre-war days nearly all the writers of books on British birds deplored the shooting, trapping and collecting which occurred, but until the 1954 Protection of Birds Act there was very little concerted opposition to any of these activities. Not much was known about the feeding habits of birds such as Hen Harriers. Ornithologists and game preservers were each apt to make categorical statements based on small amounts of local evidence. When the Hen Harrier started to recolonise the Scottish mainland, partly as a result of the lapse of gamekeeping on grouse moors during the 1939–45 war, there was no escaping the fact that it preyed partly on grouse, and keepers were understandably scornful of ornithologists who stuck by the statement in the *Handbook of British Birds* that it only occasionally did so. As any reader of this book will soon realise, I am an enthusaist for Hen Harriers and I hope I shall succeed in persuading some sceptics to share my views, but they can rest assured that I shall give an honest account of all I have learned about their habits as predators. No hawk continues to arouse more anger among grouse shooters and their keepers, so many of whom still destroy Hen Harriers ruthlessly in defiance of their legal status as a specially protected bird. Sometimes, its greatest crime is considered to be an ability to scatter driven grouse, as Golden Eagles, or even Herons, can do. In the words of the recently published booklet on predatory birds in Britain, 'whether [its] predation on game is significant is a matter of much debate but certainly the number taken varies from area to area and individual to individual'. The same booklet, however, makes it quite clear that game species *in the wild* (such as grouse) are not regarded in law as property and it is therefore against the law to destroy harriers of any kind for taking or disturbing grouse. Later in the book I return to this controversial subject and discuss the harrier as a hunter in Chapter Four, 'What kind of Predator?'. The postscript, Chapter Nineteen, is my 'case for the defence' of the Hen Harrier.

La Rochelle and that wonderful plateau in the Auvergne were already a distant memory when, in 1944, I discovered the unimaginable richness of bird life in the Arakan district of coastal Burma. Here, from October onwards, amid the devastation of war, the Pied Harrier, most beautiful of the tribe, sailed silently past our gun positions on many days; and Marsh and Pallid Harriers were frequently on view as well.

In all the brilliant diversity of resident birds and Siberian migrants, few were more satisfying to see than an old male Pied Harrier, in black, silver and white plumage, quartering the green, yellow and gold strips of the ripening paddy fields. I also liked to watch the delicate grey and white male Pallid Harriers but, without adequate reference books, it was difficult to identify females and the many young of the year. Back in the Indian Deccan, in 1945–46, vast expanses

Male Pied Harrier

of wilderness, interspersed with cultivation and vivid blue lakes, were the winter hunting grounds of large numbers of Pallid, Montagu's and Marsh Harriers. They often had little fear of man and one day a companion, for devilment, shot a magnificent cock Pallid as it pounced to the ground within easy range. For him it was just 'some kind of dicky bird' and he thought I was being ludicrous to protest.

There are several reasons why harriers, and particularly the Hen Harrier, have a special fascination for me. First, their rarity in my homeland, when I was young, made them something of a challenge. Then, when I first met numbers of them in France, they seemed to embody an exceptional combination of grace and power in flight, something which none of the old bird portraits had in the least conveyed. Also, there was the startling contrast in appearance between the sexes. No book illustration, even less any museum specimen, had given any idea of the conspicuousness of the light grey male when sunlit against a background of rich colour. This, no doubt, was why a cock Hen Harrier over heather moorland pleased me even more than the slightly darker Montagu's over cornfield, meadow or marsh: the male Hen Harrier was once aptly named the Seagull Hawk.

Like other harriers, a pair on their breeding grounds performs a food pass in which prey is dropped by the incoming male and caught by the female as they come together in flight. This is always a delight to watch. Even more arresting is the extraordinary display flight in which the male, and sometimes the female, abandons all restraint, rising and falling steeply in the sky above the nesting ground with a curious loose wing action, suggesting a wader more than a bird of prey. It is now seventeen years since I found my first Hen Harriers' nest. Each year I have learned something new. At times there is no more fearless bird in defence of its nest, yet some individuals are quite unaggressive. One of the rewards of a continuing study of one species is the realisation that the character of individuals differs widely and very little behaviour is predictable. An attacking Hen Harrier courts disaster from its human enemies but, for myself, this was yet another reason for admiration, doubtless unashamedly anthropomorphic.

The life history of the Hen Harrier is not in itself any more remarkable than that of many less dramatic birds. Among its most puzzling features are the tendency to colonial and often polygynous nesting and the association of quite large numbers in communal winter roosts. Similar manifestations occur, for instance, in the drab and exceedingly undramatic little Corn Bunting, studied in Cornwall by Ryves (who was also an enthusiast for Montagu's Harriers) and by my friend, Donnie Macdonald, in Sutherland. Perhaps I am a less dedicated ornithologist for choosing as my subject a bird which has been described as glamorous. When Trevor Poyser asked me to write and illustrate a bird book for publication I saw it as an opportunity to gather together what I have learned about a fine and controversial bird.

The study of birds in a particular region seems to me generally more worthwhile than scampering in all directions after anything unusual, and so this book contains a large section on the Hen Harriers of Galloway, in south-west Scotland. The breeding population of the species has never become high in this region but it is one of the more important wintering areas in the British Isles. Over the years I have kept detailed records of nesting and, in a particular area, have followed with interest the change from moorland to conifer forest sites. Not long ago I should have been very surprised to find nests in 14 year old forest but, in 1975, the three nests in one area were all in forest of that age. Nevertheless, there is evidence that open moorland continues to be the most important summer hunting ground. These matters are discussed in the section on The Hen Harrier in South-west Scotland, which also includes an account of observations made from a hide over a period of a month.

The re-discovery of the communal winter roosting habit, hardly mentioned in British writings since Jardine described it in 1834, encouraged me to pay equal attention to the life of the Hen Harrier in winter, so this also has an important place in the book. When Eddie Balfour, the acknowledged master of Hen Harrier study in Orkney, began to find winter roosts there, he said, with his slow smile: 'Isn't it wonderful?—now I can watch harriers all winter as well as summer'. If this sounds obsessional I can only add that some of my most unforgettable times with these birds have been in the cold and murk of winter dusks; and perhaps the most interesting problems of all are concerned with the purpose of communal gatherings and the dispersal of the birds which join them.

There was certainly an element of laziness in my liking for harriers. They are big, easily spotted birds and often most can be learned about them by sitting (or standing, in winter) in one place for a long time. I have never been short of patience for this sort of non-activity which many people find intensely frustrating. I claim that it allows me to combine an artist's work with an enjoyment of birds and landscape.

I have always been attracted, as a bird painter, by birds which bring a small focus of life to spacious surroundings and well understand the feelings of Henning Weis, the brilliant Danish pioneer of harrier study and photography, when he wrote of his Montagu's Harrier: 'It provides the enlivening element in its melancholy surroundings and has brought life to places that were waste and desolate before'. As a painter I am stimulated by birds with a range of plumage from the cryptic to the highly conspicuous. As a gleaming drake Goosander and his grey, chestnut-maned duck were irresistible in a setting of loch or river, so a pair of Hen Harriers could be related to great sweeps of hill and sky. The charm of nearly white subjects lies in their maximum susceptibility to every change of light and shade. They are like a sensitive instrument on which every colour note can be played. Dark, cryptically marked birds, like the female Hen Harrier, are at the opposite end of the scale, often merging subtly with their surroundings but, when brightly lit or silhouetted, they can provide the strongest note in a landscape. Never a facile draughtsman of flight, I found the rapid wing action of pigeons, Peregrines or ducks very difficult to suggest, but the apparently more leisurely flight of harriers, with frequent gliding and soaring, could possibly be conveyed without losing the all-important sense of movement. This book contains many pictures of Hen Harriers and some of their neighbours, including sketches made in the field, and it seemed appropriate to write one chapter of the text from a bird artist's point of view.

The opening chapters of this book discuss and compare all the different species of harriers. Next, in Part One I have dealt in some detail with the Hen Harrier's history and present status in Britain and Ireland, and continued with chapters on its hunting behaviour, food, breeding habits, migration and winter distribution. Part One concludes with the short chapter on the Hen Harrier as an artist sees it. Part Two consists of an account of my own field studies in south-west Scotland and includes data on breeding and food. The penultimate chapter of Part Two describes a long study of communal roosting in this region.

While the greater part of my own fieldwork on the Hen Harrier has been done in south-west Scotland (Galloway) I have watched Hen Harriers in many other important haunts and discussed the species with numerous ornithologists. It has been particularly interesting to find regional differences of breeding habitat and food. I have also researched into the most important European and American studies and have referred to relevant work in the other parts of the world.

Note: The Tables referred to throughout the text are to be found, for convenience of reference, at the end of the book, pages 281–99.

Marsh Harrier

CHAPTER ONE

HARRIERS OF THE WORLD

GENERAL AND SPECIFIC CHARACTERISTICS

The harriers (genus *Circus*) are all fairly large hawks with long, broad wings, long tails and legs and slim bodies. Different authorities recognise either nine or ten species (see Origins and Structural Adaptations, p. 34) and one or more species is found in every continent and on many islands. Their rather low wing-loading (the ratio of body weight to wing surface area), facilitates buoyant, sustained flight and even enables them to make considerable sea crossings in steady flapping flight. In such crossings they are less dependent than many raptors on assistance from rising air currents. Nick Picozzi, however, has seen a harrier, probably Montagu's, use thermals in company with other raptors when crossing the Bosphorus, but he noted that Hen Harriers used a high travelling flight on migration through the Pyrenees. Jeffrey Watson has observed Montagu's and Marsh Harriers on spring migration, crossing the Sahara in direct flapping flight at about 15 metres above the ground.

Harriers are capable of very high soaring flight in the manner of buzzards and eagles and most of them regularly soar at heights of a hundred metres or more when displaying in spring, and at such times perform spectacular aerobatics. All harriers have a remarkably similar outline in flight. When hunting the wings are flapped in an apparently leisurely manner, much interspersed by glides on stiff, slightly raised wings held in a very shallow 'V'. A non-ornithlogist once commented aptly on the 'hunch-shouldered' silhouette of a gliding Hen Harrier. Most harriers habitually hunt close to the ground, though some, like the Marsh Harrier, which frequently hunts over tall vegetation, tend to cruise higher than others. Prey is generally caught by a pounce or grab in which the long legs are used to maximum effect. While some species, including the Hen and Cinereous Harriers and the African Marsh Harrier, can take flying prey, the majority of harriers capture most of their prey on the ground.

All harriers are birds of relatively open country. Their long wings and comparatively laborious searching flight do not equip them for successful hunting in closed woodland. In Europe the Marsh Harrier is the most typical species of marshland but in its absence in North America the Hen Harrier (or Marsh Hawk) occupies this habitat as well as drier ground. Aversion to large tracts of high forest is well demonstrated by the distribution of the South American Long-winged Harrier. It occurs in Trinidad and Surinam, north of the equator, is entirely absent from a vast area of mainly tropical forest in Brazil, but is common further south in the pampas of Paraguay and Argentina. Apart from the Marsh Harriers, it is the only species of harrier which breeds both north[1] and south of the equator.

Most harrier species are wholly or partially migratory, exceptions being some of the island races of the Marsh Harrier and possibly the two entirely African species, the Black Harrier and the African Marsh Harrier. Some, like the Spotted Harrier of Australia, make restricted movements within a continent, while at the other extreme, the Pallid Harrier is a long distance traveller between breeding grounds in Central and Northern Europe and Asia and wintering grounds as far south as Sri Lanka in Asia and Cape Province in Africa. Some Pied, Montagu's and Marsh Harriers must also cross the equator on their migrations.

It is not surprising that a bird which generally shuns woodland almost invariably nests and roosts on the ground, in spite of the many risks which this entails. The only exception, at least in nesting, is the Spotted Harrier of Australia, which is, in many ways, the least typical member of the genus. It builds a large nest in a tree, sometimes in a tree-top, and is most often seen perching in trees though its hunting habits and food are very similar to those of other harriers.

The communal roosting of Hen Harriers in their winter quarters is described later in this book, but the habit is common to at least six of the ten species—Hen, Marsh, Pallid, Montagu's, Pied and Long-winged Harriers.

---

[1] Breeding of the Long-winged Harrier in the north of South America may be uncommon.

Montagu's   Imm.

Pallid   Imm.

Hen   Imm.

Pied   Imm.

Cinereous   Imm.

Marsh Hawk   Imm.

Black   Ad.   Imm.

Spotted   Ad.   Imm.

African Marsh   Ad.   Imm.

Light phase

Dark phase

Long winged   Imm.

Marsh (European)   Imm.

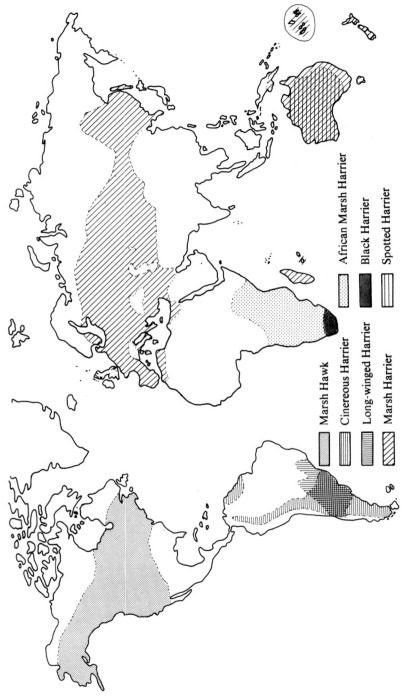

Marsh Hawk

Cinereous Harrier

Long-winged Harrier

Marsh Harrier

African Marsh Harrier

Black Harrier

Spotted Harrier

Fig. 1 Breeding ranges (for scientific names see Table 1, page 281)

Dresser (1878), recorded an observation of thousands of Montagu's Harriers collecting to roost in the Department of Vienne, France—sadly, such numbers of this species can only be dreamed of today. There are several accounts of smaller roosts of Montagu's Harriers, both in Europe and Africa. A spectacular roost of 160 Montagu's and Marsh Harriers in Kenya was described by Meinertzhagen (1956), and Delacour (1966) has told how, in the 1920s, he watched many Pied and Oriental Marsh Harriers settling noiselessly to roost in a marshy depression among the sand dunes near the western seaboard of Annam (Vietnam). In New Zealand, Gurr (1947) found a swamp roost of more than 100 Australasian Marsh Harriers. Communal roosts of Pallid Harriers are described by Ali and Ripley (1968) and others, both in India and Africa, while in Surinam Reussen (1973) observed up to 32 Long-winged Harriers gathering to roost in a flooded rice-field. Several writers have commented that the birds must collect from a vast area to join these roosts. While the habit is most common in winter quarters, Pallid Harriers have been found (Ali, 1968) to roost communally in ploughed fields or other bare ground during migration and Weis (1920) recorded roosts of Montagu's Harriers after the breeding season. He noted that adult males used a different part of the roosting ground from adult females and juveniles.

Most, and probably all, harriers have a similar pattern of behaviour in the breeding season, with the female incubating while the male brings the food, but the Spotted and Black Harriers are not sufficiently known for a positive statement to be made on this subject. The transfer of prey in flight in the food pass from male to female, in the nesting area, probably occurs in all the species. One remarkable feature of the Spotted Harrier, mentioned by Brown and Amadon, is the great length of the incubation and fledging period, which together are said to be 95–100 days, but they comment that this needs checking.

Some of the island races of the Marsh Harrier, like the Reunion Harrier, which might be classed as distinct species, are among the rarest birds in the world, but the rarest acknowledged species is the Black Harrier of Southern Africa. According to Peter Steyn this beautiful bird is found mainly in dry country. It hunts the Karroo regions of Cape Province, quite often over snow-covered slopes of the foothills. Steyn writes that virtually nothing is known of its breeding habits, but he believes that some nests are in wheat fields and one was found in fairly tall dry grassland.

While the categories of prey taken by the various harriers show considerable overlap—small mammals and birds being very generally taken—Schipper (1973) has shown that differences in size and structure affect their hunting agility and killing efficiency and reduce the overlap of species living in the same district beyond what might be expected from their superficially similar hunting behaviour. For instance Marsh Harriers, with the largest and most powerful feet, exploited heavier, less active prey while

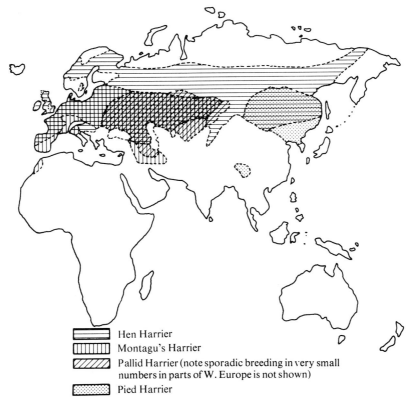

Hen Harrier
Montagu's Harrier
Pallid Harrier (note sporadic breeding in very small
  numbers in parts of W. Europe is not shown)
Pied Harrier

Fig. 2   Breeding ranges of Hen, Montagu's Pallid and Pied Harriers

the smaller footed Hen Harriers were particularly agile at catching full
grown passerine birds, but Montagu's Harriers, with the weakest feet, relied
particularly on young passerines, lizards and insects. Sexual dimorphism, in
size and structure, permits diversification of prey within a single species. The
breeding seasons of the three species, in Holland, began at different times
and this was a factor facilitating co-existence. Harriers which showed the
greatest differences in average weights of prey were most often hunting at
the same period. Nieboer (1973) considered that Montagu's Harrier was a
more agile hunter than the Hen Harrier, as might be expected from its
slimmer build and more buoyant flight, but Schipper suggests that the
relatively shorter, 'more fingered' wings of the Hen Harrier (more like those
of Accipiter hawks) provide greater manoeuvrability in capturing flying
prey.

Some harriers, certainly, occasionally kill young poultry but there is little
evidence that this is ever a major prey item. There are a few records of birds'
eggs as harrier food. Carrion, either road casualties or kills of other
predators, is probably more important to some harrier species than com-

monly recognised. Ronald Lockley tells me that the Australasian Marsh Harrier is very often seen on roads in New Zealand, feeding on birds or rabbits which have been killed by traffic. Brown and Amadon mention both Marsh Harriers in Africa feeding on the kills of larger predators, while the North American Hen Harrier depends to a large extent on roadside carrion in severe winter weather. Food studies (see Chapter 4) have shown that a single species of harrier may concentrate on quite different prey at different

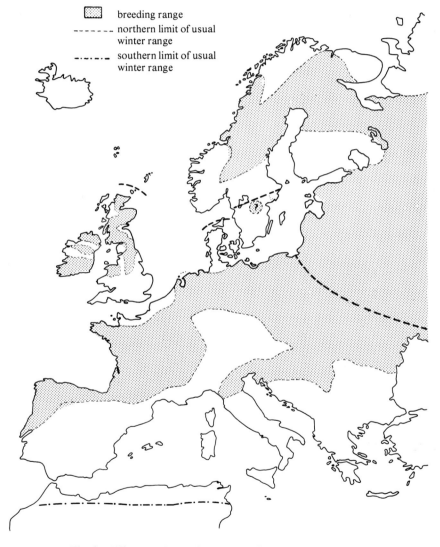

Fig. 3   Winter and breeding ranges of Hen Harrier in Europe

breeding range
northern limit
winter range
southern limit
winter range

Fig. 4   Winter and breeding ranges of Marsh Hawk in North America

seasons, even in the same locality. Montagu's Harriers, for instance, feed largely on birds and voles in the early part of their breeding season, but as summer advances lizards and large insects become important in their diet where they are available in Europe, and probably form the bulk of prey in African winter quarters. Neufeldt (1967) found that rodents made up 85% of the food of the Pied Harrier on its breeding grounds in Amurland, USSR, but in Burma, frogs and large insects are the main prey. Even the more powerful species such as the Marsh Harrier, whose food has been studied in detail by Schipper and others, take mainly young or injured specimens of their larger prey items such as pheasants, waterfowl and rabbits. Schipper has proved that the same individual Hen, Marsh or Montagu's Harrier takes prey of differing composition in different seasons, switching from voles to birds when the former are at a low density. There are many records of harriers feeding on fish but I have only found one observation of fish being caught alive, Ali and Ripley (1968) citing Willoughby P. Lowe's account of migrating harriers, probably Pallid Harriers, pursuing and catching flying fish as they skimmed over the waters of the Red Sea.

Females in harrier species are generally longer-winged and heavier than males. Schipper's studies of prey taken by Marsh and Hen Harriers show that in both species the average weight of prey taken by females was heavier than by males but Nieboer attributes this to the greater foot-size of the females. In the Montagu's Harrier the sexes are of nearly similar size and in the Pallid and Pied Harriers the size differences between the sexes are less than in most other members of the genus. No significant difference in average weight of prey taken by male and female Montagu's Harriers was established by Schipper. Nevertheless, male Montagu's Harriers, like male Hen Harriers, did capture more fledged or full-grown passerine birds, than did females. The possible hunting significance of the pale colouring of males in these and other harriers is discussed below.

Nieboer considers that sexual dimorphism of plumage in harriers is a special adaptation to life in open country, of relatively recent origin. He stresses that it is most marked in the harriers of the Holarctic region; its occurrence in the South American Cinereous Harrier favours the argument that this bird derives from North America.

No sexual dimorphism of plumage is found in the Spotted, Black or African Marsh Harriers and Nieboer considers that there is none in the Long-winged Harrier either. According to Brown and Amadon, however, the female of the latter species is most commonly browner than the male in the normal 'light phase' plumage. I have not seen any of the American harriers in life, but ever since I first saw a fine mounted specimen of the Long-winged Harrier in the Royal Scottish Museum many years ago, I have supposed this to be one of the finest members of the genus. With a wing length of over 480 mm in the largest females, it exceeds all other harriers in wing span. It is particularly handsome in the black, grey and white plumage phase and is described by Brown and Amadon as 'unmistakable and beautiful as it beats its way slowly across the rich green of the pampas'.

From my own field experience of the five European and Asiatic harriers I rate the Pied as the most beautiful. The species has been described as the eastern counterpart of Montagu's Harrier, which it much resembles in its slim elegant form, and there is a very similar distribution of darker and lighter areas in the plumage of the adult males, the grey parts in the Mon-

Pied Harriers, Arakan, Burma

tagu's being mostly replaced by black in the Pied. The latter species is strikingly longer in the leg than other harriers in its size range, and Nieboer considers that this may be correlated with a preference for hunting wet terrain with high vegetation. The main breeding grounds of the Pied Harrier are in south-east Siberia but it also breeds locally in Burma and in North Korea. A huge intervening area comprising Central and South China may, according to Neufeldt, have been made unsuitable for them within historic times as their breeding habitats were converted into cultivated fields.

Another very beautiful species must surely be the Black Harrier of Southern Africa. With its silvery underwing, white upper tail coverts and grey and black barred tail, the adult is really another pied bird. In both sexes of the Australian Spotted Harrier the slate-grey upper parts and chestnut below are spotted with white, but it lacks a definite white rump. It may perhaps be regarded as the most primitive type of harrier and is considered by Brown and Amadon to show affinities in plumage with the Serpent Eagles (genus Spilornis). The complicated group of Marsh Harriers has been divided into two species; the variable Marsh Harriers breeding in Europe, Asia, North Africa and Australasia, and the smaller, resident African Marsh Harrier. Anthony Buxton aptly described the Marsh Harrier as ruffianly in appearance, but an old cock is a striking bird, with silver grey on wings and tail contrasting with rich chocolate and orange-brown on his body and inner wing coverts. The flight is heavier, less buoyant-looking than that of other harriers—it is less dexterous at catching agile prey than Hen or Montagu's Harriers—but it is capable of magnificient aerobatics when displaying in spring. In the eastern race *C. a. spinolotus* the male is even more eye-catching, with head, neck, upper back and underparts white, streaked with black. Some other races are much darker—one has a black form—while all the females and immatures are predominantly dark brown birds, usually creamy or whitish on the crown of the head.

The reasons for the marked sexual colour difference in most harriers may be complex. The generally brown, rather inconspicuous colour of females has protective value when they are most vulnerable, on the nest. This adaptation probably arose during the early development of harriers when the birds nested in open country. The light-coloured and pied males are easily spotted by the human eye, particularly when they are making display flights, and this conspicuousness is certainly exhibited to the female during courtship. Jacques Delamain (1932) wrote of the male Montagu's Harrier at this stage: '. . . the bird successively exhibits to his companion [the female] his light breast and the silvery underside of wings'. The conspicuousness of adult males of most harrier species, from above, is increased by the openness of the terrain which they frequent and by the high proportion of time they spend on the wing, and this is particularly true when breeding grounds are first occupied in the spring. The intensity of aerial display by paired males in colonial groups might suggest that a striking plumage pattern is either a stimulus or a deterrent to other males.

Some species of harrier certainly show little territorial exclusiveness, so it would be difficult to support this explanation for the plumage colour of males. That their striking patterns have value as some kind of signal I do not doubt and it may be important in this respect that harriers, unlike many eagles and falcons, tend to nest in comparatively featureless country without obvious perching places where they could be quickly spotted by others of their kind. Also, some harriers, notably the Pallid Harrier, have a strongly nomadic tendency, sometimes seeking out new breeding areas distant from those formerly occupied if, in spring, the latter are unsuitable owing to fluctuations in the population of major prey such as voles. The conspicuousness of the male Pallid Harier could well have an important signalling value in a nomadic search for areas with adequate food. It might be significant, in the same way, that the Rough-legged Buzzard, with its conspicuous black and white tail pattern, is much more nomadic in its occupation of breeding grounds than the usually more uniformly coloured Common Buzzard. It can hardly be doubted that the striking white tail base, which occurs in so many of the otherwise protectively coloured female or immature harriers, also acts as a signal and may assist in attracting other harriers to good food locations. I have often wondered how widely scattered harriers, many of which may be strangers to an area, succeed in finding a communal roost and it seems reasonable to suppose that newcomers must first observe the flight direction of established birds, and they may even be able to spot the white tail base of brown harriers at great distances.

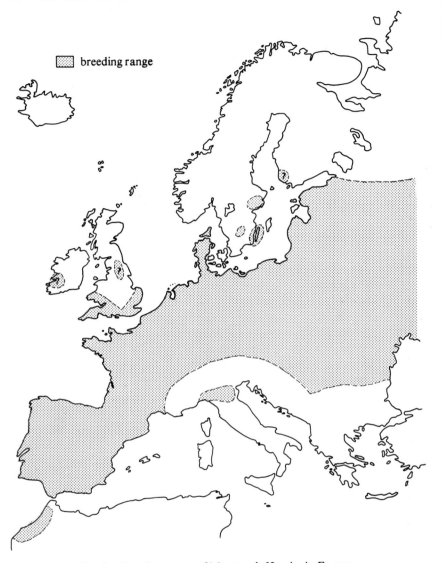

breeding range

Fig. 5   Breeding range of Montagu's Harrier in Europe

Nevertheless, there may be a more important hunting advantage in the pale grey plumage of male harriers, particularly their white undersides. It is said that the white underparts and generally pale colouring of gulls and other sea-birds make them more difficult to detect from below. Certainly, the vole's eye view of a hunting harrier must usually be a shape against the lightness of sky; so the paler tones of males may reduce their conspicuousness to such earth-bound prey. To some extent, even the darker

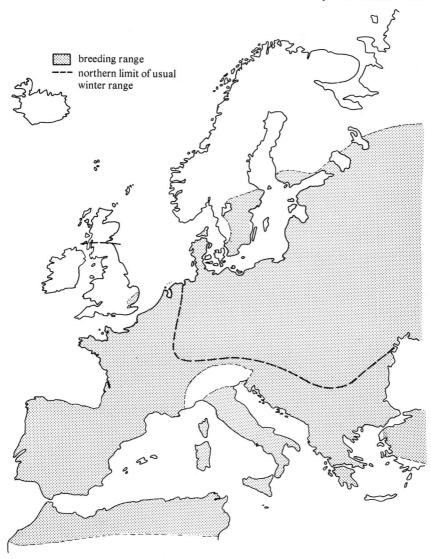

Fig. 6   Winter and breeding range of Marsh Harrier in Europe

females are relieved by pale or variegated tones on their underparts. A light-coloured bird, hunting in sunlight, casts a less dense shadow than a darker one. Since adult males bear the brunt of hunting for several months of the year, it is tempting to look for an advantage in their plumage colour; and it is interesting to learn that the Dutch ornithologist, Nieboer, in his study of the morphology of harriers (1973), concludes that pale colouring in males is indeed an advantage for hunting keen-sighted prey in open country. Support for this view comes from Schipper's findings that male Hen and Montagu's Harriers took more free-flying passerine birds than females did. In Montagu's Harriers, the size difference between the sexes is too slight to explain the males' greater efficiency in capturing agile prey. Yet light colouring is by no means universal in male harriers, the most obvious exception being the Black Harrier, which is blackest on its underparts.

Colour patterns can only be understood as a result of a balance of factors. While the conspicuousness of many male harriers may indeed have a visual importance, as I have suggested, and almost certainly has a hunting advantage,[1] the range of variation from the extremes of the Pallid to the Black Harrier, appears to be influenced by climatic factors. It is well-known that the intensity of melanistic pigmentation tends to decrease as the mean temperature decreases, and that humidity combined with heat favours dark pigmentation. Clearly, in females and immatures these factors have been much modified for survival, but they seem to provide a neat explanation for the general trends in the colours of adult males which, by taking no part in incubation or brooding the young, have much less need for cryptic colouration, although they are to some extent cryptically coloured as hunters. Certainly the palest male harriers are found in northern climates and the palest of all, the Pallid, breeds in an area of low summer rainfall, while the Pied Harrier is at least partly associated with a monsoon climate. Both the Black Harrier and the dark phase of the Long-winged Harrier, without definite sexual dimorphism, are predominantly dark birds and are found nearest the equator. The Montagu's Harrier, which ranges over similar latitudes to the Pied, has a melanistic form which occurs not infrequently. A study of its incidence would be interesting.

Montagu's, Marsh and Pallid Harriers in Britain and Ireland

The recent increase of the Hen Harrier in Britain, Ireland and Holland has occurred over a period when the breeding range of Montagu's Harrier has suffered a marked retraction. Nicholson estimated the Britain population of Montagu's Harriers as 40–50 pairs in 1957 and nests had been found as far north as Perthshire in 1952, 1953 and 1955 and in Kirkcudbrightshire in 1953. Parslow (1973) said, however, that a decline had begun in Britain by the mid 1950s, while by 1960 there had been some decrease in almost all the main British breeding areas. This has continued until in 1973 and 1974 there was no evidence of successful breeding at all in this country, although nesting was reported again in 1976.

Montagu's Harrier has lately been described as 'probably our rarest diur-

---

[1] Nieboer points out that the larger females (of Palearctic harriers) may be equally effective hunters, taking larger prey, but the pale colour of males may give them some compensatory advantage in hunting small, agile prey, within the limits of their capabilities, set by their smaller size and weaker feet.

Adult male Pallid Harrier

nal bird of prey' (Sharrock, 1973). It is a summer migrant (mid-April to October) to Britain where it has bred in a variety of habitats, but especially in young conifer forests and marshes. There have been a very few recent breeding records in Ireland. At the World Conference on Birds of Prey in 1975, a sharp decrease of Montagu's Harrier in many western European countries caused particular concern, but the reasons for this remain obscure. The possibility that climatic change is involved in the retraction of the Montagu's Harriers' breeding range, and the expansion of that of the Hen Harrier, springs to mind in view of the many examples of changes in the breeding ranges of other birds in which climatic change may be involved. Nevertheless I know of nothing to suggest how such changes could affect these harriers.

At the present time the Marsh Harrier is another very rare breeding bird in Britain. In 1974, breeding was reported from four sites, three of which were in Suffolk (Sharrock, 1975). This represented little change from the immediately preceding years but, earlier, in 1957–58, the British breeding population was apparently higher, at 12–14 pairs in East Anglia and about five pairs elsewhere, than at any time since the middle of the 19th century. In recent times nesting has been confined to low level marshland but prior to about 1840 the Marsh Harrier also nested quite widely on moorland bogs in England, Wales, southern Scotland and Ireland. Its disappearance from these haunts was partly the result of intense persecution by gamekeepers and others, but also it was probably more severely affected than the Hen Harrier by the drainage and reclamation of much bogland. It still, occasionally, appears in summer in this kind of habitat, in upland country, where I have seen it myself in southern Scotland. Since the middle of the 19th century its status as a breeding bird has nearly always been precarious and it became extinct in Britain for some years at the beginning of the 20th century and ceased to breed in Ireland after 1917. That it is a British breeding bird at all today is probably due to careful protection at its main nesting sites. Marsh Harriers are seen in all months of the year but most breeding birds appear to be summer visitors.

The Pallid Harrier is a very rare vagrant to Britain. It breeds mainly from Rumania eastwards but occasional irruptive movements have produced breeding records as far west as Sweden and South Germany.

ORIGINS AND STRUCTURAL ADAPTATIONS

Most authorities recognise ten species (see Table 1) but others (Voous 1960, Vaurie 1965, Nieboer 1973 et al) give the number of species as nine and regard the South American Cinereous Harrier as conspecific with the Hen Harriers (Hen Harrier and Marsh Hawk).[1] According to Nieboer, the whole group of harriers probably originated in the Palearctic region or at least in the Old World. He suggests that antecedents of the Hen Harrier may have colonised North America rather early in the Pleistocene era and fairly soon reached South America. The Hen Harrier may have originated as a species in North America and recolonised the Palearctic across the Bering Strait about the time of the last interglacial period. After this colonisation, the isolation of the most westerly population of these birds, in one of the glacial maxima, probably led to the specific separation of the Pallid Harrier, which developed a longer wing than the Hen Harrier as an adaptation to life in arid, open habitat with large seasonal fluctuations in temperature (Nieboer, cf Moreau 1955, Flint 1971). To escape severe winters it developed migratory habits. Nieboer further postulates that the Montagu's and Pied Harriers speciated in the Western and Eastern Palearctic respectively during one of the earlier glaciations. Their small size has probably resulted from sympatric living with larger species of harrier, especially the Marsh Harrier which hunts similar wet habitats to the Pied Harrier.

The Black Harrier of South Africa, the Spotted Harrier of Australasia and the Long-winged Harrier of South America may all, according to Nieboer, have originated from the common Palearctic stem. Both the Spotted and the Long-winged are presumed to be old forms, long established in their respective regions, and they show no close affinity to each other. Nieboer considers that it is a matter of speculation whether the Marsh Harriers originated in the Palearctic or in Africa.

The sympatric existence of up to four species of harrier of fairly similar size and weight in the Palearctic region has resulted in the development of

[1] Although the adult male plumage of the Cinereous Harrier differs considerably from the corresponding plumages of the Hen Harrier and Marsh Hawk Nieboer points out that some adult male Marsh Hawks are heavily marked suggesting an intermediate stage of colour pattern between them and the Cinereous Harrier. Possibly the strongest argument for specific separation of these harriers is the large gap between their geographical ranges. No harriers occur in apparently suitable habitats in the intervening area but they may have been there in the past and become extinct. The Cinereous Harrier may well be best regarded as the Hen Harrier of South America.

specialised differences in wing structure, length of tarsus and the structure and size of feet, claws and bill. A detailed account of these morphological differences has been given by Nieboer (1973). He has much interesting information on the ways in which structural differences are connected with hunting techniques and preferred hunting habitats. Schipper's study of sympatric Hen, Montagu's and Marsh Harriers is referred to later in this book.

Some examples of the operation of specialised structure may be cited from Nieboer; in Western Europe the larger species of harriers have absolutely, and relatively, longer legs than the smaller species and this may be correlated with the height of vegetation preferred for hunting. Thus, the Marsh Harrier hunts tall vegetation, the Montagu's low and open vegetation, and the Hen Harrier is intermediate in this respect. In Eastern Asia, the rather similar sized Hen and Pied Harriers prefer respectively drier and wetter hunting grounds, and there it is the Pied and Marsh Harriers (both long-legged species) which are sympatric, particularly favouring bogs and marshes. Hunting competition between them appears to be limited by a considerable difference both in body size and in the dimensions of the toes, claws and bill. In the central Palearctic the Hen, Montagu's and Pallid Harriers live in association and differences in wing structure may be important in enabling them to select different ranges of prey.

Nieboer emphasises the close affinity between the Hen and Pallid Harriers and likens the latter to a specialised Hen Harrier. He speculates on the possibility that hybridisation between these species might occasionally occur. Frank King believes that a male Montagu's Harrier may have been mated to a female Hen Harrier at a nest in southern Ireland. No proof of this was obtained and it must be said that hybrids between these two species seem very unlikely to occur.

Various explanations have been offered for the general rule that females are usually larger than males in birds of prey (except the vultures). It is certainly true that in the harriers the role of nest defence, in the prolonged absence of the hunting males, is largely assumed by the females. Their size preponderance, as Nieboer believes, might have developed as an adaptation to this role.

Immature Montagu's Harrier

Montagu's Harrier, female

Hen Harrier, female

Pallid Harrier, female

CHAPTER TWO

IDENTIFICATION AND PLUMAGES

COMPARISON BETWEEN HEN, MONTAGU'S AND PALLID HARRIERS

The very striking difference between the male and female Hen Harrier, in adult plumage, is shown in colour plate 1. The brown female (about 50 centimetres long) is noticeably larger and heavier than the grey male (about 45 centimetres long). Although the latter is pale enough in colour to suggest a gull, in the distance, his broad, black wing-ends are very distinctive. The characteristic outline and wing action, already described, further preclude confusion with gulls. The female's white rump, contrasting with her much darker plumage, is correspondingly more conspicuous than that of the male.

Field identification of all Hen Harriers is generally only difficult in so far as separation from other species of harrier is concerned. Yet, when seen from below as a silhouette in soaring flight, a Hen Harrier might sometimes be confused with a Goshawk, since both have long broad wings and fairly long tails. There is little difficulty in distinguishing buzzards from harriers at such times, as the former have relatively shorter tails and are more heavily built.

The difference in outline and build between Hen and Montagu's Harriers has been likened to the difference between gull and tern but this, of course, is an over-simplification. I recall watching a grey cock harrier approaching from a great distance in the foothills of the Auvergne mountains in France. In the bright summer light it looked as pale as the cock Hen Harriers I had lately seen in Scotland and it was only when it came near enough to see the

36

black centre lines on the wing and the red brown streaks on the underparts that I was certain it was a Montagu's. The absence of a white rump in adult male Montagu's is not always helpful in very strong light. Nevertheless, there *are* real differences in shape and flight between Hen and Montagu's. The wings of the latter are more slender and finely tapered, showing only three distinctly long flight feathers against the Hen Harrier's four. (Caution is needed here as I have seen a female Hen Harrier in summer moult with only three long primaries on each wing and no obvious gap where the fourth had been moulted, see p. 186).

In males, the wing of the Montagu's is distinctly longer than that of the Hen Harrier, but in females there is little difference in this respect. In both sexes, however, the wing-tip primaries are distinctly longer in the Montagu's. The wing movements of the Montagu's are generally looser, more willowy than those of the Hen—hence the comparison with tern or gull. Family groups of Montagu's over the tamarisks and reed-fringed creeks of La Vêndée, looked to me altogether slighter and more buoyant in flight than Hen Harriers. I also thought their tails seemed relatively longer and narrower. The shape of the head is another useful distinction: Hen Harriers have broader, more owlish heads and shorter necks than Montagu's and have a much more obvious neck-ruff.

The American Marsh Hawk is regarded as conspecific with the Hen Harrier of the Old World, but in the adult male Marsh Hawk the black wing ends are not so clear cut, the grey upper parts not so clean looking, and red-brown spots are retained on the underparts throughout life, while these are a mark of comparative youth in male Hen Harriers.

Although many female Hen Harriers have a less contrasted facial pattern than the typical female Montagu's this cannot, in my opinion, be taken as a reliable distinction. There is great variation among individuals of either species, some Hen Harriers having very striking whitish eyebrows and faces, contrasting with dark ear coverts, while Anthony Buxton photographed an old female Montagu's which had almost no facial pattern.

Adult females of the Marsh Hawk and Hen Harrier are similar, but juveniles differ as described below. The Marsh Hawk is a slightly heavier and longer-legged bird.

Female Pallid Harriers are about the same size and shape as Montagu's and look very similar in the field. In a discussion of all the possible ways of distinguishing females of these two species, Lars Svensson concluded that the most useful field character was the pattern of head and neck; in the Pallid the dark ear coverts are contrasted with a light ruff which is virtually absent in the Montagu's. Thus, in females, both Hen and Pallid Harriers show a more prominent neck ruff than Montagu's. In the Pallid this looks especially noticeable because the neck below the ruff is darker. Svensson also showed that the contrast between the light cheeks and the dark line through the eye was clearest in the female Pallid. The adult male Pallid

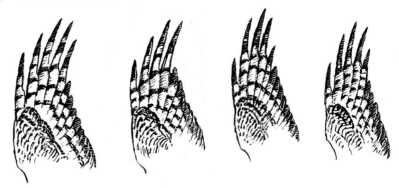

Underwings of (l. to r.): Hen Harrier, female; Hen Harrier female with 5th primary moulted; Montagu's Harrier; Pallid Harrier

Harrier is the palest of the three, but may not look obviously paler than an old male Hen Harrier on the back and wings. It is, however, much paler on head and breast which do not contrast markedly with the white underparts and it has noticeably less black on the wing tips than male Hen or Montagu's. It has no white rump.

Male and female Montagu's differ little in size, but male Pallids, like male Hen Harriers, are distinctly smaller than females. Between Pallid and Hen Harriers there is a noticeable difference in the shape of the wing, caused by the distinctly longer wing-tip primaries of the Pallid (in both sexes), but these are still longer in the Montagu's Harrier.

Juvenile Hen Harriers of either sex look very much like older females, but the ground colour of their heavily streaked underparts is a deeper tawny shade. For the first few weeks after fledging, they can be recognised at a distance by their shorter wings and tails, their darker upper parts with some fairly distinct pale cinnamon edgings on scapulars and wing coverts, and their more contrasted tail bars of sepia and cinnamon with a definite, narrow pale terminal band. None of these features persist for long and it must be remembered that freshly grown feathers on adult females may show almost as much contrast in the tail.

Nestlings can be sexed by iris colour and leg thickness, usually when about two weeks old (even at ten days, according to Scharf and Balfour, 1971), but in some instances this cannot be done reliably for a further week. Small chicks have very dark brown eyes which become chocolate brown in females and cloudy grey in males. It is usually fairly easy to distinguish the stouter legs of females from the thinner legs of males but special care is required if there is much difference in the ages of a brood. Details of the changes in the appearance of nestlings are given in Chapter 6. At fledging, females may be over 100 grams heavier than males. Young Montagu's and Pallid Harriers can be distinguished from young Hen Harriers, as soon as they are feathered, by their unstreaked vinous brown underparts. Some

European readers may be surprised to learn that the underparts of young Marsh Hawks are the same rich colour, streaked on the upper breast only.[1]

Throughout the first year young male Hen Harriers remain in brown plumage, similar to females. According to the *Handbook of British Birds*, however, moult into grey plumage occasionally begins as early as March of the first year, but generally the first grey feathers on head, breast and greater wing coverts do not appear till July or August.

[1] Nieboer (1973) found two specimens of juvenile Hen Harriers (both females) from East Asia with nearly unstreaked underparts like young Marsh Hawks. This clearly raises the possibility that the report of an immature Marsh Hawk (*C.c.hudsonius*) at Cley, Norfolk, in winter 1957–58 (Wallace, 1971 et seq), might have referred to an immature Hen Harrier (*C.c.cyaneus*). I have not read any plumage details of a more recent unconfirmed report of a Marsh Hawk at Saltfleetby, Lincolnshire, 18–30 November 1973 (*British Birds 67.2*).

Hen Harrier, female

Hen Harrier, male

A breeding male, which I presumed to be just over one year old, was parti-coloured on 16 August; grey on head and breast, with prominent red-brown spots or streaks on the flanks and belly, two or three new black feathers among the old, brown, barred outer primaries, and the tail had one or two new grey feathers. From above, the wings showed a grey middle area, caused mainly by the new greater coverts. Most of the back and scapulars still looked dusky brown, making the white rump conspicuous. I saw this bird well enough to establish that its iris colour was not yellow or light at all. I could say positively that it was dark but not precisely what colour. Montagu, in 1805, noted that his captive yearling male had 'dull yellow' eyes by June, changing to orange by 20th August, but Eddie Balfour gave the iris colour of one year old males in the wild as bright yellow, with no subsequent change.

I have examined a range of skins of males, not one of which was of known age, but a bird killed in February matched closely with a February bird preserved by Eddie Balfour and known to be 20 months old. These specimens suggest that throughout their second winter male Hen Harriers are distinctive enough to be aged fairly accurately. The most striking feature of these second year birds is the very dark area on the scapulars and mantle which contrasts with the mainly grey wings and tail. The wings are, in fact, much less pure grey than in older males but they are quite grey enough for the contrast mentioned to be picked out easily at considerable distances. When watching birds at a winter roost I have seen many males in this plumage. In some cases it may not be possible to decide whether a fairly 'dark-backed' male is in its second or third winter, as even third winter birds may show appreciably more contrast between 'back' and wings than older birds.

There are really three plumage features which indicate that a male is a relatively young bird: (1) dark brown-tinged mantle and scapulars; (2) red-brown spots and lines on flanks and belly; (3) a patch of buff and brown streaks on the nape. I do not know at what age all these features are lost. A high proportion of skins of 'grey' males show the streaked nape patch and it appears in an old illustration of an adult male. I suspect that birds which completely lack this feature are at least four or five years old. As Anthony Buxton (1946) noticed in his Norfolk Montagu's, there is a great range of variation in the aesthetic beauty of individual Hen Harriers, especially males. Very many of these fall sadly short of the perfection of really old males with their immaculate pattern of blue-grey, white and black. The latter retain the merest wash of brown on some of the long scapular feathers, only detectable at close range. Montagu, who originally demonstrated the moult of a captive first summer male from brown to mainly grey plumage, said that this took three to four months and was completed by mid-October.

Identification plates of grey males in flight are sometimes misleading on the colour of the trailing edge of the wing. This varies according to age. In

older males this border is grey on the white under-side and absent altogether on the upper surface. In younger males it is darker grey below, often looking blackish in the field, and there is a similar but much fainter border above.

There is great variation in the ground colour of mature females. Eddie Balfour found that the palest and most grey-brown birds were among the oldest but there is probably much variation independent of age. An important point to remember is that freshly-grown feathers are darker than old ones and, therefore, the same bird varies in appearance; and moult makes the upper parts of females look patchy, dark and light brown. The most important guide to age in females is the iris colour, as Balfour demonstrated. His original assessment, in 1970, was as follows: pale chocolate at one year, amber at three to four years, and bright yellow at six to seven. On close examination he found that the brown in a one year old bird was present as numerous small flecks on a background of yellow. In 1974 he told me that the above assessment needed qualifying as he had found that three to four year old females occasionally had bright yellow eyes. He also had some evidence that very old females had the palest yellow eyes.

ALBINISM AND MELANISM IN HEN AND MONTAGU'S HARRIERS

Albinism

Bryan L. Sage (1962) listed the British species in which albinism and melanism had been recorded. The only harrier in which albinism was known was the Hen Harrier. Melanism, among British harriers, was then only recorded for Marsh and Montagu's, the latter having a well-known melanistic form.

Wholly or largely white Hen Harriers have been killed at least six times in Scotland. One has almost certainly been seen in Wales, and one has been killed in Ireland. The details of these are as follows:

(1) 'A beautiful female', shot, Loch Carron, Ross-shire, May 1870. Mentioned by Robert Gray.

(2) 'A very fine albino', sex not given. Preserved at Barrogil Castle, ?

Studies of albinistic Hen Harrier: top left, male, Ireland; top right, male (chick), Orkney; bottom left, female (immature), Orkney; male (adult), Orkney

Sutherland. Before 1887. Mentioned by Harvie-Brown and Buckley.

(3) Juvenile, shot in Orkney, August 1937. Seen by Eddie Balfour earlier that summer. Now preserved as a mounted specimen in Stromness Museum. (See drawing on p. 42.) Almost all white except for brown nape, sides of head, streaks on upper breast and wash on inner secondaries; white claws. (see below).

(4) Male, adult, shot in Orkney, June 1938. Skin now in the Royal Scottish Museum, Edinburgh. I have seen this specimen; the entire plumage is almost pure white and it must have been a most beautiful bird in life. Eddie Balfour told me that he had watched the bird in 1938 and that it disappeared during a few days in June when he was absent from the island. It was evidently killed by someone on behalf of the late F. Nisbet of Pitlochry, whose collection was left to the museum. Some 20 years later Eddie Balfour was looking at the harrier skins there and so discovered the fate of the bird whose disappearance had always been a mystery to him.

(5) Male, age unknown, Perthshire, 194?. The late Dr J. W. Campbell told me that he had seen this bird which was virtually all white. Believed shot.

(6) Male, preserved at Treumland House, Orkney. I have no details.

Eddie Balfour told me that in Orkney (in over 40 years) he had seen about twelve birds which had had a 'large amount' of white. He remembered one other pure white bird which was alive when he was a boy, before 1920. He had seen many birds with a crescent, only, of white and over twenty with traces of white. Birds with white claws are fairly common. It is therefore clear that there is a strong tendency towards albinism in the Orkney population and it is, of course, possible that all the specimens described originated from Orkney. Sage cites inbreeding as one cause of albinism and this might be true in Orkney, but the recent catching and marking of breeding adults there has shown that only 23% of the 83 caught had been ringed as young on the island, though a large proportion of the young have been ringed for many years; it is therefore likely that immigrants are continually mixing with the island stock. There is, presumably, some form of hereditary albinism in the Orkney population, but Nick Picozzi reports that he found no trace of albinism in 44 young and 24 adults in 1975.

(7) Sex unknown. On 31 May 1970, D. J. Bates, R. J. McCann and J. R. Mullins had a brief view of a creamy or buffish white harrier, almost certainly a Hen Harrier, over a young forest plantation in North Wales.

(8) Male, Ireland; shot in the north of Co. Tipperary, early 1971; examined in the flesh and photographed by David Scott. It was almost pure white with a few dark dots on the head and a trace of grey on the wings.

None of the birds listed can be described, positively, as true albinos; there are no records of iris colour. Frank King has seen a male in Ireland with two white primaries on one wing.

Melanistic Montagu's Harrier

Melanism

Sage said that this was certainly a much less frequent occurrence than albinism, but went on to distinguish between 'normal melanism' which is found regularly in some dimorphic (or polymorphic) species, such as the Montagu's Harrier, and 'abnormal melanism', which occurs in isolated individuals of species with no melanistic phase but which occasionally becomes established and replaces the normal form. There is no evidence that the Hen Harrier has a normal melanistic phase, but an example of melanism has kindly been reported to me by David L. Clugston. This was first seen on 6 July 1968, when the bird was a downy chick in a brood of three (the other two normal) in a nest in North Wales. David Clugston's photograph clearly shows that the melanistic chick was sooty grey, much darker than the others. Very fortunately, all three chicks fledged and were seen on 28 July by D. L. C., J. R. Mullins, R. J. McCann and Dr R. J. Raines. The melanistic juvenile was described by D. L. C. as follows: 'Whole body, wings and tail plumage brown-black showing no sign of pale or white rump. At close range, wing coverts, tail and upper parts showed grey-brown tinge. Legs bright orange-yellow. The other two juveniles resembled the female with prominent white rump, but underparts rich red-brown, heavily streaked black-brown'. Good views were obtained of both parents. The female was typical but the male was considered less so; no white rump was apparent and the male also had a few dark feathers 'near the hind wing . . . . and in the tail'. These perhaps might have been due to comparative youth, but not the absence of a white rump. Strangely, also in July 1968, I saw a chick in a Galloway brood of three which was appreciably darker than its fellows when in down, but it appeared normal when feathered.

On 29 June 1976, again in Galloway, one chick in a brood of three was dark leaden-grey at the downy stage, strikingly darker than the others. It appeared to be a female and when almost fledged its plumage colour differed from the others (both males) in the following ways: all the white upper tail-covert feathers had conspicuous drop-like dark brown mesial streaks; the ground colour of the underparts was richer red-brown and the streaks heavier and darker; the general colour of the upper parts was darker brown, almost black on the primary wing feathers and nearly obscuring the cross bars; the rufous-buff on ruff, nape and wing-coverts was darker and so less prominent; the normal cinnamon-buff tail bars were replaced by distinctly deeper more rufous colour. Although this bird had the dark brown iris

Melanistic and normal Hen Harrier chicks

colour of a female the legs were not as thick as expected, and the possibility that it was a male was not conclusively ruled out. It appeared to be an example of partial melanism and it seems possible that this may have had a darkening effect on the iris colour.

The melanistic form of Montagu's Harrier is generally brownish-black with a greyish tinge on the throat and upper parts, including the wings and tail. Some are more or less coal-black—Ryves (1968) saw a 'magnificent coal-black female' at a nest. In this form both sexes are without any white on the rump. It is notable that neither Weis in Denmark nor Buxton in Norfolk, both of whom saw many pairs of Montagu's over a number of years, made any reference to melanistic individuals, but in south-west England, Ryves and others noted them fairly frequently, and Delamain described melanistic individuals in France. Lawrence G. Holloway informs me that on many visits to Andalusia, Majorca and Morocco, during which Montagu's Harriers were often seen, he had no records of melanism. He did, however, see one apparently partially melanistic male near Zahara (Provincia de Cadiz) in September 1971.

PART I

THE HEN HARRIER

CHAPTER THREE

HISTORY OF THE HEN HARRIER IN BRITAIN AND IRELAND

THE DECLINE

The inhabitants of these islands must have been familiar with the appearance of Hen Harriers long before any written reference was made to the species. It may be speculated that, in mediaeval times, the very extensive forest cover limited the amount of suitable habitat in many parts of the country and Hen Harriers may well have increased as more forest disappeared. There is evidence that they were already well-known in the 16th century.

Writers, however, were not aware that the grey male and the brown ringtail were the same species. No doubt illiterate countrymen who had found the birds' nest could have enlightened the scribes on this point. The earliest written reference to the Hen Harrier that I have seen occurs in a colourful poem, in Middle Scots, by William Dunbar. This poem, 'The Fenyeit Freir of Tungland' (Tongland, in the Stewartry of Kirkcudbright), was written about 1504. In it, over 20 kinds of birds are named as attacking the false Italian abbot, John Damian, when he made his disastrous attempt at flying with a pair of 'wingis of fedderis'. According to Bishop Leslie he 'flew of the castle wall of Striveling, but schortlie he fell to the ground and brak his thee (thigh) bane, bot the wyte (blame) thereof he asscryvit to that thair was some hen fedderis in the wingis, quhilk yarnit (which yearn for) and covet the mydding (midden) and not the skyis'. Dunbar's sympathy was all with the birds whose element was being invaded, though his main concern was to ridicule a personal enemy who had won favour with the King for his alleged skills with drugs and medicines. There is no doubt that in the following passage from the poem, 'Sanct Martynis fowle' was the male Hen Harrier—Le Busard St Martin survives today as the French name for the species.

> *The myttane and Sanct Martynis fowle,*
> *Wend he had been the hornit howle,*
> *They set upon him with a yowle*
> *And gaif him dint for dint.*

The name 'myttane' has not been ascribed to any particular bird of prey, merely 'some kind of hawk' according to dictionary definitions, but it is probable that Dunbar was referring here to the ringtail harrier, the female. In making this suggestion I am influenced by the fact that in this and other poems he identifies no less than nine kinds of eagle, hawk or falcon specifically—Golden Eagle, Sea Eagle, Sparrowhawk, Goshawk, Peregrine, Merlin, Kestrel, Buzzard and Kite—and the one obvious gap would be filled by ascribing 'myttane' to a ringtail harrier. It seems to me very unlikely that a man so knowledgeable on birds of prey would have used 'myttane' in a purely general sense. The linking of the 'myttane' and 'Sanct Martynis fowle' in a joint assault, as on 'the hornit howle', strongly suggests that Dunbar had observed a pair of harriers diving at a Long-eared or perhaps an Eagle Owl exactly in the manner that has been exploited by shooters and research workers in modern times.

Dunbar was probably brought up in the shadow of the Lammermuir hills, in East Lothian, where Hen Harriers must then have been an everyday sight—they were still breeding there into the 19th century. As an envoy of King James IV of Scotland he is known to have visited France and may have seen them there as well—and possibly seen Eagle Owls used as lures. There, also, he might have learned the French name, l'oiseau St Martin, derived from their customary arrival as migrants in France about 11 November, St Martin's day.

The first real description of the Hen Harrier in the British Isles, was written by Dr William Turner, in his *Avium Praecipuarum* of 1544, the first printed bird book. James Fisher has called Turner the father of British Ornithology. A. H. Evans, author of *A Fauna of the Tweed Area* (1903), translated Turner's Latin into English. Turner's object in writing his treatise was to determine the principal kinds of birds named by Aristotle and Pliny, but he added his own first-hand observations which reveal him as a percipient field ornithologist of his time. Of the Hen Harrier he wrote (Evans' translation): 'The Rubetarius I think to be that Hawk which English people

name Hen Harroer. Further it gets its name among our countrymen, from butchering their fowls. It exceeds the Palumbarius[1] in size and is in colour ashen. It suddenly strikes birds when sitting in the fields upon the ground, as well as fowls in towns and villages. Baulked of its prey it steals off silently, nor does it ever make a second swoop. It flies along the ground the most of all. The Subbuteo I think to be that hawk which Englishmen call Ringtail from the ring of white that reaches round the tail. In colour it is midway from fulvous to black; it is a little smaller than the Buteo, but much more active. It catches prey in the same manner as the bird above'. Turner, therefore, did not recognise the relationship between the (male) Hen Harrier and the ringtail. His note is, however, important in other ways; it leaves no doubt about the origin of the name 'Hen Harrier' and proves that in the 16th century it was already an unpopular predator, ripe for persecution because of its partiality for poultry, and not averse to hunting among human habitation, as it still does in Orkney and the Outer Hebrides. All 'ashen' plumaged harriers were then known as Hen Harriers, the Montagu's not being distinguished until Montagu described it in 1802. Sir Robert Sibbald, in his *Scotia Illustrata* (1684), jointly lists the *Subbuteo* (Ringtail) and *Buteus albus* (White Hawk) and has some claim to be the first writer to recognise the relationship between the male and female Hen Harrier; at least he says that some people consider them the same kind of bird.

How numerous or widespread the Hen Harrier may have been in these distant times is a matter of conjecture. It might have been otherwise had it been valuable to falconers, like the Peregrine—one Peregrine eyrie, still occupied in the twentieth century, is recorded as far back as 1564, and others

[1] Possibly the Goshawk, but the reference to size is more suggestive of Sparrowhawk.

can be traced back over 300 years. Before the period of large-scale enclosure and improvement of 'wasteland', in the 18th–19th centuries, there was clearly a vast amount of heath and moorland, even in regions like the English Midlands. W. G. Hoskins (1955) considered there were about seven million acres of 'heaths, moors, mountains and barren lands' in England and Wales alone. Such ground, with the extensive undrained bogs and marshes, must have provided much greater areas of suitable nesting country for harriers than have ever existed since. There is plenty of evidence, as I shall show, that the bird was common in many places even at the beginning of the 19th century, when land improvement and the killing of predators in the interests of game preservation had begun to take effect, and it can hardly be doubted that it was much more plentiful still a hundred or so years earlier.

It is extremely difficult to say how far its numbers were kept down by the rather haphazard attempts to reduce predators in the 16th–17th centuries. An act of the English Parliament of 1566, 'for the preservation of Grayne', included the 'Ryngtale' among birds and mammals for whose destruction a payment of two pence was made. 'Busardes, Shagges and Cormorants' were given the same rating, but Ospreys and Herons, at four pence a head, rated higher on the vermin scale, so it looks as if the Act was more concerned with the preservation of fish than grain. Doubtless harriers and buzzards were outlawed, principally as dangerous to poultry, the Bullfinch as a destroyer of fruit buds and the Green Woodpecker (Woodwall) for damage to trees, perhaps especially orchard trees. Heads of these last two and 'Kinges Fysshers' (these were sometimes Dippers) made only one penny each.

Details of predator destruction and payments made are recorded, to a varying extent, in the Churchwardens' Accounts of English parishes. N. F. Ticehurst (1920) examined these for Tenterden, Kent, for a long period, 1626–1712. All the harrier entries were entered as ringtails in these and others I have seen—only 20 individuals in the whole period at Tenterden, all between 1679–1689. Obviously 'vermin' control was spasmodic, but Ticehurst concluded that Hen Harriers were not common in the Kentish Weald, probably because it was still heavily wooded. The taking of four birds in May 1681, however, probably indicates nesting. At the other end of England, in Lakeland, H. A. Macpherson only mentions two entries, for ringtails, in 1645, while he lists numerous Ravens and Eagles. Probably at this period there was no very concerted attempt to destroy harriers, and there was, of course, no shortage of man- or boy-power to spend all day merely scaring raiders away, as the young poet Clare was later set to do.

In J. C. Cox's assorted lists from Churchwardens' Accounts, 1566–1734, there is only one reference to 'ringteals' along with 'Kiets and a Heron', in 1657, at Prestwich, Cheshire. It is clear, too, that buzzards, kites and harriers were often lumped together in the lists, so the comparative status of the large hawks cannot be deduced from them. Tubbs, in his book, *The Buzzard*, concluded that from 1720 onwards the Churchwardens concentrated on the control of House Sparrows. The golden age for birds of prey perhaps continued almost to the end of the 18th century, though large scale destruction sometimes occurred earlier, as on Deeside, where 2520 hawks and kites were killed in the parishes of Braemar, Glenmuick, Tulloch and Glengarden in 1776–86. Doubtless Hen Harriers featured among these. More specifically, it is recorded of the Border country, that around 1797 the Duke of Buccleuch's gamekeeper had destroyed some hundreds of Hen Harriers.

More serious for the species, at that time, was the growing impetus of land improvement. W. G. Hoskins wrote of Norfolk, where Turner had watched Hen Harriers: 'the greatest transformation of heathland into cornfields was to be found on the estates of Coke of Holkham, in the north of Norfolk. In the course of a long lifetime (1752–1842) he changed the entire face of this part of the country, through his own efforts and those of his imitators'. True, as Gilbert White and John Clare observed, Hen Harriers hunt over fields of corn, and Turnbull (1867) described them 'hovering over the reapers' at harvest time in East Lothian, but there is no evidence that the Continental habit of nesting in cornfields was ever common in Britain. Undoubtedly, agricultural improvement drove back the frontiers of their breeding range well before the full fury of persecution took effect. W. G. Hoskins, again, has described how the landscape of the English Midlands was redrawn by the Parliamentary enclosures of the 18th and early 19th centuries. The small, heavily grazed fields which replaced so much open arable ground and heathland would have little attraction for harriers.

The eloquent voice of John Clare was nostalgic for the open heath in the East Midlands:

> *Ye commons left free in the rude rags of nature,*
> *Ye brown heaths beclothed in furze as ye be,*
> *My wild eye in rapture adores every feature,*
> *Ye are as dear as this heart in my bosom to me.*

Clare often observed harriers hunting in his homeland near Peterborough. In prose written in praise of hawks he wrote this description of a male harrier: 'There is a large blue (hawk) almost as big as a goose they fly in a swopping manner not much unlike the flye of a heron you may see an odd one often in the spring swimming close to the green corn and ranging over an whole field for hours together—it hunts leverets, partridges and pheasants'. A male harrier also features in his long poem, The Shepherd's Calendar, (1823):

> *A hugh (huge) blue bird will often swim*
> *Along the wheat when skys grow dim*
> *Wi clouds—slow as the gales of spring*
> *In motion wi dark shadowed wing*
> *Beneath the coming storm it sails.*

Clearly he had been struck by the wonderful spectacle of the light blue bird against a dark sky. It is only fair to agree with James Fisher, that Clare's harriers hunting over the spring corn were perhaps Montagu's, although with Peterborough Great Fen so near, they could almost as likely have been Hen Harriers.

The wilderness was retreating even in northern England and southern Scotland. In Northumberland, in the late 18th century, improving farmers were clearing great stretches of broom, thorn and bramble 'in which cattle could be lost for days', while in Galloway the 18 miles of country between Castle Douglas and Dumfries were no longer as described by the Provost of Glasgow in 1688, 'a wide expanse of bleak moss, extending for miles on either side, overgrown with whins and broom and destitute of enclosures of trees' (Donnachie and Macleod, 1974).

Between 1783 and 1796, Dr John Heysham of Carlisle made a remarkable study of the Hen Harriers nesting within a mile and a half of that city (Macpherson, 1892). In those years he made accurate observations on over 20 nests on Newton Common (long since absorbed by the growth of Carlisle city). Heysham's evidence that the bird nested, more or less colonially, so close to a town might have been duplicated, at that time, in many places where large tracts of moor or bog still remained. Newcastle Town Moor was another old nesting site which seems to have been occupied into the 19th century (Bolam, 1912), while, in the south, Desmond Nethersole-Thompson (1933) referred to nesting 'within the memory of those living in what are now the tram-lined streets of Bournemouth'. All this suggests that harriers were often left unmolested. Perhaps the old ethic that gave protection to Kites and Ravens, as useful scavengers in the stinking streets of mediaeval towns, was not quite dead, but more probably Hen Harriers simply attracted no attention unless they were seen to kill poultry. They were no bother to sheep, cattle or crops.

Dr John Heysham was a pioneer, preceeding Montagu, in establishing beyond doubt that the ringtail was the female of the Hen Harrier, both by shooting pairs of adults at the nest and by keeping young birds alive and noting their plumage changes. Two chicks taken in 1783 lived nearly 21 months in captivity and Heysham also noted the changes of iris colour in the young male. Three nests were within 500 yards of each other, a likely situation for polygyny perhaps, but this cannot be deduced from Heysham's notes. The Doctor and his companion shot two of the ringtails, wounded a male and caught another in a rat trap, 'taking' the young as well. All this was, of course, typical of the methods of ornithologists then and much later, but Heysham's curiosity and discoveries mark him out as much more than a mere collector of skins. (He was in the habit of collecting specimens for Dr John Latham, one of the leading ornithologists of the day). The Newton Common harriers must have been part of a flourishing population as nests continued to be found over the next ten years, in spite of 'almost all' the adults being shot, again by Heysham in 1785, 'as they flew about us at the nests'.

John Heysham was a man of his times in more than ornithology. According to the author of *Fauna of Lakeland*, H. A. Macpherson, he did much as a medical man to advance the health and happiness of his fellow townsmen, but spent his declining years as a magistrate 'adjudicating upon conjugal amenities and hushing the altercations of rival washerwomen'. In such cases he and his colleagues invariably mulcted one side, and frequently both sides, in costs, while fines inflicted were appropriated by the magistrates themselves.

George Montagu began his *Ornithological Dictionary* in 1802. He was the discoverer of Montagu's Harrier and researched on Hen Harriers. Like Heysham, he took young from the nest and kept them alive until he was able to demonstrate the plumage change of a yearling male, from brown to predominantly grey, carefully noting the progress of moult between August and October, when the bird was killed and put in his museum. He even went so far as to 'pluck some wing and tail feathers' from the living bird to force premature change, in June. Only a decade before, Gilbert White still referred to the 'Ring-tail Hawk' as though it were a distinct species. Montagu's field work on Hen Harriers was done in Devon, where the local names of Furze Kite and Blue Furze Hawk indicated its association, particularly in summer, with gorse-covered 'wasteland'. Montagu was puzzled that he saw grey males more often than ringtails in the breeding season, perhaps because he did not realise how much time the females spent concealed on the nest. The brood which he studied was taken from a nest on Dartmoor in 1805. As he regularly saw three or four males on the wing at one time, it is clear that Hen Harriers bred plentifully in Devonshire at this date. Of particular interest is his note that the irides of a male became orange in August when it was a little over a year old, a statement which seems to have been overlooked in a recent discussion[1] about the age at which iris colour of harriers changes.

Muirhead, author of *The Birds of Berwickshire* (1889), considered that it had already left many old breeding places in that county, in the 18th century, as a result of drainage of bogland. The inaccessibility and dangerous nature of bogs had provided it with particularly safe breeding places. The most famous bog in the south of Scotland was Billie Mire, in Berwickshire, fascinatingly documented by Muirhead. It extended for five miles from Chirnside to near Ayton. Clumps of willows and alders grew on the drier parts, with deep black pools between, regarded with awe by the local people as the haunt of 'Jock o' the Mire'. Here the Bittern boomed in spring and wildfowl bred in abundance. Muirhead was able to talk to old men who knew it before it was totally drained in 1830–35 after many unsuccessful attempts. 'Mr White used to find Hen Harrier nests every season among

[1] *British Birds* Vol 65, No 8, p. 358.

sedges and rushes in the swamps. Thomas Hewit found a nest with young and took one of the fledgelings home and kept it till it was full-grown when it attacked some of Mr Logan's chickens and had to be destroyed. He said that boys used to visit the Mire on Sundays to search for the Gled's (Harrier's) nest, providing themselves with long leading-in ropes . . . giving the loose end to some of their companions who remained on firm ground ready to pull them out if necessary'. Muirhead said that 'in the mornings and evenings the Hen Harrier could be seen passing slowly over the rushes and quartering the wet meadow . . .'. He might have been describing the flight of birds arriving at, or leaving, a communal roost—there could have been no better site for one.

In so far as it is possible to judge the status of the Hen Harrier in the early 19th century, it can be said that it bred in all regions where moor, marsh, heathland and bog occupied sizeable tracts of the country. It certainly bred plentifully over much of Scotland, Ireland and northern England and there is evidence, as I have said, that it was not scarce in Devonshire. It also bred in west and north Wales and in parts of central, eastern and southern England. In many parts of these regions it may have been quite scarce and may not have bred in every county, but it evidently did so in some numbers in the Fen districts of eastern England whence five clutches are listed, 1840–56, in *Ootheca Wolleyana* (Newton, 1864). Forrest's *Fauna of North Wales* (1907), tells little more than that it bred regularly in the Montgomery–Merioneth border country, on the Berwyn moors, as late as the 1860s, and that Eyton saw birds frequently near Corwen about 1835.

Thompson's account (1849) of the Hen Harrier in Ireland begins picturesquely: 'In snipe-shooting it is often met with'. Evidently, then as now, Ireland was a notable wintering haunt but he shows, too, that nesting was fairly widespread. According to Thompson, breeding strongholds at this

PLATE 1   Male and female Hen Harriers in forest breeding habitat.

PLATE 2 Nestling Hen Harriers: top, 1–3 days; centre, about 2 weeks; bottom, 26–28 days, male at left and female on right.

PLATE 3   Studies of female Hen Harrier brooding and feeding chicks.

PLATE 4 *(Top)* adult Hen Harriers over moorland breeding habitat.
(Centre) Marsh Hawks: left, 1st winter female and 2nd winter male; right, adult male.
(Bottom) Hen Harriers at winter roost; top left, 1st winter male: centre top, adult female; centre, adult male; bottom left, 2nd winter male; lower right, 1st winter male.

time were in Wicklow, Kerry, on the borders of Waterford and Tipperary, and in counties Antrim and Londonderry in the north. Ruttledge (1950) said that it bred in Co. Galway fairly plentifully up to 1872 but that it seems to have been scarce in Co. Mayo. Shawe-Taylor (Moffat, 1889) said that it was 'common on all the hills in Connemara' in August 1851, but Thompson gave its breeding status there as rare. He added that the nesting haunts in Connemara were in swamps, generally on the margins of lakes, but reports from other localities in Ireland referred to nests 'on the heath'.

The clearest evidence for some decline in the numbers breeding in Ireland by the mid 19th century comes from Thompson's statement that, near Clonmel (Waterford), it was very scarce in 1849 whereas in 1838 he had been told that eggs and young were easily obtained there. Persecution by 'vermin killers', sportsmen and collectors was probably causing a more general decrease in Ireland at this time, but at least in the more remote breeding haunts a good many pairs continued to breed. Thompson quotes an emotive article on Highland Sport and the enemies of grouse, in the *Quarterly Review* for December 1845: 'Hawks of all sorts, from Eagles to Merlins destroy numbers. The worst of the family, and the most difficult to be destroyed, is the Hen Harrier. Living wholly on birds of its own killing, he will come to no laid bait and hunting in open country he is rarely approached near enough to be shot, skimming low and quartering his ground like a well-trained pointer he finds almost every bird and with sure aim strikes down all he finds'. No sporting writer at that time, of course, would have paused to reflect that such deadly efficiency in a predator would long since have caused its own extinction from the exhaustion of its food supply.

It is to writers in the north of England and Scotland that we are indebted for the most informative, and sometimes vivid, accounts of Hen Harriers in the first half of the 19th century. The Celt, Macgillivray, and the Lowlander, Sir William Jardine, were both able to draw on personal experience, as did the Northumbrian Selby. Through Macgillivray's eyes we are introduced for the first time to the sheer delight of a field naturalist enjoying the sight of a pair of harriers in the sky. In 1836, Macgillivray wrote in his *Descriptions of Rapacious Birds of Great Britain*: 'Should we, on a fine summer's day, betake us to the outfields bordering on extensive moor, on the sides of the Pentland, Ochil or the Peebles hills, we might chance to see the harrier, although hawks have been so much persecuted that one may sometimes travel a whole day without meeting so much as a Kestrel. But we are now wandering amid thickets of furze and broom . . .'. He goes on to write of the moorland plants and birds, like Golden Plover, Lapwing, Whinchat, Snipe and Red Grouse and continues: 'but see a pair of searchers not less observant than ourselves have appeared over the slope of the bare hill', so introducing his description of the behaviour of a pair of Hen Harriers above their intended nesting ground.

Later, in his *History of British Birds* (1837–52), he again shows a birdwatcher's delight in passages such as this: 'Kneel down here, then, among the long broom and let us watch the pair that have just made their appearance on the shoulder of the hill. . . . How beautifully they glide along, in their circling flight, with gentle flaps of their expanded wings, floating, as it were, in the air, their half-spread tails inclined from side to side, as they balance themselves, or alter their course'. Yet it was to Jardine that Macgillivray was in debt for an account of the Hen Harrier's habit of communal roosting in winter, and the rather curious description of behaviour at the nest which shows that Jardine mistook the food pass for the hen 'not suffering' the cock to come to the nest—no doubt a mistake easily made when visual aids hardly existed. Selby (1831) also described communal roosting but as he was in close touch with Jardine it is not clear whether he discovered the habit independently. According to Jardine, Macgillivray had never seen a nest, which may seem surprising for one who had walked virtually the length and breadth of Scotland—and on one occasion all the way from Aberdeen to London via the Cairngorms and the Solway coast. Macgillivray's summing up of the Hen Harrier's status in 1840 (? in Scotland), was 'although nowhere very common is generally dispersed and in some districts pretty numerous in the breeding season, (frequenting) hilly tracts from the middle of spring to autumn (and) in winter lower cultivated districts. (It is) frequently killed by gamekeepers and easily obtained'. As Baxter and Rintoul (1953) pointed out, a comparison between the references to Hen Harriers in the Old and New Statistical Accounts of Scotland (1797, 1834–45) indicates a marked diminution in many districts, but around 1840 it was the commonest large raptor in many parts of the Highlands, the Outer Hebrides and Orkney.

After reading a large number of 19th century accounts of the Hen Harrier, I am in no doubt that the great decrease took place in southern Scotland and northern England between 1820–1850; in the Highlands it was later, occurring mainly in the second half of the century. Compare, for instance, the statement by Dr Charlton of Hesleyside (Bolam, 1912) in Northumberland, in 1861: '30 years ago we could have pointed out half a dozen nests of the Blue Hawk or Hen Harrier, but it is now seen once or twice in a season', with that of Osborne (Harvie-Brown and Buckley, 1887), writing of Caithness about 1855, that it was the commonest bird of prey except the Kestrel and possibly the Merlin. Clearly, in the north of England and Scotland as a whole, loss of breeding places due to land improvement was quite insufficient to cause a catastrophic decline and there is abundant evidence that the main cause was intensive gamekeepering, especially on grouse moors. It was probably true in some districts—as in Berwickshire —that as some of the old breeding haunts in bogs disappeared and, at the same time, grouse stocks were boosted by moor management, there was a tendency for Hen Harriers to resort increasingly to the best grouse moors, thus ensuring their own demise.

If large tracts of more or less inaccessible bog or fen had remained, Hen Harriers would probably have survived here and there in spite of game preservation, but on the moors they were the easiest of predators to destroy because of their ground nesting habit, their large size and their often bold behaviour towards intruders in the vicinity of the nests.

By the middle of the century the shooting of driven grouse was firmly established as the fashionable sport of landowners and their friends. True, not all moor owners were quite so explicit as the Marquess of Bute who, as far back as 1808 (Richmond, 1959), had required his keepers to take an oath including the words 'finally I shall use my best endeavour to destroy all birds of prey with their nests, so help me God', but hardly any would have disagreed with his sentiments. The purchase of Balmoral estate by Queen Victoria, in 1852, gave the ultimate accolade to the Highlands as a centre for field sports. At the same time the adoption of the breech loading shotgun made shooting driven birds far more practicable and attractive to sportsmen, while the new railway provided them, for the first time, with swift transport from London to the Highland grouse moors. So a number of factors combined to reduce the survival chances of Hen Harriers, as predators on game birds, even in the most remote districts.

Ritchie (1920) and others have quoted the numbers of predatory birds and mammals claimed as 'trapped' on the Glen Garry estate in Inverness-shire, 1837–40. These include 68 'harriers' and nine 'ash-coloured hawks', thought by some to be Montagu's Harriers but more probably, in my view, male Hen Harriers in their second year. Specific identification in such lists must be treated with reserve; 317 Rough-legged Buzzards to 285 Buzzards and 63 Goshawks, without mention of Sparrowhawks, is puzzling to say the least, but the impression remains of the extraordinary wealth of predators and, implicitly, the abundance of prey for them in these early days of intensive game preservation. Of course, there had been campaigns against hawks in the Highlands long before the 1830s, but the main effort had been inspired by sheep farmers against Eagles and Ravens. The great spread of hill sheep farming in Scotland in the early 19th century undoubtedly contributed to the decline of the Hen Harrier, as heavy grazing by sheep and widespread moor burning by shepherds reduced ground cover for safe nesting. I believe that the importance of these factors has generally been overlooked.

The most startling evidence for mass killing by gamekeepers is the oft quoted figure of 351 Hen Harriers said to have been killed, on two south Ayrshire estates, between 25 June 1850 and 25 November 1854. Even if these figures are exaggerated, it is fair to assume that the Hen Harrier was numerous on the extensive moors of south Ayrshire, at a time when its numbers had already been much reduced in most parts of southern Scotland and the border counties of England. Only a few years later (1869), Gray and Anderson regarded it as virtually extinct in the counties of Ayrshire and Wigtownshire, clear evidence of the speed with which a flourishing population could be eliminated by teams of gamekeepers. Gray and Anderson describe the technique of destruction at the nest: 'Keepers, on finding the nest, usually wait until the eggs are hatched, and are in the habit of killing all the young birds except one, which they fasten by the leg to a stake and thus oblige to remain there, even after being fully fledged, until an opportunity occurs for shooting the old birds. This is sometimes but too easily accomplished as they continue to bring prey to the tethered captive long after it should have been hunting the moors on its own account'. South-west Scotland is an important wintering area for Hen Harriers today, and it is tempting to speculate that the same held in the 1850s; if so, the keepers were probably busy throughout the year.

The growing body of 'sporting and natural history' writers helped to spread the word that the only good harrier was a dead one. William Robertson was typical of the day. There is a macabre interest in his account (Harvie-Brown and Buckley, 1895) of a nest with five young, found on the moors near Carrbridge, Inverness-shire, in 1857: 'as far as I remember there were 23 young Grouse and 2 Ring Ouzels beside (the young). I killed all but 2 which I took home and put in a cage with the 25 birds on a Saturday night and on Monday the whole were devoured, which proved to me they were the very worst vermin we could have'. Such an accumulation of uneaten prey at a harrier's nest is outwith my own experience. Possibly the female had been killed and the young were not old enough to tear up the prey for themselves, but this seems to be confounded by the speed with which only two of them finished the whole offering in less than two days. I feel bound to conclude that Mr Robertson's imagination was better than his memory. Another contemporary, Henry Davenport Graham, showed in his *Birds of Iona and Mull* (1852–70) that there was still dislike of the Hen Harrier as a chicken stealer. Acting on his experience that a hunting harrier took the same route at about the same hour for several days (most of the old writers made the same comment), he often 'waylaid the depredator of the chicken yard'. Refreshingly, he acknowledged that the male was a very pretty bird. One windy day he let one pass him on the seashore, mistaking it for a seagull. 'Only the different mode of flight suddenly awakened me to the fact that I had allowed a "white hawk" to escape'. And only the oaths escaped getting into print.

Among the rare spokesmen in defence of hawks, J. C. Langlands (Bolam, 1912) in Berwickshire, was perhaps a keen gardener or fruit grower. He wrote: 'We still fortunately possess a few choice specimens of the little blue hawk, (?Merlin), the Kestrel and the Harrier. How long these active little police may be allowed to keep in check the small bird depredators may be doubted'. One of the most articulate opponents of the prevailing persecution of birds of prey was Robert Gray, the Glasgow banker, whose evocative description of the Hen Harriers in North Uist (1871) is still as fresh as the day it was written. 'From where I sat I could see the Clamhan Luch (Hen

Harrier in Gaelic) like a light blue sea-gull skimming the purpled sides of Ben Eval and gradually nearing the summit. Twenty yards behind came another of a darker hue, not so readily perceived as her mate but as quick at perceiving; then the two came abreast and passed within 10 yards, beating the ground like a well-trained couple and making alternate stoops at the poor mountain mice as they sat at their thresholds'. It is interesting that in the Uists, where crofters might have been expected to fear for the safety of their chickens, the Hen Harrier's reputation was never very bad. The Gaelic name Clamhan Luch means mouse-hawk and reflects the importance of voles as harrier food in those islands.

By the turn of the century, the continuity of breeding in those islands, along with that in Orkney, was to prove vital to the survival of the species in Britain. Gray and Anderson appended to their *Birds of Ayrshire and Wigtownshire* (1869) a plea for a more tolerant attitude to predators, which has a distinctly modern ring. One passage is particularly relevant: 'We have only to consider the vast diminution of species that has taken place during the past 30 years in order to learn the mischief that has resulted from one cause alone—viz. the over-zealous destruction of creatures that are supposed to be enemies of game. . . . Birds of prey have suffered to an almost inconceivable extent—eagles, falcons, buzzards, hawks and owls having been subjected to such continual persecution as to be now [1869] in some places on the verge of extinction as native species'. Yet many of the naturalists who lamented this destruction, themselves helped to write the final chapters in the story of near extermination, by their activities as collectors of specimens and eggs.

The best known example of this ambivalent attitude was Charles St John, in the 1840s. He writes as if shooting Ospreys and Eagles was a duty, to be borne stoically at the time, 'for their skins were wanted'. Nevertheless, he did have a genuine delight in watching the living bird. He kept tame Peregrines and Merlins in his garden in Sutherland and was sentimental about owls, even taking down the pole traps which were set for hawks all round his house, because 'the poor fellows [owls] looked so pitiable as they sat upright, held by the legs'. St John was not especially interested in the Hen Harrier—he commented that it was plentiful enough (in Sutherland) in the hilly districts and 'though very destructive to game it compensates for this in some degree by occasional preying upon rats, vipers etc.' He particularly noted that it resorted to the lowlands in the autumn, hunting stubble fields where he observed it after Partridges and catching rats in the twilight.

St John's *Tour of Sutherlandshire* was published in 1849, and in the following passage he shows how the men of the hills had already welcomed the chance of supplementing their meagre livelihoods by supplying the wants of wealthy collectors. 'I found that all the shepherds, gamekeepers and others in this remote part of the kingdom had already ascertained the value of the eggs of this [the Red-throated Diver] and other birds and were as eager to search for them and as loth to part with them, except at a very high price, as love of gain could make them. Nor had they the least scruple in endeavouring to impose eggs under fictitious names on any person wishing to purchase such things'. Other long forgotten Victorian collectors were journeying north; in 1860, for instance, A. W. Crichton was shooting Hen Harriers and sea birds in Orkney and recounted his exploits in *A Naturalist's ramble to the Orcades* (1869). Bruce Campbell has kindly drawn my attention to an article (1970) in which he referred to this little book, showing how Crichton echoed St John's habit of moralising about *other* peoples' destructiveness while enjoying his own. After failing to collect a male Hen Harrier which he had fired at and wounded, he wrote: 'so, swallowing my disappointment as best I could, I then as humanely as possible consigned the youthful members of the family to a premature decease'. In his book this incident follows hard upon the following comment: 'sad, indeed, is it to hear such melancholy comment . . . of the influence which thoughtless man is continuously and culpably exerting to thin the number of, if not to exterminate from among us, the charming companions which the Creator has formed for our mutual enjoyment'.

I am indebted to Desmond Nethersole-Thompson for some colourful notes on some of the 'Trophy Hunters' in the Scottish Highlands. After mentioning P. J. Selby (1834) and Sir William Milner MP (1847), both of whom shot Hen Harriers in Sutherland, he writes of his favourite villain, E. T. Booth of Brighton: 'an obsessive collector and alcoholic whose glass cases of stuffed birds are still on show in his museum in Dyke Road, Brighton. For many years on the move in the Highlands, Booth was a most unusual man, paranoiac, exceptionally devious and bitterly jealous of rivals whom he loved to deceive by publishing false scents and locations. Some of his manuscript diaries are fascinating human and natural history documents. On 15 June 1868 Booth was in Sutherland where he invited two keepers, Matheson of Achfary and Andrew Mackay of the Mound, to dinner at the Inn of Lairg. There, over bottles of whisky, he planned his next forays. Among many subsequent successes were the rape of a couple of Hen Harriers' nests, the first of which a shepherd had found on a hill near 'Beannach'. Doubtless wearing his familiar bowler or a rather grotesque cloth cap, Booth tramped out to the nest where he impatiently watched the female attacking a gull. 'At last she had settled on the heather and came right on the nest where I killed her as she flew off. There were five eggs in the nest. I watched the nest until midnight to see if the cock came in, but he was by no means a dutiful parent and never appeared. We thereupon set two traps, making a new nest and also five nest eggs'. The ungracious cock, however, dismally failed to accept the honour of being stuffed and mounted in a showcase.

'On 25 June Booth also shot a hen, at a nest near Loch Meadie. This contained a single young. There with the hen safely in his game bag, he set two traps at the nest. This time the cock harrier was more accommodating. "The keeper brought in the cock harrier" which had been trapped less than an hour after Booth had returned to his horse and trap'.

In his gargantuan book, euphemistically titled *Rough Notes on the Birds observed during 25 years shooting and collecting in the British Islands* (1881–87), Booth is indeed much less explicit about his exploits, but he records a bizarre moment beside a harrier's nest when he discovered, as he reached for his gun, that he had laid it down on the back of an old Greyhen with three fresh eggs, only six or seven paces from the Hen Harrier's nest with five eggs and one young. Perhaps the most remarkable case on record of neighbourliness between a grouse and a harrier! The colour plate in Booth's book, by Edward Neale, is of interest as showing a very fine grey old male, white at the carpal regions, no doubt selected as the finest model from Booth's extensive range of specimens.

Nevertheless the gamekeeper, not the collector, was the principal cause of the growing rarity of the Hen Harrier in the second half of the 19th century. Very many of the stuffed harriers that found their way into glass cases in country houses had been shot or trapped by keepers as vermin. Many more rotted on the keepers' gibbets; before they had become rare in the Lammermuirs for instance, in 1837, '4 or 5 might be seen in a row, one nail through the head and one each at the tip of the outstretched wings', (Muirhead). Did anyone pause, I wonder, to admire the wonderful chequered pattern on the underwing of the ringtail?

In 1865 *The Ibis* published A. G. More's much quoted paper, 'On the Distribution of Birds in Great Britain during the nesting season'. This was an unusual piece of work for its time, the format looking forward to modern enquiries by the BTO. A large number of correspondents supplied answers to a questionnaire but sadly there is no means of telling how reliable these were and, for the Hen Harrier, the results suggest that the estimates of status were not abreast of the rapidly declining situation. More's summary states 'still common in Scotland' (as a breeding bird) but the regional books of the period show that by the 1860s it was extremely rare in Scotland south of the Forth–Clyde valley except, probably, in south Argyll and Arran. Further north in Stirlingshire and Perthshire, keepers had driven it a long way towards extermination; a nest destroyed by a keeper in Stirlingshire in 1868 was considered rare enough for comment, while Booth said that not more than six specimens had come under his observation in Perthshire. Nor was it plentiful, at this time, in Inverness-shire. It was still fairly common, however, in much of the north and north-west, especially Caithness, West Sutherland, Mull, Jura, Islay and Skye and in much of the Outer Hebrides and Orkney. More, erroneously, said it was absent from the Inner Hebrides. There is no evidence that it ever bred commonly in the Shetlands, where Saxby found a single nest on Yell prior to 1874. Unfortunately, the least well documented areas of Scotland at this period are the south-west Highlands—Argyll and Arran—a region where Hen Harriers were to hold out into the 20th century.

More's paper suggests that, in England, breeding still occurred sporadically in the south-east and Midlands but some of the reports refer to earlier years. Harrison (1953) said that Hen Harriers bred in Kent until the latter half of the nineteenth century when, 'no doubt, industrial expansion along riversides and marsh drainage accounted for its disappearance'. A brood of young were taken in Norfolk in 1870. It was certainly a rarity in England by this time, except in the south-west peninsula and from west Yorkshire northwards. Even in these areas it probably held on precariously. Writers like Macpherson for Lakeland and Bolam for Northumberland, nevertheless suggest that a few pairs were still breeding just south of the border: On the Solway Flow in Cumberland nesting was reported into the 1880s and one or two pairs bred in north Northumberland in the 1890s, and it still bred occasionally in Higher Wyresdale, Lancashire, about 1885 (Oakes, 1953).

The last recorded breeding of Hen Harriers in Devon was in 1893, near Ilfracombe, but there were evidently still later records of breeding on Exmoor, Somerset (Palmer and Ballance, 1968). More reported that it still bred in north and west Wales and this is confirmed by Forrest's statement that it bred regularly on the Montgomery–Merioneth border in the 1860s. His comment that for some years previous to 1861 a grouse moor in that district had no keeper and 'the place was given over to hawks and other depredators', after which it was keepered, may be taken to infer that persecution there was only then beginning to reduce what may have been a flourishing harrier population. There was occasional nesting in north Wales later—a pair bred in Caernarvon in 1902—but there is no firm evidence that Welsh Hen Harriers survived in any strength after about 1860, except perhaps for a few years in the extreme south-west (More, 1865). In Wales and south-west England the old status is particularly difficult to judge as there was some confusion with Montagu's Harriers where the range of the two species overlapped.

In Ireland, the population had been greatly reduced by the end of the century compared with the situation described by Thompson in 1849. 'Notwithstanding the suitability of the country', said Ussher at the turn of the century, 'it only nests, and that sparingly, in Kerry and Galway, possibly in Antrim, Queen's County, Waterford and Tipperary'.

Returning to Scotland the tale of destruction in some of the remaining strongholds in the north-west can be told in greater detail, as gamekeepers became more active in outlying districts in the 1870s and 1880s. In Skye (Harvie-Brown and Macpherson, 1904), for instance, Macdonald, a keeper at Ullinish, killed 32 harriers old and young in 1870, but only three between 1876–86. Angus Nicholson, head keeper at Dunvegan, knew five nests in 1873 and accounted for 25 old and young in that year. He saw no more

Breeding status

good evidence

probable

possible

Fig. 7(a)
c. 1825

Fig. 7   Maps (a) to (g) show approximate areas within which breeding is believed to have occurred in the period c. 1825–1975. The c. 1975 map is largely based on the Hen Harrier provisional map for *The Atlas of Breeding Birds in Britain and Ireland*, and I am grateful to the British Trust for Ornithology and Dr J. T. R. Sharrock for allowing use of the material. David Scott kindly checked all my Irish maps and supplied much information on recent changes.

until a female was trapped in 1883, but nesting birds were still occasionally being trapped on Skye up to 1889. On the neighbouring island of Raasay the campaign against harriers was equally swift and sudden. George Temperley (1951), described the changing regimes on this island. In 1846, 94 families of crofters were evicted, as sheep farming took over. Then, in the 1890s game became the landowner's priority, pheasant rearing began and harriers, Merlins, Peregrines, Rooks and Herons were all destroyed ruthlessly. Collier (1904), who lived there from 1896–1902, states that previous to 1896 there had been six pairs of Hen Harriers nesting regularly on the moors, very much the size of population that might have been expected in undisturbed conditions on a predominantly moorland habitat of about 6,000 hectares. Charles Dixon (1898), one of the few voices speaking out against the persecution, visited Skye about this time and saw a Hen Harrier's nest 'in an almost impenetrable heather thicket'. He was told by a keeper that sheep trampled on many harrier nests—this could have been true where sheep stocks were heavy but it may have been a convenient explanation by the keeper to a protectionist. What is very clear is that in Skye, as earlier in Ayrshire and elsewhere further south, the keepers wrought a fairly sudden and devastating change in the status of this bird whose habits marked it down for easy destruction on the open moorland.

On the north-west mainland, Harvie-Brown and Macpherson, in 1904, said it was approaching extinction. It was still attempting to breed at Inchnadamph in the 1890s and large clutches of six in 1893, and eight in 1894, were laid but the eggs were taken and the birds shot. When Buckley was in Attadale, West Ross, back in 1881–83, he had seen no harriers and only three old nests of former years, near Loch Monar. In 1887, Buckley and Harvie-Brown said it was 'resident and still fairly common in the east', of Sutherland and Caithness, 'though killed down on every occasion that offers'. The remote moors of south Caithness, where Osborne had found many nesting 'on open wastes or in thick furze coverts', provided one of the last hideouts for harriers on the mainland. I have been unable to discover when it ceased to nest in Caithness but it was probably about the turn of the century, when, according to Ian Pennie (1962–63), it no longer nested in any part of Sutherland. Sim wrote of Deeside in 1903 that it was 'almost exterminated' but it was probably rare in this heavily keepered area long before then.

Much later, in 1922, a pair was killed at a nest at Logiealmond, Perthshire. Desmond Nethersole-Thompson, in his long experience of Speyside from 1932 onwards, found only one nest there, in Abernethy Forest in 1936. He also saw birds in Donside and believes that there may have been a pocket of survival there from the old days.

The most intriguing question in the history of the Scottish Hen Harriers at this period is, did they survive in the south-west Highlands long after they were virtually extinct everywhere else in Scotland apart from Orkney and

Breeding status

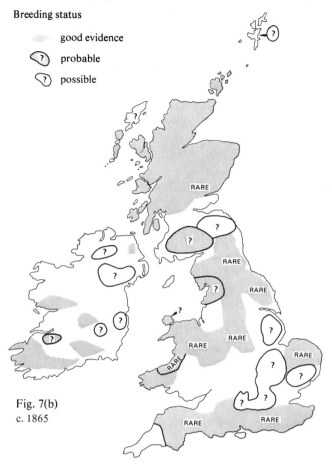

Fig. 7(b)
c. 1865

the Outer Hebrides? The evidence is worth examining. While Harvie-Brown and others were writing comprehensive accounts of most of the faunal regions of Scotland, Argyll lacked such a chronicler. We have to consult later writers. McWilliam said that it was extinct at Inveraray by 1892 but makes no reference to Kintyre. Dugald Macintyre, gamekeeper and author of books on wildlife, wrote in 1936 of Kintyre: 'The Hen Harrier was on daily view on a "moss" in my early days and I saw a couple on it in March 1919'. At one time he had seen three males hunting a snipe bog within sight of each other and he had found a nest from which five young flew. As a gamekeeper he showed no animosity to harriers in his writings. He even found the spot, on a bank of very tall heather, where the old male and 'his less perfectly plumaged son' (presumably a 2nd year male) roosted in winter. He examined their castings which showed that they fed mainly on small rodents and snipe. His conclusion that the two males overwintered, while 'the female and the other young' had left, fits with present day observations that grey males predominate in southern Kintyre in winter. To what date was he referring when he wrote of 'my young days'? Did a pair nest in 1919? The answers to these questions might show that Hen Harriers never died out in Kintyre, where landowners were more interested in varied rough shooting and wildfowling than grouse, and harriers were acknowledged as hunters of voles and young rabbits.

There is perhaps even stronger evidence that Hen Harriers lived on in Arran at least until the 1914–18 war. Baxter and Rintoul (1953) stated that they nested there, about Shiskine, in 1909, and Nicol Hopkins wrote in 1917: 'They are still to be seen in Arran and I believe still nest there—at any rate they still did at a very recent date'. Even though McWilliam quoted a keeper as saying they had gone by 1912, there seems no reason to doubt Nicol Hopkins—lack of keepering during the war should have allowed them to maintain their hold. It is, however, very doubtful whether breeding continued after this war period. I do recall, nonetheless, that when my brother and I made youthful bird-watching trips to Arran in 1933 we found that little had been recorded of the birds in the immediately preceding years, though we saw no harriers. Prior to the early 1890s, they were common in Islay and Mull, probably in Jura as well, but it can only be surmised that they did not survive much later in these islands. Baxter and Rintoul quoted Scott Skirving (1895) on Islay: 'I regret to note that for the first time for nineteen years I saw no Hen Harrier last August or September. Formerly they were numerous'. Baxter and Rintoul commented: 'One cannot help wondering if these were the autumn wanderings of birds from the Outer Hebrides or whether he was only there during these months, and referred to birds bred on the island'. In 1934–36 when I stayed on Islay with Lionel Smith he saw harriers more than once in August or September. Very likely these were migrants from the Outer Hebrides.

As a postscript on south-west Scotland south of the Clyde it is worth noting Richmond Paton's statement, in 1929, that they attempted to breed 'till recently' in the Barrhill area of south Ayrshire, and the Renfrewshire record, by John Paterson and Thornton MacKeith (1915), of a pair prospecting at Inverkip in April 1906. Further south in Dumfries and Galloway, the only published evidence of breeding between the 1860s and recent times is a probable record for the Dumfries–Cumberland border about 1925 (Witherby, 1939). Derek Ratcliffe, however, was told by Ernest Blezard that a keeper destroyed at least three nests on moorland near Langholm, Dumfriesshire, during the 1920s and Blezard himself had seen a ringtail harrier in this area during the breeding season, in the same period and a pair possibly bred successfully near Closeburn, Dumfriesshire in 1920 (Gladstone, 1923). When it is considered that an enormous area of moorland in south-west Scotland was little traversed except by shepherds

Breeding status

good evidence

probable

possible

Bred
1899

RARE

Bred
1902

Fig. 7(c)
c. 1900

Bred
1893

and keepers and that keepers might be secretive if a nest was found, the strong possibility remains that nesting never entirely ceased in south-west Scotland. If so, it is unlikely that many broods escaped the keepers. As harriers became increasingly rare, as breeding birds, reports from many parts of Britain showed, not surprisingly, that they were becoming very scarce in winter.

Throughout the whole of the first half of the 20th century, Hen Harriers bred extremely rarely in England and Wales. *The Handbook of British Birds* (1939) said: 'has nested in last 30 years Cornwall, Hants, Surrey (1932), Anglesey (1924, 5 and 6, W. Aspen) and Caernarvon, and possibly Devon'. In none of these areas was there any continuity of nesting into the recent period of recovery. Most were probably isolated occurrences, like the remarkable record for a Surrey heath in 1932, graphically described by Desmond Nethersole-Thompson in the *Oologists' Record*, 1933. The nest had five eggs, four of which hatched. The Devonian nesting is obscure. Robert Moore, in his *Birds of Devon* (1969), acknowledges no definite nesting after 1893, though he believed there were records in 1942 and 1943, details of which were suppressed. Nevertheless, Jourdain certainly had knowledge of breeding somewhere in 'the Devonian peninsula' in the 1930s. (See his summary of the British status in the 1932 edition of Kirkman and Jourdain's *British Birds*.) According to Palmer and Ballance (1968) nesting occurred on Exmoor, Somerset, up to 1910, possibly again in 1920 and 1925 and a pair were present on Sedge Moor in May 1934.

In 1948, Ryves knew the bird only as a winter visitor to Cornwall. Clifford Oakes (1953) suggests that in 1943 a pair may have bred (or attempted to breed) on the 'southern mosses' of Lancashire, where a Hen Harrier was shot while carrying food. In Suffolk breeding was 'probable' in 1918 and again in 1929 (Payn, 1962). Bolam concluded that by 1913 there was only a memory of Hen Harriers breeding in Wales, and made a strong plea for the same protection measures for harriers as had been started for Kites, hoping presumably that the occasional wintering birds might stay to nest if given the chance. At Llanuwchllyn, near Bala, Bolam described the signboard of the inn, called The Eagles. On it, he said, 'the King of Birds is represented by three very dove-like harriers in pursuit of a hare'. He thought this was the work of a local artist. Perhaps the artist had witnessed at least one harrier attacking a hare. Sadly, when Graham Williams visited the inn in 1975, no trace of the sign survived.

The Outer Hebrides, Orkney and the South of Ireland deserve special historical attention as the three regions where continuity of breeding was maintained.

Back in 1841, Macgillivray had said that the Hen Harrier was rather abundant in the Outer Hebrides, especially in the Uists. Macgillivray's homeland was Harris and he must have known whether harriers bred in the Long Island; unfortunately there is much doubt whether there were ever many there—the statement by a Mr Greenwood that it was 'tolerably abundant' at Stornoway in 1879, quoted by Robert Gray, is not confirmed by later writers. Dr J. W. Campbell (1957) wrote that it survived on well-keepered ground in the southern islands and evidently considered it absent from Harris and Lewis, as a nesting bird, because voles were absent. Voles are plentiful in the Outer Hebrides south of Harris and, with rabbits, probably form a major prey item for the breeding pairs. Quite clearly the Clamhan Luch's survival was partly due to the view that it was not a serious predator on game birds, aided by the fact that keepers and their employers were much less concerned with grouse than wildfowl. Most importantly, some landowners had a genuine desire to preserve harriers.

I have already quoted Gray's description of a pair of Hen Harriers in North Uist. He wrote further that he had seen '12 or 14 in one day on

Breeding status

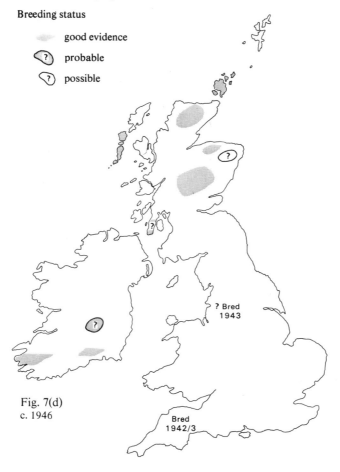

good evidence

probable

possible

Fig. 7(d)
c. 1946

? Bred
1943

Bred
1942/3

Benbecula and North Uist and likewise on South Uist'. This passage has often been taken as evidence that numbers were much higher in those islands about 1870 than in the early 20th century, but there is no certainty of a big decrease. Very likely Gray's high numbers were seen in late summer, when broods were newly on the wing, and they cannot be taken as evidence that there were great numbers of pairs. It was probably no less plentiful in 1901 when C. V. A. Peel said the bird was 'very common, especially in the southern islands and Benbecula'. That nesting took place long ago on the same heathery hills as today is witnessed by a reference (1918) in a diary by Abel Chapman's brother, Alfred, to the finding of a nest close to Mount Unavall in North Uist in May 1883. N. B. Kinnear, in 1906, said: 'a few pairs nest and are now strictly protected in the Uists'. P. H. Bahr saw a nest with young in 1907 and added: 'I am glad to report that the keeper, acting on instructions from headquarters, did not attempt to shoot the old birds and spared the life of their offspring'.

It is pleasing to be able to add that in 1950, and again in 1974, I found keepers in those benign islands continuing to 'spare' the Hen Harrier. F. M. Ogilvie (1920) saw seven or eight in a day on his winter visits to the Outer Hebrides between 1900 and 1914, and noted, most interestingly, that adult males outnumbered 'females' (? ringtails) by five to one. The evidence for a decline seems to be based chiefly on F. S. Beveridge's account of his observations, 1917–18. He said it was still fairly common and resident though in greatly diminished numbers, but as his visits seem to have been in winter this cannot be taken as proof of a large decrease in breeding birds. Rintoul and Baxter did not quote their reasons for saying there had been a marked decline, in 1953. Soon after this, in 1957, Jimmy Campbell, who visited the islands for many years, said the 'present trend is towards increase'.

I believe that in the Outer Isles—North and South Uist, Benbecula and Barra—unlike anywhere else in the country, the numbers of breeding Hen Harriers may not have changed dramatically throughout the past hundred years. Any decline earlier in this century may have been due to the activities of egg collectors more than to any other cause. It was remarkable and of great importance for the birds' survival that the tide of destruction by game preservers stopped short only 15 miles across the Minch in Skye. Perhaps, indeed, old memories of the Clamhan Luch as a bird of good omen, boding success in marital and money matters, were not without influence among the islanders.

Historically, there are several references to show that the Hen Harrier bred plentifully in Orkney during the 18th and 19th centuries. Baxter and Rintoul cite Low's statement that, in 1774, it was frequent all the year round, and Harvie-Brown and Buckley in 1891 considered it 'probably the commonest hawk throughout the islands'. A parallel may, possibly, be drawn between Orkney and Shetland on the one hand and the southern and northern Outer Hebrides on the other. Orkney and the southern Outer Isles have long had both harriers and voles. Shetland and Lewis and Harris are without voles (Southern, 1964) and have no history of a flourishing nesting population of harriers. The evidence for a real decline in the early 20th century is stronger for Orkney than for the Outer Hebrides. There is no doubt that when John Walpole Bond was nest hunting in Orkney in 1907, there were quite a few pairs of Hen Harriers. He found four nests on one hill, at distances of about 500 metres between nests, but in 1914 he believed that the total number of breeding pairs had been reduced to two.

Desmond Nethersole-Thompson, who went there in the 1930s, has given me his own vivid account of the Hen Harriers and their nest hunters in the Orkney scene between 1900 and the thirties: 'By the turn of the century the bird-shooting trophy hunters had largely been replaced by an extraordinary group of nest hunters and egg collectors about whom more is known in

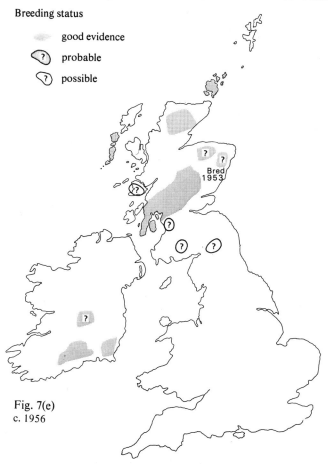

Breeding status

good evidence

probable

possible

Fig. 7(e)
c. 1956

myth and legend than in fact. In the next 15 years they advanced the sport of nest hunting almost to a science. In this period almost all that was known about the breeding biology of some of our rarer birds was based on their knowledge and observation. Among the outstanding egg collecting or- nithologists who visited Orkney before the First World War, were John Walpole-Bond, Edgar Chance and Norman Gilroy. Jock Bond, who was a friend of mine, spent a spring and summer in Orkney in 1907. His essays on the Hen Harrier and the Short-eared Owl in *Field Studies of some Rarer British Birds* (1914) were among his results. Bond was an exceptionally successful nest hunter and a remarkable field naturalist. He was an unusual character who always dressed like a tramp on his birding expeditions, but was inordinately proud of his social origins. A direct descendant of Sir Robert Walpole and a son of a Vicar of Horsham, Bond never ceased to mention that he had been to school at Winchester and rowed for St John's College, Oxford. He was one of the nest hunters who could both search and watch and he was a quite exceptionally bold and courageous tree and rock climber who, in his time, climbed to over 200 Peregrine eyries.

'In 1907 Edgar Chance had also been in Orkney. . . . Many considered that Norman Gilroy, a London timber buyer, was the most successful of all the contemporary nest hunters. Gilroy, who made several trips to Orkney, particularly after Hen Harriers, was a most devious character. He usually accepted the patronage of some rich man to pay the expenses of an egging trip and then concealed his trophies and complained that he had been out of luck! In one year a famous bird hunting Highland laird sent him to Orkney in advance to locate Hen Harriers' nests for him. Gilroy had a curious habit of blowing the eggs and then leaving them to dry on the eiderdown of his bed. When the laird arrived Gilroy was out hunting the hills but the inn-keeper directed him to the bedroom where he could not fail to notice a good clutch of Hen Harrier's eggs drying out on the bed. On his return Gilroy promptly told his host that he had been right out of luck and had not even seen a harrier. A man of rectitude, integrity and spirit, the laird departed by the next boat, leaving Gilroy to foot his own bill.

'In the pre-war and inter-war years many eggers crossed the Pentland Firth. These included the ship-builder, Sir Maurice Denny, who took Gilroy to Orkney. In 1924 Arthur Whitaker, the Sheffield architect, was there. He was another outstanding all-round field naturalist . . . and a most deter-mined and almost obsessional hunter who died of a heart attack after spen-ding a long day thrashing out a cornfield in Gloucester in a last hunt for the nest of a Quail, one of the few birds, the nest of which he had not found somewhere in the British Isles or in Ireland.

'These were a few of the amateur eggers and hunters from south of the border. But wherever they went, particularly in the haunts of rare and at-tractive birds, they almost always had "link men" to advise, guide and spy out the land in advance. Some of these were remarkable self-taught or-nithologists, of whom there were several in Orkney. In the early 1900s and in the last years of the 19th century, J. R. Gunn, the Kirkwall taxidermist, corresponded with a wide circle of English ornithologists who included Richard Kearton, the pioneer photographer. Those who knew Gunn told me that he had agents in every part of Orkney and that he frequently supplied the wants of collectors in the field and by post. For the first 40 years of the century and before Eddie Balfour was in his prime, John Douglas, a cattle farmer at Howe in Harray, was undoubtedly the greatest expert on Hen Harriers in Britain.

'I first met Douglas in May 1932. I remember a spare, tallish, well-built man, with bright eyes set in a brown and weather-beaten face. He was dressed in rough tweeds and he had his cap peaked backwards to save it blowing off in the high wind. He had a remarkably puckish sense of humour

Breeding status

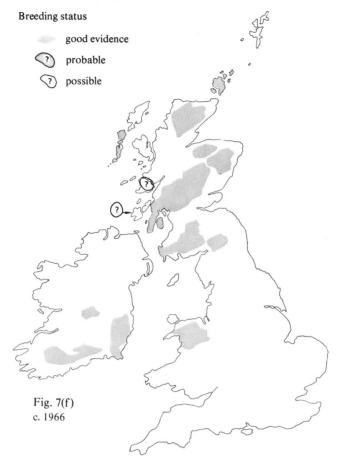

good evidence

(?) probable

(?) possible

Fig. 7(f)
c. 1966

and a most beautiful lilting Orkney accent. He was already a legend among egg men, who sometimes called him the Iron Man of Orkney, for he could keep going on the hill from the first glimmer of light, which is pretty early in an Orkney May, until very late at night. . . . I used to meet him on the hill at 4 o'clock in the morning and then after we had spent some hours together he tramped back over the tops and mosses to his farm and got on with his work. He knew his country like the back of his hand and could watch as well as search and interpret what he saw. In a few days we saw 7 Hen Harriers' nests and could have found more as we watched several other cocks hunting. When I was with him he showed me a cock breeding in brown plumage and told me about the polygamous cocks which he had sometimes found. Indeed one cock in a long valley almost certainly had 2 hens that year. . . . Unfortunately Douglas, like so many of his contemporaries, kept few notes and his knowledge died with him.'

Desmond Nethersole-Thompson ends his account by paying tribute to those who set out to conserve a stock of breeding Hen Harriers in Orkney. Foremost of all among these, in the inter-war years, was George Arthur. I well remember the day, in 1946, when George Waterston introduced me to him and his wife, Jean. He was an impassioned protectionist and it was fortunate for the Hen Harrier in Orkney—and for its survival as a British bird—that it found a protagonist in this influential and popular Orcadian. It has been argued whether the activities of egg collectors or the guns of local poultry keepers and others did most to bring it so near extermination. No doubt the absence of visiting egg collectors during the First World War helped it to climb back from the brink on which it stood in 1914.

John Douglas told Desmond Nethersole-Thompson, in 1932, that the harrier's chicken stealing habit threatened its existence and reckoned that 'the migration of rabbits to the hills' was coincident with an increase of harriers at this time. Yet, it cannot be doubted that so many determined collectors in search of clutches were a threat, especially when the harrier's general rarity was common talk. George Arthur, Duncan J. Robertson and Eddie Balfour argued and acted for Hen Harrier protection, creating above all a climate of opinion in the islands that was increasingly tolerant and sometimes proud of the bird as an adornment of the Orkney landscape. Protection was George Arthur's role—he recorded almost nothing about harriers—and it was left to the quiet dedication of Eddie Balfour, whom Desmond Nethersole-Thompson so rightly acknowledges as 'the king of Hen Harriers', to embrace a monumental field study. When I last spoke to Eddie Balfour, a fortnight before he died in August 1974, he told me that he was sure there were fewer pairs in the 1930s than in the 1940s. Nonetheless, Desmond Nethersole-Thompson, from his own experience and contact with John Douglas, estimated the breeding population as 'high' in the 1930s. In any event, by then, there had already been a considerable increase since the desperate state just before the First World War.

In later Chapters of this book, the habitat and food of the Hen Harrier in Orkney and the southern Outer Hebrides are compared. The Hen Harrier's survival in both areas owed much to the fact that its feeding habits did not bring it into serious conflict with game preservers. In neither were Red Grouse generally abundant enough to attract great attention, either from keepers or harriers. In both, voles, rabbits, passerine birds and young waders were in plenty and offered a wide range of prey and, in both, hunting grounds, rich in such prey, were sufficiently close to moorland haunts. It is often forgotten that active protection measures contributed to harrier survival in the southern Outer Hebrides as well as Orkney. The two groups of islands thus had several common features favourable to the Hen Harrier.

In Ireland, continuity of breeding into the present century has been more difficult to trace owing to the scarcity of ornithologists until recent times.

Breeding status

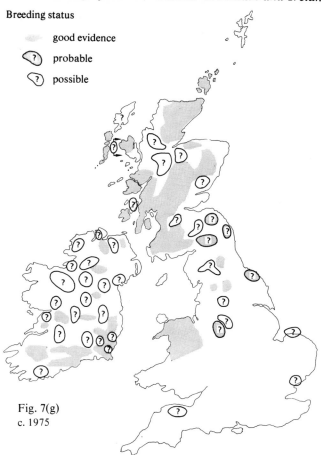

Fig. 7(g)
c. 1975

Humphreys (1937) said that it was still probably resident in a few of its original haunts in the wilder mountain districts, but had greatly decreased, and Ruttledge (1966) stated that it never became extinct though its survival was precarious early in the 20th century. I am greatly indebted to David Scott for further enlightenment on the history of the Hen Harrier in Ireland. As far as the problem of survival in the lean years is concerned, he has evidence that it never died out as a breeding bird on the Tipperary–Waterford border and that it may well have survived in the Slieve Bloom mountains on the Leix–Offaly border. He sums up the situation in the first half of the 20th century by saying that Hen Harriers continued to breed regularly in a few areas and sporadically in others, all in the southern half of the country. Frank King is further able to confirm that at least one pair was still present and probably breeding in the Iveragh peninsular, Co. Kerry, in 1945. He writes that they were seen in July of that year by the then District Court Clerk of Caherciveen who was keenly interested in birdlife. King adds that they do not now breed in that far western part of Kerry, in spite of much suitable habitat, but he does not know whether they disappeared from there (probably shot out), before or after re-colonisation of eastern Kerry began in about 1966 from Co. Cork.

In Southern Ireland, as in Orkney and the Outer Hebrides, the Hen Harrier did not come into conflict with the most rigorous grouse preservation. According to David Scott, grouse are 'almost rare birds' in Ireland and he has only once found grouse remains at a harrier's nest. So, although farmers and sportsmen certainly killed many harriers because they regarded birds of prey as harmful to game and poultry in general, persecution was not tightly organised and harriers must often have escaped unscathed on their remote and widely dispersed breeding grounds on the moors and mountains. Ewart Jones comments pertinently that the harriers' present day breeding moors in Co. Limerick are not so extensive as to preclude most pairs from having valley farmland in their territories. As I have already pointed out this is true and important both in Orkney and the southern Outer Hebrides and may be an important factor in Ireland too, especially in the absence of voles or large populations of grouse, by providing access to an abundance of small birds and mammals such as rabbits.

THE RECOVERY AND PRESENT STATUS

One day in 1947, the late John Murray Thomson R.S.A. told me, with some excitement, that he knew of Hen Harriers breeding in Sutherland. In February 1948, he gave some details in a Nature Note to *The Scotsman*. This was later quoted by Ian Pennie as the first definite evidence of re-colonisation in Sutherland. Two nests had been found in 1946 but both were destroyed by a keeper, the females being killed at each. The nests were only 200 metres apart and only one male, which escaped the keeper, was seen. Next year a brood survived to fledge.

J. W. Campbell (1957) considered that nesting occurred intermittently in the 'northern Highlands' before 1939, but there can be little doubt that the absence of keepers and the consequent neglect of grouse moors during the 1939–45 war opened the way to regular nesting. As Campbell pointed out, it was not only the lack of persecution that helped the harriers; the cessation of routine heather burning provided an abundance of good nesting sites. There is not, in fact, much indisputable evidence of widespread recolonisation during the war years. All that can be said of that period is that Hen Harriers bred in Moray in 1944 and 1945, according to Desmond Nethersole-Thompson, and that, in addition to the Sutherland nests, two were found in Perthshire in 1946 by J. W. Campbell not half a mile apart.

Campbell said that these Perthshire nests were not isolated cases of breeding, while Blake (1961) went so far as to say that the Hen Harrier was already common in the Highlands by 1945, but gave no details of localities. Most ornithologists, indeed, were wisely reticent about breeding localities and as late as 1953 Baxter and Rintoul said no more than that it was 'attempting to recolonise the country' and they greatly hoped it would succeed. However, the firm evidence that a few pairs were breeding in such widely scattered districts as Sutherland, Moray and Perthshire, suggests that recolonisation of the mainland had advanced considerably by 1946. This colonisation may have begun from Orkney but this is no more than speculation.

Before 1950, the only suggestion from ringing that Orkney birds might be colonising the mainland, rests on a single recovery in Banff on 17 June 1950. The bird had been ringed in Orkney on 15 July 1948, as a chick, but recovery details, 'loose ring dug up in garden', show that the date of finding is worthless as evidence that the bird was in Banff in the breeding season. In later years, however, there is evidence from ringing that some Orkney bred birds were summering in the Highlands, recoveries in the nesting season being reported between 1952 and 1970 from Sutherland, Caithness, Kincardine and Angus.

It is tempting to speculate on the origins of the few Hen Harriers which nested during the inter-war years in such surprisingly scattered localities in England, Wales and Scotland. Were some of them visitors from Scandinavia, pairing on their wintering grounds and remaining to breed? Could the same be true of some of the colonists of the 1940s and later? There is no proof of this but it is perhaps worth recalling the comment by the Editors of *British Birds* in 1957 that the start of the spread back into Scotland coincided with a peak in the Norwegian breeding population, though this was always small. The discovery in recent years that at least two Orkney ringed birds were in the Netherlands in the breeding season—one of them a six year old—suggests that some Hen Harriers may settle to breed at great distances from their birthplace.

By 1950, Eddie Balfour had noted a further increase in the Orkney population. In fact he recorded a peak in numbers in that year, after which they fluctuated at a slightly lower level during the 1950s and 1960s. The colonisation of new areas on the mainland was proceeding apace. Most significantly nests were being found increasingly in recently planted conifer forests of the Forestry Commission. John McKeand, now the Head Forester at Carradale in Kintyre, recalls that the first nest in Minard Forest, by Loch Fyne, was in 1949. The keeper who found it did not know what the bird was at the time. A pair nested there again in 1950, two pairs in 1951, three in 1952, four in 1953 and about five pairs by 1955.

In the early 1950s, large tracts of the Highland foothills, in the Aberfoyle district of south-west Perthshire and Argyll, were changing from heather moor to young conifer forest where the Forestry Commission, supported by the RSPB's payment of rewards for successful nests, looked kindly on the spread of the Hen Harrier. The Ornithological Reports for the Clyde area made no mention of breeding in 1951, but recorded a nest from which young fledged in 1952 and seven pairs in 1953. At this time small colonies were establishing themselves in the forests from Aberfoyle to Kintyre, and prospecting birds were seen in summer as far south as Renfrewshire. A male in partly grey plumage had been seen further west, in Mull, in July 1948. The first post-war nesting record for Arran was in 1953, according to Dr J. A. Gibson (1955), and there was soon a small increase there, in spite of persecution on grouse moors. At Carradale Forest, well down the Kintyre peninsula, a pair or two began to nest, perhaps in 1950, certainly in 1951, increasing to a remarkably concentrated colony of 18 pairs by 1958–59, nine of these being on one partly planted heathery hill of about 500 ha in extent (P. Strang, pers. comm.).

Meanwhile, further north and east, on the grouse moors of Perthshire and north of the Caledonian canal, nesting continued, but by the mid 1950s gamekeepers were on the look-out for harriers, their old unpopularity on large grouse moors had thoroughly revived and many nests and adults were being destroyed. J. W. Campbell noted a decrease on the Perthshire moors after 1954. The extent of the increase on these and other moors before that may never be accurately known, but it must be remembered that the six almost unrecorded seasons of wartime could have given the opportunity for great advances by the Hen Harrier. Blake (1961), said that by then it had lost much ground on grouse moors. Even so, the continuing general trend was strongly towards increase, the forest nesting colonies providing a reservoir which probably spilled over on to the heather moors. Nick Picozzi was told of a nest in Drumtochty forest, Kincardineshire, in 1953 and has traced nesting on the moors of Lower Deeside back to 1957, with an increase thereafter in spite of heavy persecution.

Much of the Cairngorms area has never been widely occupied by nesting Hen Harriers. Adam Watson commented interestingly in 1966: 'A pair oc-

casionally nests in Rothiemurchus and Lower Glen Feshie. . . . By contrast grouse moors not far away to the east of Braemar and north of the
Cairngorms are visited every autumn by many juveniles and sometimes
adults which stay till March, if not shot or trapped, living mainly on grouse
and small rodents. General absence and complete absence of breeding on
the Mar side cannot be due to persecution. On the Mar side birds of prey
have been left alone at least since 1945, yet harriers continually try to
colonise grouse moors not far to the east where they are persecuted worse
than eagles or Peregrines. Their absence from the Cairngorms must be due
to something else, possibly a deficient food supply or inhospitable climate'.
Picozzi, in Desmond Nethersole-Thompson's and Adam Watson's *The
Cairngorms* (1974), said that the main breeding area around these mountains was on Lower Deeside, Lower Speyside, Donside, Angus and
Perthshire, numbers having increased greatly since the 1940s in spite of
persecution. Of Sutherland Ian Pennie wrote, in 1962: 'a few pairs nest annually in different parts of central and east Sutherland—they are easily shot
and very easily caught in pole-traps so do not increase much'. Had it not
been for the comparative safety of the young forests, Hen Harriers, in many
parts of the Highlands, would have been faced with not much better
prospects than in the heyday of 19th century persecution.

The Protection of Birds Acts of 1954 and 1967 placed the Hen Harrier in
the List of First Schedule species, given special protection. It thus became
an offence, punishable by a £25 fine or imprisonment, to kill or take a Hen
Harrier, its eggs or young, or knowingly to disturb this species at the nest
without a special licence. The continued destruction of Hen Harriers by
various illegal methods, particularly on many grouse moors, bears
testimony to the toothlessness of the Protection Acts.

By the late 1950s, there were signs of a southward expansion in both
forest and moorland, and, at first, there was a readiness to accept the return
of a rare and little known bird on the part of some gamekeepers and moor
owners in the south of Scotland. I learned something of the delicate balance
between the forces of protection and persecution when I found the first nest
in the Stewartry of Kirkcudbright in 1959, on a moor where grouse preservation had some influence. (A pair probably nested in 1958, perhaps
earlier). The late Alan Mills and I spent many hours with the 1959 nest
under our surveillance. Gamekeepers were extremely curious about what the
young were being fed on and one assured me that he would shoot any
harrier he found with a grouse kill. In the following years, as the number of
pairs slightly increased in the Stewartry, I believe that some moorland nests
were destroyed but, by 1965, the great expansion of young forest near by
had provided safer nesting sites, and a small population of four to six pairs
established itself there.

In 1960 I found a moorland nest in south Ayrshire—a repeat laying after
a clutch had been robbed. At the time both the landowner and the keeper

were happy to see the young harriers fledge, but over the next few years, as a few more pairs appeared, a less tolerant attitude developed; but in a different part of the county two or three pairs have probably nested, more recently, in young forests.

On the Dumfriesshire moors a pair nested unsuccessfully in 1961, a few miles from the 1960 nest in Ayrshire, and there may have been earlier nests. More recently there have been a few pairs nesting in young forests in the same area. In Wigtownshire, particularly, they were greeted with a policy of extreme repression on the grouse moors. In 1965, when I saw my first pair of harriers in the west of that county, I found two pole traps set within sight of a public road. In more recent years there have been continued attempts by two or three pairs to nest on the moors there, but the young usually disappear from the nests.

The southward expansion of the late 1950s and 1960s did not include recolonisation of the old haunts in south-east Scotland. In the Lammermuirs, birds have lately been seen in summer. If nesting has occurred it has not been proved, although there is much suitable-looking ground, with the possibility of safe nesting sites in some recently afforested parts of Berwickshire, not far from where Billie Mire once gave them security. Across the border into Northumberland, Kielder Forest was reached about the same time as Galloway, in the late 1950s, and a small colony of at least six pairs flourished in the young plantations there during the 1960s, but had mysteriously declined to only one pair by 1971. There was no real expansion south of the border until three nests were found in North Wales in 1962; in one locality, a pair was present in 1961 and breeding may have occurred then and possibly in earlier years (Williams, 1976). After 1962, Hen Harriers began to spread fairly quickly on the extensive moorlands of North Wales.

R. F. Ruttledge and David Scott agree that the recovery in Ireland began about 1950. In 1956 Ruttledge and Peter Roche found breeding pairs in Wexford, Waterford, south Tipperary and Cork. In certain areas the birds were back in some strength, but there was no sign of nesting in western Cork or Wicklow. Scott, however, says that nesting in Wicklow began very soon after this. Already, in 1958, the Irish Bird Report mentioned that Hen Harriers were breeding in five counties and there was a gradual further extension of range during the following years, to seven counties in 1967, and eleven in 1970. Scott and Frank King (1976) point out that the main spread in Ireland has been westward and northward from a nucleus in the south, but Scott also comments that there has been some expansion from a central area—the Slieve Bloom—where a small population may never have died out. Although Ruttledge (1966) stressed that Hen Harriers in Ireland showed a marked preference for afforested areas, Scott, King, Ken Preston and Ewart Jones have all found that nesting sites on moorland, near forest plantations, are commonest in some districts.

The results of my own studies and enquiries, including reference to the provisional map for the *Atlas of Breeding Birds*, show that in the first half of the 1970s, there has been continued increase and spread in some areas, but in others there has been no definite change and there have even been some local decreases. In Orkney, Balfour considered that the population was still increasing in 1974, with 63 nests found (many polygynous matings) and an estimated minimum of 75 nests on Mainland, six to eight on Rousay and three on Hoy. In Sutherland, Nethersole-Thompson reported a good many pairs in 1975 and an evident increase, but Pam Collett told me that nesting was still rather sparse in Caithness in 1974 and 1975. In the Outer Hebrides, Peter Hopkins doubts if the breeding population is increasing, with a minimum of 13 pairs divided between North and South Uist in 1975. The results of my own enquiries and observations, in 1974, suggested about 15 pairs in the Outer Hebrides including one nest on a third island. There was still no confirmed breeding in Lewis or Harris during the *Atlas* years (1968–72), but there were records for Skye, Mull and Islay. Extensive plantations of young conifers are at present favourable to an increase on Mull, but on the moors of Islay, Graham Booth (1975) said that Hen Harriers are still only attempting to re-establish themselves in the face of persecution.

There are large areas in the West Highlands where breeding has not been reported and the main strength on the mainland continues to be in parts of Deeside, East Sutherland, Perthshire and Argyll.

On 18,000 hectares (70 square miles) of Deeside, where Nick Picozzi has studied moorland nesting, displaying harriers were seen in 17 moorland localities in spring 1974, but young fledged from only six nests. Here, and on the Perthshire moors, persecution is heavy and although a moor owner in southern Perthshire assured me that harriers were common and increasing in 1974, he made it clear that keepers are generally encouraged to destroy nests and birds, and it is unlikely that many young survive there. Geoffrey Shaw, however, found birds present in the breeding season in nine scattered localities in the Southern Highlands, between 1972 and 1975, and confirmed breeding in four of these. In 1973, he found five pairs in Dunbartonshire, where recent nests have mostly been on moorland in close proximity to forest; and single pairs, near the Perthshire/Kinross border (1972) and in Stirlingshire (1973), were in new localities. On the other hand, the maturing forest plantations of Loch Ard, west of Aberfoyle, which were an important breeding area in earlier years, had almost ceased to provide the conditions for nesting, and over the Southern Highlands in general there is a changing situation as some forests become too old for nesting and new ones are colonised.

A small number of pairs continue to breed in Arran where I found them in afforested localities in 1975, but I was also told of nesting on open moorland (Hogg, 1976). Across the water in Kintyre there has been some recent decrease from about 20 pairs in 1973 (Turner) to nearer ten in 1975. In the old counties of Ayr, Wigtown, Kirkcudbright and Dumfries not less than 12 pairs were present in 1974 but the number of nests was probably fewer than this, both in 1974 and 1975. In south-west Scotland as a whole, there is no sign of a recent increase in spite of a massive extension of afforestation on hill land. In this region there is evidence of persecution on moorland. The decline in Kielder Forest, Northumberland, which began in the late 1960s was not halted and no evidence of breeding was obtained there in 1974 or 1975.

Graham Williams estimated some 20 pairs nesting in Wales in 1975 and reports that they had 'a good year again'. He also noted colonisation of new areas in mid Wales, but he considers that the rate of increase in Wales generally has slowed down in recent years. Apart from one site in a forest plantation, which was occupied for six years in the 1960s, all the Welsh nests have continued to be found on the moors, although in 1975 the behaviour of one male was indicative of another forest nest. Nearly all the sites are on keepered ground and Graham Williams has known four instances of nest destruction by man. Nevertheless, compared with most Scottish grouse moors, persecution seems less intense in Wales and a good proportion of pairs rear young.

There has been some recent extension of breeding in England by a small number of pairs as far south as the West Midlands, which suggests that Hen Harriers might become re-established in haunts where they were lost as breeding birds more than a century ago.[1] In Ireland there had been a spread of nesting into 13 counties by 1971 when, for the first time this century, successful nesting (two broods) was recorded in the north, in Co. Antrim.

In 1973, Parslow estimated the breeding population of Britain and Ireland as over 100 pairs, perhaps much more. It is doubtful if there has been a substantial increase since then, but in any of the last two or three years the total has certainly been much more than 100 pairs. Particular caution is needed in any attempt to give a figure for the number of pairs owing to the occurrence of polygyny in some places. David Scott's estimate for Ireland is an average of 250–300 pairs in 1973–75 and I think that the average annual total for Britain in this period may be at least 500 pairs, so that a total population of 750–800 pairs might not be very wide of the mark. In some regions it is very likely that further colonisation is being prevented by persecution, but it is difficult to account for the lack of increase, and even some decrease, in the extensive tracts of young forest in southern Scotland and northern England. Disappearance of birds in spring, after they have settled and displayed on forest breeding grounds, has been noted in Kintyre and Galloway and it is likely that in Galloway, at least, the great reduction of open moorland at fairly low elevations, which may be important for hunting, is have a limiting effect. In the absence of intensive grouse moor management,

---

[1] Michael Seago considers that the evidence for a recent nest in a coastal part of Norfolk is not entirely satisfactory.

Hen Harriers in Ireland are evidently less dependent on the new forests for nesting cover and comparative freedom from human persecution than in many parts of the mainland of Scotland. It is interesting that such a successful colonisation of the open moorland has been made in North Wales in spite of some persecution. Breeding failure by Hen Harriers in France and Scandinavia has been attributed to the effects of agricultural pesticides. Many of our own Hen Harriers must at times be at risk from these, especially those which winter at long distances from their breeding grounds, but there has been no clear evidence of increased hatching failures or egg breakage to suggest that pesticides have reduced breeding success.

Postscript. Since I completed this chapter Edward A. Blake's paper 'The Return of the Hen Harrier' has appeared in *The Forth Naturalist and Historian*, Vol. I, 1976. This paper includes interesting data on the colony at Carradale, Kintyre, where over 300 young were fledged, 1957–64. Food, habits and habitats are also discussed.

On the post-1939 recovery of the Hen Harrier on the Scottish mainland Blake repeats his earlier statement (see p. 79) that it was already common in the Highlands by 1945 but apart from a shepherd's evidence of several nests near Callander in the late 1940's, he cites no sources to add significantly to J. W. Campbell's summary (see pp. 78–79). Blake found his first nest in Glen Artney, Perthshire, in 1951. He emphasises the decline on the Perthshire grouse moors, in the 1950s, caused by persecution. Campbell also commented on this (see p. 80). Today (1977), persecution on moors appears to be continuing to prevent consolidation in Britain and David Scott tells me that in Ireland it has probably been severe in some localities and may have cut back some gains.

CHAPTER FOUR

WHAT KIND OF PREDATOR?

HUNTING METHODS

In its most usual type of hunting flight, the Hen Harrier flies low, flapping and gliding at an average of less then three metres above the ground. C. A. B. Campbell found that a female hunting rough pasture flew at 50 km/h alongside his car. Many of those who have described the manner of hunting have been shooting men and, not surprisingly, have likened it to a well-trained setter or pointer 'working every inch of the ground'. Yet, to my mind, the most evocative description was by the Frenchman, Lafond (Geroudet, 1965), who said it hunted 'comme s'il cherchait un objet perdu'. Like any expert searcher, it examines the ground selectively, often doubling back to course a promising patch of cover a second or third time. Its progress over a moor or marsh may seem slow and wayward until the observer realises how skilfully it uses variations in contour and height of vegetation to achieve the best chance of surprising prey. It flaps and tacks laboriously to reach the summit of a little hill crest, then angles downward into a hollow beyond with a sudden surge of speed. Eric Ennion (1943) described how Montagu's Harriers, in a comparable way, surprised ground-feeding Turtle Doves by a lightning drop after an approach screened by clumps of tall reeds. The technique of low-level flight, varied pace and use of ground enables a harrier to exploit its long legs to maximum effect in striking at prey on, or close to, the ground.

To a human observer the hunting flight of a Hen Harrier often seems to involve a prodigious amount of travelling for infrequent reward, but in most kinds of terrain it is extremely difficult to keep the bird continually in view for a long time. I have watched a male hunting five year old conifers and forest rides for two hours without making a capture. On the other hand, I have seen one, in autumn, catch three voles on upland pasture in little over 20 minutes. It may have been killing more than it could eat, for the third vole was dropped and the harrier flew on without retrieving it. A very characteristic way of making a kill, on the ground, begins with a swift pirouette or half-turn, with tail fanned, as the low flying harrier suddenly stalls and drops into tall vegetation. The outcome of these pounces may not be apparent for a few minutes, or longer, when the bird may rise with prey in a foot.

One June evening in South Uist, with the low sun flooding a vast amphitheatre of moor and mountain with rich colour, I watched a male hunting during the hour before sunset. In the brilliant light I could follow his movements with my binoculars as he worked a gully below Beinn Mhor, two kilometres away. He began to come nearer, following the course of a burn and was then lost among the heathery mounds of the low moor. For two minutes I had no idea where he was and had little hope of finding him again. Then he re-appeared, in the foreground of this great landscape, still following the burn, just below me. Even so, he kept so low between the steep banks of the burn that when he pirouetted and pounced I could not be certain whether the prey, a Meadow Pipit, had been taken on the ground or just above it. I glimpsed a second pipit escaping by flying to one side and believe that the other had been caught as it began to rise. The prey was taken a short distance to a prominent perch above some old peat cuttings and, after feeding, the harrier remained perched there, quite still and upright, like a tiny grey statue until, long past sunset, I gave up hope of discovering whether it would seek a more sheltered spot for the night.

From his extensive studies of Marsh, Montagu's and Hen Harriers, Schipper concluded that the last was the most agile hunter. His evidence was from observation of hunting behaviour and from a comparison of prey brought to nests. Hen Harriers caught more passerine birds, able to fly, than either of the other harriers. I can cite several instances of Hen Harriers capturing flying birds. I have seen a male take a small bird, by a sudden jink, as it flew just above a moor, while Louis Urquhart has recorded how a male, in Arran, put out a foot and caught a small flying bird, 'like a cricketer in the slips making a brilliant one-handed catch', less than three metres above the ground. Dick Orton observed another male, in Wales, taking 'the tail-end

Charlie' from a flock of Starlings, in a sudden burst of acceleration. D. H. Macgillivray, of Machrie, Arran, has seen a low-flying Snipe caught after it had been flushed by a dog. The harrier showed remarkable acceleration. I have seen several captures among 2–6 metre conifers when the prey was almost certainly in flight. Schipper considers that the Hen Harrier is even more manoeuvrable in flight than the lighter-bodied Montagu's Harrier, due to its longer tail in relation to wing-length from wrist to tip.

Long flight pursuits of prey are not often observed, but H. M. S. Blair (Bannerman, 1953) saw a male in Norway chase and capture a Meadow Pipit, 'stretching out one long talon to grip it', while Geroudet wrote that the Hen Harrier could chase and capture passerine birds with as much speed as a Sparrowhawk. The examples I have cited, of Hen Harriers taking flying prey, mostly refer to males, which are generally more agile than the heavier females. The habit of capturing flying prey is certainly commoner in the Hen Harrier than many writers suppose. A species which so often preys on full-grown passerine birds is, I believe, as likely to catch them in the air as on the ground. In this respect Jacques Delamain's suggestion that Crested Larks flew up as a harrier's shadow passed over them is intriguing.

In view of the fact that Red Grouse are an important prey of Hen Harriers in some districts (see p. 264), it is surprising how little has been recorded about the way in which they are caught. Packs of grouse usually fly when they see the approach of any broad-winged predator, such as eagle or harrier, unless it is high in the sky, but single birds or pairs may try to escape attack by crouching. Watson and Jenkins described how a cock Red Grouse, when stooped at by a male Hen Harrier, stood up and struck towards the attacker with its bill, repeating this behaviour when the harrier stooped a second time. The harrier then flew on. On another occasion a hen Red Grouse flattened herself into long heather beneath a stooping harrier. She then jumped up with wings spread and avoided the harrier's strike by 'a quick bouncing movement' back to the ground. I have observed rather similar incidents; once I saw a single grouse and, another time, a pair, rise almost vertically into the air immediately under a hunting Hen Harrier. On each occasion the harrier jinked but failed to make contact with the grouse which 'bounced' back to the ground while the harrier proceeded on its way. I have never been near enough to a Hen Harrier killing a grouse to see whether it was caught on the ground or just above it. A 19th century observer, Mr McCalla in Connemara (Thompson, 1849), who had often seen harriers attack grouse, wrote that a struggle took place, the grouse rising into the air contrary to its usual mode of flight. His account suggests similar behaviour by the grouse to that already described. Graham Williams has seen a male diving continually on to a patch of heather where there was a brood of Red Grouse; the adult Red Grouse 'jumped' out of the heather each time the harrier swooped past but in spite of this the latter was seen to pick up a young grouse and fly off with it.

William Macgillivray's son, while searching for insects on the Pentland Hills in 1835, saw a pair of Hen Harriers 'start a Red Grouse which one of them captured after a short chase'. I have often seen both Red and Black Grouse flushed by Hen Harriers on ground where all three species roosted in proximity; the grouse did not then rise unless a harrier passed very near to them. A harrier coursing low over marsh or field will flush duck, and even geese, but they do not rise until the hunter is close upon them. I have seen this happen many times in Galloway but not once has the harrier struck at or pursued the wildfowl. It has always seemed intent on watching the ground for smaller prey in its immediate path. Harriers spend much more time in coursing flight than other predators of comparable size, and they appear to husband their energies by waiting for the chance of captures easily within their manoeuvrability and grasp.

Breckenridge's verdict that it is a predator of comparatively weak grasp needs some qualification, at least in respect of females[1], which are certainly able to kill prey as large as adult Red Grouse and half-grown rabbits. Nevertheless, Hen Harriers do sometimes appear to have difficulty in retaining their grasp, even of comparatively small prey. I have seen a small bird escape after being carried a short distance in the foot—in this instance the prey was retrieved and secured—but a better example of a harrier's 'weak grasp' is given by R. C. Dickson; he observed a ringtail drop into rough grass and rise with prey, possibly a rat, which it dropped. Twice more the harrier clutched and released the prey which jumped up at it and finally escaped. During this episode a male Hen Harrier, which had been hunting near by, came close to the ringtail and itself dived into rushes, possibly after the same prey, without success. Dugald Macintyre (1936) saw a Hen Harrier turn on its back to capture a mobbing Lapwing which was then carried a short distance before it escaped, apparently unharmed. In this incident the harrier evidently took the Lapwing in reaction to its mobbing, but its release was perhaps another example of the difficulty of maintaining a firm grasp. Prey which has been secured is not always crushed to death, as I have found a fledgling Skylark still alive after being dropped to a brood of young Hen Harriers and Nick Picozzi has found a fledgling Meadow Pipit, alive but dazed, at a Hen Harrier's nest. Schipper, however, noted living prey only at nests of Marsh and Montagu's Harriers, not at those of Hen Harriers.

An unusual attempt by a Hen Harrier to lift a full grown duck, probably a Wigeon, from the sea is quoted by Bannerman (1953). The harrier (the sex was not stated) made two unsuccessful attempts to secure its prey, once carrying it for about ten metres before dropping it. In Kintyre I was told the story of a male Hen Harrier striking down a Greylag Goose. It was vouched for by five witnesses familiar with harriers, and there was no doubt about

---

[1] In summer, 1976, R. C. Dickson (pers. comm.) saw an immature male kill an adult cock Red Grouse.

the goose, which fell injured and ended up in the pot. It seems a pity to have to add a note of scepticism, but perhaps the possibility of confusion between a grey harrier and some other light-coloured predator such as a Greenland Falcon or a grey Goshawk cannot be discounted. Nick Picozzi considers that it would be impossible for even a female Hen Harrier ever to strike down a bird as large as a goose.

There is considerable agreement among older writers about one of the Hen Harrier's methods when hunting Partridges. Daniel, in his bloodthirsty but uproarious *Rural Sports* (1807), must have been one of the earliest propagandists against Hen Harriers. He advocated setting pole traps for 'ringtails', placed in specially set 'bird bushes' into which the hawk was sure to drive a covey of Partridges, then perch on the pole while seeking them out. Jardine said: 'I once shot an old female which had driven a covey of Partridges into a thick hedge and was so intent on watching her prey that she allowed me to approach openly from a distance of half a mile'. In this century, Dugald MacIntyre (1947) described how a pair of Partridges with a brood escaped from a Hen Harrier by hiding under a thorn bush. In each case it might be more correct to say that the Partridges sought safety in the cover of bush or hedge, rather than that they were deliberately driven there.

Hen Harriers do not habitually seek prey by hovering at a height, as Kestrels, Rough-legged Buzzards and sometimes Common Buzzards do, but they frequently check themselves in their progress, to hang, with beating wings and spread tail, at three to six metres above the ground. This low level hovering can be seen when a harrier is hunting over crops or other dense ground cover where small birds or mammals may be concealed. Hovering over bands of reapers, for the 'game' disturbed, was noted long ago in south-east Scotland (Muirhead, 1889).

As a group, harriers are the most owl-like of hawks in their hunting methods. Short-eared Owls and Hen Harriers each sometimes suggest the other by their behaviour and outline when hunting, though the harrier's smaller head and much longer tail are quite diagnostic, and the long tail is almost as mobile as a kite's. Harriers are also more like owls than other birds of prey in having large ear apertures, about as big as their eyes, and it might be expected that these would facilitate crepuscular hunting, which Neufeldt frequently observed in the Pied Harrier, but there is not much evidence that this occurs in the Hen Harrier. Certainly, in my own experience in Scotland, I have never observed it in summer; and in ten years of observation at winter roosts I have only seen rather desultory hunting by birds at about sunset, and none at all in near darkness. Breeding adults normally cease to bring prey to their young about an hour or two before sunset and, in winter, hunting grounds are deserted for the roost within about a quarter of an hour before or after sunset; in other words, before the light is really dim.

Hen Harriers are not very early risers in the morning. Though some will leave a winter roost in dim light they do not usually start to hunt immediately. Brown and Amadon suggest that the harriers' sharp hearing serves them in locating small animals such as mice by their squeaking and rustling, when sight alone might not detect them in the cover of long grass. I have seen Kestrels hunting much later in the dusk than Hen Harriers and it seems evident that the relatively larger eyes of falcons render them more capable of crepuscular hunting. Indeed even small birds such as Robins, which continue feeding long into the dusk, are endowed with conspicuously large eyes. St John, however, noted Hen Harriers hunting rats in rickyards at dusk. When, on one occasion, a hunting Hen Harrier passed within a few feet of the car in which my wife and I were sitting, we were quite able to hear the 'swoosh' of its wings, whereas an owl at the same distance would have been inaudible.

When censusing raptors in Michigan, the Craigheads discovered that Marsh Hawks were often not spotted because they spent so much time on the ground. The time averaged 57% of the day and was higher in wet weather, when a pair were on the wing for only half an hour in three hours. Heavy rain probably makes normal hunting almost impossible, by hampering both vision and hearing, while prey is also less active and more skulking. When such conditions occur, persistently, while chicks need food, the smaller or weaker members of broods sometimes die from starvation. I have, however, seen prey brought to nests in moderately heavy rain, and Schipper records that, in one long spell of rain, 16 items of prey were brought to a Hen Harrier's nest while, in the same period, nothing was brought in by Montagu's Harriers. He also found some indication that high wind velocity, by itself, was advantageous for hunting Hen Harriers. Both Hen and Montagu's Harriers brought a higher proportion of birds among their prey in strong winds. Louis Urquhart has told me that the spectacular capture which he observed in Arran (see p. 87) was made on a very windy day. In such conditions manoeuvrability in hunting may be greatest. It would be interesting to know how far spells of really bad hunting weather threaten the survival of Hen Harriers in winter. It might be expected that inexperienced, first year birds, which certainly have much higher mortality than older birds, would be at greatest risk.

Hen Harriers frequently perch on posts, bushes or stone dykes and no doubt these are used as an aid to spotting prey, but they hardly make any use of high perches, such as telegraph poles, which Kestrels, Buzzards and owls find convenient aids to hunting. In America, the Craigheads recorded some hunting from perches by Marsh Hawks. In Galloway, R. C. Dickson has seen a female Hen Harrier on the ground, prowling the heather, apparently stalking fledged young Meadow Pipits. It seems likely that some nestlings and beetles are located while the harrier is on the ground. I have watched a female Hen Harrier moving about in a willow bush, where a Reed Bunting was perched in the lower branches. The harrier was unable to flush it out and could not come to grips with it in the bush.

Many observers, past and present, have said that the Hen Harrier could be seen travelling the same route at approximately the same hour for days in succession. Seton Gordon (1923) wrote that one in the Outer Hebrides was so punctual that he could almost set his watch by it. Collectors and keepers killed birds by waiting for them to appear at the expected time. The date and time of over 200 winter sightings in Galloway have been collected by Louis Urquhart and myself but very few of these indicate such regularity. Certainly, a male feeding young often brings prey within half an hour or so of the same time daily, particularly in the late afternoon, but he may not follow the same route. The only occasions in our experience when birds repeatedly followed the same line at nearly the same time, were when they were travelling to and from winter roosts, but the same general areas, as much as twelve kilometres from a roost, were visited by hunting birds over many winters. At times, almost certainly, the same individual hunted the same area over a period of days or weeks.

Sometimes several individuals hunt in close proximity on particularly good feeding grounds. R. C. Dickson has seen up to five together, in winter, hunting two kale fields, of 85 hectares, where unsuccessful attempts 'by bursts of speed', were made to take Curlews, Pheasants and Wood Pigeons on the ground. It is not uncommon for two or three hunting Hen Harriers to be in view at once, in autumn or winter, where voles are abundant. K. W. Bartlett has told me of a remarkable observation of five males disturbed together from the edge of a young conifer plantation, in Galloway on 3rd January. As the birds were seen at about 11.00 hours there was no possibility of a roost-gathering, and they were presumably attracted by food, although a search of the ground provided no obvious explanation.

It is not uncommon for Hen Harriers to become involved in encounters with other predators over prey. My own most interesting experience in this respect concerned a Merlin and a male Hen Harrier on a September evening, over a flat moorland near where both species roosted. It occurred well before dark and both birds were in search of food. At first the Merlin was merely diving at the low flying harrier but when the latter flushed two small birds, probably pipits, the Merlin cut in below it and pursued one of

them upwards above the harrier which continued as before. The small bird evaded the Merlin by slanting towards the ground but by ill-luck its path took it within reach of the harrier which grasped it in an outstretched foot just clear of the heather without hesitating in its flight. The Merlin reacted with something very like fury at being baulked, buzzing the harrier at full speed when it landed with its prey. I had the impression that the Merlin, which was in attendance on the harrier for about half an hour, may have shadowed it deliberately on the chance of snatching flushed prey.

Very similar observations have been made by David Bates and Dr R. J. Raines in Cheshire, in winter. It was noted that a Merlin and a ringtail Hen Harrier were often in the air together, and closer study showed that as the harrier quartered the ground the Merlin circled above and stooped at any small birds which it flushed, whereas the harrier attacked birds which had dived to the ground after being flushed by the Merlin. Don and Bridget MacCaskill (1975) describe how a female Hen Harrier suddenly appeared, flying swiftly towards a Short-eared Owl, and robbed it 'neatly' of the prey it was carrying. Eddie Balfour recorded Hen Harriers in Orkney robbing Short-eared Owls and Kestrels of prey and once saw one in pursuit of a Merlin carrying prey.

In Co. Kerry, Frank King several times saw a male Hen Harrier make a fierce attack on a male Kestrel as it crossed the harrier's home ground on its way to and from its own nest near by. Frank King writes: 'The harrier would rise like a silver streak to intercept the Kestrel and both birds would fall down into the heather like a madly-flapping feathered ball, all wings and tails, tightly locked together. The first time I saw this happen I thought the harrier intended lunching on Kestrel, but after about a minute of silence (the birds out of view on the ground) they both flew up, the harrier now holding the mouse the Kestrel had been carrying'. He adds that both the harrier and

Kestrel successfully reared young. Piracy by Hen Harriers on such neighbouring predators may be no commoner than similar acts by Kestrels on Short-eared Owls and, occasionally, harrier, Kestrel and owl are seen competing for a particular victim, as recorded by R. C. Dickson (1971).

Many pairs of Hen Harriers have Short-eared Owls as close neighbours and sometimes Merlins or Kestrels as well. It appears that both in winter and summer such associations can be mutually advantageous in the location of prey. Eddie Balfour told me that he had seen a female Hen Harrier dispute with a Peregrine over a Mallard which the latter had killed. Although the harrier was forced to retire at one stage, it returned to take possession of the kill and feed upon it. Nick Picozzi has seen a female harrier snatch food from another female in spring; Balfour's and Picozzi's observations were both made in Orkney.

HUNTING HABITATS

The Hen Harrier hunts almost any kind of open or fairly open terrain which supports high numbers of birds or mammals small enough for capture. Woodland is generally avoided, except where the trees are mostly less than about six metres high, or are interspersed with comparatively open ground. The most common hunting habitats are moorland and heath, bogs and marshes, sand dunes, cultivated fields, rough pasture and young conifer forests. Scrub woodland, such as willow, birch or juniper is also hunted. Fernando Hiraldo writes that, in south-west Spain, wintering Hen Harriers particularly hunt the maquis of rock rose (*cistus*) and heather, and also exploit barren deforested ground. Very open ground, such as mown hayfields and stubble, are favoured seasonally, especially when exposed prey suddenly becomes vulnerable.

The Hen Harrier's hunting grounds show a wide altitudinal range. In good vole years it can find enough food at 1,000 metres in the Norwegian mountains, but in some parts of its breeding range, such as Britain, food scarcity above 600 metres confines it to lower elevations. In great contrast to the high Norwegian fjelds are the Dutch breeding grounds in the Flevo polders and on the Wadden Islands. W. Schipper finds that it hunts over meadows, dunes, cultivated fields, saltings and marshland; in Flevoland the numerous wintering Hen Harriers mostly hunted open fields when voles were abundant but, when these declined in numbers, more birds were taken from the marshes.

In Britain in winter, Hen Harriers range much more widely over lowland fields, marshes, saltmarshes and sand dunes than in summer, but upland moors and young conifer forest are by no means deserted. In the Scottish Highlands ringtails are much commoner in winter on moorland than adult males. In Galloway, where many adult males as well as ringtails winter, the range of habitat hunted at this season is wide. My analysis of sightings of hunting birds (see Fig. 12) between September and March, indicates a gradual shift to hunt lower ground as winter advances. In the lowlands of Galloway, favourite winter hunting grounds are marshes and agricultural land, especially weedy fields of turnips or kale, which attract high numbers of likely prey in the form of small birds, particularly finches and buntings. There is some indication that, at this season, males form a higher proportion of the Hen Harriers hunting open fields than they do in other habitats with taller vegetation. In the Netherlands, Schipper found that females, in the breeding season, tended to hunt 'more structured vegetation' than males.

In North America the Marsh Hawk occupies an equally wide variety of habitats but in the absence of other species of harrier, is a more important predator in deep marshes.

FOOD

In some parts of the Hen Harrier's range, mammals form a larger part of its prey than birds, although a higher proportion of the latter tend to be taken in summer than in winter. Several studies of the prey of the Marsh Hawk in North America have shown the great importance of small rodents in its diet. The Craigheads (1956) found that, in winter, Marsh Hawks on Michigan farmland preyed chiefly on meadow mice, which made up 93% of the prey items in 1942, and 99% in 1948, even though mice were less abundant in the latter year. They were still the major prey in spring and summer, at 54.9%, but small and medium sized birds amounted to 31.4% in these seasons, when much less data was obtained than for winter prey. It was noted that as vegetation grew in the spring the mice became less vulnerable. At a comparable latitude in Western Europe (about 47°) there would not be the same scarcity of possible bird prey in winter.

Randall's study (1940) of the seasonal food habits of the Marsh Hawk in Pennsylvania, showed that 'mice' were the staple food in every month, except June and July, when juvenile birds were the most important items. More than 60% of the total yearly food items consisted of 'mice' (? voles). This study was done on a 'pheasant range' and it was found that only 9 out of 829 items, (1.1%) were pheasants, all apparently juveniles. Randall commented that a large part of the avian prey was probably taken as carrion, or after the young had been exposed by the activities of man (mowing and harvesting). Errington and Hamerstrom (1937) had reported that they found no perceptible relation between the conspicuous hunting activity of Marsh Hawks and the seasonal shrinkage in size of pheasant broods. Errington and Breckenridge (1936) found some regional variation in summer prey, in different parts of the prairie country of north and central USA. In Iowa prey was almost equally made up of birds and mammals while in Wisconsin mammals (mostly ground squirrels and young cotton-tail rabbits) greatly predominated, at 81% to 14% birds, mostly passerines. Errington and Breckenridge tabulated nearly 1,000 items of prey in all. Those of minor importance included frogs and insects, the latter appearing in twice as many pellets of juveniles as of adults.

Less data were obtained on prey at other seasons as few harriers wintered in the region. They fed mainly on mammals in the cold months and often fed on carrion. Even in the fall, most observed feeding was on roadside carcasses, mainly of rabbits; and in winter the staple food consisted of mice and frozen carrion, with a few weak Bobwhites. Other studies confirm the impression that in North America the Hen Harrier feeds most on small mammals and that small birds are also important prey in spring and summer. Clayton M. White writes that it may take higher proportions of bird prey in the southern parts of its American breeding range, and reports that in Utah it relies heavily on recently fledged passerines, especially Horned Larks.

The Marsh Hawk has a traditional reputation as a killer of poultry and game and has been much persecuted on this account. Prey investigations have produced no real evidence to justify this. In one of his studies, in Minnesota, Breckenridge (1935) made the interesting comment that most of a small number of pheasants and chickens taken were the prey of one particular pair of hawks which were *not* the nearest to the poultry. He added that all the farmers in the vicinity seemed to recognise the effectiveness of Guinea Fowls and Purple Martins in protecting their poultry from hawks, and that the farmer reporting hawk damage had neither of these about his premises, whereas one or the other was present on all the other farms. Two almost full-grown American Bitterns were rather surprising prey found at a nest in saltmarsh, by Charles A. Urner (1925), who commented that young Bitterns were no mean antagonists. In Norfolk, England, Anthony Buxton (1946) often saw the larger Marsh Harrier dive at Bitterns but did not think that they ever dared to attack them in earnest. Urner did not mention the strong possiblity that such prey was taken as carrion. Although most of the bird prey identified by American ornithologists consisted of passerines, other birds taken included rather many flickers (woodpeckers) whose slow flight and habit of feeding on open ground evidently made them vulnerable. Among curiosities of prey, no less than eleven Crayfish were found among 63 items at a nest in Arkansas (Wilhelm, 1960). It will be noted that fish have also been recorded as food in Britain.

In Europe, the bulk of the Hen Harrier's prey is divided between mammals and birds and, as in America, the proportions vary both regionally and seasonally. Hagen's list of summer prey in the Norwegian fjelds, quoted by Bannerman (1953), gives a total of 333 mammal items and 228 birds, or 57% and 41% respectively of the whole, but no account is taken of prey weights. The mammal most commonly taken was the large mountain vole (*Microtus ratticeps*) and nearly all the mammal prey consisted of small rodents. Many species were identified among the birds and about a third were pipits and finches. A much smaller number of birds as large as Fieldfares, or waders such as Golden Plover and Wood Sandpiper, occurred, and the few grouse and duck were nearly all young. Bannerman says that the list included all the smaller birds of the fjeld. Nevertheless, Hen Harriers in the Norwegian mountains are rarely able to find enough food for all their chicks in years when the vole population is low. During the period covered by Hagen's list (1938–46), at least four of the years were good for voles. In Finland, Hen Harriers are considerably dependent on the fluctuating population of lemmings.

Schipper (1975) found that passerine birds made up an important part of the Hen Harrier's prey on the Flevopolders, Wadden Islands and Groote Peel (an inland area) in the Netherlands and in two areas of northern France. Young Pheasants and other nidifugous birds, rabbits and voles featured among the prey to varying degrees. In one breeding season in Flevoland, young pheasants were taken to such an extent that the percentage of passerines in the prey was considerably diminished, while in that season no small mammals were identified in the diet. Evidence of some differences in predation between the sexes was obtained; females caught more rabbits and pheasants, males more passerine birds. Although lizards and large insects were often taken by Montagu's Harriers, very few lizards and large insects were found in the food of Hen Harriers in the study. Pellets from communal roosts in the Netherlands showed that when voles were abundant they formed the principal prey of wintering Hen Harriers, but when they were scarce, bird remains predominated in the pellets. Starlings formed almost 46% of all the passerine birds in pellets from the island of Terschelling. Schipper considered that wintering Hen Harriers showed a preference for voles but could switch readily to hunting passerine birds. He also cited a food study in Baye de l'Aiguillon, France, in which the proportion of voles and passerine birds in the prey varied from one winter to the next in relation to a fluctuating vole population. Nevertheless, he suggests that the absence of *breeding* Hen Harriers from large areas of Spain and Italy may be related to the lack of voles 'or replacements' in these regions.

Geroudet said that voles were the main winter prey in France but, in summer, ground birds including nestlings and fledglings 'qui volent mal' were important food. Leverets and young rabbits were mentioned as occasional prey. Studies in Germany, Hungary, Yugoslavia and the USSR, summarised by Schipper (1975), all indicate the importance of voles and other small rodents in the diet. In Uttendorfer's German study (1952) voles constituted 80% of the prey. Pellets collected from a winter roost, at which males predominated, in Belgian Lorraine, consisted mostly of the remains of voles. Some small birds had also been taken (Mois, 1975). Schipper, however, points out that Hen Harriers wintering in Italy, where very few small diurnal mammals are available, subsist almost entirely on passerine birds.

The numerous old records of prey items in Britain and Ireland need to be treated with caution as the writers were generally more likely to record the killing of a game bird than any other prey. The rather frequent references to Hen Harriers killing Partridges in the 19th century reflect a period when Partridges were much more plentiful in the marginal upland ground than they are now. The game-books of Captain Clark Kennedy of Knockgray, in the Stewartry of Kirkcudbright, for the 1860s and 1870s, demonstrate this for many shoots in south-west Scotland. (Although hawks were quite often shot, too, none were specifically identified as Hen Harriers.) There were many old reports including some very angry ones, of Hen Harriers killing Red Grouse, notably in Ireland and the Scottish Highlands. St John claimed that prey included Black Grouse and Mallard but does not describe the circumstances and it is at least likely that such large prey was found injured or already dead. Many old regional accounts do, however, show a wide variety of small prey. In Devon the food was said to consist of mice, moles, lizards and small birds, but it is possible that there was some confusion between Hen and Montagu's Harriers there.

In his pioneer study of Hen Harriers in the 1780s, on Newton Common, Carlisle, Dr Heysham observed a male bring two Yellowhammers, a sparrow and a lark to feed its young. He also noted lizards as prey. St John's verdict on the Hen Harrier's food in Sutherland (1849) was: 'though very destructive to game it compensates for this in some degree by occasional preying upon rats, vipers etc.' The 'etc' perhaps covered all those smaller items of prey which were considered neither 'useful' nor 'harmful' in

a sportsman's balance sheet. Very few of the old ornithologists examined prey remains or stomach contents of Hen Harriers which had been killed, but F. M. Ogilvie (1920) made the following dissection notes in Suffolk and Norfolk:

10 April 1900:	an adult female contained the remains of a water vole.
June 1904:	an adult male was feeding on a small leveret.
7 January 1907:	female, immature; stomach contained the remains of a Chaffinch and a Skylark.
30 March 1911:	female, adult, feeding on Partridge; its stomach contained 4 ounces of flesh.

Macgillivray (1836) found feathers of Ptarmigan in a female's crop, possibly the only record of this species as prey of the Hen Harrier. In the Shetlands, Saxby (1874) said that Golden Plovers were the most usual prey—a rather surprising statement since harriers have apparently always been rare or absent in Shetland at the season when young, easily caught, plovers are available.

There is rather more information on the prey of British Hen Harriers in some of their major haunts in recent years, although Nick Picozzi's important findings, particularly regarding the effect of predation on Red Grouse in Lower Deeside, must be awaited. From Orkney, Balfour and Macdonald (1970) reported on prey brought to a nest and identified from a hide, rather late in the season, between 27 July and 14 August, when the chicks fledged. They recorded 23 mammals (5 rabbits, all caught by the female, and 18 Orkney voles), the same number of birds (1 Corncrake, 2 Lapwings, 1 Golden Plover, 2 Skylarks, 7 Meadow Pipits, 4 Starlings, 1 small wader and 5 small birds, unidentified) and 3 'small items'. Of 82 pellets from nests in the same year (1969), 79% were fur and 21% feather. Identifications from these pellets were:

rabbit remains in	3 pellets
Orkney vole remains in	28 pellets
brown rat remains in	1 pellets
'Large Birds' remains in	10 pellets
'Small Birds' remains in	15 pellets
insect remains in	12 pellets

Twenty-three pellets without hard remains contained fur, and 5 contained feather. Meadow Pipit, Starling, Lapwing and Red Grouse were identified in pellets. In a lecture and in conversation with the writer, Eddie Balfour said that Orkney voles and young rabbits were the commonest prey, and many young Curlews and recently fledged Starlings were brought to nests. I am informed by Dick Orton that Starlings made up all the prey identified by a photographer at one nest in Orkney. It was thought that the lateness of the nest studied by Balfour and Macdonald might have accounted for the absence of young Curlews.

Balfour believed that Orkney Hen Harriers have a food preference for voles. Chicks feeding off a young Curlew were seen to leave it for a vole brought in by the cock, but one such observation, though interesting, is clearly inconclusive. John Douglas considered that the spread of rabbits to the hills, after a succession of mild winters, was a factor in the increase of the Orkney harriers before 1933. He said that at that time the Hen Harrier's habit of taking chickens from crofts was a threat to its survival, but there is no definite evidence of how commonly this has occurred in Orkney.

The great success of the Hen Harrier in Orkney obviously owes much to the high numbers of the large Orkney vole (34–63 grams), apparently not subject to severe population crashes. Balfour and Cadbury suggest that the relative scarcity of breeding harriers on the island of Hoy may be due to the absence of voles. Fairly large numbers of harriers, though relatively few adult males, are seen in the islands throughout the winter, and Sunniva Green has told me that pellets from winter roosts suggest that voles are a main food source at this season. The harriers hunt the voles both in the lowland agricultural land and on the heathery hillsides; according to the *Handbook of British Mammals* (Southern, 1963), the voles occur 'throughout pasture and arable land and up to at least 700 feet (210 m) on heather, thinning out thereafter'. In Orkney most of the hill ground is within the altitudinal limit of vole abundance. The relative absence of grazing by domestic animals, plus the moist climate, gives much lusher hill vegetation than at comparable altitudes over most of mainland Scotland and northern England, where sheep have roamed for generations. The Orkney hill ground is thus an exceptionally good habitat for voles and, incidentally, provides the Hen Harrier with perfect nesting sites.

As a visitor to the harriers' Orkney breeding grounds I was impressed by the large number of hill breeding rabbits often feeding apparently unconcernedly on the patches of emerald grass and moss in the close vicinity of the harriers' nests. Curlews are numerous breeding birds on and near the harrier nesting grounds; Balfour remarked that they were scarce early this century and have greatly increased. It is significant that Starlings nest in the heather and their newly fledged young are thus particularly vulnerable. In a few minutes flight, Orkney harriers can hunt a wide variety of habitats including moorland, pasture, arable and marsh. Red Grouse form only a minor part of harrier prey in the Orkneys. The future of Hen Harriers in Orkney may be considerably affected if the present trend towards reclamation of moorland for improved pasture and cultivation continues, though possibly more by a reducton of nesting areas than a shortage of prey.

The food and hunting habitats of the Hen Harrier in the Outer Hebrides appear to have similarities with, and some differences from, Orkney. Robert Gray (1871) inferred that field mice (? voles) were the principal prey and Donald Guthrie, a keeper in South Uist from 1883–1905, wrote (1920): 'The food is said to consist chiefly of mice, rats and voles, while sometimes they kill young rabbits, stripping the skin neatly back from the snout before eating them. Occasionally they kill grouse, but very rarely.' Seton Gordon (1923) records that many young rabbits were taken in the sand dunes. In North Uist, in July 1974, I found a feathered young Golden Plover at a nest and in South Uist, as already described, saw a male harrier capture a Meadow Pipit on moorland. Dr J. W. Campbell told me that young waders formed a considerable part of the prey taken in these islands.

With such fragmentary evidence on prey, I can do no more than comment on the most favoured hunting grounds. The Hen Harriers hunt partly over moorland but make regular flights to hunt the croftlands, machair and marshy fringes of lochs on the Atlantic side of the islands. These are undoubtedly where most prey is taken. Mr Snow, a keeper in South Uist, told me, in 1974, that even in summer he saw harriers most often over the machair, and after the young had fledged he had seen up to five together there. At this season young waders, larks and pipits are in great abundance

on the machair and are probably the main attraction. Important differences from Orkney are the complete absence of young Curlews and the much heavier grazing of moorland by sheep; large tracts of hill ground look very bare and would be unlikely to carry a very high density of voles. In contrast, over parts of the moorland, and especially on islands in lochs, heather and willow scrub grow to heights of 120–150 cm, providing excellent nest-sites for harriers. Two such sites in South Uist were 5–6.5 kilometres from the nearest machair, which would be near the limit of hunting range for a cock feeding a hen or chicks. In one island, a nest has been found in rough ground with short heather, marginal to machair, suggesting that this site was used in preference to more suitable sites in deep heather at greater distances from the best feeding grounds.

In mainland Orkney, at the present time, an area of suitable nesting ground holds about four times as many nests as there are likely to be in an area three times as great in the Outer Hebrides. It appears that Hen Harriers in the Outer Hebrides are at some disadvantage compared with Orkney, perhaps because substantial and easily caught prey, like the large Orkney Voles and young Curlews, are absent from the vicinity of nesting grounds; or perhaps because, in general, they need to make longer journeys to the best hunting grounds. The absence of breeding Hen Harriers from the Shetlands and the northern Outer Hebrides is particularly interesting and suggests that the lack of voles in these islands may be a serious disadvantage. Peter Hopkins points out that bird prey is likely to be much scarcer in the Long Island than in the Uists and Benbecula because machair and cultivation are largely confined to a small area in Harris. Bobby Tulloch has reminded me that there are no Kestrels breeding in Shetland, and Peter Hopkins says that the same is true in Lewis and Harris.

In June 1975, I visited the nesting grounds in the Kintyre district of Argyll. In four to five year old conifer forest harriers were catching voles. The undulating hill landscape, hardly rising above 450 metres, is a little reminiscent of Orkney in spite of the extensive conifer forests on many lower slopes. Although grazed by sheep, the unplanted hill ground is lush with grasses, heather and rushes in this rain-washed peninsular, and in the south-west the lower, Atlantic-facing, cattle pastures are almost Hebridean in appearance. Before the forests were planted, Dugald Macintyre (1936) wrote that food at a nest in Kintyre was chiefly young wildfowl and 'field mice' (? voles). He said that the bulk of the winter food, identified from pellets at a roost, consisted of young rodents and Snipe. Peter Strang, a forest ranger, has been finding harrier nests in Kintyre for the past 23 years, and says that Meadow Pipits were the commonest prey, but many voles, Skylarks and young rabbits were taken, also a few young Red Grouse and occasionally young Pheasants.

In the last few years there has been a marked decline in the number of harriers nesting in Kintyre. Although some former nesting grounds in

forests are no longer tenable because of the height and density of the trees, it is difficult to believe that the shortage of nesting sites is enough to explain the decline. It is much more likely to be due to a reduction in easily caught prey, brought about by the loss of much open hunting ground and the increased difficulty of hunting within the wellgrown forests. In 1975, it was clear that the main concentration of breeding harriers was in the largest area of forest to be planted within the last five years, where voles were abundant and obviously an important prey of the harriers. In Arran, across the water from Kintyre, D. H. Macgillivray said in 1967 that a Hen Harrier at Corriecravie 'used to take Lapwings'. I have already mentioned his observation of one capturing a Snipe.

So, information on the Hen Harrier's food in the three important areas of Orkney, the Outer Hebrides and Kintyre is uneven. The range of prey taken in Orkney is fairly well established, there are some interesting indications for Kintyre but far fewer for the Outer Hebrides. In all three localities, however, prey includes voles, young rabbits and small birds. Red Grouse numbers are low in Orkney and Kintyre and harrier predation on them cannot be significant in either. Nor is there a high population of Red Grouse in the harriers' Hebridean haunts. I was informed by a game-keeper there that he was much more concerned with wildfowling than grouse shooting. Two contemporary keepers have no criticism of harriers as predators on game, while the same view seems to have been held by Guthrie while he was a keeper in South Uist from 1883–1905. Although information on the food of the Hen Harrier in the Outer Hebrides is much needed, I should be very surprised if it produced much evidence of predation on grouse.

In 1967, David Stephen wrote of the feeding habits of Hen Harriers nesting in Scottish forest plantations. The locality was not disclosed but it was probably in west-central Scotland. He said that, in 1966, voles were

Young Woodcock

scarce and wet weather made for bad hunting. 'The harriers killed mainly birds but still not enough of them. In all nests there was famine and in all of them chicks were dying and being eaten. Only the intervention of the forester, supplying rabbits, saved the broods. This season (1967) was different. Six pairs hatched full clutches and reared full broods. Voles were up, so much so that a man could see one on foot at two minute intervals on a walk over the hunting grounds'. His general verdict was that Hen Harriers fed mainly on small mammals and birds, somethimes taking eggs or nestlings of ground-nesting birds. He saw a male bring a Woodcock chick to a brood. He also noted frogs and slowworms as prey. In Sutherland Bruin Nethersole-Thompson watched a Hen Harrier skin and eat a frog. David Stephen's account is particularly interesting for its suggestion that in one Scottish forest, at least, fluctuating vole numbers had a decisive effect on harrier breeding success.

On a Kincardineshire moor in the breeding season, Nick Picozzi has found Meadow Pipits, Red Grouse chicks and leverets the most common prey items. Mountain hares, rabbits and various birds were also eaten.

My data on prey in south-west Scotland are given in Chapters 16 and 17 and Tables 17–23. They can be summarised as follows: in summer, young Red Grouse and passerine birds, especially Meadow Pipits and Skylarks, were the most common items. Most of the birds were young. Mammals, including voles, rabbits, hares and mountain hares, occurred in 30% of winter pellets examined from one roost but birds, mostly passerines, were found in 70%. Birds formed nearly 90% and mammals only 10% of remains in pellets from another roost in south-west Scotland (Dickson, 1970).

There is much less evidence of Hen Harriers feeding on carrion in Scotland than in North America, but in November 1972 a female died after feeding on a carcase (? sheep) poisoned with mevinphos, near Dunblane, Perthshire (Bell, pers. comm.); and on 14 May 1974, Nick Picozzi saw a male at a very old carcase of a mountain hare at Kerloch, Kincardineshire, while Louis Urquhart has seen a female at an old rabbit carcase in Galloway (see p. 229). Osborne (Harvie-Brown and Buckley, 1887) mentioned dead fish as food in Caithness and Jardine (1834) wrote that Hen Harriers repeatedly visited the Solway Stake nets to feed on dead fish. Saxby (1874) mentioned fish as food in Shetland, but did not know whether it had been found dead or alive. It seems likely that some of the larger items among winter prey in my south-west Scotland study were found as carrion.

David Scott tells me that in Ireland the food varies somewhat from one place to another, but most of the prey in his experience consists of small birds. He once saw a female harrier with a partly-eaten rabbit which she was only just able to lift. He comments that grouse are almost rare birds in Ireland and he has only once found remains of a grouse at a nest. At one nest in the Slieve Bloom the main food appeared to be water birds, including Water Rails. No evidence of carrion feeding in Ireland was obtained by Scott.

I have little information on the prey taken by Hen Harriers in England. In 1932, Desmond Nethersole-Thompson recorded that a pair nesting on a Surrey heath fed their young largely on young rabbits and also brought them a half-grown Lapwing, and a male Stonechat. A male on Lundy Island during a hard winter subsisted mostly on starving Fieldfares (D'Urban and Matthew, 1895). Dr Ken Brewster, however, was informed 'by a reliable ornithologist' that Hen Harriers only appeared in one part of southern England when voles were abundant. Graham Williams tells me that he once found the remains of a young Red Grouse and a young Pheasant at a nest with six large young, in Wales. As I have pointed out in my account of prey in south-west Scotland the remains of larger kills, which cannot be entirely eaten, are likely to be found in or near nests with large young, whereas small prey items, which may be more numerous, are usually only traceable from pellets.

A minor part of Hen Harrier food, in both America and Europe, consists of insects, particularly beetles. These may be of some importance to young birds in their first weeks of hunting. In America, Breckenridge (1935) found that the young ate some fruit, and he recorded blueberry, raspberry and dogberry.

I have listed in Table 2 specifically identified prey from British and Irish sources but I do not claim that it is exhaustive.

PREY SELECTION

The foregoing account has shown that small mammals, particularly voles, are the main food of Hen Harriers in many parts of their range. In the Norwegian fjelds, and probably in some afforested areas in Scotland, a shortage of voles may greatly reduce breeding success, or even inhibit breeding, even though bird prey appears plentiful. The dense population of harriers in Orkney is much dependent on the large Orkney vole, the numbers of which seem never to drop to very low levels. This rich food source is augmented by the plentiful supply of rabbits and, in summer at least, there is also a good supply of the young of passerine and wading birds.

Schipper suggests that the absence of voles or 'replacements' may explain the absence of breeding Hen Harriers from large parts of Spain and Italy. Yet it is clear that thriving populations of Hen Harriers in parts of Scotland, in Ireland (where voles are absent), and in Holland can subsist principally on bird prey. In such instances passerines often form a high proportion of the birds taken but larger birds such as well-grown young Red Grouse, Pheasants and Curlews are sometimes important, too. If voles or other small mammals are scarce, or absent, the requirement is an abundant population of birds living in habitats suited to the harriers' hunting methods. Since the average weight of prey taken by female Hen Harriers, in Schipper's Dutch study, much exceeded that of males (122 g to 68.9 g), it may be that a good supply of larger prey, such as game birds or rabbits, is important to females; and where voles are scarce, might even be essential for the most successful breeding. Schipper's very interesting evidence, that males took the higher proportion of agile passerine birds, further suggests a different emphasis in the prey selection of the sexes. The fact that females usually hunt nearer to their nests than males might explain why, in south-west Scotland, most nests are close to areas of moorland or young forest plantations, where young Red Grouse can be easily found. Analysis of sightings of harriers hunting in winter in the same part of Scotland (see Chapter 17), shows that males made up a higher percentage of those seen hunting lowland pasture and arable land than moorland, conifer forest or marsh. At this season, passerine birds were most numerous in the lowland fields.

In their discussion of predation by Marsh Hawks, Errington and Breckenridge suggested that they preyed mainly on a vulnerable 'over population' of prey species. This vulnerable element was said to be living beyond the capacity of the habitat to accommodate it adequately. An obvious example of this occurs when voles, fledgling birds, or nests are suddenly deprived of protective cover by operations such as grass cutting or harvesting. But Errington and Breckenridge had especially in mind the normal, large surplus of birds or mammals which dies from starvation, or other causes, having failed to find adequate living conditions. In their research on Red Grouse in Scotland, Jenkins, Watson and Miller (1964) convincingly showed that grouse killed in winter by predators such as Hen Harriers were nearly always surplus birds which had failed to establish themselves as territory holders. Starvation was usually their fate if they were not killed by a predator. So, grouse losses to harriers in winter had little or no effect on the breeding stock in the following season.

In the breeding season most bird prey is young and is therefore taken from the most vulnerable parts of the prey populations. It is obvious that, whatever the prey species, a high proportion of the young will not survive long enough to breed. The birds and mammals commonly killed by Hen Harriers all belong to very successful, numerous species and it would be surprising if harriers ever had any controlling effect on prey such as Meadow Pipits, Skylarks, or the huge winter finch flocks which they hunt. Nevertheless, the Craigheads did show that, in their study area, the total effect of all the predators, which included some Marsh Hawks, limited a population of meadow mice in early spring, when the mice were especially vulnerable in minimal vegetation. In Britain, Lockie (1955) considered that Short-eared Owls could hasten the decline of field voles between April and June but probably had little effect on their numbers later. It is not known whether Hen Harriers, in Britain, ever have a depressive effect on vole numbers.

It is obviously true that the creation of grouse moors offers the Hen Harrier a suitable hunting habitat, with large numbers of possible prey. Yet, even if it were proved that several breeding pairs could limit the number of young grouse available to the guns, this would appear not to be important since, according to the findings of Jenkins, Watson and Miller, not all the potential crop was shot on the moor studied by them, and a surplus of birds, most of which died before the next breeding season, always remained after shooting. In the eyes of a keen grouse shooter it is a crime to disturb a grouse shoot and no one will deny that a harrier can cause grouse to fly and scatter, but the same applies to many large, broad-winged birds, not necessarily predators. Unfortunately, the Hen Harrier is still much hated on most grouse moors, and where large sums are paid to shoot grouse, it appears that legal protection of harriers avails little or nothing. I return to this subject in my final chapter.

FOOD CONSUMPTION

The Craigheads found that a captive female Marsh Hawk in the autumn and winter months ate an average of 100 grams of food daily; and a male in spring and summer ate an average of 42 grams daily. Raptors in the weight range of Marsh Hawks and Hen Harriers required an average of 12.5% of their body weight in spring and summer, and 15.8% in autumn and winter. The average weights of male and female Hen Harriers are given by Brown and Amadon as 357 grams and 483 grams respectively, but they were considerably lighter 'on migration in China'. Marsh Hawks were noticeably heavier, averaging 472 grams for males and 570 grams for females. The approximate weights of some prey species in Britain are: Meadow Pipit (adult) 20 grams (J. Watson); field vole (adult) 25–40 grams, Orkney vole (adult) 50 grams (*Handbook of British Mammals*); Red Grouse (adult) 629 grams (D. A. Ratcliffe). Young of any of these are of course in a lower range of weights.

I do not know what proportion of prey weights can be counted as 'food' but some speculations on the amounts of prey a Hen Harrier needs to kill for itself can be made. A female in winter, having the maximum requirement for a Hen Harrier, might need to kill up to four Meadow Pipits or two Orkney voles, while a single Red Grouse could be sufficient for two–three days. It would seem that if Hen Harriers could readily kill full-grown Red Grouse, life would be easy for them. It is probable that only females are commonly able to kill adult Red Grouse and even they are most likely to capture those which are already weakened from food shortage, disease or injury. On the other hand, the hunting capabilities of males presumably make it easier for them to live off a larger number of small items, than off a small number of large ones.

Hen Harrier over Orkney Moorland

CHAPTER FIVE

THE BREEDING CYCLE: COURTSHIP TO INCUBATION

NESTING HABITATS

My account of Hen Harriers breeding in a particular region (south-west Scotland) is given in Chapter 9 et seq. The present chapter traces the general pattern of behaviour throughout the breeding season and refers to a number of specialist studies, particularly those of Balfour in Orkney, and Hamerstrom in Wisconsin, USA.

The breeding habitats of the Hen Harrier include most of those which I have summarised as hunting habitats in the previous chapter. A few of the hunting habitats, such as bare grassland and saltings, are unsuitable for breeding owing to lack of cover for the nest, which is always built on or very near the ground. Provided adequate hunting grounds are available in the vicinity and the site is undisturbed, Hen Harriers can nest successfully in a variety of moorland or marshland vegetation, in the dense cover of young conifer forests, in scrub of birch or willow, and even in fields among crops such as wheat or kale. Nevertheless, in Britain and Ireland during the present century, the breeding grounds have been almost exclusively on moorland or in young conifer forest.

The contrast between the landscape and atmosphere of the harrier nesting country in Orkney or the Outer Hebrides, and that of the great tracts of conifer forest of south-west Scotland, is extreme. In Orkney, the background is the seemingly limitless sea from which the spume often flies from a multitude of white crests all the way across the Pentland Firth. Between rain showers, the towering headland of Hoy is caught in pearly sunlight, and the jigsaw of brightly patterned cultivation with its clear-cut

109

farmsteads contrasts sharply with the spongy moorland above the waists of the hills. These, the harrier nesting grounds, have been evocatively described by Desmond Nethersole-Thompson: 'squat hills, brown, barren and storm-swept, rise gradually from those countless lochs and lochans which twinkle in the sunlight like blue eyes in the deep brown faces of the valleys'.

In North and South Uist, the nesting grounds lie in that mysterious heartland of moor and bog, so deviously intersected by lochs and arms of the sea that the whole forms an unbelievably intricate mosaic, from which protrude hills of glistening, almost naked rock. To my mind these islands, where the Hen Harrier is inclined to be elusive, are the most delectable of all the nesting grounds which I have visited. Often all is obliterated in smearing rain, but when the clouds lift, the colours of the islands and the sea beyond have an almost magical freshness.

I shall describe the nesting grounds on the moors and in the forests of a mainland area of Scotland in Chapter 14. I confess that the serrated outlines of afforested hills seem to me to provide a less becoming setting for harrier watching than the open moorland, with its infinite variety of colour and texture, changing almost imperceptibly through the seasons. Yet the forests hold a certain charm, not least in early spring when the blue-green richness of sitka spruce seems to belie the time of year. In Kintyre, although the nesting places are mostly in the forests, the surroundings have a charming variety, with hints of both Orkney and the Outer Isles.

Every ornithologist knows the thrill of discovering familiar birds in strange lands. So it was with special pleasure that I met the Hen Harrier, evidently breeding, in the conifer plantations of the Auvergne, some 600 metres up, in the heart of the Massif Central—a countryside remarkably reminiscent of harrier haunts in the Galloway forests. Further north in France, Hen Harriers were almost certainly nesting neighbours to Marsh and Montagu's, in the parched heathland near a cluster of lakes in the district of La Brenne. Bannerman said that in Scandinavia the Hen Harrier has two distinct breeding grounds: 'one in the lowlands of central Sweden with their great reed and sedge-fringed lakes, the other on the high plateaux'.

As I have shown in the historical section of this book, fens and marshes were formerly regular nesting haunts in Britain and it seems possible that, where sufficient habitat of this kind still exists, they might become so again, especially since an increasing colony now flourishes not far away in Holland. Two birds ringed as young on the moors of Orkney have been found during the breeding season in Holland and may well have been breeding there. The habit of nesting in standing crops has long been known in Continental Europe, but in 1964 Terrasse said that, in France, modern agricultural methods did not give harriers enough time to rear young in cultivated fields. Geroudet knew of nesting in France in corn and kale fields, among whins and heather on heaths, in a little copse among dense reeds and in sedges bordering a marsh. Although there is no proof that Hen Harriers

ever nested in cornfields in Britain (as Montagu's have done) it certainly seems possible that 'modernised' agriculture, in the form of the so-called 'prairie' farming of eastern England, might provide a possible nesting habitat. It is probably true, however, that Hen Harriers are generally attracted by the habitat of their birth unless, perhaps, the presence of already established birds (as in Holland) acts as an introduction to different nesting terrain.

My own belief is that nesting in conifer plantations, in Scotland, was begun by birds moving a short distance from adjacent moorland, probably because of persecution, and since in the early years of afforestation the habitat change is gradual this was not as great a change as it might appear. The recent remarkable increase of the Dutch breeding population of Hen Harriers has taken place largely in low-lying coastal habitats, mainly sand dunes in the Wadden Islands and reed-beds in the polders; according to Schipper vegetation in the dunes is principally marram grass *Ammophila arenaria*, sea buckthorn *Hippophae rhamnoides*, bog rush *Schoenus nigricans* and creeping willow *Salix repens*. So far as I am aware there is only one certain contemporary instance of Hen Harriers breeding in sand dunes in Britain (anon). If there is indeed an interchange between British and Dutch breeding stock perhaps dunes and reed-beds may become established breeding haunts in Britain.

Although Short-eared Owls almost invariably colonise young conifer plantations which contain an abundance of voles, the requirements of breeding Hen Harriers are evidently more complex. Those who knew the colony which flourished for some years in Kielder Forest, Northumberland, are still puzzled by its recent disappearance, as they consider that there is no obvious lack of young plantations or moorland similar to those which used to provide food for the colony. In Wales, Graham Williams reports that the nesting habitat is largely moorland and there has been hardly any colonisation of the extensive young forests; and in southern Scotland vast areas of such habitat, where Short-eared Owls and Kestrels abound in good vole years, have gained only small numbers of nesting Hen Harriers.

When I was shown some of the Welsh harrier ground, in 1975, I was immediately captivated by the spaciousness of these rather high heather-clad moors. Nest sites there are commonly at between 375 and 600 metres, but most nesting in Britain occurs at elevations between 150 and 450 metres. David Scott and others inform me that the same applies to Ireland, where the nesting environment is commonly a mixture of moorland and young conifer plantations. David Scott tells me that moorland in the vicinity of the plantations is undoubtedly the most usual nesting situation, but there is some local variation. King, for instance, has found that most nests in Kerry are well clear of forest; and Scott attributes the siting of a number of nests in the Wicklow forests to inadequate cover on neighbouring moorland. Jones, who describes four nests in open moorland and two in young forest, suggests that the association of Hen Harriers and trees in part of Munster may be fortuitous, since forests are now so widespread there that any nesting site is bound to be fairly near a plantation, and Scott agrees that the same applies to Wicklow. It may well be that the lack of nesting in some districts, either in forest or moorland, is due to food shortage at higher elevations, particularly during the period when males do all the hunting and need to find an abundance of small prey.

In North America, Bent (1937) gave many examples of the Marsh Hawk nesting in swamps, often much overgrown with bushes, but he also mentioned nesting in dry habitats such as open grassland and wheatfields. Hamerstrom's study area of 6,500 hectares, in Wisconsin, which held up to 25 nests in one season, included both dry grassland and low-lying swales of willow and sedge, but over 60% of the Marsh Hawks' nests were in the latter.

RETURN TO BREEDING GROUNDS; PAIRING AND COURTSHIP

Anyone who has watched an area where Hen Harriers have bred over a number of years is bound to be struck by their faithfulness to established territories and their apparent reluctance to colonise other areas which appear equally or more suitable, not far away. Although Hamerstrom (1969) found in North America that conifer plantations were deserted as nesting grounds when the trees were 4–6 years old, my experience in Scotland (see Chapter 12), has been that in some instances nesting continues until the trees are at least 14–15 years old. In a few instances, I have been reasonably certain that an individual bred in the same territory in successive years. Balfour wrote that many harriers in Orkney did so, and one female bred in the same area for six years, but he also knew of cases in which known birds moved around from year to year, and in one case a hen nested in 'five different stations' in six consecutive seasons. Hamerstrom, working with colour marked birds in Wisconsin, found that pair fidelity from year to year was extremely rare. In both the Orkney and Wisconsin colonies there was a strong suggestion, from the low percentages of marked birds which returned, that the colonies were replenished by immigration. As I have said in Chapter 7, a few recoveries of Orkney-ringed young indicate that, later, these sometimes breed or attempt to do so in widely scattered parts of the northern and central Highlands of Scotland. There are, therefore, strong hints that Hen Harriers often settle to breed in areas distant from their birth place. My own observations, at a winter roost in south-west Scotland, lead me to believe that this may be facilitated by individuals from different breeding areas mingling and even pairing there.

Over a large part of its breeding range—in northern and eastern continental Europe and Asia, and much of North America—Hen Harriers are absent in the winter. Bent reported that the males returning from the south reached Manitoba in mid-March, as much as three weeks ahead of the females, while Hamerstrom found that males arrived on the nesting grounds in Wisconsin about the same time, and the females followed 5–10 days later.

In the less severe winters of western Europe, Hen Harriers hunt over some breeding grounds in any month, but these individuals may or may not include those which nest there. Certainly, in Orkney, a few ringtails, wing-tagged there in summer, have been seen roosting not far from the nesting grounds in winter. In Scotland generally, there does not appear to be the same clear-cut distinction in arrival times of males and females in the nesting territories as has been found in regions where the species is fully migratory. In south-west Scotland I have the impression that males visit the breeding areas increasingly on fine days in February and March, and these may well be birds which will breed there. On one such day, about the middle of March, a pair may be seen together, lazily floating above the territory where nesting took place in the previous year. They may not appear until early April or even later, but the first pre-nesting flights of the pair do not seem to be delayed by cold weather. Balfour found that pairs were also seen over the nesting grounds in Orkney in March, and he did not indicate that males preceded females there. On 18 March 1976, I visited a forest in south-west Scotland where there had been three nests in 1975 and found that a pair were already flying conspicuously above the old sites, in very cold but sunny weather. Sometimes they drifted apart but during the afternoon the two birds, in their beautifully contrasted plumage, kept near together for long periods, the cock most often a little above the hen. This is characteristic behaviour at the pre-nesting stage. Now and again the cock loses a little height, dives playfully at his partner who may turn on her back, or he

touches her, wing to wing. From afar, silhouetted against the pale cerulean sky, the birds are like tiny arrow-heads, only distinguishable by the bulkier form of the hen and the occasional flash of silver-grey as the cock wheels in the gentle sunlight. They glide on tense wings, rising and falling almost imperceptibly. Time seems to stand still for them. As they work slowly over a wide expanse of forest or moor, they are not hunting but appear to be scrutinising the ground in which the nest will later be sited. On breezy days they lean into the wind on sharply flexed wings, their long tails often fanned and for ever in motion. At this early date they separate towards evening, no doubt to seek a meal before dusk, but in early April I have seen a pair settle to roost not far apart, very close to a nest of the previous year. On warmer days they soar together to a great height, with wing tips almost in contact, until the watcher strains to keep them in sight through binoculars. Jacques Delamain referred to similar 'magnificent and calm ascensions' by a pair of Montagu's Harriers. Yet, at any time in early spring, the advent of stormy weather, or more especially a blizzard, will drive them away from the nesting grounds and they may not be seen for days.

I have seen the first tentative versions of the full display flight before the end of March. This, surely one of the most arresting of all avian displays, has been most aptly christened 'skydancing' by Frances Hamerstrom. At first the male, after spiralling upward a little, angles downward only to rise and fall again in a series of undulations. There is nothing spectacular about these trial runs, but an observer might be forgiven for wondering if this can be the same bird which has previously behaved with such quiet restraint. The wing tips taper sharply to points, so that the outline is quite different from usual, more like a large wading bird as it whiffles down to land on a still day. The contrast between the black wing-ends and the white underparts is revealed to the maximum. The combination of this pattern and the uninhibited manner of the undulating display flight, often remind me of the spring flight of the Lapwing. For many days, until well into April, the most heady 'skydancing' is likely to be withheld. In its most intense form it consists of a steep climb, for perhaps 30 metres or more, when the bird rolls on its side 'like a wing-nut turned on a bolt' (Breckenridge), or turns a somersault followed by a seemingly reckless earthward dive which is suddenly checked, just above the ground, either by the start of another ascent or by flying slowly onward to alight, often at a possible nest site. In fine weather the performance may be repeated many times—the exceptional number of 105 successive dives was once recorded by Balfour. All the time the wings are flapped rather slowly and loosely, as if the bird were acting in a trance. At no time is a harrier more conspicuous. In this way it may advertise its presence to other Hen Harriers by displaying over several different possible nesting stations, travelling from hill to hill and rising high above each in turn. Although some of the most prolonged display flights are made by young unmated males, or by males whose mates have died or been killed, 'skydancing' commonly takes place when one or more females are in the vicinity. It is most intense when two or more pairs or polygynous groups are nesting within sight of each other, and my own experience indicates that when pairs are separated by a few kilometres the full display is not likely to be seen at all. Hamerstrom discovered that a number of different males 'skydanced' during April over the same site and, when a pair finally nested there, the male was not one of the 'skydancing' birds. Typically, however, the behaviour is quickly followed by the inspection and selection of the nest

Flight path of 'skydancing' Hen Harrier

site. Females often display, also, 'especially when they outnumber males' (Brown, 1976), but according to Balfour their flights usually take a 'switchbacking' course rather than one of steep ascents and descents, as I, too, have noted. The hen usually watches her displaying mate from the ground and it may be that the display helps to establish a bond between the pair, but it does not appear, from what I have said, to play an indispensable role for pairs in isolated situations. Once, when three other Hen Harriers were in the vicinity, Balfour saw a male and female 'skydancing' together. The male's aerial display generally ceases about the time that eggs are laid, but according to Brown (1976), diving displays by females continue late into the fledging period.

During display and courtship both sexes call frequently. Display flights are often accompanied by bursts of chattering ('yikkering'), similar to the alarm calls made when a nest is threatened, but not as loud. The female's 'yikkering' is high-pitched and was compared by Walpole-Bond to the trilling of a Little Grebe. Frank L. Beebe (1974) writing of the Marsh Hawk, gives a good rendering of the call as 'kek-kek ke, check-quik-ah-ek'. The male's version is distinctly lower-pitched, but I once heard a first year male's call that was almost as high-pitched as his mate's. It is, however, the squealing whistle (or 'squeal-wail') of the female which is the dominant sound during the courtship period. Transcriptions of this sound hardly agree in more than assigning it two syllables. At different times I have written it 'swee-uk' and 'twiss-you', and it may vary in different situations. It is best-known as a begging call, urging the male to release food which he is carrying, but it also solicits copulation during courtship and may be continued with piercing insistence as the female follows the male about the nesting ground. The complementary call by the male, typically given when he approaches with prey, is a much quieter and lower-pitched 'dyouk-you' or 'tchiou'—almost a chuckle—but I have occasionally heard a male give a loud 'swee-uk' call when he was, perhaps, frustrated by a female refusing to come to take food from him. On one such occasion the male's call sounded to me like a sharp bark. It is obviously difficult or impossible to be sure, from a long distance, which bird is making a particular call and this has no doubt led to incorrect statements by some writers that the 'swee-uk' call usually comes from the male.

The following passage translated from the French of Delamain describes a facet of courtship which is unknown to me and does not seem to have been observed by others: '. . . the Hen Harrier . . . mimes, to pay his court, a carving scene. Taking a stand on a clod of earth, not far from his female, he repeatedly lowers his hooked beak towards his empty talons, as if he were mangling a prey then, standing erect again, exhibits his white breast'. He compares this to other well-known examples in which male birds exhibit prominent features of their plumage to females, such as the cock Chaffinch showing his 'white epaulettes'.

THE FOOD PASS AND COPULATION

About the time that the nest site is selected and building begun, the male begins to supply food for the female. At first he may fly in with prey but no aerial transfer or 'food pass' ensues when the hen approaches him. She may assert herself by dispossessing him of his prey after he has landed with it. On such occasions he appears very much the weaker partner but she will very soon be totally dependent on his hunting skills for all her food, which she will receive by the food pass. She will, however, continue to hunt for herself to some extent until she has begun to lay and incubate the eggs. Possibly, the male's first presentations are important in providing extra nourishment at the time of egg formation.

After a brief period of hesitancy, the food pass is nearly always achieved unerringly. The cock approaches, usually with the prey held in his conspicuously lowered foot, but sometimes carried pressed back under the tail. His manner of flight varies from a calm slow glide to steady almost hurried flapping. Very often he first comes into view a little above the horizon of the nesting hill and slowly loses height until he is almost above the nest. These never fail to be moments of tingling expectancy as the watcher waits for the hen to rise. If incubation has begun, and sometimes even before the start of laying, the nest can be approximately located by noting where she breaks cover at the start of her short flight to take the food pass or, of course, by watching for her return afterwards. During incubation she usually stays off the nest for some minutes while she feeds, and she may take a brief flight before returning to the eggs. The details of the food pass have many variations but in its most usual form the cock, keeping slightly above and ahead of the hen, drops the prey which she catches in an outstretched foot. This is achieved either by turning on her side or completely over onto her back, but she rights herself so swiftly that it is often difficult to be sure from a distance precisely how the catch has been made. Sometimes the prey is exchanged, talon to talon, and occasionally the hen takes prey from the cock on the ground. Later in the season, particularly when the chicks are near to fledging, hens often fly further from the nest—as much as 400 metres—for the food pass. Balfour saw a female take prey from the male, by a food pass, even though she was already carrying prey herself, but Dickson commented that the male in a similar situation flung his prey in the air so wildly that the female failed to catch it.

It is tempting to regard the food pass as a ritual, perhaps preserving the bond between male and female through the long period when their separate roles, as hunter and guardian of the nest, permit hardly any other contact between them. Yet, I wonder, is it not reasonable to suppose that the habit of aerial food exchange developed simply as the most efficient method for birds nesting in extremely tall dense cover, sometimes in marshes, where

The 'food pass'

prey, which is usually small, would be easily lost if it were dropped to the ground? Obviously, too, the long legs of harriers are advantageous for exchanging prey in the air. Presumably, the nest would run a greater risk of predation if the conspicuously plumaged cock habitually brought food for the hen directly to it.

Balfour wrote that coition will follow almost every food presentation until the sexual urge has been subordinated by that of brooding. He described the sequence of events as follows: 'After the "food pass" both birds will be grounded and perhaps about 50 yards apart. Instead of getting on with her meal, the hen crouches over it, giving vent to the food call with more urgency than ever. She is soliciting the male and he will respond unless he is not yet ready to do so.' The act of mating takes place on the ground, near where the nest will be built, or is already being constructed. It is accompanied by wing flapping of the male as he maintains his balance on the female, while she crouches with half open wings and raised tail. Food presentation, however, by no means invariably precedes mating. Of Montagu's Harriers, Delamain wrote that 'during two weeks and almost at every bringing of prey the nuptial rite will be the same, always provoked by the female after the food offering, and barely solicited sometimes, with sharp cries or an impatient flight, by the male'. I have observed a female Hen Harrier which had not been brought food before mating, continue to give begging calls afterwards, perhaps urging the male to hunt for a meal!

Surprisingly, Hamerstrom very rarely observed copulation in her long study of a breeding colony. I imagine that this was because the terrain where she worked was much less open than Orkney and birds on the ground more difficult to see. I have found, in south-west Scotland, that the only occasions when I could observe this behaviour clearly were when the birds were in open moorland. Those nesting in forest plantations are so often hidden by trees when they land that many details of their behaviour can only be surmised. In this habitat copulation is most likely to take place in forest rides.

NEST BUILDING

I have already mentioned that the cock at the end of a display flight may land in a possible nest site, where the hen follows him. When, in April or early May, the pair are to be seen slowly cruising close to the ground, with tails widely fanned, it is often the cock which drops first into a patch of tall vegetation. Nor is it rare for him to carry nest material at this stage. It is interesting to learn, according to Neufeldt, that the cock Pied Harrier glides above the hen with a small twig in his feet and is dominant in the selection of the nest site. Yet there is general agreement that the final choice of the nest site is made, and nearly all the building done, by the female Hen Harrier. It is not difficult to tell, from a distance, when nest-material rather than prey is being carried. Small bundles are sometimes carried in the bill, larger ones in

the feet. Long strands of grass for nest lining trail most conspicuously beneath the tail, or like straggly moustaches from the bill. Balfour considered that Walpole-Bond's description (1914) of the female nest building could not be improved upon: 'sometimes she walked rather clumsily for a short distance, sometimes she would jump rather curiously in the air ['endeavouring to uproot some heather' comments Balfour]; otherwise she indulged in low flights of a few yards and alighted again. Eventually she tore off a thin rod of ling, then flew by a circular course, low down and in a rather guilty manner, to a certain area of tall heather, into which, hovering momentarily, she let herself down gently.' Nest materials are all collected from within a couple of hundred metres of the nest. I have watched a hen make eight short flights to collect material in half an hour. Often, a nest is begun and abandoned for a different site, and at this stage the birds are easily upset by anyone misguided enough to walk over the ground in search of a nest.

THE NEST AND NEST SITES

Although Hen Harriers' nests are generally built among tall vegetation, it is remarkable how open the actual site often appears at close quarters; this may be partly because the birds do a certain amount of trampling in preparing the site, but I believe they choose a small, relatively clear space at the start. The material most commonly used for nest building is heather, varying from stout twigs to fine stems and sprays. Many nests are partly made of old bracken stalks and I have also found twigs of birch used. In my own district, however, few nests are close enough to birch trees for these to be used commonly. Balfour also found old withered thistle and foxglove among nest material.

In two out of four Irish nests in plantations of Scots pine or spruce, described by Garry Doran (1976), the foundation was made largely of gorse. Heather was a component of all four nests. Other materials used were straw, birch, larch, spruce, bracken and a little grass. This basic material is loosely woven together. A softer lining is then added, usually of grasses or rushes, often mainly the papery strands of dead molinia grass; sometimes bracken alone is used. Woodrush, the Golden Eagle's favourite, is also used as lining by some Hen Harriers. All through the nesting season the hen sometimes adds material, both to the outer structure and to the lining. Until the chicks are three or four weeks old, nests usually look quite clean and there is often an attractive contrast of colour between the dark outer material and the pale yellow or orange grass in the lining. The neatest nests have a 'soup-plate' appearance, but are often very flat with hardly any depth to the cup. I noted that one nest, poorly built by a first-year female, was made almost entirely of grasses. Some are much bulkier, 'at least ten inches high' according to Balfour. He gives the diameter as, generally, thirteen to twenty inches (32.5–50.0 cm)

The work of building a nest to the stage when it is ready for the first egg occupies a hen for 'fairly short spells', over a period of 'a few days, even a few hours in the case of a replacement nest, others taking a fortnight or more' (Balfour).

Male Hen Harriers sometimes build 'nests', which they do not line, although Balfour in his long experience never met the habit among Orkney harriers. Blake (1956) wrote that he had seen over twenty 'cock's nests' and had watched several being built, while Dickson has found several nests, which he attributed to cocks, on a moor in south-west Scotland, but he has not observed any being built. He described these as 'platforms, two feet or so in diameter, of dried grey heather stalks'. I have only once seen a male, which had apparently lost its mate, building a similar structure (Chapter 12). David Whitaker watched a cock adding material to an old nest over a period of an hour. At the time he had no mate but was displaying frequently. Later a female joined him but took no interest in the nest he had been building. I have found several platforms, hardly more than bundles of long heather twigs carelessly thrown together, which were close to nests with young, and I observed that well-grown chicks received and ate prey there. In the latter instances I had no proof that the 'nests' were the work of

the cock. P. H. Bahr (1907) found a chick, only fourteen days old, using a 'second nest, of a few twigs of heather, 30 yards from the original nest'. Dickson has found feathers and faeces at 'cock-nests', suggesting that they were used for roosting and this might possibly be their primary purpose. Yet, since Hen Harriers choose extremely wet situations for roosting in winter, I cannot imagine why they should build up a platform for roosting on relatively dry moors in summer unless, perhaps, to gain a better field of observation. Weis (1923) said that, in Denmark, male Marsh Harriers regularly built 'cock-nests' without lining, and used them as feeding and resting bases. He found no sign of this habit in male Montagu's and claimed that they had no need of it because they could find dry ground to sit on. It seems to me most likely that 'cock-nests' are only built where cocks out-number hens or when a cock has lost his mate. In Orkney, of course, there are only about half as many cocks as hens in the breeding population. Generally, it may be no more than a 'frustration' activity, but the platforms used by chicks as feeding bases, whether built by cock or hen, are possibly due to excessive human disturbance at the nest. Balfour, at any rate, con-sidered that a photographer had upset the birds at one Orkney nest where such a platform was built.

Within some of the nesting habitats which I have already described, some preferences in the choice of the nest-site may be cited.[1] Balfour, for instance, found that the more favoured nesting areas in Orkney always contained enough damp vegetation to escape damage by fire. About two-thirds of a large sample of nests found were in mixed heather and rushes, while more of the rest were in pure rushes than in pure heather. In North America, Charles A. Urner (1925) found that some nests of the Marsh Hawk built in very marshy ground were exceptionally built-up (to 37.5–40.0 centimetres), so escaping floods which washed out the nests of Short-eared Owls in the same marsh. Balfour said that in Orkney, nests were built up higher in tall or wet vegetation. Dixon (1898) described a nest site in Skye 'in an almost im-penetrable heather thicket', and this is still a good description of some sites in the Outer Hebrides where the surroundings of the nest are sometimes a dense mixture of tall, chest-high heather and willow. Some of these sites are on ungrazed islands in lochs. I noticed that rushes were growing among the heather around a nest in North Uist and, according to Hopkins, one site in South Uist is in a damp low-lying area of tall grass. Sites in 'beds of rushes' in the Border Hills were known to Bolam in the nineteenth century and I have seen a nest in Galloway, at a height of 420 metres, placed in a big tract of rushes with no heather in the vicinity. Bolam said that his father, long ago, knew of nests 'in the thickest hawthorn and gorse glens' on Alnwick Moor. Ruttledge (1966) and Scott, commenting on the recent spread of nesting in Ireland, have also remarked on the attraction of sites with a

[1] See also details of nest sites in south-west Scotland, Chapter 14.

strong growth of gorse among young conifers; and King has found some moorland nests which were built between the bare stems of flattened gorse bushes, the prickly extremities of which provided shelter and some concealment (see sketch). He has also found that small islets of heather and bracken situated in river beds, and measuring only about 100 × 150 centimetres, are often favoured in Kerry. Sometimes these are completely surrounded by a moat which may deter predators. Over a period of five years, a pair nested successfully in such sites in two different rivers. Other island nests are in almost dry river beds. Scott stresses that, in Ireland, nests are generally in well drained situations. Blake (1961) said that nest sites in the Norwegian mountains were typically in thickets of hoary arctic willows, at elevations between 870 and 1,050 metres. On a much-favoured hill in Kintyre where until recently a colony of pairs nested, the eye was surprised by numerous purple rhododendrons flowering among the conifers in a luxuriant underbush of heather. Many sites in conifer plantations are surrounded by heather, bog myrtle and grasses 60–120 centimetres tall, and are thus well sheltered and concealed throughout the summer, but many moorland nests and some in the youngest forests are very exposed early in the season. As shown in my regional study (Chapter 11), the most exposed sites of all have a high incidence of failure. The frequency with which the Hen Harrier chooses a site with a mixture of vegetation, such as heather and bracken or heather and rushes, is striking. The birds seem able to recognise that bracken, which is hardly out of the ground when the nest is built, will later provide valuable shade and shelter for the chicks.

I have tried to discover a pattern in the selection of situations for nests. Very few are on exposed hill-tops and steep, rugged slopes always seem to be avoided, even if there is plenty of ground cover, though King has found one remarkable nest on a steep slope, about six metres above a river bed, in Kerry. It was built on one of a series of the horizontal track-like lines caused by the stretching and splitting of the land surface. In this instance the ground rose steeply above the nest and fell equally steeply below it.

The most common situations are on gentle slopes, often just above or in a gully, generally well sheltered from the prevailing wind. In such places, of course, there is often a small stream near by. Delamain said that Montagu's

Harriers never visited a water hole which was within a few paces of their nest, but Hen Harriers certainly visit water for bathing, sometimes. This has been noted both by Balfour and Brian Turner.

There seems to be no evidence that sites which provide a wide outlook over their surroundings are preferred—the bird on the nest is often much too surrounded by vegetation to see any distance and must then depend on her ears for warning of approaching danger. In conifer forests, nests are quite often in virtually flat ground at fairly low elevations but here, I think, it is significant that females with young in the nest make much use of perching places on trees as look-outs. Nesting in marshy ground could obviously have an advantage in reducing accessibility to mammalian predators—the old sites in the almost impenetrable bogland of Billie Mire, in Berwickshire, must have been excellent in this respect. Island sites could also provide a high degree of safety. Yet, the more typical nesting sites in Britain and Ireland at the present time are easily accessible to man or fox and generally depend for their survival (where they are not actively protected) on being located in large tracts of fairly uniform country without obvious features to advertise where they may be sited. In Orkney, John Douglas told Nethersole-Thompson of a nest within 500 metres of a crofter's cottage. Hen Harriers are not commonly deterred by regular human activities such as peat-cutting, farm work or the passage of a shepherd and his dogs near the nest, but Jones suggests that the great amount of peat digging on the moors in Co. Limerick may sometimes compel birds to change their choice of site. Even moor fires, which often destroy good nesting cover early in the season, do not necessarily drive the birds very far away. Balfour said that the Orkney colony thrived among war-time manoeuvres!

Bannerman quotes evidence from Blair and Hagen that many nests in Norway are built close to some handiwork of man, such as a ditch, fence, snowbrake, railway line or station. He said that three nests were within ten metres of the main Oslo–Trondheim line. In my own experience a number of nests in south-west Scotland have been less than 100 metres from forest roads, and several have been less than 50 metres. More have been close to a forest ride than deeper into blocks of forest; there was sometimes a dead conifer nearby, conspicuously red or orange among the general greenery, which might have served the birds as a recognition mark. However, I am not sure that these features had any special significance as nest-markers for the birds. Balfour found that birds did not rebuild on the actual nest of the previous year, except sometimes when this had failed at an early stage, but there is widespread evidence of nests built within 20–200 metres of sites used the year before.

SOCIAL NESTING

Delamain said of the Montagu's Harrier: 'It is sociable and when it has at its disposal vast uncultivated expanses it tends to form colonies.' Hen Harriers also tend to nest in groups, but their nests are very rarely so close together as the Montagu's'. Weis observed a colony of six or seven nests of Montagu's barely 20 metres apart, and Chris Knights tells me that very similar spacing occurs in southern Spain at the present time. In the largest and best documented colony of Hen Harriers, in Orkney, Balfour had never seen two nests closer than 200 metres apart, but had heard of an exceptional instance in which only 15–20 metres separated two nests. Few nests in Orkney, however, are closer together than 500 metres. Remarkably, when I asked Peter Strang about the peak period (1958–60) for the largest colony in a Kintyre forest, he also gave 200 metres as the minimum distance between nests, and said that nine pairs had nested in an area of 250 hectares, the same number as that given by Balfour for an area of the same size in a particularly favoured moorland valley in Orkney in 1949. So the highest known density in Britain has occurred in two widely separated areas, at different times, and in very different habitats. Peter Strang believed that all the matings in the peak years in Kintyre were monogamous, and as far as can be judged from Balfour's account there was little if any polygyny in Orkney in 1949. (Polygyny is discussed below.)

In North America, Breckenridge found two pairs of Marsh Hawks nesting within 200 metres of each other. C. E. Douglas told me that only 150 metres separated nests of Hen and Montagu's Harriers in a Border forest in 1965.[1] In south-west Scotland, the shortest distance between two Hen Harriers' nests, in a polygynous group, has been 500 metres, but here, in a comparatively sparse population, pairs are generally much more scattered, nests being commonly separated by at least two kilometres. In Ireland, the nearest nests in David Scott's experience were one kilometre apart within sight of each other, but closer when separated by a ridge. Densities of nests, comparable to those cited for Orkney and Kintyre, probably occur here and there in Scottish forests at the present time but, in general, it is likely that they are prevented by limitations of food or hunting habitat; and on grouse moors persecution nearly always acts as a check on the more social nesting.

The tendency to social nesting is matched by mutual toleration on the hunting grounds and only the near vicinity of the nest is normally defended against other Hen Harriers—this may be an area of about 600 metres in diameter, according to Brown and Amadon. Even at the nest a bird may show no aggression to visiting individuals or pairs. Balfour observed two pairs nest-prospecting together and up to six individuals flying amicably together over a nesting site. Once he watched a strange, immature male alight at a nest and mate with the female in full view of her acquiescent mate. Dickson, on the other hand, has seen two first year males driven away

[1] Frank King tells me that a female Hen Harrier incubating eggs in Munster was attended by a male Montagu's Harrier.

by the older resident male[1] and Geroudet (1965) saw two males confront one another and grasp talons, after apparently trying to intimidate each other by flying with wings partly folded and tails fully spread. Errington (1930) recorded frequent conflicts between three pairs of Marsh Hawks whose nests were close together, at 130 and 400 yards. The characteristic form of mild defensive behaviour shown by males, chiefly to other males, has been described by Balfour as 'escorting flight', in which a male shadows an intruder on the borders of his nesting area by flying just below it, as if preventing it from alighting. In polygynous groups, males defend the home areas of two or more nests in this way, against other Hen Harriers. Further away, on the hunting grounds, Schipper found that there was not even any conflict between harriers of three different species—Hen, Montagu's and Marsh Harriers.

POLYGYNY

Polygyny occurs most often where there is a high density of nesting. Its most remarkable development has been in Orkney, where it was first noticed by John Douglas, at least as early as 1931, since when it has greatly increased. Balfour and Cadbury say that 'in recent years the sex ratio among breeding birds has been approximately two females to one male but each year there are a few males with three and even up to six females,[2] usually simultaneously'. Elsewhere in Scotland, polygyny has been observed in Kincardineshire by Nick Picozzi, in Kintyre by Peter Strang (only once), at least once in south-west Scotland by myself, and by Donald Macaskill in an unnamed forest further north. It has also been noted in Ireland (where Scott considers it uncommon), in the Netherlands and in North America. Schipper tells me that there are 'many more females than males' in the breeding population on the island of Ameland in the Netherlands; but Hamerstrom knew of only seven bigamous matings, and one case of trigamy, in 99 nest histories in her study area in Wisconsin, USA.

One obvious effect of polygyny is that some females are not supplied with sufficient food, or with no food at all, by the male and are forced to spend more time hunting. The Orkney study has shown that this may have an adverse effect on hatching success; this was lowest when two females shared a male, but higher again with four females. Although in polygynous situations losses of young occur on account of inadequate brooding by females which must hunt from an early stage, Balfour and Cadbury state that overall breeding success is not significantly affected. According to Brown, fledging success (66%) was actually higher with four females than with two or three, in a polygynous group. This is attributed by Balfour and

---

[1] See also Chapter 12; the subsequent disappearance of some of the males, which I saw in a Galloway forest breeding area in March–April, might have been due to conflict with and exclusion by other males, but I saw no direct evidence of this.

[2] Up to seven females (Brown, 1976).

Cadbury to the fact that older, probably more experienced, males tend to associate with more females. First year males are nearly always monogamous and older males sometimes acquire additional females which have been mated to young males. Although the available evidence suggests that polygyny was much rarer in a comparably dense nesting group in Kintyre, observation there was not detailed enough for a valid comparison on this point.

One explanation for polygyny might be that it reduces the time spent in the conflicts which can arise when pairs are extremely close, and so releases more time for hunting. Balfour and Cadbury have shown that in Orkney more females than males (1.2:1) have been fledged since 1953, and this might favour the growth of polygyny. Evidence for differential mortality of the sexes after fledging is inconclusive, but in this respect it is interesting to note that both Balfour and Nethersole-Thompson firmly believed that males had the higher mortality rate in the Orkney population. It is likely that on some mainland nesting grounds the reverse is more probably the case because, where there is no protection, females are more likely to be killed at the nest. If this is true it might explain why polygyny appears to be exceptional on the Scottish mainland.

The possibility that polygyny is largely the result of social behaviour, by which a proportion of males is excluded from the breeding population, was put forward by Balfour and Cadbury. Further research may be enlightening.

NEIGHBOURS

Possible prey species often nest successfully very close to a predator's nest. I recall, for instance, Wrens feeding nestlings within a metre or two of a Merlin's nest and Ring Ouzels habitually raising broods in the shadow of a Peregrine's eyrie. I have seen the fledglings of several passerine birds, such as Robins, Wrens and Willow warblers, unconcernedly feeding among the conifers beside a harrier's nest with young. Eventually, of course, some of these may have been taken as prey (see Chapters 9 and 11), since female harriers do some hunting close to their nests. As a rule, however, there is probably a degree of safety for small birds in the immediate vicinity. There are interesting examples of several larger species of birds breeding close to harrier nests and no suggestion that such nests were ever raided by the harriers. I have already related Booth's story of the Greyhen nesting at 'six or seven paces'; and Picozzi found a Mallard on nine eggs at only 1.20 metres, in Orkney. Also in Orkney, Balfour recorded a Kestrel's nest at 14.5 metres, and Merlins often nesting at distances of less than 100 metres. The close association of Hen Harrier, Merlin, Short-eared Owl and Kestrel nests has often been noted in Orkney where Kestrels, too, like the others, breed among the heather. In Galloway, I have found Short-eared Owls nesting within 200 metres but Merlins never so close. Dickson, in a different part of

Galloway, found a Greylag Goose on its nest at less than 140 metres from a Hen Harrier's and, another time, a Teal nesting closer than this. I have already mentioned that Hen, Montagu's and Marsh Harriers sometimes nest in neighbourly association.

Bent has told how a Marsh Hawk once incubated twelve eggs of a Prairie Chicken. Only one chick hatched and 'promptly ran away'.

LAYING AND INCUBATION

The start of laying may be delayed by a sudden cold spell, or even a snowfall, but in Scotland the first egg is usually laid between late April and about 20 May. Blake, however, referring to the 1950s, said that laying began as early as mid-April in Central Scotland; more recently, in 1971 and 1972, nests found by Bremner and Macdonald (1970; 1971) in east Sutherland must have contained their first eggs by 10 April, calculating from fledging dates in mid-June. This is about the time that laying begins much further south, in the Netherlands, for instance. It is possible that the early Sutherland nesting originated with birds from a southerly locality. In the south-east of Ireland (Kerry), King has found a full clutch on 4 April but Scott has found that birds did not usually lay until mid-May in Co. Wicklow. Balfour's earliest date for eggs was 19 April in Orkney and generally he found that few had full clutches before the end of the month, while the peak laying period was 11–20 May. This is very similar to my own experience in south-west Scotland and there is little if any difference in the laying season in Kintyre (Strang). Early failures are followed by repeat layings in which the clutch may not be complete until well into June.

There is generally an interval of 48 hours between egg laying but longer intervals, of up to eight days, were recorded occasionally by Balfour, and Hobson told Nethersole-Thompson that one hen, in Ireland, took twelve days to lay two eggs. According to Brown and Amadon, and from my own observations in south-west Scotland, the commonest clutch is five eggs. Clutches laid by a single female range between three and eight eggs, but first clutches of only two eggs probably occur and I believe that a clutch of nine in south-west Scotland was laid by a single female. Bent gives the clutch size of the Marsh Hawk as from four to nine eggs. In Balfour's experience, larger clutches of up to twelve eggs were generally laid by two hens, although they may have been the result of one female laying a repeat clutch in the original nest (Brown). Repeat layings, after loss of eggs, take place within a fortnight according to Nethersole-Thompson (1933); in my own experience one female, in south-west Scotland, which would almost certainly have laid a clutch of seven, lost a nest with five eggs, built a new makeshift nest immediately and laid another two eggs within three days.

When freshly-laid, most eggs are very pale blue but this colour soon fades and they become off-white within a week or ten days. Their only claim to beauty lies in the ice-green colour inside the shell. Rarely, however, clutches occur with rust-coloured spots or streaks, while Balfour said that some eggs were blotched or spotted with 'mid-green'. Nethersole-Thompson wrote that Staines Boorman had two heavily marked clutches and that John Douglas twice found sets of marked eggs during many years of nest-hunting in Orkney. Spotted eggs are apparently more common in the Marsh Hawk, amounting to some 10% of sets (Bent). During incubation, eggs frequently become stained and their rather 'coarse-grained and chalky shells . . . tend to become polished' (Balfour). Eggs of the Hen Harrier may be difficult to distinguish from those of Montagu's Harrier, as I have good cause to remember (see p. 186). Although Hen Harrier's eggs on average are distinctly larger, their dimensions can overlap with Montagu's, according to the *Handbook of British Birds*. The mean dimensions of 901 eggs of the Hen Harrier, measured by Balfour, were 46.3 × 35.6 mm; and the average of 100 Montagu's Harrier's eggs, given by the *Handbook*, was 41.5 mm × 32.7 mm. Eggs of both species are therefore small for the size of the birds. They vary in shape from rounded to quite elongated.

In the case of the Hen Harrier, incubation is usually entirely by the female and is said to start with the second egg, but it does sometimes start with the first and, according to Geroudet, may even be delayed until the last egg is laid. The only British evidence of a male incubating, apart from a suggestion by Richmond, comes from a single Hebridean record, mentioned by Brown, involving a clutch of addled eggs which the female had continued to incubate long after they were due to hatch. R. D. Lawrence (1975) cites an instance of incubation by a male Marsh Hawk. Certainly, male harriers normally refrain even from alighting at nests during the incubation period.

Incubation usually takes about 30 days for each egg, but according to Brown the period varies from 29 to 37 days. However, Wilhelm (1960) found that the last egg of a Marsh Hawk hatched in 24 days, an exceptionally short period. The normal incubation period for the Montagu's Harrier, which on average lays three or four weeks later than the Hen Harrier, is 27–28 days for each egg. Neufeldt found that, in the Pied Harrier, irregular brooding caused the embryo of the first egg to take up to two days longer to develop than in the other eggs.

When trying to find all the Marsh Hawk nests in her study area, Hamerstrom was sometimes aided by observing that the female frequently left the eggs to preen herself in the early morning. The incubation period is much the most difficult time to locate a Hen Harrier's nest. This is particularly true where nesting is sparse and it is impossible to spend the necessary time overlooking all the possible areas where a pair might nest. The hen sits very close and, once incubation has properly begun, she rarely leaves the eggs except twice or thrice a day for the food pass or, as already said, for a brief excursion at the start of the day. The cock usually disappears from the precincts of the nest very quickly after delivering food.

CHAPTER SIX

THE BREEDING CYCLE: HATCHING TO FLEDGING

HATCHING

Since incubation has usually begun well before the completion of the clutch, hatching is usually spread over several days. At one nest I noted that three eggs hatched over a period of six days, and in large broods the time between the hatching of the first and last eggs may be as long as 10–11 days. The newly-hatched chicks are clothed in very short pinkish-white down, sparsest on the underparts, but their pink appearance is increased by the skin showing among the down. At first their eyes are closed but they are opened, blearily, within a day. The eyes are then seen to be very dark; though actually dark brown, they look black from any distance. These and their little black, hooked bills (tipped with the whitish egg tooth at first) are their most striking features. All young harriers have broad flat skulls which give their heads a rather reptilian look. The waxy cere at the base of the bill is elongated, dull pink in colour, and the limp legs and feet are flesh-pink. Delamain pointed out differences between the young chicks of the Hen and Montagu's Harrier; the former, he said, have rounder heads with a more prominent superciliary arch while the Montagu's can be distinguished at this early stage by their yellow legs and cere; but he added that melanistic chicks of Montagu's have dark brown legs and cere. Scharf and Balfour give the average weight of a newly hatched Hen Harrier as 19.8 grams.

While chicks are actually hatching, or immediately afterwards, it is usual for the hen to remain on the nest when the cock arrives with food. Indeed, if the cock is seen to fly low and almost stall above the nest as he drops the prey, but the hen does not rise, an observer may guess that hatching is imminent or has begun. The hen may be equally reluctant to rise at any time while the chicks are small and require continuous brooding in bad weather.

The shells of hatched eggs are often removed by the hen quite soon after hatching and may be dropped some hundreds of metres from the nest. Sometimes, they are also left by the nest; or eaten by the hen, as David Whitaker tells me was observed by F. G. Hollands.

FEEDING OF CHICKS: HUNTING RANGES AND RHYTHM

Small chicks are fed by the hen from small items of prey brought by the cock. I describe the delicate manner in which the food is presented to the chicks, in Chapter 13. Bird prey is already well plucked when brought to the chicks, and usually headless, until they are at least three or even four weeks old, when they begin to tear up unprepared prey for themselves. Differing views have been expressed on how far hens ensure an even distribution of food among the chicks. Certainly, a hen may make deliberate attempts to feed each chick in turn, but Balfour and Macdonald (1970) noted that chicks in a brood of four lunged forward to grab food, and the quickest often got the prize. The largest chick in this brood received more, and the smallest less, than a fair share. I have made similar observations. However,

Balfour and Macdonald also noted that, when the oldest chick was able to feed itself, the hen sometimes took food from it and distributed it among the brood. Hamerstrom made the interesting suggestion that the hunger calls and white down of the smallest chick in a brood inhibited the others from taking food and caused them to move away, thus allowing the smallest a larger share, but Balfour and Macdonald did not observe this behaviour.

When watching a nest from a hide I saw the first evidence that the hen was deliberately feeding gristle, bone and feather to a chick when it was 22 days old. From this stage, at least, chicks produce pellets of indigestible matter; these, like uneaten remains of food, are fairly soon removed by the hen who thus keeps the nest clean. Shortly before fledging time, however, when chicks are feeding themselves, pellets and remains begin to be left in or around the nest so that in the final stage nests with large broods tend to become messy and fly-ridden. As I stress, in Chapter 16, it is usually only the skeletal remains of larger prey which are uneaten and these can give a misleading impression of the true range of prey brought. I have seen quite clean nests with young almost fledged; in such instances it is likely that all the prey has been fairly small. Very soon after hatching, nest-sanitation is always ensured by the chicks defecating over the edge of the nest.

Heysham (1783), who killed many Hen Harriers at the nest, said that he had seen a cock feeding chicks and further claimed that a cock could rear a brood after his mate had been killed. It would not be unusual for a cock to continue to bring food to the nest in such a situation, but I can find no recent evidence of a cock *feeding* chicks and they would only be likely to survive if they were well advanced and able to tear up prey for themselves. Breckenridge said that males' visits to nests were like 'forced landings'; they 'dropped in, released their talons from the prey and literally bounced back out of the nests with the evident attitude of an intruder'. This, however, is not invariable behaviour and I have seen a male which alighted repeatedly at a nest and stayed there for a minute or more, but I do not know whether he ever fed the chicks. Anthony Buxton described how a cock Marsh Harrier, which had lost its mate, continued to bring food to a larder 20 metres from the nest—too far for the chicks to reach it. He was not the only harrier enthusiast to take a hand in helping chicks to survive in such circumstances. Neufeldt, however, saw the male Pied Harrier tearing up food and feeding it to the chicks when the female was absent.

For the first two, to two and a half weeks the chicks require much brooding by the female, especially in wet or cold weather. In this period she does not normally stray far from the nest and, when not feeding or brooding the chicks, she can often be seen patrolling the neighbourhood, circling to a considerable height or drifting down to perch for a long time on a favourite look-out, ever watchful for the cock's return with prey. As already stated females which are insufficiently supplied by the male, in a polygynous group, are compelled to start hunting for themselves and their chicks while

the latter are still small. Some hens, even in monogamous situations, delay taking their share of hunting longer than others, but it is usual for both sexes to hunt for the second half of the period that chicks are in the nest. Hens bring in a greater share of larger items of prey and their role in food provision at this stage is clearly of great importance. Schipper has listed the numbers of prey items supplied by male and female, after hatching, at 13 different nests in the Netherlands: during the first ten days males brought 82%, females 18%; during days 11–20, males brought 54%, females 46%; and from day 21 onwards males provided 41% and females 59%. As these figures suggest, some cocks supply a lesser share of the food as fledging approaches and it is not uncommon for a cock to disappear altogether during the last week before the chicks are fledged. In my own experience, however, this has only occurred at a minority of nests. Schipper found that, with one exception, spells of prolonged rain reduced the supply of prey to nests, but there was some indication that more prey was brought when the wind was strong.

Females tend to hunt nearer the nest than males, but many females regularly travel two to three kilometres to hunting grounds and two marked hens have been observed by Balfour hunting at five and eight kilometres from their nests with young. Schipper found that males were often hunting more than three kilometres from nests in the Netherlands. Some cocks in south-west Scotland hunt at least four kilometres from nests and probably considerably further. Geroudet gives two to four kilometres as the hunting range of 'a pair'. Clearly the distances travelled from nests vary according to the availability of good hunting grounds, as Neufeldt found for Pied Harriers, some of which hunted no further than one and a half kilometres from their nests while others, separated from open ground by a belt of forest, ranged up to five kilometres. Breckenridge stated that the nesting Marsh Hawks which he studied in Minnesota, hunted over an area of 'only one square mile' (259 ha).

When watching Hen Harriers' nests containing young, I have always noted the times at which food was brought and, when possible, whether the kill had been made by the male or the female. Using notes for 136 hours watching, at four nests of known brood sizes, I have calculated that the mean number of prey items brought per chick in a 14 hour hunting day was 3.2. This agrees closely with Schipper's result from his much more systematic study, which gave a mean figure of 22.3 items per chick 'per 100 hours of nest observation', or an average of 3.12 prey items per chick in a 14 hour day. Clearly the number of deliveries of prey to a nest may depend greatly on the number of mouths to feed, but I found no lessening in the feeding rate after a brood of two was reduced to one. Variable hunting success, due to weather conditions or fluctuations in easily available prey, may also affect the feeding rate. Tinbergen (1940) found that prey supply by Kestrels gradually increased until the chicks were about three weeks old; and A. J. Watson, in a study of Merlins (1973), demonstrated an increasing feeding rate until chicks were 25–29 days old, followed by a decrease. Breckenridge (1935) recorded changes in the feeding rate for a family of five young Marsh Hawks (only three of which fledged). The rate rose from less than four feeds per day for the brood on the eighth day, to a maximum of 24 on the twenty-fifth day, with a decline to only six feeds on the thirty-second day, near fledging time. Schipper, however, said that in his study of Hen, Marsh and Montagu's Harriers, it proved impossible to conclude that at any particular stage of development of the young, more prey was supplied than at any other. In any attempt to calculate weights of food supplied to chicks, it must be remembered that some proportion of the prey items brought is eaten by the female parent. A surprisingly high figure of 19.9 grams is given by Schipper as the average weight of prey, per chick, per hour.

Hen Harriers, in the breeding season, do not usually hunt with equal consistency at all hours of the day. I have suggested 14 hours as a hunting day in south-west Scotland, during the breeding season, from my impression that very little hunting is done before about 06.30 or after about 20.30 hours. In my own experience, there are peak periods of hunting activity, most often between 08.00 and 10.00 and between 14.00 and 19.00 but the 'hunting rhythms' of individuals vary to some extent. Schipper found little sign of a pattern in hunting activity.

DEVELOPMENT OF CHICKS; MORTALITY AND CANNIBALISM

Within a week, the chicks begin to lose their first rather naked pinkish-white appearance and grow a longer, dingy covering of down, well described by Richmond as 'rabbit grey' in colour. On the crown of the head, however,

this down is distinctly paler, like a 'skull cap' sprinkled with hoar frost. The size of the body increases rapidly and the head soon ceases to look absurdly and disproportionately large. Compared with most other young birds of prey, harrier chicks of any age have a very distinctive head and bill shape, caused by the combined effect of the broad skull with eyes frontally set, like an owl's, and the long tapering base to the bill (see illustrations).

The legs and cere of a week-old chick are already becoming yellow, very pale at first and tinged with green on the cere, while the legs are a different, more creamy tint. I have found variation in the rate at which these parts become brighter yellow, but it is not usually until chicks are nearly four weeks old that the legs turn an astonishingly brilliant chrome yellow and the cere becomes bright lemon. I suspect that good feeding hastens these changes. In small chicks, the inside of the mouth is flesh-pink at about ten days and later crimson. The long tongue is notched, mid-way, with black and tipped pale pink. The gape is outlined with yellow, becoming orange at the base.

Towards the end of the second week, dark feathers on scapulars and wing-tips break their sheaths, forming double chevrons among the down. The feather sheaths are steely blue. An almost bare patch of grey-green skin remains on the lores, between eyes and bill, and a fringe of dark brown and chestnut feathers begins to show on the ear coverts. Between the ages of three and four weeks, feather growth rapidly changes the appearance of chicks and most of the down is lost, with the help of much preening. The forehead and crown of the head are the last parts of the body to lose their prominent tufts of down and as long as these remain a chick is far from ready to fly.

In their first complete feathering the young are dark chocolate brown[1] on the upper parts, with numerous narrow salmon-buff fringes to wing and scapular feathers especially prominent on the wing coverts. Their freshly-grown tail feathers are strikingly beautiful, with their broad bands of the same colour and a lighter more creamy salmon-coloured terminal bar. Unless the wings are raised or spread, the white upper tail coverts are generally concealed but, when revealed, are very striking: some or all of these white feathers may have a narrow or fairly broad dark brown mesial streak. Further study of this feature is required to find out whether only females have the broad mesial streaks—it is possible that this might prove to be an additional way of sexing young birds. Below the dark crown the pale, almost white eyebrows and face set off the frowning deep-set eyes, and the deep russet fringe to the dark ear coverts overlaps the delicate lace-like border of the facial ruff.

The underparts in feathered chicks of the Hen Harrier (see Chapter 1) are rich warm buff, streaked heavily with dark brown on the breast, more sparsely with red-brown below. On the underside of the wing the leading edge is bright salmon-buff, the axillaries and under wing coverts rich reddish buff, splashed with red-brown streaks, and the flight feathers are pale grey below, with a most arresting chequered pattern of dark brown wedge-shaped markings. I have described in Chapter 2 how the chicks can be sexed, when two to three weeks old, by iris colour and leg thickness. Female chicks are heavier and look altogether bulkier than males of similar age. As fledging time approaches, males are more inclined to escape into surrounding vegetation when approached, females tending to stay in the nest. Similarly, males usually fly sooner than females. During the last week or so before flying, the young harriers increasingly stand up on their long legs but they still sink back to rest 'on their haunches'. The strength to hold down prey comes gradually, but well-grown chicks require judicious handling if laceration by their sharp black claws is to be avoided.

Scharf and Balfour (1971) studied the growth of chicks and stated that the size difference between the sexes never obscured the size differences due to asynchronous hatching. Older chicks were dominant and so competed better for food. It was usually the latest hatched which succumbed to stresses of cold, rain and food shortage. They were surprised to find no difference in the pattern of development between young Hen Harriers in Orkney and young Marsh Hawks in Wisconsin, in spite of apparently greater hunting activity and more frequent feeding by the parents in Orkney. All those who have seen many nests of the Hen Harrier have found that the weakest chicks in broods often die in bad weather. There is sometimes presumptive evidence from picked remains that a chick which has died has been eaten by its siblings, and Balfour observed one female fly off with a

---

[1] I have recently noticed that the brown upper parts of some young males are slightly lighter than in some young females. See also Chapter 2. (Melanism.)

dead chick, return with its decapitated body and feed it to the remaining chicks. Breckenridge observed a similar incident in the Marsh Hawk. Balfour thought it probable that chicks were sometimes killed by the female parent, or by their siblings, but he had no proof of this. Blake, however, said that he had seen 'young males, almost fledged, plucked alive, killed and eaten by young females'. However, if the hierarchy in the nest is according to age, as Scharf and Balfour stated, there seems to be no reason why males should die or be killed by their sisters more often than the reverse. Weis and Buxton both recorded larger chicks of the Marsh Harrier killing and eating smaller members of broods; indeed Weis regarded this as usual behaviour in that species, but he found no evidence of killing, or even fighting, within broods of Montagu's Harriers. It seems clear that in harriers, as in some other flesh-eating birds such as owls, cannibalism can sometimes ensure the survival of a proportion of a brood when there is a diminution of the normal food supply. Ingram (1959), commented: 'it is eugenically preferable to rear, let us say, two or three well-nourished progeny rather than six or seven weaklings', and further emphasised that 'without a marked disparity in the age and size of the fledglings, fratricide would be virtually impossible'. The disparity, of course, is the result of the intervals between hatching due to incubation starting soon after laying has begun.

The normal fledging date is between the thirtieth and thirty-fifth day. A single chick in a nest, which I watched from a hide, did not take its first flight until it was at least 38 days old (see Chapter 13). This was a male, although, as stated above, males can generally fly earlier than females; Scharf and Balfour, however, also recorded two single chicks which did not fly until the thirty-eighth day and concluded that they were too heavy to fly earlier; this was probably the case, too, with my male chick. Early fledging dates should be treated with caution; first flights may be hastened by human disturbance, and this may explain my earliest record of a chick which flew at 29 days. The average weight of chicks, at fledging time, is given by Scharf and Balfour as 472 grams, but female chicks may be as much as 100 grams heavier than males at this stage.

OTHER BEHAVIOUR OF CHICKS

Many aspects of chick behaviour are described in Chapter 13, and elsewhere in Part Two, the Study of the Hen Harrier in South-west Scotland.

Hen Harrier chicks do not stray far from the nest, but from about the age of three weeks they often retreat a few feet into the surrounding vegetation and so form 'hide-outs' which provide shade, or shelter and some concealment. Balfour and Macdonald suggest that this habit also aids nest sanitation. As fledging approaches, they may spend much of their time just outside the nest and, as already described, they are sometimes fed at roughly-built platforms some metres from the actual nest. They are, however, much less prone to pre-fledging dispersal than the chicks of some other ground-nesting birds, such as Short-eared Owls. When closely approached by a human intruder the chicks vary in their reactions. Docile when very young, they soon begin to assume a menacing posture, with tongues lolling from wide-open mouths and wings half-raised as they stand their ground, or back slightly away, gazing fiercely at the intruder. Sometimes, on the other hand, even quite small chicks try to escape into hiding and half-grown chicks, especially males, may bound out of the nest. They will turn on their backs to strike with their claws if handled, but not with the rapidity of, for example, young Merlins.

BREEDING SUCCESS AND FAILURE TO BREED

In Orkney, Balfour and Cadbury found that the mean clutch size for 288 nests was 4.6; 60.5% of eggs hatched, 61.9% of chicks fledged; and the mean number of young reared for 223 successful nests was 2.5. My figures for much smaller samples in south-west Scotland are similar; a mean clutch size of 4.8, 57% hatching success, 60% fledging success and a mean number of 2.85 young reared per successful nest. In this region, however, nests in forests were significantly more successful than those on moorland (see Chapter 15).

Balfour and Cadbury found some evidence that high fledging success (over 70% of young fledged) was associated with fine weather in June, but that there was little relationship between hatching success and weather conditions in May. They also considered the possibility that periods of low hatching success might be caused by organo-chlorine pesticides, as has been demonstrated by Ratcliffe (1969, 1970) for the Peregrine, but they found no convincing evidence of this for the Hen Harrier in Orkney. Bell's analyses (pers. comm.) of eight livers and nine clutches of eggs of Hen Harriers in widely scattered parts of Britain are given in Table 3. He comments that, with two exceptions, the organo-chlorine residues in livers were all at 'background' levels and could have had little bearing on the deaths of the birds. The exceptions were numbers 347 and 1534, 'where the dieldrin levels were exceptionally high and were undoubtedly responsible for the deaths of these two birds'. It will be noted that the number of clutches analysed is small and none is more recent than 1965.

It may be said that there is no evidence that organo-chlorine pesticides have significantly reduced breeding success of Hen Harriers in Britain, or Ireland (Scott). Bell commented that the DDE residues in Hen Harrier eggs were considerably lower than those found in Sparrowhawks, in which species this metabolite has been primarily responsible for egg-shell thinning. There is, however, some evidence that in parts of Continental Europe breeding success in Hen Harriers has declined due to the effects of pesticides. Bijleveld (1974) mentioned a sharp decline of Hen Harriers in Sweden during the 1960s, in agricultural and forestry ground, due to pesticides; and also suggested that 'agricultural pesticides' may have been implicated in the complete breeding failure of five pairs in Marne, France, in 1970. In North America, Hamerstrom recorded a remarkable decrease of Marsh Hawk nests, from 25 in 1963 to four in 1965, on her study area in Wisconsin. By 1968 the decline had continued further. The paucity of nests was not associated with a comparable decrease in the number of adults on the study area during the breeding season. During the period of decline, birds showed abnormalities of behaviour; almost no 'skydancing' was seen and there was a marked increase in 'almost frantic, talon to talon food transfers'. Hamerstrom speculated that an apparent lack of sexual drive, and consequent breeding failure, might have been due to the effects of pesticides possibly working through the avian component of the harriers' diet. A recovery in breeding numbers reported by Hamerstrom in 1974 (per Newton) occurred, perhaps significantly, after a ban on DDT.

In Britain, the possibility that pesticides have been implicated in some un-explained instances of apparent failure to breed cannot be discounted. In June 1973, Brian Turner estimated that there were some 20 pairs in one area of Argyll but concluded, after careful observation, that many of these did not have nests with eggs or young. In Galloway I have repeatedly noted that some pairs which have been present in spring either did not breed, or failed at an early stage, and then disappeared from the area; Picozzi has noticed the same behaviour in Kincardineshire. In all these instances, however, the explanation may be that the birds which failed to breed were unable to find adequate food in the area. It is possible that some moved on and found more favourable conditions to breed elsewhere.

Balfour and Cadbury said that first year birds were less successful at hatching their eggs than older birds, but Hamerstrom found that they bred equally successfully. In south-west Scotland, of the four first year males, two failed to rear any young, suggesting a slightly higher failure rate than for older birds, but the difference is of no statistical significance.

Nest failure at the egg stage is likely to be followed by a repeat laying in a new nest, often not far from the first. After later failures the birds usually disappear from the nesting area within a day or so. In these instances their whereabouts for the rest of the season may remain a mystery unless, of course, they are known to have been killed. In one case, in Orkney, an albinistic female which had unsuccessfully courted a male with two other females, was subsequently seen by Balfour living a solitary life on a different island.

AGE OF BREEDING BIRDS

It has been known for a long time that some Hen Harriers breed in their first year. Gray (1871) was told that the male of a pair with young, shot in Sutherland by Crawford of Lairg, was in brown plumage and other first year males had been 'repeatedly seen and killed at the nest' by the same man. Harvie-Brown and Buckley (1884) stated that the male of a pair shot at the nest in Dunrobin Forest, Sutherland, in 1881 'had not attained adult plumage'. According to H. M. S. Blair (per Nethersole-Thompson) breeding by first year males was also noted in Norway from about 1885. Douglas first drew attention to instances among the Orkney birds (Nethersole-Thompson, 1932), and more recently Balfour has frequently found males and females breeding in their first year. Nevertheless, the proportions of these, in the Orkney population (13% of the females and 20% of the males) were considered (by Balfour and Cadbury) to be less than they would have been if all the surviving Orkney-born young of this age group had bred. It was also found that there were more breeding females above five years old than expected. A few were known to be nine or ten years old, and a female which was nesting in 1975 was twelve years old (Spencer pers. comm.). Balfour told me that one male was almost certainly aged thirteen. The age structure of the Orkney breeding population was considered by Balfour and Cadbury to lend support to the view that social behaviour was excluding some younger birds from breeding.

I have found males and females breeding in their first year in south-west Scotland. I can give no reliable figure for females but four out of 47 males (8.5%) known to have nested were first year birds. In her study area in Wisconsin, Hamerstrom had 14 first year birds (male or female) among 46 breeding birds of known age (30%).

REACTIONS TO DISTURBANCE; PREDATION ON NESTS

The spectacular attacking flights made by Hen Harriers against human visitors to nests have been the subject of much comment. It has been said that one or other parent is always aggressive in these circumstances, but this is far from the truth. I have found that at some nests neither bird flew nearer to me than about 35 metres, but the majority of females and a few males flew closer, at least when they had chicks. My notes of 34 nests show that attacks were pressed to the point of striking at only 13 (38%); at the other 21 nests aggression was mild or non-existent and, occasionally, females flew almost out of sight after rising from the nest. At 12 of the 13 nests the attack was pressed only by the female, and a very aggressive male was encountered at only one nest. At the majority of nests, males rarely came closer than about 45 metres. The same bird, of either sex, showed variations in degree of aggression at different stages in the nesting period. A few were highly aggressive at all times, but most reached a peak of boldness while chicks were under three weeks old. Interestingly, some males which had previously been quite timid dived fairly close, and were very noisy, when chicks were nearly fledged, attacking not so much near the nest as near the limit of the home ground which is defended, to some extent, against other harriers.

Balfour found that about 50% of females, and a few males, were 'aggressive' in Orkney; and Peter Strang told me that about the same percentage of females in Kintyre showed some aggression, but only about two-thirds of these attacked strongly. Richmond thought that an old male with an inexperienced female was inclined to be more demonstrative at the nest than most, but the only very bold male I have seen, an old bird himself, was mated to an old, though timid, female. While examining a nest of Montagu's Harriers, which kept their distance, Blake received repeated diving attacks from a male Hen Harrier. In contrast to the abundant evidence from Scotland that females are generally the chief defenders of nests, some American observers have found that the male Marsh Hawk is often dominant in this respect. Urner even said that all males were aggressive to human beings, and Saunders that the male was much more so than the female, though Bent found little difference between the sexes in this respect. Balfour believed, as I do, that the offspring of a bold parent tend to show similar behaviour when they breed; and it is certainly true that, even when newly fledged, young sometimes join a parent in her attacks, in apparent imitation. I have observed a female and her family diving at man and sheep in the nesting area. Similar diving attacks are made against foxes and other mammals on nesting grounds and at winter roosts (see Chapter 18).

The results from my sample of 34 nests (Table 4) suggest that Hen Harriers which showed most aggression to man at nests were the more successful at rearing young. Nevertheless, one or two of the mildest females had outstandingly good nest histories over successful seasons, although one of these may have been fortunate, one year, in having a bold male as her mate. Richmond said that birds which were most timid towards a man at the nest were prone to desert at the slightest pretext. No doubt he was referring to desertions of eggs and, since I have generally refrained from visiting nests at this stage, to minimise risk of desertion, I am not qualified to comment from personal knowledge.

An attack by a really bold Hen Harrier is at once a thrilling spectacle and an unsettling experience. It is thrilling because the bird displays its utmost mastery of flight, appears to be totally regardless of its own safety and presents a most exciting series of swiftly changing images to the eye. It is unsettling because the bird so obviously resents the intruder's presence with every fibre of its being that, whether or not the intruder is physically discomforted by her buffeting, he is made to feel that he must retire as quickly as possible to allow the bird to regain her composure. These at least are my own feelings, but to their many human enemies the boldest birds are the most sacrificial. At first, after rising from the nest or its vicinity, the bird quickly gains height and flies away for 20 or 30 metres. Then she banks steeply, catching the light on the beautifully chequered undersides of her wings and turns, full-faced and yikkering, into the assault. She slants downward and assumes a strangely menacing outline, with broad wings angled sharply back from the wrists and wing-tips widely splayed. If her course is set low enough she will, certainly, rake a man's scalp with her talons as she sweeps just above him and, presumably, it is the trailing hind claw which sometimes draws blood. More often, the clenched foot inflicts a thumping, quite startling blow, but the speed with which the bird can turn and repeat the attack is its most devastating skill. This is most impressive when a bird continually varies the line and height of its approach, sometimes flying in so low that it seems about to strike a man's face, but at the last second it always rises a little. Some of my own memories of these occasions are described in Chapters 10–12, but I particularly like Eddie Balfour's story of the female harrier which lifted his beret and carried it 50 metres before dropping it in the heather. 'I had an awful job finding it', remarked Eddie, admiringly. Over the years I have noticed that a bird will unquestionably attack the man it knows—usually myself—in preference to a newcomer, and Eddie Balfour had the same experience. Once, at a nest with Ian Munro, who was visiting Orkney, he tested a bird by an exchange of headgear but after a moment's hesitation the harrier ignored the familiar beret on Ian's head and continued to attack the rightful owner. I suspect that this power of recognition lasts longer than a single nesting season. Aggressive birds often break off their attacks, temporarily, to perch and continue calling from the ground or from a tree and, in frustration, sometimes start to preen.

Clearly, this aggressive trait is a disadvantage where Hen Harriers are in danger of being shot at the nest but, of course, it must have been established long, long ago and it is easy to see that it might deter many potential predators of eggs or chicks. Dalmen and Lorig (1970) found that in polygamous situations, in the persistent absence of the female, nests near a colony of Herring Gulls sustained heavy losses of eggs and young from the gulls; but one nest, which was equally close to the gulls, remained undisturbed on account of the continuous protection given by the female (Nieboer, 1973).

Is it possible that the recent spread of nesting into conifer forests has, in some way, favoured the survival of less aggressive birds? In a small sample of nests in south-west Scotland (see Table 4), I have found a much higher proportion of relatively mild females at forest sites than on open moor; and David Scott tells me that Irish Hen Harriers, many of which nest in forests, are 'much less vicious than they were' in defence of their nests. The numerous examples of successful colonisation of this habitat seem to indicate that any such loss of aggression has not been disadvantageous.

Apart from man (the Hen Harrier's greatest enemy), what are the main threats to nests? The evidence is scanty. A well-grown nestling was found in a fox earth in the Southern Highlands (G. Shaw, pers. comm.), but there was no proof that it was taken alive; and a brood was probably killed by a fox in Galloway (Chapter 12). Hagen (1957) said that dogs killed broods in Norway, and Hamerstrom listed nest failures due to predation by skunks, and trampling by deer and cattle, in North America. Dixon (1898) was told by game keepers in Skye that sheep broke many eggs. Crows, and possibly Black-backed Gulls (see Table 15), destroy eggs, though it is doubtful whether they can do so, often, once incubation has properly begun. Weis,

however, found that a Jay succeeded in snatching all five eggs of a Montagu's Harrier while the female was briefly absent for a food pass. I am informed by Dr K. W. Brewster that badgers are a danger to Montagu's Harriers' nests. Probably, even the least bold Hen Harriers attack birds such as crows, Ravens, large gulls, Buzzards and Golden Eagles in the vicinity of the nest. It is likely that eagles occasionally kill young harriers and I have presumptive evidence that an eagle killed an adult female (see p. 193). I have found a young Short-eared Owl among prey at a Golden Eagle's nest. With regard to the possibility that forest nesting sites might be more favourable to unaggressive birds than sites on open moorland, it is worth noting that, in forests, there is no threat to nests from wandering sheep, cattle or dogs. Foxes are usually common in forests but the dense cover which surrounds nests in this habitat must be some safeguard against these animals. Foxes are absent from the important nesting grounds in Orkney and the Outer Hebrides, but very successful nesting has occurred in many regions where foxes are plentiful.

It may be asked why the remarkable habit of attacking man, and other large mammals, occurs in some harrier species, such as the Hen and Pied, but not, so far as I know, in the Montagu's or the Marsh Harrier? Possibly this disparity derives from an original preference by Hen and Pied Harriers for drier, more open nest-sites, which would be most at risk from mammalian predators and the trampling feet of herbivores; but if its ancestors invaded North America from the Asian Steppes, why did the Marsh Hawk retain the aggressive habit while becoming a predominantly marshland nester in the absence of other harriers? Or is there some significance, which eludes me, in the reported tendency for the male to be more aggressive than the female in this race of the Hen Harrier?

The question must be asked whether human visits to nests increase the risks of predation by foxes or other mammals such as badgers. Scharf told Balfour that human visits to Marsh Hawk nests could increase such risks. It is possible that my own visits to nests have occasionally had a similar effect but the high success rate of nests in forests (Table 12), where it is difficult to avoid some tell-tale trampling of surrounding vegetation, suggests that this did not happen. I have, however, generally refrained from disturbing a bird on eggs and, with one exception, have kept an interval of a week or, usually, longer between visits to nests with chicks. The exception was the nest watched from a hide. There, regular visits inevitably left a beaten path but no predation occurred. Nest photography from a close hide sometimes brings unexpected hazards, as Don Macaskill honestly admitted when he discovered that one female reacted to the sound of the camera shutter by flying away with the food which she had just received from the cock. The male landed repeatedly at the nest, but would not leave food, and photography had to be abandoned. Unfortunately, not all photographers are as scrupulous. It is only fair to add that there has been no evidence that nest failures have been significantly increased even by research work involving the capture, by dho-gaza nets, of birds which had chicks, either in Scotland or in North America (Balfour, Hamerstrom).

Shortly before fledging time, when the nest is littered with prey remains, flies settle increasingly on chicks, especially about their eyes and bills. This is particularly noticeable at forest nests, and on hot days in July I have seen chicks with their eyes totally obscured by flies. Clouds of flies accompany a man to a nest and then transfer to the chicks. I have found some chicks infested with flat flies and fleas. Broods of Pied Harriers in south-east Siberia were sometimes found by Neufeldt to be injured, their nostrils blocked and eardrums perforated, by the larvae of flies of the genus *protocalliphora*. Hamerstrom found one brood of downy young Marsh Hawks eaten alive by carrion beetles.

MOULT OF THE ADULT

Females begin to moult during the incubation period and continue to do so until after the young are fledged; but Balfour found that females were never missing more than two flight feathers and some tail feathers at one time. Middle and inner primaries with their coverts, the greater wing-coverts, tail feathers and some body feathers are moulted and renewed first. The complete moult may extend over several months but I do not know precisely for how long. Grey-plumaged males begin to show signs of wing and tail moult later, usually not until the chicks are a few weeks old. Though wing and tail moult is gradual, it might be thought that it would reduce hunting efficiency; and it may indeed be a factor in the reduction or cessation of hunting by males, for their broods, late in the season.

In Marsh and Montagu's Harriers, as observed by Weis, the females also moulted ahead of the males and the latter then become sole providers for the young. In Pied Harriers, Neufeldt found that females began to lose feathers soon after incubation started and in this species, too, moult began considerably later in the male, which changed only six primaries and half its tail feathers before migrating south. Hen Harriers in their first summer might be at some disadvantage in providing for chicks since males, and probably females also, start to moult wing and tail feathers earlier than older birds.

Female Hen Harrier, second summer. Note dark new feathers; inner primaries and their coverts, greater coverts (all newly grown), bastard wing, tertials, lesser coverts, all tail feathers *except* central one (2 outer, growing); some new feathers on mantle and rump

Male Hen Harrier, first summer (July). Note four new grey inner primaries and their coverts; old greater coverts mostly moulted and some new feathers growing; a few new feathers on breast and one in bastard wing

According to the *Handbook of British Birds*, some first year males have begun to moult as early as March and I have myself seen partly grey-winged males in this month.

THE POST-FLEDGING PERIOD

After they have made their first flight, young Hen Harriers continue to use the nest or its near vicinity as a base at which to receive food, and to roost, for two or three weeks. During the day they are often well scattered, perching quietly among the heather, or on small conifers, for long periods. Lengthy intervals pass between visits by the adults, chiefly the female, with food. Frequently, the food is dropped in the air to be caught or missed by a flying youngster, which thereby gains some experience at taking a food-pass, though it may be argued that this can only have value as practice for a young female. Young give the squealing food call as they fly towards their parents for food, but they also make this call at other times—I have heard it from a fledgling as it rose in front of me in alarm. As mentioned earlier, the fledged young of a bold parent are sometimes aggressive to man. Within a week of fledging they become fairly proficient on the wing, improving their skill by diving and playing together in the air. They also dive towards the ground and pounce frequently. As already stated, young Marsh Hawks soon learn to capture insects but the majority of their pounces bring no reward.

The rich dark colours and shorter tails and wings—the latter are also more rounded and Sparrowhawk-like—distinguish the young at a distance from the old female, and size differences are quite evident between young males and young females. Among the bronzy-green and purple heather clumps the young harriers can be difficult to spot but they become conspicuous against a background of vivid green bracken or conifer trees. I have seen them alight and perch without difficulty on tall bracken tops.

Lewis O. Shelley (1930), quoted by Bent, related his experience with a family of young Marsh Hawks which he reared from the nest. He said that their sight and hearing were unsurpassed. 'Any noise, and a good many too slight to be detected by human ears, was noted instantly.' One flew from 150 metres to take a small cube of meat from his finger tips, seizing it in one foot without slackening its flight.

To a harrier enthusiast it is always a satisfying sight, though tempered with end of season regret, to watch the young venturing further and further from the nest site. I have watched them for hours as they float just above a long slope of dark green forest, but never drop to make a successful capture.

At what stage are they totally independent of their parents? I confess I do not know precisely, but unless the family keeps together after leaving the nesting grounds, and such wandering groups are rarely seen, they must fend for themselves by the time they are about eight weeks old. Shreds of evidence which suggest that some young may stay with the female parent for longer periods come from observations by R. C. Dickson and Balfour. Dickson saw a female with a young male and a young female fly in to a winter roost site only days after a similar family had left a moorland nesting ground some 15 kilometres away; and Balfour told me that he had seen a female with her brood of two at a roost that was distant from their nesting ground. Weis said that groups of Montagu's Harriers consisting of old females and young of the year roosted together before migrating in autumn, the old males roosting separately. The flocks of up to 40 Marsh Hawks seen moving together in autumn over the western prairies, by Audubon (Bent, 1937), may have included family parties.

From their data on Orkney Hen Harriers, Balfour and Cadbury concluded that only 32% of young Hen Harriers were alive a year later; and Hickey found that 80 of 102 Marsh Hawks which had been shot in their first year were under five months old. To survive these early months of independence the young birds need to become not only expert hunters, but to avoid a whole range of man-made hazards such as guns, traps and overhead wires. They may also run some risk of being killed by a few predators such as foxes, and possibly Golden Eagles or Peregrines.

Short-eared owl

CHAPTER SEVEN

MIGRATION AND WINTER DISTRIBUTION

Hen Harriers begin to migrate southward from most of their more northerly breeding grounds in Continental Europe, Asia and North America in late August and early September. In the less severe climate of Western Europe, however, overwintering birds are found as far north as southern Sweden, Denmark and Scotland, where Orkney (Lat. 59° N) is the most northerly, major wintering area in the world. In North America, few remain further north than Lat. 50° N. Mead (1973), writing of European Hen Harriers, gave the normal southern limit of winter range as the Mediterranean but noted that there are records from north-west Africa (Vaurie, 1965).

In Asia, the winter range extends as far south as Iran, north-west Pakistan, northern India, Upper Assam, Burma, Indo-China and possibly the northern Philippines (Brown and Amadon). Ali and Ripley (1968) described it as 'probably the commonest harrier in the Sikkim Himalayas', but Smythies (1953) cited only one positive record for Burma. My own records for the Arakan district of Burma in 1944–45 included only occasional, probable (ringtail) Hen Harriers.

The winter distribution of the Marsh Hawk extends as far south as Panama in Central America, but it occurs only rarely in the West Indies. There are very occasional records in South America, from Colombia and one in Venezuela (Bent, Brown and Amadon). Most Marsh Hawks winter in the southern states of the USA but several have wandered as far west as Hawaii.

Families of Hen Harriers have generally left the immediate vicinity of breeding grounds three to five weeks after the young have fledged but, in Britain, most recoveries[1] of young birds before November of their first winter have been close to where they were hatched. Apart from two possibly exceptional recoveries,[2] only five out of thirty show movement of more than 30 km in this period and the longest journey by a juvenile, in the period August–October, was only about 140 km, from Orkney, to Shetland, by 4 September. The next longest journey by a juvenile in the same period was also in a northerly direction—82 km from Kincardineshire to Banff by 9 August.

The record of a ringtail seen crossing the Wicklow coast, on 17 August (Irish Bird Report, 1961), suggests the possibility of an early long distance movement. Autumn movement over the Irish Sea is further indicated by the comments from bird observatories in this area; at Calf of Man, the Hen Harrier has become a regular October visitor since about 1965; and at Copeland Island, off the coast of County Down, it appears especially often in late September (Durman, 1976). There is also a record of one seen flying in over the sea at Clogher Head, County Louth, on 19 September 1973 (Irish Bird Report, 1973). Hen Harriers are much less frequent late autumn migrants at the Isle of May, off the east coast of Scotland, and further south at the Gilbraltar Point observatory they are seen more often in January and February than during the usual periods of passage migration. The only observatory in Britain or Ireland which notes them as most frequent in spring is Walney Island, off the Lancashire coast (Durman, 1976).

From late September onwards, there is widespread evidence from parts of Britain where few or none are seen in the breeding season, that Hen Harriers are either passing on migration or arriving in winter quarters, but few reach southern England before October. The main period of southward movement at Falsterbo (Rudebeck, 1950) and at Col de Bertolet (Thiollay, 1966) is between late September and late October and the first migrants reach Belgian Lorraine from 25 September (Mois, 1975). There is evidence, in Europe and North America, that some ringtails precede adult males on southward migration. The earliest autumn arrivals in southern England are generally ringtails, which also predominate throughout most winters (Reading Orn. Club Reports, Buxton 1946, Bryant pers. comm.).

In America, Maurice Broun's records for 1934, at Kittatinny Ridge,

---

[1] In my analysis of ringing recoveries I am greatly indebted to the Ringing and Migration Committee of the British Trust for Ornithology for permission to examine all the recoveries of Hen Harriers ringed in Britain and Ireland, and those ringed abroad and recovered in Britain (none of the latter have been found in Ireland).

[2] Two chicks, illegally taken from a brood in North Wales, were ringed and 'hacked back' in Anglesey, and released on 14 and 19 July 1973. The first was found shot on 29 July near Oswestry, Shropshire (100 km ESE) and the second was 'shot' on an unspecified date in August near Basingstoke, Hampshire (290 km ESE).

Pennsylvania (Bent, 1937) showed that most of the 51 birds seen up till 19 October were 'females' but of 38 observed between 1–12 November, 28 were males. It is interesting to recall that the French name, Busard Saint Martin, which undoubtedly referred originally only to the adult male, arose from the belief that it arrived in France about 11 November (St Martin's Day). It is possible that the majority of those ringtails which travel south in advance of the adult males are birds of the year.

According to Brown and Amadon, Hen Harriers are distinctly gregarious on migration, except in America where they usually migrate singly. Audubon (Bent, 1937), however, wrote of the Marsh Hawk in 1840: 'I have observed it in our western prairies in autumn moving in flocks of 20, 30 or even as many as 40 individuals and appearing to be migrating, as they passed along at a height of 50 or 60 yards, without paying any attention to the objects below; but on all these occasions I could never find that they were bent on any general course more than another; as some days a flock would be proceeding southward, on the next to the northward or eastward'. Apart from one not wholly convincing description of a flock of ten travelling south in a mountainous part of Gwent, Wales, on 16 September (Gwent Bird Report, 1975), I know of no British records of migrating flocks.

There is convincing evidence, in Europe, that as winter weather becomes more severe some northern regions are almost entirely deserted by males but a number of females remain behind. No doubt the females' ability to hunt larger prey, even when ground is under snow, enables them to survive better than males in such conditions. Sorensen, for instance, found that in Denmark females noticeably outnumbered males in the coldest periods of winter (Mois, 1975) and the same is true of north-east Scotland (Picozzi, pers. comm.). At the same time there are strong indications that a higher proportion of males winter in the milder western parts of Britain than in the north or east. F. M. Ogilvie, for instance, remarked that during a number of winter visits to the Outer Hebrides, 1900–1914, when he sometimes saw seven or eight Hen Harriers in a day, adult males exceeded 'females' by five or more to one, 'the exact opposite of his experience in East Anglia'. Peter Strang told me that most of the Hen Harriers which he saw in the southern part of Kintyre during the winter were adult males. In Galloway, another western region, the proportion of adult males and ringtails in the winter population is variable but the former sometimes equal the latter or even exceed them in numbers during the early part of the winter. Immigration to this region evidently occurs on a considerable scale, especially in October–November, although the only proof of such immigration comes from a December recovery of a first-winter male, ringed in Kincardineshire in July.[1]

The recoveries of ringed birds, discussed below, do not at present provide

[1] Since this was written, R. C. Dickson has seen a ringtail with a white wing-tag at a roost in Galloway on 24 October 1976. Nick Picozzi tells me that this bird must have been tagged as an adult, by him, in Orkney during the summer of 1975.

enough data to confirm the impression, from field observation, that a high proportion of adult males, wintering in Britain, are to be found in the west of the country. Although counts at winter roosts (see Chapter 18) may give a good indication of the proportion of adult males and ringtails in a particular region, this cannot be completely relied upon in this respect owing to the difficulty of ensuring that all roosting sites, communal or solitary, are known. Nevertheless, it can be noted that very few adult males are seen at winter roosts in Orkney (Balfour and Green, pers. comm.) or on Deeside (Picozzi, pers. comm.), but Frank King found a roost occupied entirely by adult males in Kerry, south-west Ireland during October.

In Belgian Lorraine, Mois noted that males exceeded females by two or three to one between October and the beginning of March, and females usually predominated in March and April. The winter climate of this region is not particularly severe and so generally provides suitable hunting conditions for males. It appears that, with the onset of the most severe weather in Denmark, especially in late January and early February, a number of harriers, including a majority of adult males, travel south to Lorraine and the Grand Duchy of Luxembourg (Mois, 1975; Wassenich, 1968). It is also likely that there is a westerly movement into Britain in mid winter; this may explain why Hen Harriers are most often seen at Gibraltar Point observatory, on the Lincolnshire coast, in January and February (Durman, 1975). The record of an adult male ringed in Belgium on 11 November and found in Norfolk on the following 9 February could be consistent with such a late westerly migration. The decline in the proportion of adult males at winter roosts from February onwards, which has been noted in Galloway and Lorraine, may be due to a tendency on the part of males to seek breeding grounds in advance of females.

Before 1974, a total of 1544 Hen Harriers had been ringed in Britain and Ireland, and 143 (9%) had been recovered (Spencer and Hudson, 1973). All but twelve of those recovered were ringed as chicks or juveniles. In Fig. 8 and Fig. 9 I have plotted all recoveries of birds ringed in Britain and Ireland, and British recoveries of birds ringed abroad, up to November 1975, at distances greater than 80 kilometres from the ringing localities. Mead (1973) has published an earlier analysis and I am indebted to the guidelines set by his maps.

The great majority of the records are of birds ringed in Orkney by Balfour. Mead noted that the British evidence showed a southerly movement during the winter with exceptional birds travelling 500 or even 1,000 kilometres. Even so, the remarkably scattered pattern of recoveries is illustrated by the two most distant, one (January) from Argyll south to the Basses Pyrénées and the other (February) from Orkney north-eastward to Buroya islet off the Norwegian coast. The wide dispersal of some Orkney birds is further illustrated by recoveries in south Norway, Denmark, the Netherlands, West Germany, south-west Ireland and East Anglia. The eight

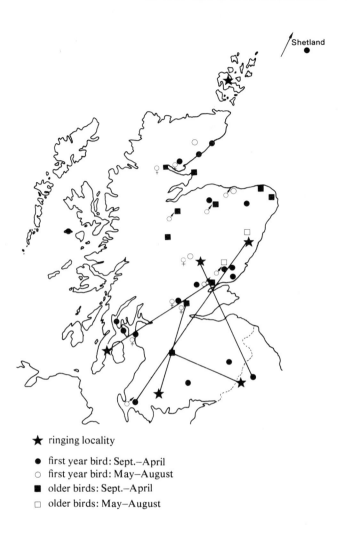

★ ringing locality

● first year bird: Sept.–April
○ first year bird: May–August
■ older birds: Sept.–April
□ older birds: May–August

Fig. 8   Recoveries of Hen Harriers in Scotland (one recovery of a male, Kincardineshire–Banff in August, age c. 2 months, is not shown

breeding season recoveries of Orkney birds at distant localities are of particular interest, suggesting, as Mead pointed out, that there has been colonisation of fresh areas by the 'vigorous Orkney population'. Although five of these records are in eastern Scotland, including at least one shot at a nest, three are much more distant, two in the Netherlands and one in West Germany.

Four winter recoveries give evidence of immigration into England: from Finland, the Netherlands, Belgium, and one from Noord Holland having

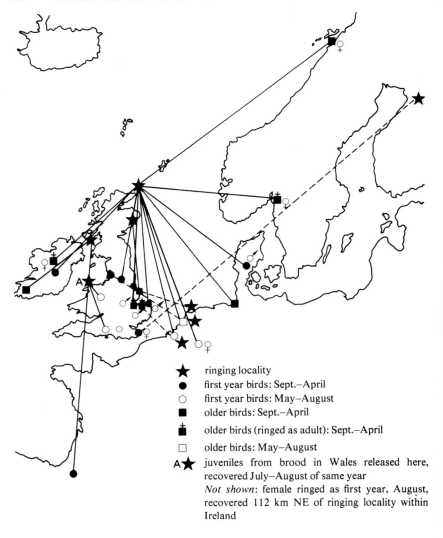

ringing locality
first year birds: Sept.–April
first year birds: May–August
older birds: Sept.–April
older birds (ringed as adult): Sept.–April
older birds: May–August
juveniles from brood in Wales released here,
recovered July–August of same year
Not shown: female ringed as first year, August,
recovered 112 km NE of ringing locality within
Ireland

Fig. 9   Recoveries of Hen Harriers outside Scotland more than 80 km distant

travelled as far north as Lancashire. Goethe and Kuhk (1951), quoted by
Mead, listed German recoveries and showed that a few Hen Harriers remain
in Germany and the Netherlands, but most winter in France and Italy.
Bernis (1966) records two north German birds, one in north-east Spain and
one on the north Portuguese coast. Most of the Hen Harriers wintering on
the south-east shores of the North Sea originate in Norway and Sweden
(Mead).

I have examined the ringing recoveries for evidence of any differences in the migratory pattern of first year and older birds, or of males and females. Considering all the acceptable reports[1] there is a close similarity between the proportions of first year and older birds found distantly from the ringing locality (see Table 5). If first year birds are not significantly more migratory than older birds, as the table suggests, then the Hen Harrier differs in this respect from some predators in Britain, such as Kestrel and Merlin (Mead, 1973).

Table 6 gives the proportions of first year and older birds found more than 80 kilometres distant from ringing localities in the period September to April. The suggestion, in Table 6, that a higher proportion of older than first year birds winter distantly from breeding grounds, is supported by a different analysis, using only Orkney ringed birds recovered in the mid-winter months, November to February. According to this, 13 first year birds were found in Orkney and the same number outside Orkney, while only five older birds (33%) were recovered in Orkney compared with ten (66%) elsewhere. Although, as has been shown, many British Hen Harriers travel a long distance from breeding areas in autumn or winter, it seems remarkable that so many appear to make no appreciable migration at all.

If, however, a comparison is made between first summer recoveries (May to August, i.e. including birds recovered in the August of the year after they were hatched) and those in later summers, there is a strong suggestion that older birds are more likely to spend the breeding season in or near their natal area. Nevertheless, the results of this comparison cannot be regarded as conclusive owing to the small sample of first year birds available (Table 7).

Whereas older birds recorded in Table 7 are likely to have been breeding, only a proportion of first year birds may have been doing so. It is interesting to find that some of the oldest birds recovered have been found in the breeding season, close to where they were ringed as chicks; one of the most remarkable was a female, ringed as a chick in Orkney in July 1963, which was alive and breeding only 15 km away almost twelve years later. Similar faithfulness to the home region, after a long period, was shown by an eight year old female in Galloway. Males do not appear to differ obviously in this respect: two breeding season recoveries, in the home area of Orkney, being of birds approaching five and six years old.

There are 51 recoveries, for all seasons, of British ringed Hen Harriers of known sex. Of these, eight out of 23 males (35%), and twelve out of 28 females (43%), were recovered more than 80 kilometres from the place of

---

[1] Recoveries up to and including August of the year hatched are excluded from the tables as some may have been of birds which never fledged and others are certain to be of birds still dependent on their parents. I have also excluded any in which the circumstances of the recovery made it impossible to judge whether the bird was first year or older. Birds recovered up to August of the year after hatching are counted as first year.

ringing. There is therefore only a slight suggestion that females may be more migratory than males.

Balfour and Cadbury found that although a large proportion of the young in Orkney had been ringed each year, only 19 out of 83 (23%) breeding adults captured there had been ringed as chicks in the archipelago. They considered that immigration, particularly of males, might be necessary to maintain the population level in Orkney. As I have pointed out in Chapter 6, they also found that the proportion of females over five years old (42%) was higher, and that of first and second year birds lower, in the Orkney breeding population than was expected, and they considered exclusion of younger birds by social behaviour a possible explanation.

In Table 8 I have given the age groups of all ringed Hen Harriers known to have died, or been killed, after they had fledged. This table demonstrates the high mortality in the first year, and shows that in later years life expectancy for the survivors declines very slowly. There is no apparent difference in survival of males and females. According to Brown and Amadon, the average life of a Hen Harrier, 'once mature', must be about seven years, and length of life is occasionally as much as 16 years.

Man was responsible, deliberately or by accident, for most deaths of Hen Harriers for which the cause was known. Out of 37 recoveries of ringed birds for which the cause of death was certainly or almost certainly known, ten were reported shot, five trapped and one poisoned (43%), and 13 (35%) appeared to have been killed by overhead wires. When Balfour and Cadbury (1975) analysed the recoveries of Orkney ringed birds for which the cause of death was known, they pointed out that 16 out of 26 (62%) found outside Orkney had been shot, trapped or poisoned, compared with none out of ten found in Orkney. They also commented on the high proportion of casualties from striking overhead wires in Britain as a whole; deaths of Hen Harriers from this cause were more than three times as common as of Kestrels, a proportion which was thought to reflect the different hunting methods.

There can be little doubt that awareness of the protection laws has resulted in many cases of deliberate killing being reported as 'found dead' and, probably, of more not being reported at all. I have found that nine (18%) of the first 50 ringing recoveries (1939–59) were reported as shot or trapped, compared with only two (4%) of the last 50 (1967–75). It might be argued that this suggests that fewer harriers have been killed by man in recent years, but my own subjective impression is that the reverse is likely to be true. A. A. Bell (see Table 3) has reported two instances, in Perthshire and Norfolk, of deaths 'undoubtedly due to exceptionally high levels of dieldrin' and one of death from eating carrion bait containing mevinphos. As these chemicals were found among only nine birds analysed, it seems possible that mortality from toxic chemicals or poisoned bait may not be uncommon among British Hen Harriers. As I have said in Chapter 6, however, evidence that toxic chemicals have impaired the breeding success of British Hen Harriers is lacking; but this has occurred elsewhere.

Three Hen Harriers were killed by road traffic, one was found dead on a railway and another 'pursued a bird into a building and could not escape'. Wild predators probably killed two adult females: one was found 'freshly-killed in a fox den' in Caithness in June, and the other was probably killed by a Golden Eagle in Galloway (see pages 193–94). At least two birds probably died from starvation. Perhaps the most curious reports were of one 'freshly dead on a rose-bush' and another 'stuck in a tree'—and released!

Male Hen Harrier in South Uist

CHAPTER EIGHT

THE HEN HARRIER AS AN ARTIST'S BIRD

Since the illustrations play a considerable part in this book it may be appropriate to give some account of their origins. I realised, many years ago, that for a bird artist with a special interest in depicting his subjects in their environment, harriers offered exciting possibilities. Even so, my early attempts at painting Pied Harriers over the Burmese paddy fields and Hen Harriers hunting the Hebridean machair, were frustrating, to say the least. I could capture nothing of that elegant flight and only succeeded in spoiling a promising background with birds whose impossibly angled wings seemed pinned to their bodies.

I only began to make tentative progress when I spent a whole summer watching my first pair of Galloway Hen Harriers with a sketch book always at hand. I did not particularly want to make static close-up portraits of the birds. These, of course, had been done to great effect by artists like Wolf, Thorburn and Lodge but, when the great illustrators painted birds of prey in flight, I thought they sometimes diminished their impact by too much detail of feather markings. In this respect it is interesting to note how Liljefors, the master of European wildlife art, increasingly eliminated detail in his later, most monumental works. It seemed to me that few bird artists had tackled Hen Harriers as I saw them, small in scale yet making a vital focus in a spacious setting, though Charles Tunnicliffe and J. C. Harrison had each done impressive studies of Montagu's Harriers in flight, capturing the elusive moment of the food pass. I had also seen and greatly admired some small flight studies of Hen and Montagu's Harriers by Eric Ennion. These convinced me that I had everything to learn.

I am often asked whether I use photographs as aids to bird drawing and when I answer that I only do so sparingly the questioner seems to think, sometimes, that I am being perverse and making unnecessary difficulties for myself. So I had better explain. Of course, I admire and enjoy good photographs of birds and, as Talbot Kelly said, 'no painter can ignore the photograph'. In his beautifully written book, *Bird Life and the Painter*, he said almost all there is to say about how and why a bird artist goes to work. 'If we are to absorb birds as the Chinese artists did,' wrote Talbot Kelly, 'we must begin by sharing something with them, whether it is the plum blossom among which the myna sits, or the trough of the sea that embowers the petrel. . . . The artist must see bird and environment, and the bird's actions, as one whole.' For myself, at any rate, the study of photographs cannot be a substitute for such experiences. As Russow, the biographer of the painter Liljefors, said: 'our eyes always combine several movements into an impression and therefore have a different conception of truth from the photograph.'

No doubt, if field study is impossible, the wonderful modern *films* of wildlife could provide a vicarious reality from which an artist might work, but it must be remembered that the best films are already creative to a high degree and cannot therefore be regarded by the painter as the raw material of nature. Surely the wildlife artist needs to experience the excitement, the difficulty and, often, the discomfort of observing and selecting his subject matter in direct confrontation with nature. Even the best photographers admit that colours and tones in their pictures can be capricious. This, of course, is not to say that reference to photography and museums is not of great value in increasing an artist's stock-in-trade of knowledge, especially in regard to details of plumage and structure which may elude him in the field. Tame birds, in zoos or elsewhere, provide marvellous models for sketching and study of detail, but here a caveat must be sounded. I think it was Charles Simpson who spoke of 'the beauty of detail lost'. How easy it is when faced with the close-up zoo animal or dead specimen in the studio to become obsessed with the charm of detail, and entirely lose the liveliness of the swift impression which belongs to a few particular moments in time. It is particularly risky to rely on even the cleverest taxidermy in a mounted specimen as a guide to the posture of a living bird.

To return to the Hen Harrier, it must be said that it is no better as a subject for the artist than many other birds. Yet it has several features which I find extremely stimulating and I can honestly say that I never tire of trying to master the bewildering variety of its flight postures. I have watched the swift manoeuvre of the food pass countless times but have never yet achieved a satisfying drawing of the actual exchange. Undoubtedly the dimorphism of male and female Hen Harrier is particularly attractive to an artist. Then, too, as some politicians are natural subjects for the caricaturist, I find Hen Harriers with their rakish outline more tempting to draw than the blunter short-tailed Buzzard or eagle; yet I much admire the best flight studies of these, such as Liljefors achieved and Douglas Weir seems able to manage with a deceptively throw-away ease. I need only to look back at my own sketch books to be reminded that year after year certain species recur unfailingly while others, as often seen, are rather neglected. Not all are favourites for the same reasons but it is certainly true that such diverse examples as Spotted Flycatchers, Great Grey Shrikes and Hen Harriers share a kind of élan which makes my fingers itch for a pencil and paper.

I have already explained, in the Introduction to this book, how a pair of harriers make a compelling focus of life in a spacious landscape. Whether in its pallid mood of spring ochres and browns or, later, when the high green of bracken beds and bronze-purple heather shimmered beneath a summer sky, the pictorial interest of the setting filled as many pages of my sketch books as the birds which related to it so intimately. The sketch book was no less important on winter days when a harrier might appear unexpectedly, brushing the skeletal grass heads, or at the roost with its special opportunities for flight studies. Some of the drawings in this book are the results of the many encounters with other wildlife on days when harriers were the principal objective.

I usually carry a small 'Bushey' sketch book, 17.5 × 11 cm, which fits easily into an anorak pocket. In a car I like to have a much larger one. Sketch books must be able to withstand rough usage, in all weathers, and I detest those which fall apart after a couple of outings. One or two pencils (B or softer) still seem to me adequate for my purpose, though I have tried several kinds of pens. For me, the essence of sketch book drawing lies in concentrated observation, watching the bird perform the same action over and over again—but of course it often doesn't do that.

July is an excellent time to make flight drawings, when a female in charge of fledged young will sometimes fly a long way from the nesting site to mob you. Both she and her fledged brood can then be watched through binoculars, from a comfortable vantage point, without causing them undue disturbance. At this season, however, there is no certainty that a male will be seen. Observe the female overhead: it is close enough to reveal, momentarily, every detail of the splayed flight feathers but the wings are continually changing angle and appearance as it twists and banks. It is approaching you

in a half dive but, in a second, is rising again and leaving you. Watch her make another run and perhaps one more. Has some impression of that wonderful, emphatic outline imprinted itself on your memory? You must hope so and concentrate rapidly on the sketch; no, not one sketch, but several, put down like writing, for in seconds the bird has assumed a whole range of flight shapes. The results may be mostly worthless, but the effort should be made. Something true may emerge. If not, the memory will have stored an image which may isolate itself half-an-hour later when you can recollect those breathless moments in a little tranquillity. I have been told that Joseph Crawhall stood for hours leaning on a gate watching farmyard bantams or ducks; so good was his visual memory that he drew nothing at the time but could produce a masterpiece in recollection.

It is a little easier to absorb the attitudes of a pair of harriers as they float and play at a distance, in the sky above their nesting ground. On a windy day they move slowly and can be held in the binoculars for a long time, but wings and tails are constantly being trimmed and many sketches are needed to record the full variety of postures. The most intriguing flight positions are always the most difficult and some, I find, are totally elusive. Perhaps this is as well, since if the best were attainable I might be tempted to give up. One such moment is when a cock harrier hurls himself earthward, or threshes upward in full display. I can only begin to suggest this extraordinary perform-ance in a drawing.

Like all nearly white birds, the male harrier is a superb subject for tonal study. One moment it is so dark against a bright sky that it is hard to dis-tinguish from its mate. Banking a little, it catches a silver gleam of light on its upper surface. When this happens, the artist rapidly tries to note the ex-tent of light and dark; it may bank enough for the white underparts to flash but the area of shadow cast on them by the wing needs to be noted. If the upper parts are caught in bright light the black wing ends will be lightened a little too, even warmed almost to purplish-brown by the sun, while the black on the underside of the shadowed wing-tip remains intense. In brilliant top-lighting the black almost merges with the rest of the pale wing. I recall Tun-nicliffe's Rooks sparkling white in a top light. Who has not seen this in Rook or Crow, but an artist needs some courage to portray them so. Too much reliance on field guides has perhaps left us expecting birds to present a norm in appearance. (Pictures in such books, with mass reproduction, are often far drabber in colour than the artist painted them.) When a cock Hen Harrier flies to the roost on a snowy, leaden-skied evening it can look a dark grey bird even in the best of plumage, but reflected light from ice or snow turns the underparts creamy-yellow. The chequered grey underwing of a female careening above moor or forest looks gilded and almost translucent in low sunlight.

When sketching birds in the field I am often struck by the effects of weather or temperature on their appearance and note, too, how this changes strikingly according to whether the bird is at ease or alarmed. Never before the tropical summer of 1976 had I noticed Spotted Flycatchers looking almost as sylph-like as Swallows, and even the often loose-plumaged female Hen Harrier can look remarkably slim and well-groomed on a hot day.

Talbot Kelly said that when the artist studies birds in the field he must always be conscious of the setting and learn to look at both at once. In some of my favourite bird paintings a bird plays only a small but vital part in the whole. Edwin Alexander, for instance, made a diminutive Dipper the focal point in a composition of boulders and trickling water; both bird and setting are simply stated and correctly related in scale. Sometimes a small-scale harrier, or a pair of harriers, seem to fit truthfully into a landscape painted out on the hill, but much greater problems are involved in selecting and synthesising the raw material of field sketches when the birds are to occupy a large part of the picture space. Then, in the studio, the artist aims to achieve a satisfying composition without losing the urgency of the field sketch. Too often, in my own experience, something is lost and if the result appears staged it must be considered a failure. The final setting for a Hen Harrier painting may include only a small patch of sky or hillside, or a balance of both, but somehow the illusion of space in the picture must not be diminished.

Bird artists are sometimes scorned by art critics as mere zoological recorders (some, of course, are scorned for different and more justifiable reasons). Yet good bird pictures reveal a great variety of approach and it is usually easy to recognise the work of different artists at a glance. There is no reason why art should cease where ornithological illustration begins. Not without reason, Audubon remains the art critics' favourite bird artist, although his main purpose was to leave a faithful record of what he had seen and, often, discovered for himself. As I look now at his dynamic study of a Marsh Hawk devouring its kill I marvel at his attention to such details as the grasp of the bird's foot on its prey. So insatiable was Audubon's appetite for work that he complained when he was prevented by sweltering heat from drawing for more than 16 hours in a day. Even within the limits set by the needs of identification guides it should be remembered that Peterson's neatly summarised birds were an innovation not so many years ago.

Sketches of Hen Harrier

Modern photography can produce a beautiful and efficient record of a bird's appearance, nevertheless, anyone who tries to draw birds must find that his powers of observation are sharpened in the process. He will have the satisfaction of discovering many surprising details of plumage and posture for himself. Each time that I stop to make a few rapid sketches of a brood of feathered young harriers, some new aspect of their complex appearance attracts my attention. At the end of another nesting season I have just had my first encounter with a partially melanistic nestling. I am by no means convinced that the slightly unpredictable colours and tones of a photograph would be the best method of recording its appearance.

To some artists it seems right to distort or simplify bird shapes to such an extent that the model becomes barely recognisable. Probably I am not adventurous enough to go very far in this direction, but I confess that I have much sympathy with the splendid Dutch artist, Rien Poortvliet, when he says of animals in art: 'it is impossible for me to deform them; perhaps I know too much of them to see them as circles or something like that' (Buerschaper, 1975).

Sketch book study of female Hen Harrier

PART II

A STUDY OF THE HEN HARRIER
IN SOUTH-WEST SCOTLAND

This account of the Hen Harrier in my home region begins in the long, fine summer of 1959 and spans 17 years, finishing in the even warmer, sunnier summer of 1976. During this period I studied Hen Harriers at all seasons.

Initially, from 1959–1965, most observations in the breeding season were made on Area A, an area of moorland of about 2,000 hectares, which consisted principally of two hill sheep farms. There was some grouse shooting and game keeper activity. Much of the ground was below 200 metres, sloping north and south from a higher ridge of 270–330 metres. Heather, grass and bracken covered most of the drier ground, and bog myrtle, bogcotton, deer grass and sphagnum mosses were plentiful in the lower and wetter parts. There were numerous small outcrops of rock on the steeper slopes. Moorland nesting in a different area, Area B, some 48 kilometres away, was also studied, mainly by R. C. (Bert) Dickson, from 1968 onwards. This was mostly undulating heather moor and some more grassy or boggy valleys, with a high population of Red Grouse and active gamekeepering. It was also part of a sheep farm, and lay between 210–240 metres. Two nests were studied on other moorland, one on a keepered heather and bracken covered moor, at an elevation of about 300 metres, Area F, 64 kilometres away; the other on an unkeepered sheep farm, at about 420 metres, Area G, 40 kilometres away, where the vegetation was mainly grassland with extensive tracts of rushes.

Hen Harriers were also studied in 1–20 year old conifer forest, especially in Areas C, D and E. Areas C and E were contiguous with Area A and Area D adjoined Area C. Areas C and D, together, covered about 9,000 hectares, including some unplanted ground. The planted ground in Areas C and D was largely between 100 and 300 metres and the unplanted ground was mostly between 300 and 500 metres. Area E, with no unplanted high ground, covered about 400 hectares, all between 200 and 275 metres. These areas were part of a much wider extent of forest, parts of which were over 20 years old by 1959 and probably already unsuitable for harrier nesting.

Observations were also made, to varying degrees, in neighbouring forests, especially in Areas H and J, in both of which nesting occurred at least once, and one forest nest was studied in Area K. The trees in these forests were of similar age structure to those in Areas C, D and E; Area H consisted of about 900 hectares, mainly between 225 and 360 metres, area J about 1,400 hectares, mainly between 165 and 820 metres, and Area K was part of a much larger area of forest in a similar range of elevation. From the nearest part of Area D, the approximate distances to Area H, J and K were respectively 6.4 kilometres, 9.6 kilometres and 24 kilometres.

In reading the following narrative accounts, it will be helpful to refer at times to Figure 10. This shows the annual number of known nests, excluding

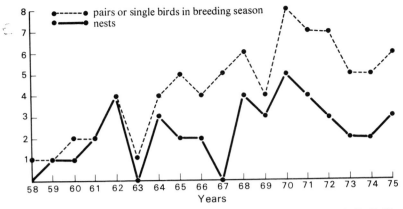

Fig. 10   Hen Harriers and nests in south-west Scotland in Areas, A, C, D, E, H and J

repeats (and the number of extra pairs or single birds when nests were not found) in Areas A, C, D, E, H and J, about 12,000 hectares and some adjacent ground. It was considered that Areas H and J were sufficiently well watched and close to the special areas to justify the inclusion of the two nests and the sightings of pairs there, in the graph.

As described in the historical section of this book, an increasing number of pairs was noted in south-west Scotland as a whole during the 1960s but it is doubtful if there has been a further increase since about 1970. In recent years I have had increasing contact with people who might know of breeding Hen Harriers over a wide area and it is therefore impossible to make accurate comparisons with the early years for south-west Scotland as a whole. Nevertheless very few reports of proved nesting outside my special area have been received, apart from those in area B, where R. C. Dickson has made thorough observations since 1968.

In Chapter 15 I have given some breeding data using nests from all areas detailed above and particularly comparing success in moorland and forest.

In Chapter 16 I have discussed food and hunting grounds in the breeding season for my special area and given details of prey remains identified in various ways. This section is followed by an account of food and hunting grounds in the winter. Diurnal sightings of Hen Harriers within 24 kilometres of a major roost have been recorded for a number of years and I am greatly indebted to Louis Urquhart for the work he has done in plotting these. They have been used in an attempt to discover which types of habitat are locally most favoured by hunting Hen Harriers, and whether males and females have different preferences. The final section in this part of the book gives an account of observations at a winter roost (Roost 1), on bogland, adjacent to Area C, and makes some comparisons with studies made by R. C. Dickson at a different roost (Roost 2) about 16 kilometres from Area B, and discusses the problems arising from the study of winter roosts in south-west Scotland.

AREA A – MOORLAND

300 m

150 m

AREAS C and D – FOREST

450 m

300 m

150 m

AREA E – FOREST

300 m

150 m

height above
sea level in
metres

Sketch/diagrams of characteristic habitats in Areas A, C, D and E. Note: Area B
(Moorland) is somewhat similar to Area A, mostly 210–240 metres altitude

Male Montagu's Harrier

CHAPTER NINE

THE BEGINNING: THE NINETEEN FIFTIES

Before 1959 the only Hen Harriers I had seen in the Stewartry of Kirkcud-bright were occasional birds in winter, hunting the marshes of Loch Ken or the fringes of the hills. Even before the 1939–45 war, they had been seen not uncommonly in autumn and winter on the extensive moors of South Ayrshire and Wigtownshire where, in 1930, Maurice Portal recorded (Seigne, 1930) the arrival of one Hen Harrier about 12 October, for five successive years. Such harriers were very likely to be shot or trapped. Reflecting on the scanty local information on the bird before 1959, I have often wondered how, long before that year, it had bred undetected or un-reported. Strangely, it was the attempted breeding of a pair of the even rarer Montagu's Harriers in a young conifer plantation at Corriedoo, near Dalry, in 1953 (sadly, the female was caught in a gin trap placed at the nest), that first alerted me to keep a special look out for nesting harriers. This occurred at a time when the British population of Montagu's Harriers was in a far healthier state than now and when breeding records as far north as Perthshire raised hopes of continued nesting in Scotland.

The considerable local interest aroused by the Galloway incident com-plicated the problem of establishing when Hen Harriers began to recolonise the region, and any harrier seen was likely to be reported as a Montagu's. Derek Ratcliffe had a distant view of a probable pair of harriers of unknown species in the High Ken valley in 1950; and it will never be known which harriers were seen near Lochinvar in the same neighbourhood by the Dalry postman, Hugh Clark, in the summer of 1951. He later described what he saw to Louis Urquhart and there is little doubt that it was a pair of harriers

170

in the act of the food pass. 'He thought it was a seagull of some kind, though a most unusual-looking gull which made him remember it. Following the "gull" had been a big "Sparrowhawk", long-winged, apparently chasing the gull. There had also been a Great Black-backed Gull around and the grouse were alarmed and flying in all directions, which he attributed as much to the presence of the "gulls" as to the "Sparrowhawk".' As already mentioned, a distant view of a male harrier is easily confused with a gull; even the great naturalist, Sir William Jardine, misinterpreted the food pass as 'the female not suffering the male to approach the nest'.

Although there is little doubt that the pair of Hen Harriers which nested in 1959 had been preceded by others, there cannot have been many nests in earlier years, for none of the keen-eyed nest hunters who regularly combed the Galloway hills for Golden Eagles, Buzzards and Peregrines had any knowledge of Hen Harriers' nests at this period. During the mid 1950s, however, adult male Hen Harriers were occasionally identified in summer, in south Ayrshire, by the late Sir Geoffrey Hughes-Onslow and others. The first clue that a pair might be breeding in the Stewartry came when Commander Graham reported to Arthur Duncan (later Sir Arthur) that a male harrier in grey plumage had flown across a hill road in front of his car, one day in the summer of 1958. Then, one snowy winter's night in 1958, I took that same road on my way to give a talk and, en route, dropped Frank Dalziel, from Dalry, at the road-end to the remote house on the moor where his brother and nephew were shepherds. It seemed just worth while suggesting that he might ask them if they had ever seen any large hawks fitting a description of harriers. When I collected Frank in a whirl of snow, near midnight, he had a positive report—they had seen such birds—and I knew that next spring I should be there.

CHAPTER TEN

WATCH IN THE HEATHER—THE FIRST NEST

My first visit to the likely nesting ground, in 1959, was not until 21 May. On this and many subsequent days my companion was the late Alan Mills, already nearly 70 years old, but fit and eager for the search. He brought a blend of enthusiasm, patience and quiet humour to our watches. Our first call was at the shepherds' house. Will Dalziel said he had seen the birds for some weeks past, a 'white yin' and a 'broon yin'. This was the first year he and his father had seen a white one, but brown birds had been about for eight seasons. They pointed out the hill recently frequented by the pair.

Our first move was misguided. We walked all over the hill, which was well covered with old, tall heather and steep in places, lost a lot of sweat, and obviously did not find a nest. With hindsight it is easy to say that even if we had flushed an incubating hen, we ought to have been ashamed for disturbing her without need. As we came down, a little disconsolately, I looked back and was just in time to catch a dazzling glimpse of a cock harrier, white as a gull and black wing-tipped, as it swept away on the wind and breasted the slope of another hill across the valley. I could hardly believe our good fortune—there could be little doubt that somewhere a hen was on eggs and there was no more likely site than the deep heather on the hill we had just left. Yet, as I learned from experience later, that first sight of the cock might have been miles from a nest and, of course, there might not have been a nest at all.

Fortunately, our next move was more sensible. We retired to watch our hill from a distance, choosing a sheltered, grassy spot, concealed from the road above by a convenient little rocky bluff. In retrospect we were, perhaps, too near to the likely nesting hill. At 500 metres from its base we ran the risk that the birds would be disturbed by our presence, and if the cock had kept away we should have discovered nothing. But we had all the luck that day. At 17.45, when we had been watching for nearly three hours, the cock flashed into view from behind us, approaching the hill in a long, fast glide. A lowered foot, carrying prey, was at once apparent, and in seconds the big brown hen was up beside him, the two flying almost together before the cock jinked and passed the prey to her. The cock flew on and was quickly out of sight behind the hill.

Meanwhile, the hen had alighted in the heather to feed. When, 15 minutes later, she rose, circling slowly in the evening sunlight above the now shadowed heather slopes, I knew that I must keep her in view and that, this time, she would surely return to a nest. She was crossing the lower slope of the hill, just above eye-level from our view point, conspicuous in her rich buff and brown plumage with the clear white patch at the tail base, when she suddenly vanished, dipping neatly into the heather where the nest must be. As the old collectors might have said, 'the nest was ours', but should we permit ourselves a look at its contents? Neither of us had ever seen a Hen Harrier's nest before. We started forward, but, within yards of the nest, when the female had still not risen, I thought that to flush her from eggs almost at our feet might conceivably cause desertion. So, at the last moment, we withdrew, content with the certainty that she was still safely on the nest. On this first day I had begun to learn. One lesson was to stay well away from a suspected nesting area and watch patiently for the food pass if you hope to locate a nest; and another, that the female Hen Harrier may be a very close sitter. Later, I was to discover that this was the general rule. Indeed, at all the nests in my experience, a female with eggs or small young has sat tight at less than 20 metres, and usually at less than five.

May 23 was a day of broiling sun, blue, hazy distances and the lightest puffs of east wind. I had enticed Arthur Duncan away from Dumfriesshire, always eager at the prospect of a new ornithological experience in Galloway. At 10.45 the nest site was under observation from the same point as before. Almost seven hours later no harrier had shown itself. Arthur had, by then, had to leave for home, generously casting no hint of scepticism on my story that a certain patch of heather concealed a bird on its nest. I am not sure if I still believed it myself, as I continued to gaze at the quiet hillside and watched the shadows lengthen. Then at 17.45 the cock came out of the sky and I heard the hen's food call as she went up to him for the pass. A Short-eared Owl barked and suddenly the two owls and both the harriers were over the nest, the female sparring with an owl.

Arthur has exceptionally sharp eyesight and there is no doubt that if the cock had been anywhere in view during this long period we should have spotted him. So a day which was so nearly a non-event taught me that, when a female Hen Harrier is incubating eggs, the cock may not approach the nest for many hours at a stretch. In later years I found that some cocks may behave differently, making fairly frequent visits to the vicinity of nests during incubation, but I am convinced that there is a tendency for the male to avoid such apparently unnecessary appearances at this time. For the hen to remain for seven hours without stirring from the nest proved to be not at all exceptional.

Over the 17 years of this study, I have noted the times of food passes at many nests. During the incubation period, food is brought at least once in the early part of the day, and at least once in the afternoon or evening, but it may be usual for the hen to be fed three times a day in all. We came to regard the hour between 17.00 and 18.00 as the magic time when the cock's arrival could be most confidently expected.

After the first two or three watches, we began to develop an almost proprietry familiarity with the environment of the nest and all that lived there. No doubt some will say that sitting still, watching birds and the ever changing face of a moorland landscape, is lazy and boring. Lazy it may have been but we were never bored. When, for long periods, there was no harrier activity, other moorland birds claimed our attention. Between us and the nesting hill the ground was flat and partly boggy, dammed at one time to form a loch. Some 400 metres away, just in front of the hill, ran a very small burn and a fence, this forming the march between two sheep farms. Everywhere, the landscape in view was sheep country, a patchwork of grassland, heather and bracken, rising to a skyline of 325 metres, with here and there the higher, bluer hill tops showing beyond.

In 1959, the advancing tide of conifer forest was hardly, if at all, visible from our viewpoint, though a mile and a half behind us, the first block of young trees in the near neighbourhood was being planted that spring. Apart from this, the nearest young plantations were over three miles distant. A long history of sheep grazing, with sporadic burning, had left only a few tracts of old, deep heather, much the strongest growth being on the rather rugged hill which the harriers had selected for their nest site. Yet several other patches of heather, bog myrtle and moor grass provided sufficient cover in later years for harrier nests. Until 1967, moorland habitat extended unbroken on a broad front from here to the west, but that year a belt of new forest reduced the special area of moor to about 500 hectares, and it became an enclave among the plantations. This proved an important change for the harriers and other birds of the neighbourhood.

In May 1959, the most obvious and vocal of the harriers' avian neighbours were the Curlews, while Meadow Pipits, followed by Skylarks, were the most numerous passerines. There were three pairs of Curlews nesting between us and the base of the hill. With young recently hatched, the adult Curlews often flew to attack possible predators which passed near

them. Crows invariably received this treatment but the harriers worried the Curlews less. If the cock harrier was perched, usually on a fence post, the Curlews ignored him, though one pair had chicks 50 metres or so from one of his favourite resting places. There was some sparring between the Curlews and the cock harrier when he was in flight but, at this and later nests, Curlews paid less and less attention to harriers as the season progressed, and it was not unusual for them to breed successfully within 100 metres or so of a harrier's nest. Once, at the 1959 site, an attacking Curlew flew at the female, in characteristic, straight, fast flight when she was just above her nest. She feinted to avoid the attack and then made a savage dive at the Curlew when it had landed again, and probably struck it momentarily. Sheep, advancing close to Curlew chicks, caused the greatest outbursts of parental alarm—once, I saw a ewe turned aside in its path by a pair of Curlews barring its way with upraised wings, using both wings and bill to dunt its nose.

Young Curlews are commonly taken by Hen Harriers in Orkney, yet in Galloway I have not found a trace of them in prey remains or pellets gathered over the years, but Bert Dickson has two records of young Curlews as prey on the moorland Area B. The two next commonest waders on the moor were Golden Plover and Snipe; of these only Snipe have been detected as prey of local harriers. Allowing that my prey sample is by no means conclusive, the absence of young Curlew or Golden Plover invites speculation on the reasons why. It is possible that, on this very open type of moorland, the warning cries of parents are particularly successful at foiling the harrier's method of capture by surprise approach.

The harriers' predatory neighbours were Short-eared Owls and Kestrels, both nesting quite near. There was only occasional buffeting between owls and harriers but the cock Kestrel, carrying prey to its mate in an old Raven's nest on a rock face, was chased or dived at by either harrier if he passed close to their nest. Carrion Crows and Ravens were assured of an onslaught whenever they appeared with 500 metres if the male was about, or the female off the nest. We soon learned to listen for the protesting calls of harassed crows—though they were sometimes the attackers—to lead our

eyes to the male harrier approaching with food. We occasionally saw a Merlin slip across the hill but there was no sign of its nest that year, though a pair have bred there more recently. Many, but by no means all, of the Galloway harrier nests have had Short-eared Owls breeding fairly near them, twice at 200–250 metres distance, but I am not sure if any special association between the two species could be argued. Short-eared Owls' nests are very difficult to find and the chances of locating one, if it happened to be near a watched harrier's nest, were obviously much higher than elsewhere in the same area.

We were aware from the beginning that there was some gamekeeper activity on the moorland and that questions would be asked about the harriers' feeding habits. No attempt was being made to manage the heather in the interests of Red Grouse and the keepers did little more than wage a sporadic war on crows and foxes. The population of grouse was low compared with the major grouse moors, but considering the sparseness of heather it was not negligible. Red Grouse could probably be bracketed with Curlew as the most numerous of the larger birds nesting on the moorland. To the casual observer, they appear much less numerous than they really are, during their time of incubation in April–May. I recall that, in 1959, neither Sir Arthur Duncan nor I expected that grouse would be an important prey of Hen Harriers. Jimmy (J. W.) Campbell had suggested that young waders formed the major part of their diet, probably from his experience in the Outer Isles; and the most recently published summary of their prey in Britain, in the *Handbook of British Birds*, mentioned Red Grouse as only occasional prey.

Over the ensuing years a good deal of evidence has been gathered about prey taken by harriers in Galloway (Chapters 16 and 17). At the first nest only one of eleven identified kills was a Red Grouse (young), found after the harrier brood had flown. The rest were Meadow Pipits (3), Skylark (5) and Whinchats (2), the latter being probably the fourth commonest passerine species on the moor, exceeded only by the first two and the Wheatear. More than once, the shepherds told me, keepers would have shot the harriers if they had not known that the nest was being watched—once we overheard them discussing the fact that 'bodies in the heather were watching the birds' and I have no doubt that, if they had found one or two kills of grouse, the harriers would have been destroyed. It is fair to add that, in recent years, I have had some very friendly talks with the principal keeper in the district, who now prefers photographing birds of prey to killing them, though I doubt if he will ever rate harriers among his favourites.

We were fortunate in having found a nest ideally situated for observation, set in one of the most delectable landscapes in Galloway, and luckier still that the pair were particularly fine examples of their kind. It now seems hard to believe, but it was 27 May before I was fully convinced that we had been watching Hen Harriers and not Montagu's; or, riduculous thought, Pallid Harriers! We certainly did not know the harrier species well enough to distinguish the females at a distance and it was not easy, in dazzling sunlight, to swear that the cock *did* have a white rump and did *not* have a black midline on the wing. In fact the cock was one of the palest of his sex that I have ever seen, causing a note to be made that the blue-grey head and breast hardly stood out from the white below; and that the back and tail were so pale that the white rump was scarcely noticeable. So he did look a little like a cock Pallid Harrier! Both birds must have been old, the cock from plumage colour and the hen from her brilliant yellow eyes, and it seems almost certain that they had bred for several years before, most likely locally.

On 27 May I made my first morning watch, reaching the look-out at 06.00 hours. The cool grey early light slowly brightened, bringing the first

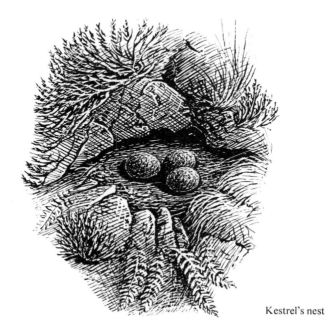

Kestrel's nest

hint of blue to the far away hump of Cairnsmore. In the still morning air
Cuckoos called almost without a break, and the songs of Whinchat,
Whitethroat and Reed Bunting carried up from the scatter of willow bushes
along the burn. Neither Whitethroat nor Reed Bunting had been evident
during previous watches at later hours. In this study of Montagu's Harriers
in Cornwall, Ryves maintained that small birds nesting close to the harriers'
nests were immune from attack. This was probably because his female Montagu's did not hunt till the young were fledged. At this, and many other, Hen
Harriers' nests, we were to see the female hunting very close at hand, once
even jumping about in the crown of a big willow bush, shadowing the
movements of a Reed Bunting in the branches below. The cock, like Ryves'
cock Montagu's, very rarely hunted near the nest. We did not know the extent of his hunting range although, by watching him till out of sight, it was
possible to say that he regularly travelled well over a kilometre from the nest
and probably much further. The size of hunting areas in Orkney is being
studied by observing colour-marked birds, but no colour marking has been
done in Galloway, so precise information on this subject remains lacking in
the region.

On the first morning watch I expected to see a food pass fairly soon.
Possibly the hen had already been fed, but from 06.00 she received nothing
till 10.45. The cock had flown in at 06.50, heralded by a little excited Curlew
chatter, but not the prolonged alarm calls signifying danger in the form of
man or fox. The cock harrier remained for nearly an hour, perched on
different fence posts, but sometimes he made his low-pitched yikkering call,
indicating for the first time that he was uneasily aware of my presence. It
may have been a flash of light on my telescope which bothered him; through
it I was able to see his fierce-looking yellow eye and note the quick owlish
swivelling of his big grey head. At later nests we often found that it was well
into the morning before a sitting female was fed, but the nagging thought
that we *might* sometimes have missed a pass soon after first light could not
be discounted.

We maintained our cautious policy of not visiting the nest until we were
sure that hatching had taken place. On 2 June, after a food pass, the hen
stayed off the nest for only eight minutes, instead of her usual 15–20, and
obviously carried in most of the prey. It seemed certain that one or two
chicks had hatched and, next day, Alan and I went to look at the nest for the
first time. The hen was off, having just taken a food pass. She was much less
aggressive at this first visit than later on, coming no lower than six metres
above our heads. Her yikkering alarm call, on first hearing, reminded me of
a Song Thrush's alarm notes. I wrote in my diary of this first exciting look at
a nest: 'As we approached the now well-known spot through deep heather, I
feared treading on the nest but the first view of it was startlingly clear—a
clear space in the heather with neat, spotless nest, black heather stalks, grass
lined, somewhat flattened—by no means large—with two very small young

and three eggs, piled in the centre. Young much of a size, a day or two old, pinkish with scarcely any down yet, some blueish skin especially above eyes, flat, broad skulls, pitch-dark eyes, jet-black bills, pinkish ceres and flesh-pink, weak looking feet and legs. Made no sound, only just able to raise heads to look blearily at us. Eggs surprisingly small, dull whitish, slightly brown stained.'

We stayed only a few moments, lest the diving, yikkering female attracted notice from passers-by on the road. She followed us down the hill, in some frenzy, alighting and glaring from rocks, but did not come out over the moor. The male did not appear. As soon as we were back at the look-out below the road she returned to the nest.

If the first chick had hatched on 31 May, incubation had begun about 1 May. It may have begun after the first egg was laid or later.

During the ten days of the pre-hatching period since the nest had been found, it had been under observation for 31 hours, the longest period I have watched a nest with eggs. We had seen only five food passes in this time, so that, on average, the female sat for over six hours at a stretch. During the early days of June, with young to be fed, the cock's visits with prey greatly increased, but we had some puzzling and slightly disturbing watches. Was it time to retire to a more distant or less open look-out? On 6 June, the cock came five times with prey between 10.30 and 18.00 hours, but there were no food passes and only his last catch reached the nest. This was dropped by the cock when almost stalled over the nest. Later, I learned that this was common behaviour, especially around the hatch.

It was a coldish day with some heavy rain at mid-day and the chicks evidently required much brooding. We had noticed that the cock sometimes flew with prey to a gully beyond the nest, where an old hawthorn was a favourite perch. Beneath the tree we found the plucked, headless, but un-eaten carcases of a Meadow Pipit and a fledgling Skylark. I made more, but similar, finds at a cock's 'look-out' post at a 1961 nest. In both cases it seemed possible that the cock had become nervous of us, although in 1961 I had a more concealed observation point. Eddie Balfour always considered that male harriers had, in general, more nervous temperaments than females. On the other hand, a more plausible explanation may be that, when the young are very small, some cocks bring more prey than the hen will accept.

Back in 1959 I was only beginning to learn. It is easy to say that it was imprudent to go to the nest in the rather poor weather of that 6 June, but we had watched for a long time and were puzzled to have seen nothing of the hen, and eager to make certain that some disaster had not struck the nest. We were relieved to find four chicks had hatched and we received some spectacular head-high onslaughts from the hen; but, again, the cock did not come into view. The hen returned to brood her chicks as soon as we were back at our look-out.

In early June we were still having difficulty in deciding whether it was always the female which made the far carrying 'squealing wail', or food call, 'twiss-yew', just before the food pass. Although this is typically the begging call of the female to her mate, later experience showed that males make a very similar call, notably when a female refuses to rise for a pass. The low call which the male may always make, as he approaches with prey, is audible to human ears for less than 100 metres.

On 12 June, Willie Austin joined me on an evening watch. At 19.30 the sun was already dropping behind the rather commanding skyline of hill which we had christened the 'Lion's Head'. It was a radiant evening, with long banners of sun-topped cloud over the far hills and a flawless sky above. The harriers' nesting slope was in deepest shadow and the cock was engaged in a magnificent exhibition of leisured, soaring flight over the other, still sunlit, side of the hill. At 19.55 he had a small kill but apparently consumed it himself, re-appearing as a black silhouette floating in the sunset sky. He was still up there, in the glow of sundown, at almost 22.00 hours. One previous night he had been perched high up on the hill above the nest, where he would probably remain to roost. How to explain the apparently effortless, so evidently enjoyable, high flying? It seems to me that there is really no need for the scientist and the layman to fall out on this. If such behaviour *must* have 'survival value' for it to persist, there is no need to deny enjoyment, too. There can surely be two sides to the same coin, as an athlete or a primitive hunting man for that matter, may be exhilarated by keeping himself to the peak of fitness.

By mid June, after we had tried out some new, more distant observation points, we were back at the original spot. The hen sometimes came over and circled us, yikkering, but the business of feeding the young was not being interrupted by our presence. By now the hen, in good weather, was no longer brooding the chicks for much of the day, and she often sailed about over the road and would fly as far to meet the cock for the food pass. The pair must have become obvious enough to passers-by but, apart from the shepherds and keepers, few people took any notice of them. We were concerned one day when a boy left his bicycle on the road and made great speed for the hill. For 20 minutes we boy-watched anxiously, then laughed at ourselves as he reached the summit and came smartly down again, perhaps getting in trim for the school sports, and certainly not interested in birds' nests.

We could now make out the actions of the female as she fed the young. Surprisingly, although this nest was watched for 43 hours after hatching we never had much evidence of hunting by the hen, not even when the young were fledged. For instance, on 7 and 8 July, when they were 5–5½ weeks old, during seven hours of watching, all the prey came by way of the cock, either by food passes to the hen and once, probably, to a flying youngster, or by direct drop to the young still using the nest as a base. The cock at this nest never flagged in his attentions, as many do towards fledging time, and the hen was more zealous than some in her role of guardian. So the division of labour was more like that observed by Ryves, at his Montagu's nests, than is usual at a Hen Harrier's nest when the young are large and the hen is hunting at least as much as the cock. (Henning Weis and Schipper each found that female Montagu's often hunt before the young can fly.) Consistent with the cock continuing to do most of the hunting, nearly all the prey looked small, as far as could be judged.

The hen, always bold, reached a peak of aggression when the young were about three weeks old. Head-covering on visits of inspection became prudent. More than once, at this stage, she clawed hat from head, and a shepherd claimed that she dived so fiercely at a keeper, 'looking for pluckings', that he came away quickly. She was succeeded in following years by other aggressive hens, so that, for some years, I thought this behaviour was the rule at almost every nest. Further experience has shown that many hens show little or no aggression towards man.

On 20 June, in the early morning sun, the hen was spending most of the time perched on or near the old thorn tree, sunning herself and preening, but very much on guard. Crows were chased vigorously from the nest area. At this period of the nesting cycle it is fairly easy to locate nests by watching a hen, as she is so inclined to perch, conspicuously, near the nest, and the young require frequent visits with food. A food pass at 07.05 was the earliest seen at this nest, the young being fed after the hen had spent two minutes plucking the prey in the heather. Watching a nest from a hide, years later, I was surprised to find that a hen was still tearing up plucked prey and feeding it to a chick 31 days old. Intervals between visits with prey were now sometimes as short as a quarter of an hour. Intervals of 5–10 minutes between some visits were recorded in later years, strongly suggesting that a brood of fledglings had been raided in quick succession. When the young were big the hen often ignored the cock's arrival as he dropped prey direct to the chicks.

We visited the nest on 20 and 29 June, and 2 July. In Chapter 6 I have detailed the changes in the appearance of chicks as they grow from birth to fledging. On this first experience I was especially struck by the rapid feather growth during the final ten days. On 2 July we went, confidently, to ring the brood, having decided in favour of this rather late in the season. The eldest chick would be hardly more than four and a half weeks old and we did not expect any to fly till they were over five weeks: we had not the benefit of Eddie Balfour's papers on the breeding cycle.

On the dull, damp morning we were up at the nest soon after 07.00 hours, Bobby Smith, young Lars Svensson and I. Lars, now famed far beyond his native Sweden as an ornithologist, had come to us to improve his English, with the strong proviso that he would get some bird-watching. We had chosen an hour when we were unlikely to attract attention from the road. But inexperience caught us out again—one of the brood flew as we approached and could not be found again. Although the other three were no problem, that morning taught the lesson that young Hen Harriers, if disturbed, can often fly at little over 30 days, and ringing should never be left so late. Nor were we too happy at causing a premature flight, even though the hen, for once ignoring us at the nest, immediately flew after the escaper.

Apart from a few flecks of grey down on wings and head, the young harriers had become superficially like darker and more richly coloured replicas of their mother. A host of details were rapidly noted or sketched, as the young crouched on the flattened remnants of the once tidy nest, the almost purple bloom on their backs emphasised by the bronze-green tangle of heather that overshadowed them. Their most arresting features were their, now brilliant, chrome yellow legs and their beautiful tails, banded creamy-red and sepia, some partly-grown feathers still looking like little darts in their blue sheaths. The bird which had flown was probably a male and the others were two females and a male, sexed quite easily from iris colour and leg thickness. The grey-eyed young male was slimmer both in body and leg than his sisters. In the steamy weather, the nest was infested with flies, and this brood were more heavily afflicted with fleas and flat flies than any I have seen since. Even at this late stage the hen had removed uneaten remains of prey and the only food in the nest was an apparently adult Skylark, which must have been the prey we had seen the cock drop at the nest before we left the road. It had been delivered plucked. In the heather near by, a very young Whinchat, not very fresh, was also uneaten.

Interest did not cease after the young could fly. For at least a week after fledging the young birds often flew back to the nest to find prey dropped there by either parent. They were extremely difficult to spot from a distance when they sat, for long periods, well scattered about the hill face, but often they could be seen circling or diving at one another on the wing. At this and later nests I saw recently fledged young fly up to catch prey dropped by the hen, as in a food pass. Sometimes they were too slow and did not get near enough to the hen to make the catch.

The hen, ferocious as ever, became particularly angry when sheep happened to come close to any of her brood, often diving at a sheep's head for minutes at a time and even striking with her feet. The sheep seemed unimpressed and the shepherd was merely amused. The whole family stayed about the nesting hill until at least mid-July, and harriers were still to be seen not far away until the end of the month. Then, as generally happens, the nesting area was deserted, though I saw a single young bird quartering the brown bracken at the roadside on 9 October—as likely, at that date, to be a wanderer from elsewhere as one of the local brood. It may have been no coincidence that, in November of this first year of proved nesting, I had my first sighting of a Hen Harrier at the bog, five miles away, where in later years a communal winter roost was established.

CHAPTER ELEVEN

MOORLAND NESTING: 1960–1968

After the successful nesting in 1959, I looked forward to the return of a pair in the following season. In view of the reports of increase further north, there seemed good prospects for the establishment of a breeding population in Galloway over the next few years. This did, indeed, happen, but much more slowly and hesitantly than might have been anticipated.

On 8 February 1960, a male was seen near the old nest site, and on 14 March I saw a ringtail, probably a female, there. Then, on 4 April, came a shock. Almost all the long heather on the slopes of the 'Lion's Head' had been burnt in an uncontrolled moor fire on 30–31 March. Looking at the bare blackened hillside I despaired of a nest that year. On that fine spring morning nothing looked promising for the harriers. Close at hand, men were working on road improvement, two boys with a gun were on the next hill and, just over a mile away, I could see the big red forestry plough turning up long lines of glistening peat. Yet, as I was to learn many times over, the magnetism of last year's nesting ground is a most powerful force in the life of the Hen Harrier. Ryves (1948) has told how, in Cornwall, a pair of Montagu's Harriers returned, to his amazement, to nest in the one small, unburnt patch of bog myrtle in a marsh devastated by fire. But I had not read this, and when I spotted a pair of Hen Harriers quartering the burnt heather slopes by the old site, I was astonished and delighted.

183

Because we had found the nest late in the incubation period in 1959 we had so far seen nothing of display, courtship or nest building. At once I began to consider the possibilities of a nest in one of the few oases of old heather which remained. At least, it seemed, the choice was so narrow that there would be no problem in locating a nest if one should be built. That first day's watch in 1960 is still one of my most vivid memories of the birds. They were surely the same pair as before, the cock translucently pale and clean grey, the hen big, richly-coloured and yellow-eyed. When they alighted close together among the charred, blue-black heather stalks, the whole made an arresting, even startling, colour spectacle.

The pair did not, after all, choose one of the obvious heather clumps on the old hill for their nest. Instead, they moved across the burn, into a patch of sparser heather and bracken on a lower adjoining slope that was in dead ground from where I had been watching. On 1 May, Louis Urquhart joined me in a final attempt to pinpoint the nest. It was the beginning of a long partnership in harrier watching, for which we had equal enthusiasm and patience, and to which Louis brought the astuteness of a first-rate field ornithologist, tempered with salutary caution, when there were problems of nest finding or interpreting features of the birds' behaviour.

The hen, in fact, had begun to incubate before the end of April—the first chick hatched about 27 May—but the behaviour we watched on 1 May gave the impression that the nest-site was still being selected. The pair gave a beautiful exhibition of slow-motion circling flight, keeping close together, the male always a little above his mate, who sometimes almost stalled when low over patches of deep heather, as if inspecting them as likely nesting places. For half an hour or so they seemed to float in the air with scarcely a wing-beat. Both were noisy, bursts of yikkering alternating with the squealing food call. Earlier, we had seen the cock arrive with prey, but there was no food pass. Instead, the hen flew at him as he was plucking the prey and seized it on the ground, literally bowling him off it. All that spring there were no 'skydancing' displays. Later experience taught us that it was un-

usual to see these performances when a pair had no other harriers as neighbours, and it was often a young male, seeking to establish himself, who gave the most intense displays.

The best place from which to observe this nest proved to be a steep gully beyond the burn, reached by almost a mile of devious walking. One of the delights of this hide-out was its remoteness from the road. The tributary burn which flowed down the gully was steep-sided, with ivy, heather and blaeberry clinging to the rock faces, and a straggle of deciduous trees, rowan, oak and ash. From here came the songs of Willow Warbler, Mistle Thrush and Chaffinch, and we saw much of the bold Ring Ouzels whose nest we found in a later year on a heathery scar of rock. Watching the Ring Ouzel pair feeding chicks, we learned that a hen can be almost as white-chested as a cock, quite unlike her text-book image. Short-eared Owls and Buzzards were never far away, and it was interesting to compare the cock harrier's reaction to the two species. The Owls, which had a nest 250 metres in front of the harriers', hardly bothered the harriers, but whenever a Buzzard appeared the cock harrier pursued it and dived at it relentlessly.

The land where the harriers nested in 1960 was under different ownership from the 1959 site, but an approach to the landowner early in the season, happily, met with a sympathetic response and strong instructions were given for the nest's preservation. It was a rather exposed nest, and the three chicks which hatched from a clutch of five, had to rely on the growth of bracken among the heather for shade on hot days. On 24 June, a four week old youngster bounded away when the nest was visited and was not easily settled again. When the young were nearly fledged, the cock became increasingly demonstrative, and began his deep-toned yikkering in fairly low level flight as soon as I came within 500 metres of the brood. On 9 July, Langley Roberts and I saw them flying strongly. A female from this brood was the first Galloway-ringed harrier to be reported. Its remains were found, bird 'apparently shot', 145 kilometres NNE, at Sherrifmuir, Perthshire, on 19 September 1961.

In the spring and summer of 1960, I looked at a number of other possible nesting grounds in south-west Scotland and followed up any promising reports. A long watch in the young forest (Area C) produced no proof that a pair was breeding there, but visits to a large grouse moor in a neighbouring county, on the strength of a report that a clutch of Montagu's Harrier's eggs had been taken there, resulted in the discovery of a nest which proved to be a Hen Harrier's. The Montagu's identification was presumed to be mistaken, and the nest I found with five eggs on 23 June was probably a repeat by the robbed pair. This nest was the only one I have watched closely on a highly-rated grouse moor. There, long ago, King Edward VII had been one of the guns accounting for some prodigious bags. The late date of the nest meant that the young might be taking their first flights just as the grouse shooting started, so their chances of survival seemed minimal, especially as the nest was just below a line of butts. But, in 1960, Hen Harriers were rare birds in southern Scotland—no nest had been found in that district since the 19th century—and both landowner and keeper seemed content to accept them as protected birds. Unfortunately, such an outlook did not persist for long when Hen Harriers returned to the locality in later years.

At this nest I had my first experience of a cock Hen Harrier breeding in brown, first year plumage. I wrote to Eddie Balfour about this and learned that it was fairly common in Orkney. Because I had been led to believe that the birds might be Montagu's, specific identification proved difficult at first, as brown plumaged harriers are notoriously confusing. It was one of the few nests where the cock was bolder than his mate, so I soon had a close view of him in flight, but never of her. Had he three long primary feathers, or four? I counted them many times as he flew swiftly overhead and was reasonably satisfied that he had four, and so must be a Hen Harrier, but he was distinctly a more slightly built cock than the one I had been watching nearer home, and just possibly slim enough for a Montagu's. A knowledgeable friend who saw the birds kept an open mind. No doubt it would have been easy with a first year cock Montagu's for comparison, but I must admit that total certainty came only when the feathered chicks showed the diagnostic, streaked breasts of young Hen Harriers. Measuring the eggs was not quite conclusive.

Years later, when looking at one of Jim Young's flight photographs of a known female Hen Harrier, I was startled to find that she had only three long primaries on each wing—correct for a Montagu's—and no obvious gaps left by moulted feathers. Yet the explanation, in this instance, *had* to be moult, and the presumed loss of the innermost (fifth) long primary was very difficult to detect.

The grouse moor nest was on comparatively high ground, at just over 300 metres, though the actual site was in a hollow of deep bracken and heather above a burn. At that time, the landscape was heather moor as far as the eye could see, showing the patchwork of varied colour and texture made by moor burning. This had been beneficial to Golden Plover, as well as grouse. It was an incomparable setting for harrier watching on clear days, when blue cloud shadows were flung loosely across the madder brown slopes of the big hill beyond the burn, but the brown cock harrier was a poor substitute for the silver grey bird at the other site. Our greatest excitement came when we encountered a cock Marsh Harrier not far away, a reminder that in days long past this species nested on upland bogs. I often used to ponder the irony that, but for grouse shooting, most of what I liked best in this landscape would disappear and be replaced by conifer forest, or something worse.

Once again there was a pair of Short-eared Owls nesting within a few hundred metres of the harriers. The moor was virtually treeless, yet Willow Warblers had young in a brackeny hollow, ten metres from the nest. A pair of Merlins—the cock diving at the harriers—and Ring Ouzels were other neighbours. Crows were notably scarce on this keepered ground.

In early August, when the young harriers were almost fledged, I was surprised to find a bulky platform of stout heather twigs, like an unshaped nest, built less than four metres from the nest itself. Both were being used as feeding places. I found similar constructions beside nests in later years but none as substantial as this. One day, the keeper accompanied us to the nest and admired the young harriers. It was evident that they were being fed, to some extent, on grouse, but he did not think this would have an important effect on his very well-stocked beat. By August the cock was partly grey on the body, noticeably on the new greater wing coverts, and had grown two or three black primaries. I saw him close enough to observe that his eyes were still dark.

One of the female chicks from this nest was found, presumed dead, 65 kilometres north-east in the Moorfoot Hills on 14 November 1962. So, of the first nine I ringed, two were recovered, but this one had at least survived long enough to breed, once, or possibly twice.

In the autumn of 1960, there was a vole 'plague' in some of the local young conifer plantations, and for the first time I saw Hen Harriers obviously hunting voles, accompanied by exceptional numbers of Short-eared Owls and Kestrels. On 26 September, two grey males and a ringtail were hunting a grass slope beside a young forest, and one male was seen to catch three voles in twenty minutes. Throughout the late autumn and winter, Hen Harrier sightings were more frequent and widespread than in any previous year; and although no full counts were made at the site of the winter roost a few birds were seen entering or leaving it. In July 1960, George Waterston had ringed three dozen chicks in Kintyre and recoveries, from this and subsequent ringing there, were widely scattered, though none were actually in Galloway.

The spring of 1961 promised well, with two pairs on the old moorland, but a double failure ensued. The presumed old pair made one, or probably two, false starts, nest-building being observed on 17 April very close to the 1960 site. They were rarely seen for most of May until on 30 May the new shepherd, Jimmy Stewart, while on his daily round, raised a hen from a single egg in a nest just below the crest of a heathery ridge a mile away. Meanwhile, the second pair had haunted the flat ground below the 1959 site, built a flimsy nest on an exposed patch of bog myrtle and molinia, much too near the public road, and had two eggs sucked by crows. The eggs may have been abandoned before the crows took them. The failures may have been due to human disturbance, as the shepherds were questioned by strangers determined to find nests early in the season. The pair on the flat also seemed to be unsettled by the Buzzards which had occupied the high ground just above.

The cock of the new pair was apparently a second summer bird, in half grey plumage. From him I saw the full 'skydancing' display for the first time. In late May, after his nest had failed, he travelled around an area about one and a half kilometres square, breaking into this extraordinary loose-winged up and down performance over much of the higher ground. Once, he took prey to a dark-coloured hen, perhaps a newcomer, which would not take the pass. By June, however, the displaying male had disappeared and the only successful nest that summer was the late one which the shepherd had discovered. The cock was probably the same as in previous years, the hen more doubtfully so. She laid seven eggs but, the summer being rather wet, two of the five chicks died. By good fortune the site could be observed from an old sheep stell about 250 metres away, where an ancient spreading larch tree provided cover and much needed shelter.

This was the fourth successive nest which had Short-eared Owls as near neighbours. The owls were much further advanced than the harriers this time, and I found a feathered young owl away from its nest on 24 June, ten days before the first harrier chick hatched. Jimmy Stewart, the new shepherd, had been recruited as a keen harrier protectionist. He took a path every day only yards above the nest, so I received full reports on the progress of the clutch—eggs were laid every second day—and, later, of hatching. In the later stages of incubation the hen sat tight as the shepherd passed a few metres away. It might seem that the hen was disturbed rather much, as 'Jock the drainer' also walked past the nest to and from his solitary

work and was duly attacked each time by the hen. Jock was a phlegmatic character and I used to be amused at how little notice he took of these assaults. I doubt if he ever actually looked at the nest.

The sheep stell was like a seat in the stalls for observing the details of food passes. Sometimes they were nearly overhead and I could see that the hen turned almost onto her back and thrust one of her amazingly long legs upward to grasp the prey. It was soon apparent that the cock had a favourite stance on a green knowe below the nest and here, at hatching time, he dumped the plucked and headless carcasses of three young Meadow Pipits, a young Skylark and a young Whinchat. At this stage he would sometimes carry prey almost to the nest, calling a piercing 'swee-uk' when the hen refused to rise, and would then return, still carrying the prey, to his stance, where he called again. Jettisoned carcasses were found to have been 'gutted' by the cock, perhaps especially for the liver. If the cock was making a food cache he made no future use of it.

Around the old stell the tall bracken was alive with small birds—Meadow Pipits, Wheatears, Whinchats and Linnets, especially. Many were young of the year, but Linnets were carrying nesting material in July. Certainly the hen of this harrier pair provided much of the food in the later stages, and she often hunted quite near by. The cock was not seen at all on 11 August when the hen and her three, fledged young were over the crest of the hill.

The 1962 season looked like being a repeat of 1961, with an old pair back, nesting in the same patch of heather by the shepherd's path, near the hilltop, and a younger pair building on the flat by the road. The first egg was in the older pair's nest on 1 May, but when five eggs had been laid, on 12 or 13 May, Jimmy Stewart found the nest 'pulled out' and empty. He blamed crows but there was no certain way of telling what happened, though Nick Picozzi suggests that a fox or dog may have been responsible.

A new nest, with a minimum of material, built 400 metres over the ridge, must have been started immediately, and the two eggs laid in it would have completed another clutch of seven, if the first nest had not been lost. I did not find the second nest till 14 June, when it contained two chicks. Their size showed that there could not have been an interval of more than a day between the loss of the five eggs and continuation of laying. Both chicks fledged.

Back on the flat by the road, the rather dirty grey male was almost certainly the bird which had displayed so much in 1961. His display flights were spectacular again, including a complete 'roll-over' at the top of the climb. On 12 May he was tearing up nest material and carrying it to the patch of bog myrtle used in the previous year. The female followed him into the site, taking more material. This nest-building followed slow-motion flying by the pair together, so low that they almost brushed the tops of the bog myrtle clumps. In this 'pre-nesting' ritual their tails were spread like fans. For the second year, this too-obvious site was abandoned, but this time the pair tried again, and on 4 July, four chicks had hatched from a clutch of five in rather sparse heather only a little further from the roadside, but in a much less obvious situation. Here, on 8 July, Langley Roberts reported what appeared to be the first definite case of human destruction. He was confident that the chicks, which he found dead, had been killed by gunshot. The female was missing and had possibly been killed, too. We had earlier suspected that the gap in one of the cock's wings had been made by a shooter.

When I recall how Louis and I went forthwith to tell our story to the rather imposing local lady, who had the shooting rights, I am amazed that she listened to us with such patience. I had only seen an empty nest and my story was second-hand. The lady was concerned that harriers were taking grouse, and wished that they would retire to the forest to nest, but she was positive that they had not been destroyed by a keeper in her employment. Ironically, it had been a Buzzard which Louis and I had seen take a grouse chick near the harrier's nest. A visit to the sheep farmer's house convinced me that, whatever had happened, it would be naive to pursue my enquiries. Perhaps the absence of any nesting harriers on the old moorland in 1963 was the strongest indication that, as a friend put it, 'measures were taken' against them in 1962, just when it had begun to seem that they were set to increase.

A happier postscript to the year was Langley Roberts' finding of the first successful nest within the forest boundaries, in Area C. The female at this nest bore a ring and might have been from one of the earlier moorland broods. The nesting place, close to a popular path, was unlike all later forest nests in being on unplantable ground. A ringed female from this brood had had the longest recorded life for the region, when it was found dead on moorland only five miles away on 3 July 1968. A keeper later assured me that a pair reared young on a neighbouring moorland in 1962, and it is possible, also, that a second forest nest was undiscovered.

The 1963 season followed a memorably hard winter and it is possible that this had an adverse effect on breeding. A male and two ringtails were about the moor in May, but did not settle. On 29 May, I spent 13½ hours watching for flight lines of a cock which I thought might have a nest in the three year old forest (Area E) adjoining the moor, but could not trace him to a nest. The only known nest, that season, was a complete surprise, on a high rushy hillside (Area G), 32 kilometres to the north. First news of this came on 18 May, from a shepherd's message that a bird 'like a hoolet with white at the root of the tail' had risen from eggs. He showed me the nest, which had five eggs, and I was surprised to find that here was another first year male breeding. The shepherd later reported a remarkable clutch of nine eggs, which might have been explained by exceptionally good food supply in a local vole plague (which also attracted a high number of Short-eared Owls). In June, however, the nest was empty, apparently robbed, and there was no

evidence of a repeat laying. So not one young harrier was seen that summer.

A young Golden Eagle had wintered on the moor, for the first time, in 1961–62, roosting below the Lion's Head, where it was sometimes seen in pursuit of blue hares. Each year thereafter, eagles were seen more often, as a young pair became established at a nesting site a couple of kilometres from the moorland perimeter. In the 1964 breeding season, the sight of a cock harrier repeatedly diving at a hunting eagle became common, and the possibility that nesting harriers might be seriously unsettled by the eagles was raised.

That year there were three harrier nests on the moorland, including two clutches of six, so there were hopes of a good crop of chicks. Yet only the third and latest nest, not found till the three chicks were well-grown, was successful. At one of the others the hen sat for at least 52 days on eggs which never hatched (analysis of three eggs for toxic chemicals showed small residues; results are given in Table 16). At the other, the death of the two-week old brood was never satisfactorily explained, although Dr John Selwyn carried out a post-mortem which showed that they had been well fed. Human predation could not be ruled out. The three nests were evenly spaced, exactly two kilometres apart. Only one cock was seen, and it is fairly certain that this was the first polygynous group of nests. Certainly, the hen with the unhatched eggs was neglected and must have been forced to hunt for herself during incubation. She was an old, yellow-eyed bird—possibly the original hen—and her nest was but 50 metres from the 1960 site, in deep heather by the burn. The hen which lost her brood was young, dark-eyed and intensely aggressive. Indeed, nearly all the hens which nested on the old moorland were bold to a degree, and timid hens were only seen at distant sites or, later, at forest nests.

In 1964, the extremely open situation, in pure molinia, of the nest in which the young died, emphasised the limitations of the moorland as nesting habitat, since the best cover had been burnt. However, the presence of three nests with, so far, no sign of establishment in the neighbouring forests, underlined the birds' faithfulness to an old nesting area. This was demonstrated again very clearly in the forest habitat, while apparently more suitable sites remained unoccupied.

The 1965 season saw the beginning of a continuous history of forest nesting in Area C (see Chapter 12). After the shepherd had found a cock harrier dead, in April, only one pair was on the moorland, but this nest, well hidden in deep molinia, reared five healthy chicks. The hen, from behaviour and plumage, was indistinguishable from the bird which lost her brood in 1964, and the nest was less than a kilometre from that site. The surrounding moorland was the best Golden Plover ground in the district; and the nearest of several pairs of Curlews raised a brood within 100 metres of the harrier nest. Neither species featured as prey at any harrier nest in the locality. The pair of eagles had a chick to feed and the cock harrier regularly chivvied the hunting male eagle. Ever since the eagles had arrived, Buzzards were seen more rarely over the moor. When my wife and I visited the nest to ring the harrier chicks, the attacking hen dropped a young Skylark almost on my head, not the first or last such experience at a nest. A female chick from this brood provided proof of later return to the natal area, when she was found dead on the moor, 400 metres away, on 27 May 1968. The bizarre circumstances of this discovery, described in detail in *Scottish Birds* (Watson, 1969), are given on page 193.

In July 1965, I searched for Hen Harriers on moorland (Area B) about 50 kilometres distant and found a pair, but not the nest which they undoubtedly had. The reported words of the head keeper, that a brood of these 'worst vermin' had unfortunately escaped him, confirmed that harrier nests would be at risk on this well-stocked grouse moor. The policy was confirmed when we found two pole traps, each with the remains of Kestrels beneath them, set in full view of a road. On an evening of drenching rain the local police helped us gather up the evidence, which I innocently expected would result in a prosecution for illegal trapping. Enquiries were made but, of course, nobody admitted any knowledge of setting the traps. So there was no case. I do not think pole traps were set in that spot again, but there is little doubt that other methods were used to destroy Hen Harriers and, probably, other predatory birds.

The finding of a ringed female in this area, from the 1964 brood on Moorland A, in July 1966, was an indication that it had been partly colonised by birds from the original nesting grounds. My attempt to obtain details of how this bird died went unanswered and increased my suspicion that it was trapped or shot. From 1968 onwards, R. C. Dickson studied Moorland B and found a very high failure rate in the small number of nests there. Destruction by game keepers was presumed to be the main cause of this.

Every winter, Hen Harriers were seen hunting moorland area A from time to time. Ringtails were seen more often than adult males. It could only be surmised that some at least were local breeding birds, but when I started to count harriers at winter roosts from 1966 onwards, it became clear that numbers were often too high to be drawn only from the local summer population.

The 1965 brood was the last that was seen on the old moorland. A pair were back in early April 1966, then disappeared when heavy snow fell in mid-April. They returned later, and I was fortunate in witnessing their courtship and nest-building on 15 May, a day of blue sky and flying clouds. Only the hen 'sky-danced', switchbacking at no great height, but the pair gave a prolonged display of soaring in unison, rising to a great height with wing-tips almost touching. Copulation took place twice, on the ground, noisily, and the cock led the hen to a possible nest site in moderately long heather, near where there had been successful nests in 1961 and 1962. There was no certainty that the hen was the same as in 1964–65 but she alighted near, and seemed to inspect, old nests of those years. (The existence of old nests is probably a factor in stimulating site selection in the same area. Eddie Balfour later told me that he thought this was true in Orkney.) The hen dropped in to more than one possible nest site and was finally seen carrying nest material. Early in June, however, Jimmy Stewart found two sucked eggs near the nest which she had built and a repeat nest, on the same part of the hill, came to the same end. On 15 May, I had seen the hen being harrassed by a pair of crows but it still seemed surprising that a very mature pair of harriers were apparently unable to protect their eggs from crows. I can only guess that some other disturbing factor, perhaps human, or possibly Golden Eagle or fox, had resulted in much straying from the nest by the hen before incubation had properly begun, and that any watchful crows might have taken their opportunities. An undiscovered nest of some previous year, showing no sign that it had ever contained chicks, was found in the same patch of heather as the first 1966 nest.

In 1966–67, about one third of the moorland area was acquired, ploughed and planted with conifers by the Forestry Commission. This must have been disturbing to the harriers initially, but its long term importance was to reduce the extent of open ground for hunting. Although in the ensuing years, harriers nesting in neighbouring forests demonstrated the great importance of the moorland as a hunting ground, only once, in 1968, was there any indication that they might nest there again.

In May 1968, a pair were soaring over the hill top above the old larch tree in the stell, and I saw and heard them battling with the pair of eagles, diving almost to strike them. A week later, John Young and I found the hen dead at this spot, unmarked except for a small wound near the sternum. As I have said, she had been hatched and ringed in the 1965 nest, just down the slope. Did she dive too close to an eagle? I believe she did, and the discovery of an eagle's pellet beside her body was suggestive of this, though no more. Ian Prestt's diagnosis that the wound was consistent with having been caused by a talon, and that there was no exit hole for a bullet, added weight to the theory. Our strangely assorted finds also included the plucked wing and partly bitten breast bone of a Snipe, which had perhaps been dropped by the harrier, and, 20 metres away, a Red Grouse nest which had been destroyed. Its ten eggs, mostly bitten through and eaten, and the trail of female grouse feathers, including a bitten off wing, pointed to a fox as the predator—a verdict supported by the late Ernest Blezard, who kindly examined all the incidental remains and confirmed that the pellet came from an eagle. It therefore seemed that, by chance, two possibly quite distinct dramas had been enacted at almost the same spot. So, the short history of Hen Harrier nesting on this moorland ended with this violent mystery.

The risk that might be run by a Hen Harrier diving too close to a Heron is suggested by an incident described by M. K. Hamilton (pers comm). In this a ringtail harrier, circling in soaring flight, was itself circled by a Heron which carried its neck outstretched and bill open. It appeared to be trying to attack the harrier but was far too slow to come within striking distance. The incident occurred in late August and the harrier seemed quite content to continue circling inside the circuit of the Heron for at least two and a half minutes before the latter folded its neck and broke off the attack. No reason for the Heron's aggression could be suggested but it may be speculated what would have happened if the harrier had reacted boldly, as it might have done in the vicinity of a nest.

Possible causes of failure and decline of nesting on Moorland A

In 1962 it seemed that a group of pairs might become established. This was the time when local gamekeepers became most concerned about the possible impact of several pairs of harriers on grouse stocks, and some persecution probably occurred. The lack of nests in 1963 may have been due to this, but an additional factor may have been the severe weather in late winter (the exceptionally large clutch that year on Moorland G coincided with a local vole plague).

The burning of much of the oldest heather in 1960 had already reduced the choice of good nesting sites and there was evidence that several nests were poorly concealed. This might not have been a serious disadvantage had it not coincided with increased human disturbance. In such a small area of open country any human activity, including harrier watching, could possibly unsettle the birds in the early part of the season. Geroudet considered that Hen Harriers in France became accustomed to farm workers in the vicinity of nests, and it is probable that they similarly accepted the shepherd and his dogs on their regular rounds.

The ploughing and planting of about 500 hectares (about a third of the area) in 1966–67, with later work on fencing, undoubtedly caused additional disturbance and temporarily reduced the amount of suitable ground for nests.

Persistent attacks by harriers on the Golden Eagles, which were over the nesting area almost daily from 1965 onwards, suggest that they may have had an unsettling effect; and the presumed killing of a female harrier by an eagle, in May 1968, may have prevented nesting on the moorland that year.

The cessation of moorland nesting may have been largely due to the fact that much nesting cover in adjoining forests reached its most suitable stage between 1965 and 1970.

CHAPTER TWELVE

FOREST NESTING: 1965–1975

In the first half of the 1960s, Langley and Madelaine Roberts regularly scoured the most promising forest areas for nesting harriers and other birds, while I spent more time on the moorland. Later, as moorland nesting faded away, I also spent much time in the forests, alone or in company with other enthusiasts, especially Louis Urquhart, my son Jeffrey, Dr John Selwyn, Dr Ken Brewster and Michael Williams. Much helpful information was given by foresters and rangers and in later years, ornithologists, such as Dick Roxburgh, Richard Mearns and Mick Marquiss, who were primarily concerned with other predators, helped me by reporting all sightings of harriers. Many others contributed useful observations.

During the 1950s and early 1960s, most of Areas C, D and E was planted with conifers, mainly sitka spruce and lodgepole pine, with a fair amount of larch and smaller quantities of other species. In these years, road-making was an important part of forestry activity, involving fairly continuous lorry traffic. Although Hen Harriers were occasionally seen in the forests from 1958, the only proved nesting before 1965 was in 1962, on un-plantable ground, as described in the moorland section (Chapter 11). The area was probably less suitable for nesting in the early period, partly because of disturbance by ploughing, planting and road-making but, more importantly, because in the very young forests there is much less concealment for nests.[1] Although the optimum period for forest nesting was undoubtedly when the trees were 6–12 years old, there was much variation in the height of trees of any age-group and it was found, in Area E particularly, that harriers could still find sites in 14–15 year old forest, where most of the trees were 3–6 metres tall, but the canopy was by no means closed up. No nests were found in forest rides although many of these appeared to have suitable sites in deep heather and grass.

After the moorland experience many new lessons had to be learned about harriers in a forest environment. The advantage of often being able to use a car as a hide in locating pairs or nesting areas was offset by the much greater difficulty in pinpointing sites. Many times a food pass might be seen but trees made it impossible to follow precisely where a bird had gone to ground. Initial observing, as on moorland, had to be done from a commanding viewpoint to avoid losing sight of the birds in dead ground, and this often involved watching from at least a kilometre away. When a hen went down to a nest site, great attention had to be paid to 'marker' features such as dead trees and rides which might help to identify the spot later. In June and July, flies and midges were often almost unendurable in the heart of the young forest. The final search for a nest which entailed negotiating furrows, folds and waist high heather, with constant warfare against sharp sitka needles, was no doubt made sufferable only by some elemental hunting urge. In blocks of uniform forest it is easy to become disoriented and many a search foundered at the first attempt when, at close quarters, marker trees could not be re-discovered and every part of the forest seemed alike.

At first, after the spaciousness and varied colours of the moorland, so sensitive to seasonal change, I had no liking for the forest with its oppressive, repetitive landscape. In time, as I came to know it in all its moods, it sometimes cast a quiet and mysterious spell. I often had the feeling that the trees concealed secrets. It was good country for observing without being observed, and there was never a day in search of harriers which did not bring a harvest of incidental sightings—a roe doe with speckled calf, a monstrous red stag in a ride, or a fox, like a flash of gold and silver against the dark underbrush of the forest edge.

Bird song on May or June mornings was a revelation of high breeding populations of Robins, Wrens, Willow and Grasshopper Warblers, Redpolls and Song Thrushes. In one harrier territory, a Song Thrush included a deceptive mimicry of the harrier's food call in its song phrases. Often the soothing sound of Blackcock in display carried from a distant lek, and Cuckoos called almost as ceaselessly as on the moorland.

[1] In 1975 I found a nest with six young in Kintyre in very young forest with almost no concealment by surrounding vegetation; there was an abundance of food (voles) to be found in the vicinity.

In the young plantations, Short-eared Owls were again the harriers' neighbours. Barn Owls, more creamy-white than cock harriers, left their nesting places in former shepherds' houses or rock cavities to hunt conspicuously, by day, among the dark trees. Until their weaker, fluttering flight and rounded wings were observed they could be momentarily confused with a cock harrier in the distance. Kestrels were never far away and a few Merlins nested in the deep heather on unplanted rocky slopes, while Buzzard, Peregrine and Golden Eagle sometimes passed overhead. The Black-headed Gulls, which continually journeyed between lochside nesting colonies and distant fields, were the jokers in the pack, looking enough like slim cock harriers when far away, to raise many a false hope.

If all this suggests that the forest was an idyllic haven for wildlife, the impression needs qualifying. Jet aircraft often roared just above the trees and sometimes a helicopter spraying fertiliser droned and spluttered for days on end. The forest, of course, existed for timber production. Rangers were under orders to shoot many of the red deer which, it was feared, increasingly damaged trees by stripping bark. Roe deer were fairly heavily culled and foxes were snared or shot. Among birds, only crows were generally destroyed, but pheasant and grouse shooting was let, and there was always a possibility of illegal destruction of predators on this account. Most importantly, the majority of the bird species which flourished while the trees were small were doomed to disappear within 10–20 years as the forest closed up and grew taller. Others would replace them, but there would eventually be less variety of species. As new plantations appeared, the Short-eared Owls and harriers might find alternative breeding sites in them for a few years, but I was already concerned that the loss of so much open moorland below the 300 metre level was reducing the numbers and variety of hill birds, and might seriously limit food and hunting grounds for harriers and other predators, particularly eagles and Buzzards. Ravens, much dependent on sheep carrion, decreased sharply as the forests spread.

When, at the beginning of May 1965, two cock harriers were seen displaying over seven year old trees near the western end of Area C, and one nest was found shortly afterwards, there seemed no reason why nesting should not soon spread over a large extent of similar-aged forest. This first nest among the trees was a failure, the hen sitting on a clutch of only two eggs till long past the time they were due to hatch. The second and more handsome cock, looking almost as white as a gull against the dark conifers, was often seen over a long valley, apparently well stocked with good nesting sites, until he disappeared at the beginning of June. In 1966, three young were fledged from a nest about 800 metres from the 1965 site. This nest was notable for the discovery of a Crossbill's head among prey remains—it was identifiable as an adult female of the Continental race, a flock of which had been seen in the vicinity shortly before. However, it was soon apparent that the forest-nesting harriers hunted much more over neighbouring moorland

Young Merlin

(especially the old nesting area, Area A) than in the forest itself. No nests were found in 1967, only a cock being seen at the 1966 nest site, though the number of harriers in the forest continued to increase slightly (see Fig. 10). Poor conditions for hunting in a very cold, wet May, possibly inhibited breeding. Increased nesting in 1968, with three broods in Area C, resulted in the highest annual total of ten fledged young. Two of these, from different nests, were later recovered: one found 'decapitated', suggesting the possibility of a fox kill, on moorland 35 kilometres SW, on 21 April 1969; and the other reported 'found' only 14 kilometres away in the same direction, probably on farmland, near a small winter roost, on 10 October 1971. Seven, or over 21%, of the first 33 young ringed and fledged were therefore recovered, a remarkably high proportion even for a predator which is killed by man. At least it can be said that all but one had survived long enough to breed. At one of the 1968 nests I found definite evidence of a chick being eaten by its siblings in the nest, though it had probably died first, during the wet weather in July and the consequent poor hunting conditions for its parents. The latest brood, fledged at the end of July, continued to use the nest as a base during the first three weeks of August. By then, the cock had disappeared and the young were flying to the incoming hen to catch prey which she dropped from a height, although they sometimes missed their catches. They had regular feeding places in a big ride near the nest and left many tell-tale remains there. This habit was often seen near other forest nests in later years.

There were now signs of a regular but unequal spacing between nests, of two to three kilometres. In this respect 1969 was a repeat of the previous season. Two nests had small broods and one, at the site first occupied in

1968, was abandoned at a very early stage. This may well have been due to disturbance by forestry work in the vicinity. The behaviour of the cock at this site followed the pattern observed at other sites where early failure or disappearance of a hen occurred. On 31 May he was making conspicuous flights, with some bouts of 'sky dancing', over about two square kilometres of forest in the nest area. Soon afterwards he had disappeared.

Nesting in Area C reached its peak in 1970. Five nests were built, young were reared in four, but broods were again small. At one successful nest a young hen, in her first or second summer, bore a ring. A second pair were nest-building only 800 metres from this nest on 17 May, but in June their nest was found abandoned and contained only fragments of egg shell. The possibility that contamination by toxic chemicals was reducing hatching existed at this nest, and at another where only one chick survived from a clutch of three or more eggs, but unfortunately no eggs were analysed.

The most surprising nest was in 18 year old forest, where none had been known before. Although most of the surrounding trees looked far too tall and dense for nesting harriers, the birds were able to find a small open patch where the trees remained stunted and bushy from early deer browsing. Such sites are extremely difficult to locate, and the nest would certainly not have been known if a forester had not found it. All the other nests were in the usual areas, where most of the trees were now 10–12 years old. Langley Roberts' observation of a hen displaying over the site unoccupied since 1962 suggested that this was still attractive for nesting.

In 1971, only single ringtails were seen at the two more recently occupied sites, and nothing was seen at either in later years. Nor was there any sign of nesting, after 1971, at the oldest site occupied since 1965. Here, in 1971, an old, very pale-eyed hen broke her eggs. She was probably the bird which had had only one chick in 1970. Only the central site continued to be tenanted by a pair in most years, but after a brood had probably been taken by a fox, in 1974, there was no sign of nesting in the following year. At this site, with a remarkable run of closely-sited nests, the same timid, pale-breasted hen was recognised for three years, and when other younger hens succeeded her, they also built within a few metres of previous nests. The cock was not always the same, so it must be presumed that some sites have a special attraction, perhaps increased by the evidence of former nests.

Very likely, as much of the forest in Area C approached 15 years, harriers were faced with a shortage of suitable nesting places, but the history of Area E casts doubt on this as a full explanation for the decline. Area E was planted in 1959–61. Harriers may have nested there from 1966 but no proof of nesting was obtained before 1971, although much time was devoted to watching the area each season. In 1971 and the following years, single successful nests were recorded, until, in 1971, after two pairs had been seen in April, there were three successful nests apparently attended by a polygynous cock. The locations of all the nests in Area E were concentrated

in an area of about two square kilometres of forest, planted in 1961 (see Chapter 14).

A rather similar history of summer sightings of pairs, or adult males alone, occurred in the forest Area D, from 1966 onwards. Here no nests were ever found—if one excludes nest-building by a cock, in the absence of a mate, on 19 May 1974. The absence of nests could not be explained by the lack of nest sites, as the terrain, and the average age of the trees, was similar in both the other areas. There was no apparent reason why disturbance should have been greater in Area D than elsewhere. The most likely reason for the absence of nesting in Area D can be found in a comparison of the hunting grounds accessible to the three areas. In this respect, Area D differed from the others in having much less open moorland, below 225 metres, within normal hunting range. The implications of this difference are considered in the discussion of hunting ranges and prey, in Chapter 16.

To some extent comparison can be made between Area D and other more distant forests, such as Areas H and J, where summer sightings were quite frequent in the later years but nesting was rarely proved, in spite of many hours of observation and close liaison with forest rangers who regularly worked the ground. In April 1972, we witnessed intense skydancing by a cock over a 300 metre slope of forest in Area H, possibly stimulated by the presence of another pair not far away. Sometimes, two hens were seen and later, when one was on eggs, the second cock hung over the nest until gently ushered away by the other. This nest, in a remote part of the forest, seemed to us well-placed for success but the chicks were found dead, and a bunch of feathers from the missing hen suggested that she had been killed or involved in a struggle. It was neither the first nor the last time that the mystery of a failed nest could not be solved. Our guess was that word of the nest had reached neighbouring keepers.

In the last five years, special attention was given to nesting in Area E, where a timid, pale-breasted hen, possibly the same bird which had been in Area C, nested successfully from 1971–1974. When the nest was visited she would rise and fly away, circling at a distance of 100 metres or more. We never saw her well enough to note the colour of her eyes. In 1974, the cock was a memorable and beautiful old bird. He was the only male, over the years, to make really low-level attacks on human intruders, sometimes striking with a wing but never with his feet lowered. He also spent much more time than most near and, even, at the nest and was a most assiduous

provider of prey. In one period of under four hours he brought prey seven times. When I visited this nest just before the four chicks flew, one of the adults had just brought a fully feathered young Skylark which was still breathing, though probably unconscious from a head wound.

The harriers in this forest were often visible to passers-by on a public road. Indeed, some food passes took place directly above the road, and the cock regularly crossed it on flights to and from hunting grounds on the adjacent moorland. Not much 'skydancing' was seen in spring but, even so, a pair were very conspicuous before the eggs were laid. On 7 April 1975, a day of bitter north-east wind and snow showers, the birds were already together above the previous year's nest, leaning into the wind on flexed wings, their partly fanned tails as mobile as kites'. A week earlier they had not been there, and several had still been using the winter roost a few miles away. Then, on the night of the 6 April, the roost was deserted. On the next day this pair were on their breeding territory, the cock even 'skydancing' a little, and at dusk they roosted among the trees. I had no proof that they were birds which had been wintering locally, but it seemed very likely, and they may well have arrived on the breeding grounds together.

In the three seasons, 1973–75, watches in April showed that the first choice of nesting place was abandoned each time. Once, the hen behaved as if she already had eggs, on 19 April, but no broods hatched before early June. Early nests were not abandoned because of any disturbance by us, but the cost of avoiding such disturbance was the lack of proof that eggs were laid. Whether or not eggs were laid, these early desertions were probably directly or indirectly due to very cold spells in May.

Early in May 1975, a second pair were over the forest, only about a kilometre from the first. The cock of the second pair apparently disappeared soon afterwards and we never, positively, saw more than one cock in this forest throughout the rest of the season. On 29 May, the cock was seen to exchange prey with two hens, one rising for the pass from the known nest; the other receiving the prey on the ground about 800 metres away. Later, I noticed that aerial food passes between the cock and the second hen were always close to the ground, the hen seeming to snatch at the prey. Further watches and, finally, some gruelling searches in hot, fly-infested forest led to the discovery of two more nests. The three nests formed the points of a triangle, about 1,200 × 1,200 × 500 metres. In the absence of colour-marked birds it was impossible to be certain that there was only one cock to the three nests, but in the end there was no reasonable doubt. On 20 June, when we found the third nest, with five fresh eggs, we were surprised on one occasion to see the hen travel about a kilometre from the nest to hunt herself, although at this stage she did not appear to be neglected by the cock, who passed prey to her twice between 10.45 and 17.30. After the young hatched, on 9–10 July, the cock was never seen to bring food to her or her chicks. As described in the next chapter, only one chick survived out of three hatched, and even this might have died if we had not provided extra food for a short period. The earliest nest was the most successful. Five chicks hatched in mid-June and four of them fledged. The second nest produced three young. On 6 July, the cock carried prey towards this nest while the hen was probably feeding the brood with prey which she herself had just brought. The cock hung low over the nest as if about to drop his prey, but flew on with it towards the nest with the largest brood. Owing to an intervening crest of the hill we could not see what ensued but it could hardly be doubted that he took the food there, or passed it to the hen at that nest. We often saw him close enough to judge his plumage colour and he was not the fine old fierce cock of 1974, but a younger bird, probably about three years old.

This group of nests provided much scope for speculation. Why did the original second pair fail to nest? There may have been a dispute between the two cocks, whose nests might have been only about a kilometre apart, which was closer than any two pairs in the region which had nested successfully. Did the hen of this pair become the second mate of the breeding cock? The hen of the third nest was probably a new arrival in late May. Her iris colour, seen from the hide later, showed her to be young, possibly only a year old. Had she tried and failed to find a cock elsewhere? What was the particular, lasting attraction of this small patch of 14 year old forest, which a casual glance would have dismissed as already far too closed-up for harrier nesting? It was forest where Wood Pigeons were already well established and Short-eared Owls had almost disappeared. It could hardly have been simply the magnetism of former, successful breeding sites. Strong as this may be, it could not be effective without the continuing proximity of good hunting grounds. Again and again the hunting flight lines of forest-nesting harriers demonstrated the importance of adjacent moorland (see Chapter 16). Within five years this forest would surely cease to have nesting sites at all.[1] Would there still be a chance, then, that a pair or two would return to

---

[1] In July 1975, Richard Mearns and I came upon an old, previously unknown nest within 100 metres of the nest with three chicks. No sign of food carrying had been seen there in previous years but, in 1974, a second cock and hen had occasionally been seen in the vicinity. This nest may have dated back more than a year. We could only conclude that there had probably been a second nest in this forest before 1975. I doubt if we would have missed any fledged broods but this may not have been the only nest which escaped us, owing to the density of the tree cover and the undulating character of the ground.

nest in their favourite hunting grounds on the moorland, where we had found the first nest in 1959? In the next five years that moorland might also be planted with a new crop of trees which could provide nesting sites for harriers only at the cost of eliminating their main hunting grounds. Even if the area remains open, it is doubtful if it now has sufficient growth of heather for good nesting sites.

Summary of 1976 breeding season

Two pairs nested successfully in the forest Area E, rearing three and four young respectively; four had hatched at the nest where three fledged. The male at each nest was in grey plumage. A first-summer brown male was also in the area, accompanying a female in late March, and there were probably three, or possibly more, grey males present in early April. A grey male was seen during the summer in the forest Area C but it is doubtful if nesting occurred there. It is fairly certain that nesting did not occur in Area D. Birds nesting in Area E again regularly hunted the neighbouring moorlands, including Area A.

One pair bred successfully on Moorland Area B. Five eggs were laid, three young hatched and two fledged. A second pair had a nest with four eggs which disappeared before hatching, and a third pair built a nest but apparently no eggs were laid. A fourth pair was present in the area but were not proved to nest. The second pair built a second nest (no eggs seen) only two feet from where the third pair had built and abandoned their nest. (Information on Moorland Area B from R. C. Dickson.)

No data for 1976 has been included in the Tables 10–15 but the above summary gives a further indication of greater nesting success at nests in forest than on moorland in the study areas of south-west Scotland.

CHAPTER THIRTEEN

WATCH FROM A HIDE

When we visited all three nests in the 1975 group, on 9 July, the possibility of watching one of them from a hide was in our minds. I had long resisted the temptation, for a number of reasons. Hen Harriers were still scarce nesting birds in the district and I knew it was no use pretending that a hide, to be used for photography, close-up observation and sketching, would be practical in the jungle of 3–6 metre conifers and waist-high heather without some disturbance and the tying back of vegetation to permit clear vision. The very late nest had two newly hatched chicks and two unhatched eggs so, if all went well, there would be time for the bird to become accustomed to the hide before anyone need occupy it. For at least the next two-and-a-half weeks the female would be likely to spend much time at this nest, feeding and brooding the chicks. This was the only nest of the three which Jim Young considered possible for photography as the other two were far too enclosed by trees. He was still pondering the question when we parted that night, after an evening in which flies and midges had been relentless. Next day he had decided that it was worth a try from a photographer's point of view. We had the necessary licences, and permission from the Forest authorities, and it seemed to me that with two good broods well on their way to fledging and with so much to learn from close-up watches at this third nest, the case for using a hide was as strong as it was ever likely to be.

Our objectives, and the limitations of observing from a hide in contrast to watching from a distance in the open air, may need explanation. Apart from

photography, which was not my concern, there was obviously the opportunity for making close-up sketches, particularly of the female as she fed or
brooded the chicks. Even when she was not present, the behaviour and attitudes of the chicks provided a range of subjects for drawing which could
never be attained by my usual visits to nests, when the chicks always
reacted defensively to a human presence.

The nest was some six metres from the hide, so it was just possible to
focus binoculars on it and we would be able to note details, such as the state
of moult and iris colour of the female, difficult to obtain even when a bold
bird is flying close overhead. More importantly, there was a good prospect
of identifying most of the prey brought in and the amount provided for the
chicks during each watch. Further, the hide could reveal precisely at what
stage of development the chicks begin to tear up prey for themselves. These
and other details of activity in the nest could only be learned from a hide,
and there was also the exciting possibility that the cock might pay the occasional visit. I very much wanted a close-up view of him, both as a model
for drawings and to clarify my impressions of his plumage detail and likely
age, but I was doubtful whether he was still in attendance at this nest and, in
fact, he never came to it during our watches. Here, one of the limitations of
hide watching, especially in dense tree cover, must be noted. Occasionally,
the female could be heard giving the food call as she flew overhead and the
most likely explanation would have been that the cock was approaching
with prey, but from the confinement of the hide it was never possible to be
sure. I was inclined to believe that although she may sometimes have seen
him with prey, she never received any from him after the young were very
small. Distant watches, at any rate, provided no evidence that she did. The
basic limitation of hide watching is, of course, the very restricted field of
view but it can also be something of an endurance test when cramp sets in or
the feeling of claustrophobia becomes strong.

Each time the hide was occupied, the watcher or photographer was 'put
in' by a companion who would then be seen by the bird (if present) to leave
the vicinity. At first this worked admirably but later, when she needed to do
less brooding, she sometimes observed our approach from a distance and
followed us to the nest, calling in alarm, and did not lose her suspicion until
an hour or so after one of us had left. If she knew that only one of us had
gone, and that the other remained, it seemed that time erased the knowledge.
Unable to detect any visible sign of man in the hide she had no lasting distrust of it.

The hide was set up by Jim and Brian Turner, on 12 July, and moved
forward into its final position the next day, after we had seen from a distance
that the female had accepted it. Jim took the first watch on 17 July,
photographing and observing from 11.30 to 17.30. Three chicks had
hatched by 12 July but the smallest was dead on the fifteenth. There were
several wet days at this period and we concluded that the female, with little

or no food supply from the only cock in the area, was probably being forced to leave the chicks too long unbrooded. Clearly, we wished to minimise the risks of total nest failure so we provided a few extra rations—three sparrows were left at the nest on 13 and 15 July, and were apparently eaten. On 17 July, Jim left a young rat and a young Sandpiper found killed on the road. The latter was removed by the female (and possibly eaten away from the nest) but she fed the chicks and herself on the rat for about 40 minutes that morning, then took away the remains. In the following 4½ hours the only prey caught and fed to the young was a Snipe which was either an adult or a well-grown young bird. My first day in the hide was 19 July, from 11.40 till 18.00 hours. Settled alone, tense and anticipatory but hardly comfortable, I felt totally detached from the world at large. Apart from the all important patch of ground where the harrier's nest was untidily framed by rank heather, a clump of purple moor grass and the pendulous branches of surrounding spruce and pine, I could see only chinks of grey sky through the slits in the hide, but my awareness of sounds was heightened. The wind rose and fell through the forest like a far away sea on a pebbly shore. Raindrops pattered the canvas over my head. A Wren whirred inches from the hide, like a distant motor bike.

After only half an hour, the swoosh of wings announced the female harrier's arrival at the nest. It was her owl-cat face which continually riveted my attention. Her deep-set dark amber eyes were offset by rippling white eyebrows and cheeks, the latter contrasting sharply with her russet brown ear coverts, bordered by the wavy fretted pattern of the neck ruff. It was hard to accept that the intensity of her frontal gaze could not penetrate the hide. She looked big, rangy and powerful; incongruous in the confines of her small nesting space so closely surrounded by trees much taller than a man. Obviously at such a site she must rely a great deal on hearing to sense the approach of danger. I quickly scanned her legs for a ring but there was none. Her dark irides marked her as a youngish bird, probably one or two years old, very likely breeding for the first time. Possibly this had some bearing on the lateness of her nesting. When she settled to brood, with the chicks snugly tucked beneath her, her head and neck looked particularly broad and owlish.

She covered the chicks without a break for an hour and a quarter, while rain fell spasmodically. Then she walked stiffly to the edge of the nest and took off. Surprisingly, she returned in five minutes with a well plucked carcase of a fairly large bird, which she may have found, caught and plucked in that short time; although it might have been killed and plucked earlier, left and retrieved. I now had a problem of identification. I could see no recognisable feathers and must decide what species it was from the legs alone. It was obviously a game bird. There seemed to be little if any feathering on the toes, but it is one thing to detect, in the hand, those sparse bristly feathers on the toes, which separate the young of Red Grouse from Black Grouse, and quite another when the carcase is six metres away, spreadeagled beneath the crushing grip of a harrier's talons. I was fearful that movement of my head or hands might show through the slit in the hide. For ten minutes the female fed the chicks small gobs of meat, offering them with a gentle half-turn of her lowered head. Swiftly though the black hook of her bill tore at the flesh, her head moved slowly, even cautiously, in the act of feeding the young chicks. She swallowed larger hunks of meat and bone herself. After ten minutes she lifted the partly eaten carcase in her bill and flew off above the trees. I was fairly sure that the kill was a sizeable young Red Grouse but it was not going to be easy to identify every item of prey whenever it was brought fully plucked.

I noted that the larger of the two chicks was quicker to grab the food, although sometimes the hen deliberately fed the smaller chick. Henning Weis, in his pioneer study from hides, found that Montagu's Harriers similarly shared out the food, but Marsh Harriers did not, with consequent, frequent mortality of weaker chicks.

When the female was absent the chicks' most energetic task was to ensure nest sanitation. These performances were amusing and possibly hazardous, as the chicks were punctilious in heaving themselves backwards to the extreme edge of the nest to defecate, and if they had over-balanced they would not easily have climbed back over what had become quite a stockade of sticks, this particular nest having been well built-up. I soon learned that even at this stage the hen was frequently bringing new material, sometimes quite large branches of old heather, and she seemed to be trying to build a screen on the more open side, facing the hide. During the early afternoon, light rain fell persistently and the chicks were brooded continuously for forty minutes. When covering the chicks the female dozed briefly although she was generally very alert and snapped at passing flies. She would turn her head swiftly in response to the sounds and movements of small birds in the trees near by, but she did not react at all to low-flying jet aircraft.

At 14.45 the sun came out and the female left, her barred tail flashing buff, white and brown as she made an almost vertical take-off. She was back in 16 minutes, again with a large plucked prey. This time there was no mistaking the long, bare, greyish legs of Pheasant—a well-grown poult, it seemed, from its size and the few unplucked wing feathers. I had not personally seen Pheasant as prey at a nest before but we knew there were broods in the forest rides not far distant. Evidently the harrier had found one of these because she brought another young Pheasant at 16.35, having been away for 26 minutes; and yet another was being carried towards the nest as I was making my departure at 18.20. This time she had been away for 75 minutes. When I saw her overhead with the prey I thought I had never seen a harrier carrying such a large burden before. Had she not dropped it in panic on sighting me, I might have guessed it was an old grouse from the reddish appearance of some of the feathers, but examination of the body proved these to be the tibial feathering of a young cock Pheasant.

So, my first day's hide watching at this nest would have given no comfort to a game preserver. He would certainly not have given the harrier a second chance, but we were to learn that on other days quite different prey was brought. The details of all the prey at this nest are given in Table 9.

On some days, fledgling passerines (chiefly Meadow Pipit and Skylark) were the sole prey and, once, the female brought two fledglings together. The occurrence of Wood Pigeon, including a squab, was notable. Shortly before Louis saw a fledged young Wood Pigeon brought to the nest, I had watched the female harrier hunting low along a ride between tall conifers where she had doubtless caught it. When the nestling Wood Pigeon was brought, I was at a loss to identify it at first as it was just a squashy bundle, covered with whitish straw-coloured fluff—no need for her to pluck this one. Only the head was diagnostic—the curiously long, almost duck-like bill, with the dark, naked patch extending to the eye. She immediately fed most of the skull contents and the eyes to the chick so I had very little time to make the identification. A quick sketch of the bill and head shape provided useful confirmation, later. I never saw any sign of the legs, and concluded that she may have eaten them before carrying the body to the nest. She was probably in the habit of lightening her larger prey burdens by consuming parts of them herself before bringing them in.

Other observers have remarked on how clean a Hen Harrier's nest is kept until the young are nearly fledged, and the hide watches showed that the female always removed the remains of prey. After she had fed the young, she sometimes consumed whole legs of birds herself, in the nest. Once it took her half a minute to gulp down a grouse leg. She made a grotesque picture as she strained and waggled her neck with the horny toes of the grouse still protruding from her gape. Yet very little sign of such large items appears in regurgitated pellets of harriers. On 31 July, it was a little surprising to see a Wood Pigeon carcase taken away and brought back for further feeding twice in the afternoon. Nick Picozzi confirms that prey which is removed is sometimes picked up later, as Jeffrey Watson has recorded for Merlins, and Dick Orton for Peregrines.

On 23 July, when Jim was in the hide, he witnessed the death of one of the two chicks. This was both a great disappointment to us and a surprise, as the weather had been fine, though cool, and both chicks had fed well. Seven passerine fledglings had been brought to the nest between 10.45 and 16.55, at which time the chick lay flat in the nest and showed no further sign of life. Photographs taken by Jim confirmed that it was the smaller chick which died and I had certainly noticed, earlier, that it was more backward at feeding times. A post mortem might have been interesting, but when Jim left that night he thought it possible that a spark of life remained, so he left the chick in the nest. However, it had been removed or eaten by 25 July. The earlier casualty had disappeared, likewise, two days after death.

The surviving chick proved to be a male and, as it was clearly the larger

of the two in the early stages, must have been the first to hatch. Balfour and Scharf found that the hierarchy in the nest depended on age rather than sex, although female chicks are as much as 100 grams heavier than males at fledging (Bannerman, 1953). We never knew the sex of the chicks that died, but our observations fit the concept of age hierarchy. Although it may be that the deaths were due to insufficient brooding by the female in the absence of food provision by the male, the following observations make this doubtful. The two chicks had been brooded for nearly an hour, in three stretches between 12.10 and 16.55, but a heavy rain shower when the hen was absent, from 13.15 to 13.30, might have chilled them. The chicks always appeared to be fed until they could take no more. This was particularly noticeable when large prey was brought, and a good deal was eaten by the female when the chicks were replete.

On 25 July, a partly-eaten young Red Grouse was left in the nest for periods of 35 and 45 minutes, somewhat to the inconvenience of the surviving chick which could find nowhere to lie down. The chick sat for a long time at the edge of the nest with its vulturine head drooped over its distended crop and looked distinctly uncomfortable.

In the latter part of its second week the chick became much more active when left unattended. Wing and leg stretching, which occurred fairly often, was a remarkable action, revealing the great length of a leg when at full stretch (see sketch). At 22 days, on 31 July, feather growth on scapulars, wings, tail and ear coverts gave the chick a parti-coloured appearance and the dark feathered areas looked a little like a pair of braces across its back. Yet it was still predominantly downy at this stage (details of plumage and other changes in the growth of young harriers are given in Chapter 6).

With the rapid growth of its feathers, the chick spent an increasing amount of time preening, probably mainly to remove loose down. The sun was hot on 31 July, and the chick passed the $2\frac{1}{2}$ hours from 13.00 till 15.30 resting or preening in the shade outside the nest. In a site such as this, with plenty of tall trees and long heather close at hand, it was much easier for a chick to find shade than at some more open nests where bracken fronds may

provide almost the only protection when the sun is high. Regular brooding of the chick was not seen after it was 2½ weeks old, but none of the later observations were made during periods of persistent rain.

At 22 days the female, for the first time, was carefully feeding the chick small feathers from prey, and sometimes gave it quite large beaksful of feathers, gristle and bone. Louis even saw the chick accept and swallow both legs of a small bird, probably a young Skylark. The whole of this meal was demolished without trace within three minutes.

On 2 August, when the chick was 24 days old, the female spent only ten minutes at the nest in seven hours (13.45–20.45). Her first appearance was at 17.00 hours when she dropped a plucked young passerine bird into the nest, without landing herself. An hour later she brought another small bird and fed the chick for two minutes. At 19.00 hours she fed the chick from two small birds, brought at the same time, for eight minutes. Jim's chances of obtaining pictures were restricted to these final eight minutes. He took some pictures using flash and found that the bird was quite unconcerned by it.

From the hide I had many opportunities of noting plumage details of this female harrier. It is probably true that no two individuals are precisely alike, while the same bird changes in details of appearance as the summer moult proceeds. This bird was growing her new outer tail feathers at the end of July and, in flight, these projected like little wedges half way along the tail. A new central tail feather was also about half grown and when she stood in the nest with her back to the hide the darker colour of this new feather was noticeable. Her wing feathers looked fresh, and certainly no flight feathers were missing or growing. I have seen female harriers, feeding young, in various stages of wing or tail moult, and have wondered that moulting should occur at a time when the bird requires to make its greatest efforts in hunting flight.

For four days we did not occupy the hide. In a summer which will long be remembered for sunshine, the early part of August was exceptionally hot, with frequent outbreaks of thunder in the evenings. During my three and a half hour watch, from 07.50 on 7 August, the chick remained out of view, a metre or so from the nest. When the female landed at the nest with an unplucked Skylark I expected the chick to run to her, but it did not appear. The female transferred the prey from foot to bill and moved out of my field of view towards the chick's retreat. Six minutes later I heard her take off and I could only guess that she had been feeding the lark to the chick. Later that morning, Louis saw part of another Wood Pigeon brought—by this time the chick was back in the nest but the female made no attempt to feed the chick. When Louis left at 14.15, the pigeon still lay untouched in the nest, the 29 day old chick apparently not yet able to tear up such large prey for itself.

On 7 August, while the chick was out of view, I took a long look at the fairyland pattern and colours of my little vista of anonymous forest. There was a cool beauty in the varied greens of spruce, pine and ling, the latter now with spikes of lilac flower. It was a morning of soft rain with beads of moisture at the top of every drooping sitka spray. The further trees receded into enclosing mistiness, full of the coo-ing of Wood Pigeons. A young, yellow speckled Robin and a Wren perched in turn, an arm's length from the hide, apparently unconcerned by the harrier's close proximity. Although the nest would have been very difficult for a casual human searcher to find, long vigils in the hide set the imagination working at times. Surely, I sometimes thought, someone will follow our tracks and emerge from the trees to blunder upon the nest, but, of course, no one ever did. I could even, occasionally, sense an uneasy feeling as though I had myself gone into hiding from unknown searchers. Such are the neuroses of hide watching deep in the forest. Mostly, however, there was no time for lapses of concentration as page after page of sketch book was filled and incidents noted.

After leaving the hide on 7 August, I visited the site of the nest where there had been five chicks on 9 July. On the way I enjoyed a brilliant spectacle of eight or ten peacock butterflies on the tall heads of marsh thistles. Even more numerous in the lush rides were the dark, little Scotch argus butterflies, fluttering ahead of me at almost every step. As I approached the harrier site, one of the young, now more than six weeks old, rose in easy flight from the side of a broad ride.

Up at the nest I collected a smelly assortment of prey remnants for later identification. As usual, at this stage, there were several fairly large pectoral girdles, but I could make only one immediate identification, from a foot of a young Red Grouse. Much of the prey had been smaller, judging from the accumulation of passerine feathers. Evidently, at the late stages, the young had been using the narrow extraction ride, a few yards from the nest, as a feeding place in preference to the nest itself. Looking at the much trampled nest platform, I was struck by its rather precarious situation at the very edge of a deep drain, which might have been hazardous for the chicks.

There was nothing by the nest to suggest that any of the five young had failed to fledge, but a chance discovery in the ride, 300 metres away, proved that one of the female chicks (recognisable by its ring) must indeed have died in the nest. It had been dead for two or three weeks and the flight feathers, only partly emerged from their sheaths, could not have sustained flight. No doubt it had been carried away from the nest and dropped in the ride by the female parent which had evidently not fed it all to the other chicks. Why, I wonder, do harriers persistently drop their unwanted remains in the open rides, so laying a trail for any curious man or fox? One very obvious heap of plucked feathers was from a young Pheasant, but with Sparrowhawks feeding young in the tall larches nearby, there was no saying whether they or the harriers had accounted for this.

On 9 August, Jim was tempted back to the hide for a final session of photography. This time the female had observed our approach and showed increasing aggression, making some beautiful, long dives at our heads with arched wings. The chick, too, was proving to be a bold character, standing his ground, quick to strike out with claws and bill, and even advancing a step or two towards us. It was now 31 days old and we were surprised to find that all the prey—three pipit-sized birds, partially plucked—was still being fed to it by the female.

On the hot, sunny morning of 11 August, I was in the hide for my last watch. One day to go to the start of grouse shooting hardly more than a kilometre away! The young harrier was hunched like an eaglet in the 'pathway' from nest to hide as I settled in. It appeared rather grey-brown on its back and wings, apart from the pronounced russet pattern on the smaller coverts; and I wondered, not for the first time, if a comparison between a large number of male and female chicks would confirm a suspicion that females are browner, in their first feathering. Flies clustered on the wings

and one leg of yet another Wood Pigeon in the nest. There was not much meat left on it. The narrow, fawn-brown tips to the unplucked wing coverts were a sure indication that this had been a young, fully-fledged bird. The pigeons could have been killed within 100 metres or so of the nest, and it was probably true that the late date of this nest meant that the female harrier had exceptional opportunities to prey on newly-fledged pigeons.

Soon the chick was back in the nest, attempting to strip the remaining meat from the wing bones, but with little success. It evidently lacked the power in its legs to hold such large prey firmly and tear it with its bill at the same time. It played with the leg for a moment, as if about to swallow it, but dropped it again. The effort of trying to feed itself soon proved too exhausting and it sank on to its 'haunches'. It looked awkward, even comical, especially when it turned its head to one side and gazed at flies with one eye; or, sometimes, to judge from its cheeping calls, at its female parent flying overhead. Sideview, the pale iris and an illusion of nakedness below the eye—caused by very short, russet feathers—gave it the facial expression of a domestic fowl. It still had a projecting tuft of down on the forehead, and more on the peak of its crown, forming an absurd little top-knot. Tiny shreds of down flew copiously from all the accessible parts of its plumage

during extensive bouts of preening. The action of combing the still partly-sheathed tail feathers with the bill, was particularly neat. At times it stood on one leg, the other furled among the rich buff feathers of its underparts, and I was reminded of the old saying that 'the harrier is lame and limpeth of one leg'.

A renewed onslaught on the Wood Pigeon remains was more effective, after which it lay prone in the intense heat of early afternoon, the picture of ennui, with its head sagging sleepily forward. It was suddenly aroused, apparently having seen the female overhead. I heard the food call but could not decide whether it had been uttered by the chick or its parent. Later, it struck me that the call came perhaps from a fledged youngster at one of the other nests. The young birds were ranging widely over the forest and probably gave the food call to any passing adult.

The hen did not come down to the nest and the chick's excitement subsided quickly. Soon afterwards, the question of how it would rid itself of the down on its head was answered. Balancing clumsily, with a wing as prop, it scratched its head with a talon and the down began to fly. It was much more concerned by aircraft overhead than its parent had been, and Louis had recorded earlier that the chick had 'a great fright' and jumped into the air when a low-flying plane roared over. It was beginning to spend more time up on its legs, sometimes preening in this position, and wing exercising for the first time, bouncing well clear of the ground. Yet, though 35 days old, it did not look ready to make its first flight for another two or three days. As males are generally quicker to fly, and this one had often seemed surfeited with food in the absence of competition from siblings, I had expected a considerably earlier fledging date.

At 15.00 hours I was due to leave the hide and had resigned myself to doing so without further sight of the female, but one final episode was enacted, swiftly and suddenly. The chick was in the 'pathway', skywatching. I heard a soft thump—something small had been dropped by the female between the chick and the hide. The chick reacted in wild confusion, hirpling first towards the new prey, then back into the nest without it, where it started to tug at the old bones of the Wood Pigeon, dragging them about like a dog greeting its master. The female pitched down beside it, seemed about to carry off the wing girdle of the pigeon, but dropped it again. In a few seconds she had gone, and the chick came down the pathway and retrieved the dropped prey from the heather. For my last few minutes I watched it competently tearing it up. When I came out of the hide, it had eaten all the hind parts from what proved to be a Meadow Pipit, brought in fully feathered.

I came away regretfully, feeling that the 70 hours we had spent in the hide still left us much to learn about the early stage of a harrier's life. The chick had survived one hazardous stage only to embark on another, even more hazardous, in the next few days. It had been reared, as far as we could tell, with little or no assistance from the male. It was due to fly at an extremely late date for a Hen Harrier, and was quite likely to blunder fatally among the guns on a grouse moor during the next few weeks. It has been calculated that 70% of young harriers die in their first year, so the prospects for a late fledgling in a fairly dangerous neighbourhood would not be rated highly. Yet, of course, I had a special hope that this young male would survive to return in a future spring, to 'sky-dance' over the forest, in the grey plumage of maturity.

Postscript

On 17 August, when the chick was 39 days old, I thought it would be well able to fly and that there would be no risk of it taking off prematurely if I visited the nest. All along the rides the heather flowering was at its peak and it was hard to accept that, so late in the season, a harrier could still be intensely protective of its young. The female indeed was more aggressive than she had ever been and, for the first time, I found myself ducking my head from her attacks. Knowing that fledged, young harriers often cling to the nest as their base, I ought not to have been surprised to find the chick still at home. It was on one of its favourite stances, a metre or so from the nest, upright, sphinx-like, its dark head now beautiful with all trace of down lost. Surprisingly, it did not rise as I came through the trees and I thought I might manage to examine the nest for prey without disturbing it, but as I bent down, it took off, yellow legs trailing, and flew rather unsteadily towards the nearest ride. Later, from a distance, I glimpsed it flying among the trees, probably returning to the nest, or thereabout. It had almost certainly made previous short flights. A couple of days earlier, a visit might indeed have made it fly too soon, with the risk of a crash-landing in an awkward spot.

There was no trace of large prey by the nest but I found many feathers of small birds, some obviously of Meadow Pipits, and a young Robin lay partly eaten in the pathway. Although the Robin is one of the commonest small birds in the forest, and there had been many late broods this summer, I had not previously recorded it as prey.

CHAPTER FOURTEEN

NEST SITES

All of the study nests were on the ground, and nearly equal numbers were found in fairly young conifer forest and on open moorland. None was found in forest rides.

Heather, *Calluna vulgaris* and *Erica spp*, was much the commonest dominant vegetation surrounding nests, both at forest and moorland sites. At more than half the moorland nests, bracken grew among the heather and provided additional shade and shelter for chicks. Some sites had a mixture of heather, *Molinia* (purple moor grass) and/or bog myrtle, often with bracken as well. Heather was absent from only three sites, one in almost pure *Molinia*, one in rushes *Juncus sp* and another in *Molinia* among young conifers. Most moorland nest sites were in fairly deep ground cover, 60–100 centimetres high or more, but a few were in very sparse cover. Such rather poorly concealed nests on moorland often failed. Two nests, in one season, in fairly short heather (about 60 centimetres high) failed early, in spite of being distant from any roads; and the most open nest of all, in pure *Molinia*, failed after hatching.

Forest nests were always well concealed in the very lush ground vegetation, frequently more than a metre high, which was a feature of the young plantations. Heather was generally dominant, with a strong admixture of *Molinia* and bog myrtle. The height of the surrounding conifers varied greatly, from about 1.50 metres to over six metres. The harriers showed a marked preference for the more open parts of the forest, where tree growth was retarded, sometimes due to early browsing by deer. All forest nests were in plantations at least five years old. In Area C it appeared likely that the difficulty of finding sufficiently open sites was a reason for the reduction, and possible cessation, of nesting after the trees were about 15 years old; but in Area E, in 1975, there were three nests in 14 year old forest, where only one had been found in any previous year. In such older plantations, we were often aided in the final search for a nest by the knowledge that it was almost certain to be in a patch of ground where the trees were comparatively sparse or stunted.

The most common tree species in the forest were sitka spruce *Picca sitchensis* and lodgepole pine *Pinus contorta*. All the forest nests were found where these two species were mixed, but there was some evidence that sites with a good proportion of pine were favoured. Blocks of larch *Larix sp* were quite widespread, but no nests were found amongst them, probably because this tree rapidly forms a close canopy. The unevenness of tree growth in plantations of spruce and pine facilitates landing and taking off at nest sites, as well as providing space for the nest itself. These conditions may continue in blocks of trees more than 15 years old, which at first glance look far too tall and dense to be suitable for nesting. Even when Hen Harriers are nesting on open moorland, both sexes make use of prominent perches nearby, either rocks or isolated trees, and it seems likely that the fairly high perching-places provided by the top branches of 10–15 year old forest conifers are an additional attraction. Females with young very often use trees as look-outs.

Very little human disturbance occurs in young forest plantations during the harriers' breeding season. Forest rangers kill deer, foxes and crows in harrier nesting areas, but usually avoid unnecessary disturbance of nesting birds. Lack of human persecution, better concealment of nests and, probably, less risk of disturbance by man in the early stages of nesting, seem to be the most likely advantages of nesting in forest rather than on moorland, in this region.

CHAPTER FIFTEEN

BREEDING DATA

The earliest nest-building was seen on 19 April. In 14 out of 27 nests for which the date was known or could be fairly certainly calculated (from hatching dates), incubation began between 1–15 May; in six nests it began between 16–31 May; in three nests between 27–29 April; and in another three between 3–11 June. In many instances the first egg was probably laid two or more days earlier than these dates.

At 14 out of 21 nests with known hatching dates, the first chick hatched between 1–15 June; at three nests between 16–31 May, at two between 16–30 June; and at another two nests between 1–15 July.

The earliest fledging date was 1 July, the latest 17 August. The shortest fledging period was 29 days (possibly due to disturbance) and the longest was 38 days. Most chicks were able to make short flights at 32–34 days.

Fifty-one nests were known to contain eggs or young. Of these, 25 were on moorland, and 26 in conifer forest. Thirteen of the moorland nests were in Area A, ten in Area B, and one each in Areas F and G. Sixteen forest nests were in Area C, seven in Area E, and one each in Areas H, J and K. There were no nests in Area D. Details of clutch and brood size and fledging success, where known, are given in Table 10. Information on clutch size is very incomplete for forest nests because many nests were left unvisited until after hatching, to minimise disturbance. Total accuracy, in numbers of eggs laid and young hatched, is impossible without more regular nest inspection than was deemed justifiable. However, my figures enable some conclusions to be drawn and comparisons to be made between the success of nests in moorland and forest situations.

Tables 10–15 do not take account of possible annual differences in breeding success due to changes in food supply, or climatic variations. The main period of nesting on Moorland A covered different, earlier years from the main period of forest nesting; nesting on Moorland B, however, largely coincided with the latter.

The percentage of clutches which hatched was higher on Moorland B and in the forests, than on Moorland A, although the percentage of nests from which young fledged was similar on the two moorland areas (Table 12). Young were fledged from a significantly higher proportion of nests in forests than on moorland probably due to the lack of human and other disturbance in the forests.

Complete failure was most common on the grouse moor B, probably due to destruction of nests with young by gamekeepers. (See Tables 13–15.)

Notes on Table 15

Unless otherwise stated all nests were found empty after failure. At nests 18 and 19, flank or tibial feathers of the adult were found at the nest, suggesting that they might have been lost during a struggle with a predator, or, possibly, that she might have been killed. Nests 1, 6 and 7 were probably deserted at an early stage, possibly before the start of incubation. They might have been raided by crows while the female was off the nest; and human disturbance may have been a factor at these nests, and possibly at nest 2. There were ten or eleven examples of total loss of a brood. Excluding those on Moorland B, it was very difficult to decide whether man, fox or some other predator was responsible. Total loss of young broods might have been caused by very wet weather affecting food supply, but this possibility could only have occurred at nests 5, 19 and 20. The three clutches which did not hatch raised the possibility of contamination by toxic chemicals, but the analysis of three eggs from nest 4 showed low residues (Table 16). The female at this nest was thought to have been neglected by the only male seen in the area, in a presumed polygynous group, and she may have been forced to hunt for herself during incubation, with possible, consequent chilling of the eggs during wet weather.

Notes on sex and age ratios in the population

A minimum of 51 females and 47 males bred during the study period. Two instances of presumed polygyny occurred: in 1964 there was almost certainly only one male to three females with nests on Moorland A; and in 1975 a single male was attending three females with nests in Forest E. In the latter case a second pair had been present on 24 April but only one male was seen in the area thereafter. There was, therefore, no significant excess of females over males, such as occurs in the much larger breeding population of Orkney, where females may be at least twice as numerous as males. A noticeable excess of females in the breeding population of south-west

Scotland might have been expected in view of the predominance of females among fledged young, but it may have been prevented by greater mortality of females. There is a little evidence for this, from ringing recoveries. Breeding females were more vulnerable than breeding males to human persecution.

A total of 59 chicks consisted of 37 females and 22 males. Of these 33 females and 19 males fledged. In 14 nests in which all the fledged young were sexed, there were 25 females and 17 males. Females outnumbered or were equal to males in 14 broods, and males outnumbered females in two broods with young surviving to an age at which they could be sexed. There was therefore some indication that, either females survived better than males, or more females were hatched than males, but the difference was not statistically significant.

Of the eight recoveries of ringed birds (excluding one male and one female found dead in or near the nest), six were females and two had not been sexed. In only two instances was the cause of death fairly certain: one female was shot and the other was probably killed by a Golden Eagle. There was a strong possibility that shooting or trapping accounted for some of the other recoveries.

CHAPTER SIXTEEN

FOOD AND HUNTING GROUNDS IN THE BREEDING AREA

Prey identification in the breeding season was made from: (1) fresh kills or remains, mainly from nests or feeding places used by well-grown young near nests; (2) observations from a hide at one nest in July–August 1975; (3) pellets found at or near nests.

It is clear that birds were much the most important prey. Field voles were the only mammals of any significance as prey and were a surprisingly small component of the whole (see Tables 17 and 18). Table 18 shows that the results from prey collections and fresh kills, observation from a hide and pellet analyses are strikingly different. The percentage of grouse or other large prey is clearly exaggerated by the figures for remains and fresh kills found at or near nests because most of these were collected when chicks were nearly fledged, or even later, when harriers commonly left only the bones of such large prey at nests, whereas smaller prey was eaten more or less entirely. The hide observations and the pellet analyses each show a high proportion of passerine birds and a much lower proportion of grouse. Beetles occurred quite commonly in pellets but were obviously of minor importance as food. Nearly all pellets contained a fair amount of plant matter, especially *Molinia* grass. A comparison with the results from analyses of winter pellets (see Table 27), shows that mammals of several species formed a more considerable part of the diet at that season.

Observations of food passes at all stages and at many nests suggested that most prey brought before the young were three–four weeks old, was small; and as, during this period, remains were rarely left in the nest, very little was identified. I thought that most small prey items were passerine birds. Larger prey was more often seen in food passes just before and after the fledging period. It is quite clear that Red Grouse were by far the commonest species in the range of larger prey, while Meadow Pipits and

Skylarks were the small species most often taken. The weight of a four to six week old Red Grouse is about eight times that of a Meadow Pipit (say 120 grams to 15 grams) so, from my prey data, the percentage of grouse by weight would be high, but if many of the grouse were less than four to six weeks old, it would obviously be much lower. I do not consider that my data permit any positive statement on proportions of prey by weight, but it is obvious, as Tubbs found for the Buzzard, that if harriers can catch larger prey, such as juvenile grouse or Wood Pigeons, the amount of time and energy required to feed their young at the most demanding stage can be correspondingly reduced. Nevertheless, there was evidence from the hide watch that much of the prey, even in the later stages, was still of Meadow Pipit size.

Table 17 shows that most bird prey consisted of fledglings (or nestlings). Indeed, the six Red Grouse and the single Crossbill were the only positive adult identifications. In 1968, when four out of the six adult grouse were found, there was a high population of Red Grouse in the young forest within easy hunting range of nests. Harriers may have found it easier to catch them by surprise in such habitat than on open moorland.

When the prey identifications from moorland nests are compared with those from forest nests (Tables 19–21), the most important difference is that none of the former could be assigned to forest haunting species, while some of the latter could. The true porportion of prey taken from forest is impossible to assess accurately as the two commonest prey species, Red Grouse and Meadow Pipit, were plentiful in both young forest and on moorland, but only those items listed in Table 23 were fairly certainly caught in the forest. Even if as many as half the Red Grouse and Meadow Pipit prey was taken from forest, which is unlikely, considerably more than half the prey found at forest nests must have been caught on moorland.

The most conclusive evidence for the importance of moorland as hunting ground came from watching hunting birds. Our own observations continually showed that adult harriers with nests in forests regularly hunted neighbouring moorland. Jimmy Stewart, the shepherd, informed me that he saw harriers hunting Moorland A almost every day in spring and summer, and quite often recognised two or three different cocks over a period of days; he saw them fly away with prey in the direction of known forest nest areas. I once saw two hunting cocks meet over the moor; they came from moorland nests rather more than a kilometre apart, and there was a brief aerial tussle when they met about half way between their nesting sites. They soon disengaged to hunt in different directions.

Typically, a cock with a nest of eggs or small young in the forest would set out from the nest area, hunting at first along the edges of forest rides, or sometimes low over the trees, and he would occasionally make a kill in this way. Usually, he continued to the open moorland and proceeded to hunt until lost to sight a kilometre or more away. It was interesting to see that he lost height as soon as he reached the moorland edge and thereafter seemed

to hunt more assiduously, mainly very close to the ground, using the contours to assist him in surprise approaches. Because hens do much of their hunting near the nest, those from forest nests often hunted among the trees or along rides. Cocks and hens were each seen to circle to a height of 30 metres, or more, over forest nesting sites and set direct course to moorland hunting grounds, slowly losing height, but not dropping to hunt the forest at all. Young harriers, fledged from forest nests, began their hunting in the forest, especially in the rides within about a kilometre of the nest, but after two or three weeks they ventured out to hunt over moorland, soon dispersing more widely. On 27 July 1974, I watched a juvenile fledged about three weeks, return at dusk from the moorland, evidently to roost in the forest at or near where the nest had been.

In Tables 24–26, I have listed the bird species which breed commonly on the moorlands and in the 5–15 year old forests, where harriers bred and hunted. I have little quantitative evidence for the relative abundance of different species, but have taken note of counts made by Jeffrey Watson in local forests and have also relied on my own long acquaintance with both habitats in the district. As already mentioned, it is surprising that neither Curlew nor Golden Plover have been found as prey in Areas A, C and E (two young Curlews were noted as prey on Moorland B by R. C. Dickson). At least 15–20 pairs of Golden Plover nested regularly, and Curlews were considerably more numerous, on Moorland A, which was hunted by at least one cock harrier throughout every season. Among forest nesting birds Chaffinches, particularly, might have been expected as more common prey, and there are several notable absentees among the numerous species, as the lists show. Both thrushes habitually made long flights to collect food out on the open, grassy moor and appeared at such times to be vulnerable to predators.

I have discussed the Hen Harrier's hunting methods in Chapter 4 and I think the limitations of these may explain some of the apparently surprising absences from the prey list, in so far as these can be taken to represent a valid sample. Forest haunting passerines, if not surprised, can often evade capture by diving into trees where harriers cannot follow. When travelling about the forest, or further, finches and thrushes tend to fly high and I have never seen a Hen Harrier in pursuit of a high-flying bird. Finches and pipits could approach a harrier soaring over forest without provoking any reaction.

Actual observations of kills or attempted kills in the breeding season have been few, partly because much more time has been given to watching nest areas rather than the main hunting areas, and partly because hunting harriers, by covering so much ground, are very difficult to keep in continuous view for long periods. One female was seen to capture a juvenile Red Grouse in or just above the heather, on moorland, and two different cocks were seen to snatch at adult Red Grouse as they rose from the ground. In one of these instances, a pair of grouse seemed to fly up at the harrier, probably in defence of chicks, and the harrier appeared as surprised as the grouse. Several successful catches of smaller prey, by cock or hen, were seen near or on the ground. A cock and a hen were each seen to capture small birds low among forest trees within a few hundred metres of a nest. On moorland, one spring, Jimmy Stewart reported disturbing a hen while she was feeding on an adult grouse. In summer 1976, R. C. Dickson saw an immature male kill an adult cock Red Grouse on Moorland B.

In recent years rabbits have become very abundant within easy hunting range of most harrier nests. Surprisingly, none were found as prey in the present study.[1] Unlike field voles, which may only be detected as prey in pellet analyses, rabbits could be expected to show up among prey remains, and would have been identified from the hide if any had been brought to that nest. Even if a larger sample of pellets might have shown a higher proportion of vole prey, mammalian prey was clearly of much less importance than in many parts of the Hen Harriers' breeding range. Rabbits were most numerous around the fringes of woodland, in rather enclosed habitat for easy hunting by harriers, though they were commonly taken by Golden Eagles.

Hunting activity by Hen Harriers in the breeding season was almost entirely confined to moorland, or its fringes, and the plantations of conifers under 15–20 years old. It was extremely rare to see harriers in summer over cultivated fields, lowland pasture or marsh—all hunted in winter—but they would have had to travel a minimum of three kilometres from nests to find much habitat of these types. Harriers were occasionally seen over moorland as high as 300 metres, but they mainly hunted over lower ground. They

[1] After this was written I found a young rabbit as prey, in July 1976, when young had fledged from a forest nest. The rabbit had been almost entirely eaten, except for the forelegs and decapitated head, and the remains had been left with other prey remains in a ride near the nest. Other prey identified at this site consisted of two young Black Grouse and a Chaffinch. There were also feathers of other passerine species and a larger skeleton, probably of a young Pheasant.

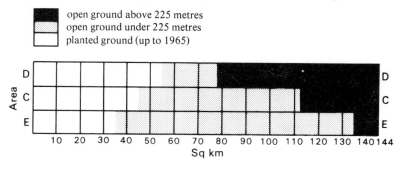

open ground above 225 metres
open ground under 225 metres
planted ground (up to 1965)

Fig. 11   Hunting grounds in the breeding season, within 7 km of centres of Areas C, D and E

were very rarely seen hunting the unplanted and ungrazed hill tops, mostly above 300 metres, within the forest areas. The extremes of distances travelled from nests were not known, but observations of cocks moving between the forest and hunting grounds on Moorland A, showed that they commonly hunted at least four or five kilometres from nests. Taking seven kilometres as a possible outer limit of hunting distance from nests, I have tried to assess the comparative suitability of hunting grounds within that distance from central points in the three forest Areas C, D and E. Figure 11 shows that hunting grounds for harriers based in Area D, included rather less moorland than the other two, and strikingly less ground below 250 metres. The puzzling lack of nests in Area D, in spite of a long history of spring and summer sightings of harriers in the area, might therefore be explained by the comparative inaccessibility of good hunting grounds. Although I do not have census figures to prove that prey is scarcer on moorland above 250 metres than below, a general knowledge of the birds of the area and the evidence that harriers usually hunted the lower ground are, in my view, strong indications that this was so.[1] Observations over all the years give strong grounds for believing that breeding success of both moorland and forest nesting harriers was greatly dependent on the accessibility of sizeable areas of *low elevation* moorland and marginal land. It is likely, as well, that the decreasing extent of such ground is an important factor in keeping the breeding numbers of Hen Harriers so low in the area as a whole. It must also be said that densities of prey species appear to vary considerably, both on moorland and within the young plantations, in different local areas of similar elevation. It may well be true that food for harriers is comparatively scarcer, generally, in the environs of Area D which

[1] Lack of grazing or burning on the higher ground, above forest plantations, made this area much less open and so less suitable for many of the birds preyed upon by harriers. Cock harriers, particularly (Schipper, 1975), may have greater difficulty in locating prey in the uniformly dense ground cover. Although the ground became more open again at the highest elevations, above 500 metres, prey was obviously scarce there.

border on the main granite massif of Galloway. It is certainly my impression that moorland birds such as Red Grouse, Curlew and Golden Plover are scarcer in this area than on the more fertile moorland close to Areas C and E. The results of censuses of breeding birds on selected plots within young forests and on open ground, presently being made by D. Moss, are awaited with interest. Differences in tree growth and survival and in types of ground vegetation within young plantations are probably important factors accounting for local differences in bird communities in plantations of fairly similar age. The distribution of breeding Hen Harriers must, of course, depend on the suitability of the terrain for their style of hunting as well as on the abundance of potential prey.

CHAPTER SEVENTEEN

FOOD AND HUNTING GROUNDS:
SEPTEMBER–APRIL

Prey identifications, out of the breeding season, were made from pellets collected at a winter roost (Roost 1) adjacent to Area C, and the results are given in Tables 27–28. Birds (70%), were the most important items but the proportion of mammalian prey (30%), was notably higher than in pellets found in the breeding season (beetles and moth cocoons are excluded from these percentages). A strikingly different feature of the winter pellets was the large amount of rabbit, hare or mountain hare which they contained (52% of mammal items). Some young rabbits and mountain hares were probably available in the period, but it is likely that some of this prey was taken as carrion. The importance of carrion food, generally, has been discussed in Chapter 4. Only one local observation, by Louis Urquhart in September 1975, of a female Hen Harrier at an old rabbit carcase, gave presumptive evidence of carrion feeding. Rabbits incapacitated by myxomatosis or caught in snares might also have been eaten. Field and water voles and a pigmy shrew made up 29% of the mammalian items, and unidentifiable fur was present in a few pellets. The highest proportion of Red Grouse occurred in 1968, a year of high grouse population in the district. All grouse taken in the period must, of course, have been full-grown, but they may have included birds which were already dead from other causes. The proportion of Red Grouse among avian prey (11%) was precisely the same as in summer pellets. It was very difficult to make specific identifications of small bird prey from pellets as harriers, unlike owls, generally reduce skeletal parts to very small fragments. Nevertheless, small, mainly passerine, birds (72% of bird

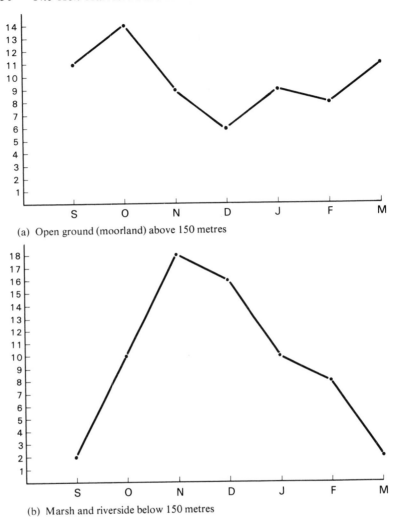

(a) Open ground (moorland) above 150 metres

(b) Marsh and riverside below 150 metres

Fig. 12 (a–b) Sightings of hunting Hen Harriers within 24 km of Roost 1, Sept.–March

prey) were clearly very important in winter, as in summer.

R. C. Dickson (1970) has published findings from an analysis of 32 pellets collected in December 1966, January 1967 and September 1968, from the other major roost in the region, on low ground near the coast (Roost 2). These showed an even higher proportion of birds (89.8%) than at Roost 1. Bird prey identified was mainly passerine, including finches, buntings, pipits, Skylarks, Starlings and a Wren; in addition there were two waders (one Redshank, one unidentified) and only one grouse (species?). Mammals (10.3%) consisted of three mice or voles and one shrew. Two

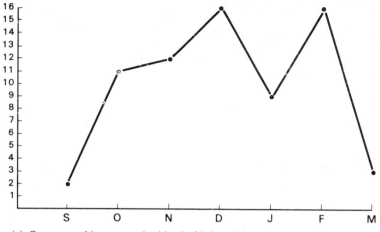

(c) Open ground (pasture and cultivation) below 150 metres

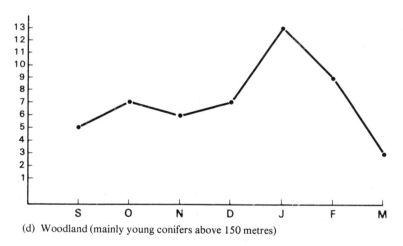

(d) Woodland (mainly young conifers above 150 metres)

Fig. 12 (c–d) Sightings of hunting Hen Harriers within 24 km of Roost 1, Sept.–March

small beetles have been excluded from these percentages. More recently, Dickson has collected a much larger number of pellets from Roost 2. The full analysis of these is not yet complete but he has kindly given me the results for 21 pellets. These contained 81% birds (mostly pipits, Skylarks, finches and Starlings) and 19% mammals (all rodents, the largest of water vole size). These later findings are therefore very similar to Dickson's published evidence on winter prey from pellets at this roost.

Winter hunting grounds covered a much wider range, with a greater variety of habitat, than in summer. Of 253 sightings of hunting Hen

Harriers between September and March, within a radius of 24 kilometres of Roost 1 (see Figure 12), 68 were on moorland above 150 metres[1], 69 on grassland and cultivation below 150 metres, 66 on marshland below 150 metres and 50 were over woodland (mainly young conifer forests, but occasionally hardwood scrub). As such these figures are difficult to interpret owing to differences in the relative extent of these habitat types and to a further possible bias due to uneven observer cover.

In the Netherlands, Schipper found that males showed a hunting preference for less structured vegetation, and took more agile passerine birds, than females. In south-west Scotland ringtails slightly exceeded adult males on moorland over 150 metres (often with long heather), woodland and marsh, but sightings of each on pasture and cultivation below 150 metres were nearly equal (Fig. 12). In general, the latter habitat had the barest ground and undoubtedly held the largest numbers of passerine birds. The tendency for males to hunt the most open ground is further emphasised by my analysis of 34 winter sightings of Hen Harriers in a particularly open area of salt-marsh and coastal fields, near the estuary of the River Nith; these consisted of 20 grey males (59%) and 14 ringtails (41%). It must be remembered that all totals of ringtails also included a number of brown, first year males. It is interesting that the proportions of males to ringtails hunting either moorland above 150 metres, or marsh with tall vegetation at lower elevations, were so similar.

There was some seasonal change in preferred hunting habitats during the winter. There was an indication (see Fig. 12) that higher moorland was hunted mainly in September–October and March, lowland marshes mostly in November–December, but the largest number of sightings on grassland and cultivation below 150 metres was obtained in December and February. There was a peak in woodland sightings, with some suggestion of a move to lower elevation woodland, in January. In general, there was an indication that Hen Harriers moved to hunting areas on lower ground between November and February, which may reflect changes in the distribution of available prey. In the early winter there are many Meadow Pipits, Skylarks, Fieldfares and Redwings on upland moors, while there is certainly a decline in small birds in the marshes as the vegetation dies down in mid-winter (a reed-bed Starling roost, for example, was usually deserted about December). The peak numbers of sightings on farmland, in December and February, may well be associated with the distribution of winter flocks of passerines such as finches and buntings. On several occasions harriers were seen hunting over fields of kale or weedy stubble where flocks of passerines gathered to feed, and a harrier was sometimes seen attempting to make a kill there. The same fields provided feeding for finch flocks for many weeks at a time and I gained the impression that harriers made regular hunting visits to such

---

[1] Less than half of these were above 225 metres, most in September and March.

sites. It is possible that the distances travelled from roost to hunting grounds were more restricted on the shortest winter days, or when the weather was particularly wet or stormy; some evidence on distances travelled is given in the following section on winter roosts.

Although duck or geese rose in alarm from fields or marshes as a harrier approached, the prey sought usually appeared to be smaller birds or mammals. It was common to see a harrier hunting assiduously over the tall grasses or reeds in the river valleys, when it would pounce into the vegetation at intervals and sometimes remain hidden for several minutes. Occasionally, two harriers were seen hunting in close proximity and once, in autumn, three were seen together in association with larger numbers of Kestrels, Short-eared Owls and one or two Buzzards, over young conifer forest and grass moor where voles were abundant. A similar association of predators, including two Hen Harriers, was seen hunting a field of unharvested oats in January. Here too the prey sought probably consisted of small mammals. As noted in Chapter 4, R. C. Dickson has observed up to five harriers at one time hunting a large kale field in winter. Harriers which hunted young conifer forests or upland moors in mid-winter were most likely to be preying on voles or grouse, as there appeared to be very little other prey available at that season in those habitats. They may, however, have found some passerine birds such as Bullfinches (present in winter pellets) in the forests. In March, I have watched a female Hen Harrier over 15 year old conifer forest, shadowing flocks of Starlings as they flew to and fro before roosting. It made no attempt to attack them at this stage but may have caught one later, as I saw it reappear in the dusk with its crop bulging. Possibly it was in the habit of raiding the Starling roost as the birds settled. Some of the invertebrate prey, such as the great water beetles *Dytiscus marginalis*, could have been taken on the marshy roosting grounds; water voles may also have been taken there. Weighing 120–180 grams in winter (Southern), a water vole would provide a substantial meal for a harrier.

There was evidently some variation from year to year in the proportions of wintering adult males and ringtails. Table 29 gives the number of diurnal sightings of each, within 24 kilometres of Roost 1, in three winters for which records were most complete. Since in these years, particularly, there was fairly consistent observer cover for all the main habitats, the numbers probably give a good indication of the true proportions. The counts at Roost 1 (Fig. 13) support the impression given by Table 26 that males were more numerous than ringtails during much of the winter 1973/74, and that they were strikingly less numerous than ringtails in the winter 1975/76. This latter impression was further supported by observations at the neighbouring coastal area of Caerlaverock, where 1975/76 was the first winter in five when ringtails were seen more often than males. In general, throughout south-west Scotland, the proportion of adult males, in winter, is much higher than in districts such as Orkney and the Scottish Highlands. As I have mentioned in Chapter 7, there is some indication that adult males are also relatively plentiful in winter in other western parts of Scotland.

The total numbers of diurnal sightings of hunting harriers within 24 kilometres of Roost 1, varied little between October and February, but were less than half as many in September and March (Table 30). These figures and the roost counts (Fig. 13) suggest that many of the harriers were winter immigrants to the area (see also discussion of counts at Roosts 1 and 2, Chapter 18).

Harriers dispersing to hunt from Roost 2, in a coastal area, frequently hunted lowland fields and marginal land. Such habitats were easily accessible to the roost and covered a wide area. Small areas of moorland and young conifer forest were available near the roost but the harriers would have had to travel at least 8–10 kilometres to find large areas of moorland and the pellet analyses from this roost suggest that they did not regularly hunt these areas. Extensive young conifer forests were considerably more distant.

CHAPTER EIGHTEEN

COMMUNAL ROOSTING IN WINTER

INTRODUCTION

I have referred in Chapter 1 to the habit of communal roosting among harriers and noted that it occurs in at least six species.

The earliest reference to this habit in the Hen Harrier appears to belong to Selby (1831) who wrote: 'It roosts upon the ground in very long heath or ling and generally in companies of five or six together, males and females indiscriminately'. There is, however, no certainty that Selby's observations preceded those of Sir William Jardine or, indeed, that he discovered the behaviour independently, as the two men corresponded and made expeditions together. Jardine (1834–38) gave a fuller account and there is every reason to believe that this referred to his native Dumfriesshire in Scotland. He noted that after the young were 'perfectly grown they, with the old birds, left the high country and returned . . . to hunt fields of grain with great regularity.' He continued: 'At night they seem to have general roosting places, either among whins or very long heath, and always on some spot of open ground. On a moor of considerable extent I have seen seven in one acre. They began to approach the sleeping ground about sunset; and, before going to roost, hunted the whole moor, crossing each other, often three or four in view at a time, gliding along in the same manner as described by Dr Richardson of the C. Americanus [the Marsh Hawk]. When they approached the roost they skim three or four times over it, to see there is no interruption and then at once drop into the spot.'

Although it was to be expected that with the decline of the Hen Harrier during the nineteenth century the opportunities for observing communal roosting would become fewer, it is perhaps surprising that during all the rest of that century and, indeed, well into the twentieth, no further references to the habit can be found. Macpherson (1892) however, gave the following account of a 'pair' roosting together in the winter of 1886. 'They were adult and had appeared in the same locality [Weddholm and Bowness Flows, Cumberland] in previous winters but had never remained to breed. Smith noticed the spot in which they roosted in tall heather and, after watching them for several weeks, killed one and then the other.' Walpole-Bond (1914), also, said that 'in Orkney a pair in winter patronise a special roosting site in very long ling' and the gamekeeper naturalist, Dugald Macintyre (1947), wrote: 'the keeper saw Circus and his less perfectly plumaged son meet together at dusk, after each had consumed a Snipe, and he noticed the direction in which the couple flew to roost. Their roosting place was on a bank of very tall heather and there were piles of castings on the ground.' In March, he watched a pair fly in company from their home glen each morning. 'They parted, on reaching the first marsh, to hunt in different directions but, the hunt over, they met and flew home together, to roost side by side in the heather.'

It is remarkable that the next British reference to communal roosting should come from Kent, a district where the Hen Harrier's status is that of a far from plentiful visitor from autumn till spring. This account of a roost of up to three males and two ringtails in Walland Marsh during November and December 1953, by F. J. Walker, appeared in the *Kent Bird Report* for that year and was later mentioned in *British Birds* 49 (1956). The birds roosted in tall grass growing in 15–22 centimetres of water. These accounts seem to have passed almost unnoticed by most ornithologists.

Meanwhile, communal roosting of the Marsh Hawk had been observed in Florida, by Stoddard (1931). He wrote: 'This species has the unhawklike habit of roosting on the ground, frequenting the same spot night after night. If numerous the hawks form a loose roosting group numbering from two to three, to as many as thirty. A large field grown up to heavy broom sedge and preferably upon a hilltop is chosen as a roosting site. Each bird has a beaten-down spot in the sedge, well "limed" with droppings.' Further accounts of Marsh Hawk roosts, in Pennsylvania, were given by Randall (1940); in Missouri by Weller (1955), in Michigan by the Craigheads (1956), and in Indiana by Mumford (1975). All these roosts were on the ground, with vegetation tall enough to provide cover for the birds, in otherwise open country. Sites were either wet, with vegetation growing in several centimetres of standing water, or dry among tall prairie grass or a luxuriant growth of weeds on stubble or wasteland. The Craigheads noted a maximum of 48 birds at a roost in late January–early February and Mumford counted at least 60 on 24 January.

Brown and Amadon suggest that communal roosts may be more common in the Marsh Hawk than in the Hen Harrier, but a number of recent
European accounts indicate that they occur in most or all of the regions
where the winter population of Hen Harriers is considerable.

Roosts in Germany have been described by Baron Geyr and Haas
(1957), by Andris (1970) and by Jakobs (1971). Wassenich (1968) studied a
roost in the Grand Duchy of Luxembourg and Mois (1975) has given an account of roosting at two sites in Belgian Lorraine, where detailed observations were made from 1968 to 1974. Several roosts in the Netherlands
have been closely studied by Schipper and others since 1969–70, in which
season a maximum count of 54 birds was noted at one roost. In cor-
respondence, Schipper has told me that more than 60 birds were seen at a
roost in Bulgaria by Johnson and Biber.

Later in this chapter the study of communal roosts in south-west
Scotland, between 1966 and 1976, is described. Maxima of at least 30 birds
have been seen at two different roosts in this region. This account adds new
material to, and modifies, some conclusions in an earlier publication (Watson and Dickson, 1972).

The late Ernest Blezard told me of a small roost in the southern
Highlands of Scotland, discovered by E. Blake in 1960, while from 1971
onwards Balfour and Green observed several roosts in Orkney. The latter
were generally small but at one roost up to 20 birds were noted. Other
roosts—none very large—have been found within recent years on Deeside
by N. Picozzi, in Speyside by D. N. Weir, in the Inner Hebrides by R. H. Hogg,
Allan Goodin and others, and in south-west Ireland by Frank King.

Descriptions of these roosting grounds generally show a similarity with
those of the Marsh Hawk, but in Europe by far the majority of sites is in
damp or marshy ground. In Flevoland, Netherlands, the birds roost close
together in small reed-beds but are well scattered in larger tracts of reeds
(Schipper, pers. comm.). All the Orkney sites are on marshy ground, especially among reeds, but in autumn and early winter when reed beds are
still dense the birds tend to favour rank, mixed vegetation, with plants such
as meadow sweet (*Filipendula ulmaria*). At the first site discovered in
Belgian Lorraine the ground was marshy but flooding apparently caused the
harriers to desert this site. Thereafter they roosted in drier conditions on an
extensive, sloping heather moor, three kilometres from the first site.

The only sites on perfectly dry ground have been reported, by Andris, on
wasteland in the Upper Rhine valley. King, however, found the most exceptional roosting site of all, in Kerry, Ireland; the birds spent the night in a low
ragged hawthorn hedge, on neglected farmland which had reverted to moor.
His observations at this site were made only in October, over two years,
when the hedge was still leafy, and he doubted if it would provide sufficient
cover later in the winter.

Counts at most winter roosts in Europe show an excess of ringtails over adult males. The most striking exception was the Irish roost where, in October, all the birds—up to ten—were adult males, although ringtails occasionally appeared at the roost but drifted away. King considers that the numbers of adult males in south-west Ireland decline, later in the year, perhaps due to emigration, while many ringtails remain all winter. In Belgian Lorraine Mois found that males exceeded females by two or three to one between October and the beginning of March, but during March and April there was usually an excess of females. A similar pattern of change in the proportions of males and females was found at roosts in Luxembourg by Wassenich and in Eifel, Germany, by Jakobs.

Elsewhere, the only region where adult males sometimes equal or exceed ringtails at roosts is south-west Scotland, most often in the autumn or early winter. The highest total numbers at roosts in south-west Scotland were recorded between November and January, but in the Netherlands and West Germany peaks were reached in February. In Belgian Lorraine the highest total was only 11 birds, but over seven winters a fairly regular pattern of fluctuations emerged. Peak counts occurred in mid November, late January–early February and in mid–late March.

COMMUNAL ROOSTING IN SOUTH-WEST SCOTLAND

When, in November 1959, I saw a ringtail harrier gliding down at dusk above a forest slope, to drop silently into a wide flat expanse of boggy grassland, the possibility that this might be a site for a communal roost did not occur to me. At that time the winter population in the region was extremely small and, anyway, I was not aware that Hen Harriers had ever formed large roosts in the British Isles.

Over the next few years, I sometimes paused on an evening above the big flat, or flow, and obtained a fleeting view of two or three harriers as they flapped and glided over the orange and ochre grasses. I saw them hesitate and drop out of sight in the tall cover, sometimes rising again to seek a different spot. Once, happening to approach in the hour before sunrise, with the moon still bright in the sky, I was listening to the calls of Fieldfares and Redwings crossing the forest, when I spotted a cock harrier on his first morning flight away from the roost. Yet it was not until 1966, after receiving a postcard from Alan Paterson, announcing that he had seen ten Hen Harriers in the vicinity of the flow (it seemed an incredible number at the time), that I decided to watch the site carefully.

At first I was disappointed, not to say disheartened. Much of January 1966 was bitterly cold, with severe frosts; sometimes wreaths of white mist settled at ground level and made observation futile. Also, some of my first watches were too distant from the more favoured roosting sites and it would have been particularly easy to miss the light-coloured males as they flickered against a background of pale grass. Later I discovered that this roost was

never occupied by many harriers in still, frosty weather, for reasons which are still a subject for speculation, so it was not really surprising that my highest score after the first four watches was still only four birds. Then, on 19 March 1967, a day of gusty north-west wind tossing the old shreds of purple moorgrass about the sky, we found a good vantage point and waited without much expectation. It happened to be one of the rather rare nights, after occupation of breeding grounds has already begun, when turbulent weather seems to force a late resumption of communal roosting. From 50 minutes before, until 20 minutes after sunset we made a cautious estimate of ten to twelve ringtails and two adult males.

Against the lingering light of a spring evening, even the grey males were darkly silhouetted and the ringtails looked black and menacing. We stayed, fascinated, till all the birds seemed to have settled and the light had become too murky for further watching. We would return, above all, to enjoy the mysterious spectacle of these gatherings in a quiet and lonely landscape, but as time went on it became compulsive to observe each facet of their behaviour and attempt to understand the motivation that lay behind it. Unknown to me at the time, R. C. Dickson had discovered and begun to watch another roost since September 1966. Later we pooled our experience and wrote a joint account of Hen Harriers roosting in south-west Scotland (Watson and Dickson, 1972). In the present account, these two major roosts are referred to as Roosts 1 and 2, respectively, as explained in the Introductory Note to the chapters on the Hen Harrier in south-west Scotland.

Over the years a number of friends have shared my vigils and others have watched independently. Many have contributed information. The interest and fieldcraft of Louis Urquhart, with whom I have shared so many watches, have been unflagging and Jeffrey Watson, apart from taking part in a number of watches, has especially stimulated discussion on roosting behaviour. Records have been kept, including counts of roosting harriers, time spanned by arrival or departure, behaviour, and weather, for nearly 170 evening watches and ten in the morning at Roost 1. Evening watches have generally been from about 45 minutes before sunset until it was almost dark; in the mornings, the period from about 40 minutes before, till half an hour, or more, after sunrise was covered. R. C. Dickson has maintained a fairly similar series of watches at Roost 2, where David L. Irving has also made a number of counts. R. H. Hogg has made several counts at both roosts. In 1970–71, R. C. Dickson found another roost near Roost 2 and obtained some evidence that individual harriers moved between these two. I occasionally found very small numbers occupying a fourth roost, intermediate between Roosts 1 and 2.

Not the least memorable aspect of these frequently damp and chilly occasions was the variety of wildlife incidentally observed. Sometimes, however, when harriers were slow to appear, the swiftly changing spectacle of a Galloway hill landscape beneath a wild evening sky was sufficient compensation in itself.

Description of roosts

The site of Roost 1 is a long inland valley, skirted on the north by a stream above which the ground rises gradually to form a range of hills heavily afforested with conifers. To the south the hills are open and grassy, with patches of short heather and bracken and many outcrops of rock.

The valley is about 75 metres above sea level, with an area of virtually flat boggy ground extending over some 125 hectares, but the usual roosting sites are in a section of about 16 hectares. The vegetation is very rank, consisting of purple moorgrass, sedges, rushes, cotton grass and sphagnum mosses, with some tall stands of reeds in the wettest parts and an occasional willow bush. The ground cover is mostly 75 centimetres or more in height. Several dry rocky hillocks are grassy or sparsely covered with heather. Apart from these, and a narrow stretch of firm ground beside the stream, almost the whole area is extremely boggy and difficult for a man to traverse unless it is frostbound. Sheep, however, are able to forage over parts of it.

The area is thoroughly water-logged by normal winter rainfall and, at first, I supposed that the harriers must sometimes roost with their feet in standing water because they continued to occupy the roost in even the wettest weather. However, after making daytime visits in search of their precise roosting places, I concluded that matted vegetation, trampled into 'beds' by the birds themselves, may always have provided a platform to support them. These 'beds', or forms, were mostly found among a strong growth of rushes; some had a base of sphagnum. From observation of birds settling, it was clear that several birds often roosted in close proximity,

though a few were sometimes widely dispersed. Examination of the ground revealed many 'beds' separated by a metre or less, and some more or less contiguous, but only a proportion of them could have been occupied on any one night. None showed signs of long continuous occupation since most contained only one pellet. A few had two, three or even five pellets, and some none at all. In recent years, the main concentration of roosting birds sometimes shifted by several hundred metres, but these changes were generally temporary and the most favoured ground is still the same as ten years ago. At times, from December onwards, a few birds roosted among the tall reeds; presumably winter weather flattened or broke down sufficient stems to make some sort of platform, even there.

The roosting area of Roost 2 has been described by Dickson as: 'a low-lying coastal moor, separated from the sea by a series of sandhills planted with a belt of young conifers. The roost proper is an area of about 23 hectares, with dense heather dominant and, in the area favoured by the roosting harriers, up to a metre tall, with a field-layer of bog moss and cotton grass; in winter the ground is sometimes waterlogged. The area is ungrazed by domestic animals and natural regeneration by Scots pine is taking place in some parts of the moor.' Heather gives way to rushes, purple moorgrass and bracken on the fringes of the moor, with clumps of willow, rowan, birch and gorse, and on one side a spread of rhododendrons. Dickson found, however, that the harriers roosted in the long heather 'creating trampled platforms, or forms, half a metre to a metre in diameter, of dead, bent grey heather stalks'. Some forms showed signs of repeated use, sometimes on consecutive nights. He commented that Short-eared Owls probably used the forms by day since their pellets were also found there. The Craigheads found that a Marsh Hawk roost was also occupied by Short-eared Owls in daytime, some owls

arriving in the mornings before the Marsh Hawks had left.

The satellite Roost 3 which Dickson found, 2.4 kilometres from Roost 2, is also on marshy ground, interspersed with dry banks of heather and bracken, and there is an extensive area of thick willows. The harriers roosted between the trees among the heather, bracken and grasses. As at Roost 1, they generally concentrated within 15–20 hectares although the entire area covers 150–200 hectares. This roost is only '200–300 metres from high-water mark'. Roost 4, never much used by the harriers, is a fairly wide expanse of level, rough grassland, partly heathery and rushy, in the vicinity of a conifer plantation. It is also on low ground near the coast.

The main features of the roosts may be summarised as follows. All are on flat ground and the three which have been occupied regularly (Roosts 1–3) are boggy, even heavily waterlogged at times. These three roosts are also virtually free from human intrusion, partly because access is either difficult or discouraged, and partly because of the boggy nature of the ground. Roost 4, on the other hand, was drier, hence more accessible, and was liable to intrusion by shooters or other people. Almost certainly this disturbance prevented it being used regularly by the harriers. Nevertheless at Roost 1 and 2 it was clear that the presence of human beings near the perimeters of the roosting areas, providing they did not enter them while the birds were in occupation, did not discourage the harriers noticeably.

At Roost 1, occasional flight-shooting of duck and geese from the stream bank, less than 50 metres from the edge of the roost, caused temporary disturbance but the harriers re-occupied their favourite sites on the ground nearest to where shooting occurred, either later the same night or within a night or two after shooting ceased. It was, however, quite likely that harriers were sometimes shot on these occasions. At Roost 2, traffic on a public road passed the perimeter of the roost and had no effect on the birds, but the possibility that birdwatchers who left their cars to obtain better views of the harriers might draw unwelcome attention to the birds, in an area where harriers are known to be disliked by keepers, could not be ruled out.

Although the roosting grounds were generally open enough to give the birds uninterrupted views of any predators from the air, their vision from the ground must have been limited by the tall vegetation, especially among the willow bushes at Roost 3. They probably relied much on hearing to warn them of danger while they were on the ground, and there is little doubt that the tendency to gather in close-knit groups facilitated mutual warning. It is likely that the choice of marshy ground for roosting is a deterrent to foxes, the most probable danger apart from man; yet, as stated earlier, large roosts on dry ground are known elsewhere. It seems to me more likely that lack of disturbance by man *on the actual roosting ground*, and the need for shelter and concealment, are the principal factors in roost site selection. In most parts of mainland Britain it cannot be too easy to find extensive areas fulfilling these conditions and they are nowadays most likely to be found in bogland.

I have often wondered why Hen Harriers appear never to roost in trees. Presumably in their traditional habitats of steppe, moor and marsh, roosting on the ground was generally obligatory. Even so, the conifer forests which adjoin the main roosting grounds in south-west Scotland seem to offer an alternative which might be safer; and it would be interesting to know how the habit of roosting above ground, in a hedge, has arisen in Ireland.

Arrival at the roost

The evening arrival of harriers at Roost 1 was generally spread over a period of 40 minutes to an hour or more. Arrivals of more than ten birds were occasionally completed in as little as half an hour; the longest period was more than 83 minutes (16 birds). Once, in November, some 30 harriers reached the roost in only 40 minutes, but most of the highest totals were spread over more than an hour. Nothing resembling the mass arrival 'in one flock', described by the Craigheads for the Marsh Hawk, was ever seen, although up to five birds very occasionally appeared together. Usually the birds came in singly, sometimes with gaps of ten to fifteen minutes without new arrivals.

Harriers approached the roost from all directions, but the majority came from the east or north and very few from the south-west. This pattern fitted well with the diurnal evidence of preferred hunting grounds and was confirmed by morning observation of flight-lines away from the roost. Habitat between the south-west and north-west was largely mountainous with extensive afforestation, compared with a mixture of farmland, moor, marsh and forest or woodland to the east and north. Most adult males arrived from points between south-east and north, whereas ringtails predominated, strikingly, among those which arrived from westerly directions.

Clearly the pattern of arrival depended greatly on weather conditions during the day and at roosting time. On wet and stormy nights with early darkness, some or all came to roost earlier than on fine evenings. It was also noticeable that when the weather cleared towards the end of a very wet day, birds were slow to reach the roost and presumably took advantage of the clearance for late hunting. The subsequent manner of arrival and behaviour

was also much influenced by weather conditions.

One or two birds sometimes hunted the near vicinity of the roost during the day, and these were almost certainly the individuals which were occasionally seen over the roost as much as an hour and a half before sunset. The earliest record of a bird settling to roost was about 70 minutes before sunset. On the very wet November night, when some 30 birds arrived in 40 minutes, all settled before sunset; but generally the first arrivals were between 15 and 30 minutes before sunset and the majority appeared during the next half hour. The last birds reached the roost up to about 45 minutes past sunset. These late arrivals nearly always dropped swiftly into cover. It may be asked how it was known that no more came in after darkness prevented observation. The long series of watches, usually maintained until five or ten minutes after activity seemed to have ceased, made this an unlikely possibility, nor was this belief disproved by any of the morning counts. No obvious segregation of the sexes, such as Weis noted in Montagu's Harriers, was observed at any of the roosts.

At our favourite observation place, some protection from the elements was provided by thicket stage conifers from among which we could command a long view of all except the northerly approaches to the roost. From that side, the first view of a bird was often when it appeared close overhead, not much above tree-top height. Some of the most memorable evenings were those when wind and rain swept across from the west and many birds came labouring up the valley from the east, in low-level flapping flight. On such occasions a procession of three or four well-spaced birds might be in view at once. On dry nights they tended to come in high; and so many were unseen until they appeared, almost miraculously, right over the roosting area, that we surmised that their initial approach may have been at a great height. Fine nights with a fresh or strong breeze were occasions for aerobatics, as many as five or six birds circling and playfully diving at each other, obviously in no hurry to settle.

Unless the weather was either very windy or wet, some of the earlier arrivals always perched for a while, sometimes for 15 or 20 minutes, on posts, hillocks, rocks or a stone dyke overlooking the roosting sites. This was particularly noticeable on the evening of 23 November 1975 when the weather suddenly cleared after a very wet day; four ringtail harriers remained perched and preening on adjacent posts, and one on a nearby rock, for the best part of 20 minutes. This may have been no more than a 'drying out' exercise but, since they represented part of a sudden increase in numbers of ringtails, they could well have been tired birds which had just completed a migrational flight. The weather pattern was almost exactly similar on 3 November 1974 when, again, four ringtails had perched close together on the perimeter of the roost for over ten minutes before flying in.

Schipper (pers. comm.) had the impression, at a communal roost in Flevoland, that birds from hunting ranges with low numbers of voles arrived late at the roost. At Roost 1, early arrivals in wet and stormy weather suggested that it was unprofitable to continue hunting late in such conditions. It seemed likely that the spread of arrival time depended to some extent on the distances to hunting grounds. On 28 October and 6 November 1975, the same number of birds (six) and the same proportion of males and ringtails came to the roost. They arrived in the following sequences:

	28 October			6 November	
male	sunset	− 3 min.	male	sunset	− 8 min.
ringtail	„	+ 5	ringtail	„	+ 1
male	„	+11	male	„	+10
ringtail	„	+15	ringtail	„	+13
ringtail	„	+19	ringtail	„	+18
male	„	+25	male	„	+24

It seems probable that the same individuals were concerned on both evenings, and the very similar intervals of time might have been due to the distances they had to travel from hunting grounds. Both evenings were fine, with light winds.

I often wondered how Hen Harriers which were newcomers to the district discovered the roost. Although hunting ranges were widely dispersed and it was unusual to see two or more harriers hunting within sight of each other, a newcomer was perhaps able to make visual contact with birds familiar with the roost and to follow their flight direction. A second year male was once seen apparently following an older male into the roosting area, and on many occasions the arrival of two or more birds within sight of each other was consistent with the above suggestion. It was not known whether the same birds ever occupied the same 'beds' on successive nights.

Most of the birds arrived at the roost with full crops. This was easy to detect in females (if they flew close enough) because a full crop bulged like a pouch, but it was much less obvious in males. The difference presumably reflects the difference in average weights of prey taken by the sexes. Further observations would be necessary to find out if a significantly higher proportion of birds regularly arrived with empty crops after days of bad hunting weather, but on 24 November 1974, a very wet day, I noted that of those clearly seen none had full crops.

Harrier relationships at the roost

Birds which had found a roosting spot were frequently displaced by others. As might be expected, this was most common when the total number of birds was high. Usually, ringtails drove out males; and I had the impression, from relative size, that if a ringtail was displaced by a male it was always a first year male. A female often flew deliberately to a spot where a male had settled and drove him out by diving with lowered feet. On one extraordinary occasion, a large female dived at a spot where we had seen a male drop and, as if by a conjurer's trick, two males sprang up from the same spot. There was also an indication of a hierarchy according to age, because some birds would be driven out more than once on the same night and whenever these were clearly seen they were recognisable as first or second year males. When the roost was most crowded, one or two of these 'junior' birds sometimes flew to and fro for a long time and only found an undisturbed spot after all the others had settled.

Gurr (1968) has suggested that in the case of the Australasian Harrier, communal roosting may facilitate pairing. At roosts of Hen Harriers in Belgian Lorraine, behaviour which suggested that birds were paired or pairing was observed several times in March or April. A male was repeatedly seen to leave a group of harriers already at the roost and fly to meet a distant incoming female. The male and female then flew into the roosting area together but subsequently separated. When, in April 1969, only one male and one female were continuing to use a roost, whichever arrived first would wait for the other and fly out to meet it as soon as it appeared in sight. The two birds then settled beside each other (Mois, 1975).

The following observations at Roost 1 may indicate paired or pairing behaviour:

(1) On 17 March 1970, two adult males—one a noticeably dark, blue-

grey bird, suggesting some melanism—had alighted conspicuously on tussocks of yellow grass, prior to going to roost. The lighter male was approached by a female which alighted within a few metres without aggression and so they remained for several minutes. Shortly afterwards, the same or a different female had settled beside the darker male and these two had also stayed together amicably for some minutes. Later they dispersed to roost separately.

(2) On 19 December 1971, a female circling over forest near the roost was approached by two incoming males. They all circled together for a minute or so; then one male closely followed the female into the roosting area and settled beside her at a 'pre-roosting' spot on the ground. The second male approached again and both males rose and flew low over the roosting ground, one just below the other in the manner described by Balfour as the 'escorting' flight of a bird 'seeing off' an intruder on the nesting ground.

(3) On 4 February 1973 (cf 17 March 1970), two adult males alighted close together, conspicuously, on tussocks in the roosting area. I observed a female rise from where she had been perched in the open and fly to a roosting site among rushes. The lighter-coloured of the two males immediately flew to where she had pitched and almost stalled above her. He then swung away and dropped into a roosting site a little distance away. There was no conflict between the two birds. Shortly after the second, darker male, evidently a fairly young bird, flew and attempted unsuccessfully to displace the light male, then settled elsewhere. The light male rose again and was displaced from another roosting site by a different female. He settled to roost a third time in a new site and a female, from the rushy site, almost certainty the bird he had 'visited' earlier, rose and flew directly for at least 50 metres, to drop close beside him without any attempt at displacement.

(4) On 6 December 1973, an adult male and a ringtail (? female) circled together over the roost for five minutes, the male flying briefly with loosely flapping wings, suggestive of display flight. They then dropped, apparently to roost, in the same area but the ringtail twice put up the male and thereafter, for another seven minutes, the two birds circled close together, much like a pair in spring, and finally settled to roost not far apart.

(5) On 24 December 1975, in the morning, an adult male and a female, after rising, alighted and perched for several minutes within a metre or two of each other on a hillock in the roosting area.

Even as late as 1 April a female was seen to displace a male in an apparently aggressive manner, but the female of a pair on their nesting ground dives at her mate in much the same way. The obvious tendency for females to displace males at the roost should perhaps be regarded as an aspect of sexual behaviour, rather than simple dominance by the stronger over the weaker. It is perhaps worth noting that the roosting 'beds' of harriers are rather similar to their actual nests.

As already mentioned, high soaring flight before settling to roost was often seen on fine windy nights. Mois recorded similar aerial manoeuvres over a roost in Belgian Lorraine, in the same weather conditions. There, however, females rarely shared in these flights, while in Galloway both adult males and ringtails, which certainly included some females, took part. Up to eight harriers were seen behaving in this manner together, sometimes diving at and buffeting one another, apparently playfully. On these occasions they looked not unlike kites. In common with the habit of perching conspicuously before roosting, these flights might advertise the presence of harriers at the roost and attract others. Newcomers, and birds which had hunted unsuccessfully, could recognise birds which arrived with full crops and might profit from observing their flight-lines from hunting grounds.

Hunting at the roost

In the early days of roost-watching, I thought that the attraction of the marshy site might be partly for crepuscular feeding. Certainly it looked an excellent habitat for water voles and there was some possible bird prey, such as Snipe, Reed Buntings, Meadow Pipits, Skylarks, Wrens and occasional Stonechats. Larger birds might also have been taken, since a few Red and Black Grouse regularly flew to roost on the same ground as the harriers. Yet the harriers showed little interest in prey at the roost, quite often disturbing small birds or grouse which they made no attempt to capture. On a few occasions, early arrivals did appear to be hunting the margins of the area; for instance, on 21 October 1970, three males were hunting and one was seen to rise from the grass with small prey, and on 15 February 1974, a ringtail dropped from a post and flew up with a small capture. On another night, a ringtail made a rather casual dive at a Snipe which had risen ahead of it but did not press the attack. Remains of water voles and beetles, including the great water beetle, were found in harrier pellets at Roost 1, and it is possible that such prey was taken after the birds had settled on the ground. The overall impression, however, is that the roosting ground had little significance as a hunting area. Red and Black Grouse were alarmed and rose only when a harrier flew close above them and they continued to share the roost with the harriers throughout the whole period. A pair of Stonechats frequented the harriers' favourite roosting patch for several weeks during October–November of one year. They disappeared later and it is possible that they were taken, but the habitat was only marginally suitable for them and it is equally possible that they moved away. Dickson records regular pre-roost hunting around the rhododendron bushes on the perimeter of Roost 2. Black Grouse also roosted among the harriers there.

Relations with other birds and mammals including man

Apart from possible prey species, the only other birds seen at the roost which ever caused any reaction from the harriers were crows, owls and other birds of prey. Harriers sometimes dived at Carrion Crows or the latter chased and mobbed harriers. A Barn Owl frequently hunted over the roost, though mostly around the perimeter. Both it and the occasional Short-eared Owl became involved in brief aerial tussles with harriers, but a Barn Owl hunting the perimeter was usually ignored. At Roost 2, aerial conflicts between harriers, Short-eared Owls and Merlins were common and I have described in Chapter 4 how a Merlin and a harrier competed for prey there. At Roost 1, Merlins, Sparrowhawks and Peregrines were all irregular visitors; of these only a Peregrine, which perched on a hillock in the roosting ground, received a sustained diving onslaught from a male harrier, which failed to dislodge it. A Sparrowhawk once joined two harriers in a high circling flight, and all three birds stooped playfully at each other.

Foxes were occasionally seen at or near all three major roosts but the tall vegetation made it impossible to follow their progress. They were never positively seen among the harriers, but Dickson saw twelve harriers at Roost 3 circling, diving at and following an unknown predator which was probably a fox. On other occasions, a number of harriers were seen to rise from their roosting places for no apparent reason, occasionally chattering in alarm, and the presence of a fox or other ground predator was suspected. Otters haunted the margin of Roost 1 in some winters and once I saw a ringtail dive at the spot where two otters had just disappeared into tall vegetation. On 8 December 1969, I experienced a communal reaction to my own presence while I was watching the roost from a slightly exposed view-point. A ringtail approached overhead, landed briefly on the stream bank some 50 metres away and began to chatter. She then flew towards me, hesitated, but returned to make a low level attack with arched wings, exactly like a bird in defence of its nest. She climbed again, without striking, then repeated the attack. Her chattering cries were taken up by at least five more birds which left the roosting ground and approached me. Two more ringtails and a male circled close above my head without attacking. As soon as I gained some concealment the chattering ceased and the birds drifted back and began to settle again. It had been a remarkable and slightly eerie episode and I could not help wondering if the ringtail which attacked me was a local breeding bird, which might have recognised me as the particular villain who had infuriated her by visiting her nest (see Balfour's comment on recognition of himself in Chapter 6). Dickson had a rather similar experience on the night when he discovered Roost 3; first a ringtail rose, chattering, after which other harriers began to call and circle overhead. This behaviour was repeated on later occasions when the birds were disturbed at this roost.

The influence of weather on numbers of harriers at the roost

Although no other roost has been found in the neighbourhood of Roost 1, at times some or even most of the harriers in the district evidently roosted elsewhere. On a number of occasions birds flew into the roost area and passed out of view without alighting, but it was impossible to be certain that the same birds did not return later. Sometimes birds rose and left the roost after they had settled; for example, on 27 December 1970, a ringtail settled and rose again three times before spiralling high into the sky where it was joined by three other ringtails; all four then flew off, losing height as they went, as if about to land, distantly, in the forest.

Throughout all the winters, the numbers of harriers at Roost 1 showed marked fluctuations in different weather conditions. The highest counts occurred in windy and, usually, fairly mild weather, and the lowest on calm and generally cold nights. The roost was always sparsely attended in hard frost. Diurnal sightings (see Table 30a) do not indicate any marked change in the numbers of harriers hunting the area, within 24 kilometres of the roost, between October and February, thus supporting the view that a proportion must sometimes have roosted elsewhere, probably within this area. The following observations may throw some light on this question:

(1) Just before sunset on 20 November 1976, I saw two ringtails drop as if about to roost in tall grass at the edge of a young forest plantation about 16 kilometres north-east of Roost 1. They had been hunting the forest area in company. Weather was cold with light wind. None roosted in this area on 21 or 22 November, although there was no marked change in the weather.

(2) About sunrise on 2 December 1976, in very cold, calm weather, Philip

Coxon flushed a ringtail from a marshy islet close to a river bank, in a valley about 8 kilometres from Roost 1. It seemed highly probable that the harrier had roosted on the islet.

I can only speculate on how and why the weather influenced the numbers attending Roost 1 whereas it did not do so, significantly, at Roost 2. It seemed unlikely that a large alternative roost remained undiscovered near Roost 1. It may have been important that the best hunting grounds appeared to be more widely dispersed from Roost 1 than from Roost 2 (see below). This may have been particularly true when hard frost or snow reduced the effective hunting grounds in the near neighbourhood of Roost 1; the harriers might then conserve energy by remaining to roost on or near the more distant hunting grounds, either singly or in groups. In contrast birds at Roost 2 could nearly always find good hunting grounds in the surrounding low-lying coastal area which escaped the worst severities of the weather. My own guess is that harriers find travelling flight much easier when the wind is fresh or strong, from whatever direction, and that lengthy journeys consume most time and energy in windless conditions (they might then remain to roost, either singly or in small groups, on or near the more distant hunting grounds). In late winter some might roost on local breeding grounds, although none were proved to do so before mid-March.

The shelter provided by the communal roosting sites could obviously be a special attraction in wet and windy weather. On particularly stormy nights the birds tended to crowd into a small area; this would be an advantage in mutual warning of danger, especially through alarm calls. Although the marshy roosting grounds were obviously more accessible to foxes in frosty weather, no other site was likely to be safer, unless it was in trees well clear of the ground or, perhaps, on an island as suggested by Philip Coxon's observation. On the very cold night of 26 December 1976, I noticed that the single harrier (a male), which came to Roost 1, dropped into the only part of the roosting ground which was not white with frost.

Seasonal fluctuations at the roosts; sex and age structure of the roosting population

Counts at Roost 1 in all the winters since 1967–68 are shown in Fig. 13. Monthly aggregates of peak counts over eight winters, at Roosts 1 and 2, are compared in Figs 14 and 15. The highest nightly totals tended to occur in November at Roost 1, and in December and January at Roost 2. These probably reflect winter immigration into the region and onward movement to lower ground as winter advances.

At both roosts adult males often made up a high proportion of all the birds early in the winter, ringtails usually predominating from November onwards. At Roost 1, adult males regularly outnumbered ringtails in October. (It may be recalled that Frank King found up to ten adult males, with no ringtails, at a roost in south-west Ireland in October.) It is possible that

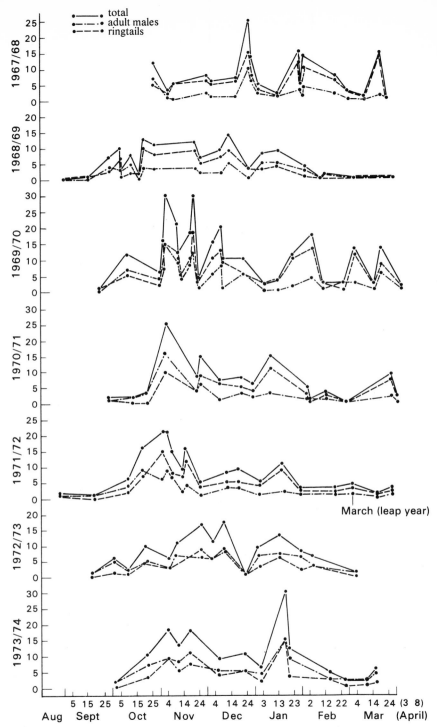

Fig. 13   Numbers of Hen Harriers at Roost 1, Sept.–March, 1967–76

252

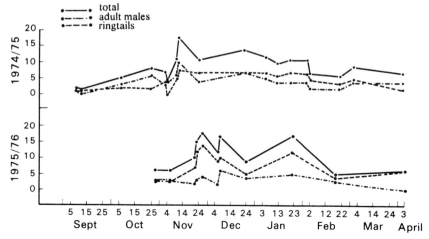

Fig. 13 (contd.)   Numbers of Hen Harriers at Roost 1, Sept.–March, 1967–76

this early winter predominance of adult males consists largely of local breeding birds remaining behind after many females and young have migrated or dispersed (see Chapter 7).

Some of the greatest fluctuations in numbers at Roost 1 appear to be correlated with changes in weather conditions, as already explained; for example an exceptionally high January count of at least 30 birds, with adult males and ringtails about equal, occurred after more than a week of westerly gales and torrential rain. It is not known whether such mid-winter peaks were caused by fairly local changes in distribution, or by longer distance immigration from regions which might have been evacuated owing to poor hunting conditions or a reduction of available prey, in unfavourable weather. No immediate correlation between changes in numbers at Roosts 1 and 2 was evident. It seems likely, however, that Hen Harriers wintering over a very large area form a dynamic population between different gathering points, at roosts, as suggested by Mois for Luxembourg, the Eifel district of Germany and north-east France.

Small peaks in March, at Roost 1, may have been caused by migrants returning to the vicinity of breeding grounds; these did not occur at Roost 2 which was more distant from any breeding locality. The strongest suggestion, that some birds which bred near Roost 1 sometimes used this roost, comes from the following observations. On 30 March 1975, I saw no sign of harriers during a day spent largely in a breeding area. On 1 April, six harriers, including at least four adult males, came to the roost. On 6 April the roost was deserted, and on the following day a pair were over the breeding area all day and roosted there.

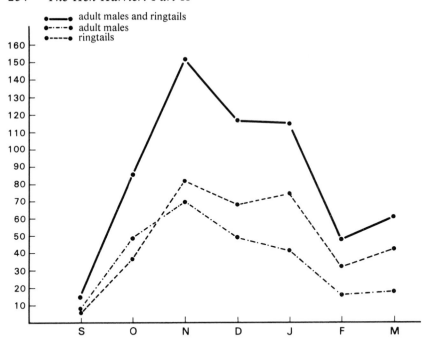

Fig. 14   Aggregates of monthly peak counts of Hen Harriers during eight winters at Roost 1

It may also be noted (see Figs 13 and 14–15) that the highest numbers occurred at Roost 1, in the winter of 1969–70, and that in the following summer there was a small peak in the local breeding population.

It was impossible to judge whether female harriers at the roost were first year or older birds. First year males could be distinguished from females, by size and shape, if clearly seen. They were never numerous but one or two were generally present among every ten to fifteen ringtails. Among the birds classed as adult males, a remarkably high proportion (usually more than 75% at Roost 1) were considered to be second winter birds, judging from their very dark (dusky or dusky-brown) mantles. Dickson commented that a high proportion of males at Roost 2 were likewise. This might be an indication that few males survive long enough to attain the full grey plumage; or possibly that, for some reason, older males were disinclined to join the communal roosts.

Departure from the roosts

Harriers were seen to leave Roost 1 between 53 minutes before, and 47 minutes after, sunrise. The majority left before sunrise. Departures from Roost 2 had later averages, the earliest recorded by Dickson being 20 minutes before sunrise and the latest 45 minutes after sunrise. It was

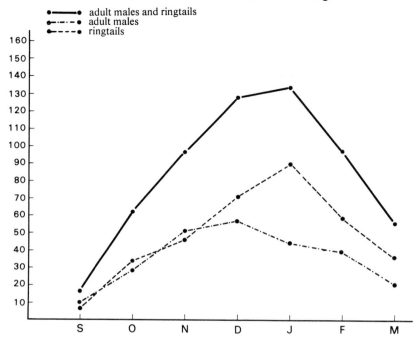

● ● adult males and ringtails
●—·—·—●   adult males
●— — —●   ringtails

Fig. 15   Aggregates of monthly peak counts of Hen Harriers during eight winters at Roost 2

generally difficult, or impossible, to obtain satisfactory counts in the morning at Roost 1; ringtails were particularly difficult to spot as they flew above the brown grass in dim early light, and mist in the valley was sometimes a further handicap. Most of the birds left the roost area quickly, and dispersed in different directions. They rose a few metres into the air above their roosting sites, often shaking their feathers, and either proceeded in direct low-level flight, or circled to a considerable height and drifted away more slowly. Once, a ringtail which had risen from the roost flew for a short distance and dipped to disturb another ringtail, as if chasing it out of bed. When first rising, the birds sometimes seemed, literally, to jump out of cover. Twice, a male and a ringtail kept close together as they flew away and, once, two ringtails behaved similarly. On 24 December 1975, I followed the course of six departing birds as far as possible; they fanned out in every direction except due west and gave the impression that they all had pre-determined routes to their hunting grounds. On another occasion, proof was obtained that one ringtail hunted within one to two kilometres of the roost; it was still hunting in this area an hour and a half after rising. A few birds perched and preened for some minutes—once for as long as an hour—on rocks or hillocks overlooking the roost. At Roost 2, Dickson saw up to six birds perched together on fence posts and rocky outcrops before they left the roost. They generally flew off singly but he once saw three males leave in the same direction and, another time, four males and four ringtails left together.

Dispersal from the roosts

In the absence of colour-marked birds it is impossible to say with certainty how widely the harriers dispersed from the roosts during the day. During November 1971, a bird which appeared to be a first year male, with prominent light patches near the carpal joints of both wings, was thought to be carrying wing-tags. On 12 December 1971, a first year male which had been ringed and wing-tagged by Nick Picozzi in Kincardineshire (240 kilometres NE), in July of the same year, was found dead near roost 2. There was obviously a possibility that the same bird had moved from one roosting area to the other. There was a sharp decline in the number of hunting birds seen at more than six kilometres from Roost 2, compared with a majority of sightings between eight and twelve kilometres from Roost 1. This difference probably reflected the relative accessibility of good hunting grounds. Many observations were made of harriers, travelling towards Roost 1 in the evening, at places up to sixteen kilometres distant.

A ringtail with distinctive wing pattern, previously seen at the roost, was recognised by Louis Urquhart at a point more than nine kilometres away. One November evening, I watched a ringtail hunting over a large reed-bed, at twelve kilometres from the roost; flocks of Starlings were gathering at the time and seemed an obvious attraction as prey, but after spending ten minutes coursing over the reeds at high speed the harrier suddenly turned away, at twelve minutes past sunset, and set a deliberate course towards the communal roost. It could have found a very similar roosting site—but liable to disturbance by shooting—in the big reed-bed which it had been hunting, but the pull of the communal roost was evidently irresistible. The Craigheads found that Marsh Hawks dispersed up to at least nine kilometres from a roost; almost certainly harriers from Roost 1 sometimes dispersed to more than sixteen kilometres.

The atmosphere of a roost (Roost 1)

For an hour or so towards the end of a short winter's day, a watcher can break all ties with the world of human affairs and enter another 'under the heavens that know not what years be', which is the world of wildlife. I often wondered how far back in the distant past harriers had first discovered and made use of the flow for roosting. There was something about the slow pageant of their gatherings which contributed to a sense of timelessness. Watching the final moments of the harriers' day seemed to underline how little I knew of their total activity. As I have said, most birds arrived well gorged from a recent meal, but how rarely on daytime excursions in the surrounding countryside had I observed one making a kill! Once we spent a full November day in neighbouring country without so much as seeing a Hen Harrier until, at dusk, twelve flew in to roost. Even on extensive wanderings it was unusual to see more than one or two hunting birds. Although the sight of harriers gathering to roost became a familiar spectacle, I was always aware of the unfathomable gulf which separated their identity as living creatures from ourselves. Often as we turned for home, after a drenching watch, and left the birds to sit it out for another 15 hours or more of darkness in their roofless beds, I thought of the marvellous protection which feathers must provide. Occasionally, some slight observation added an unexpected detail of knowledge, as when, on 26 November 1975, a ringtail showing one or two short dark central feathers in a faded tail revealed the extended period of moult.

My recollections of incidental activity at the roost are dominated by a sense of seasonal rhythm. On soft September nights, Swallows and Pied Wagtails flickered over the marsh and drab-plumaged Mallard and Teal guzzled under the stream bank. From mid-September, the first menacing roars of rutting stags were heard from the depths of the forest. Sometimes, in October's Indian summer, the evenings were warm enough to bring up clouds of midges, but roost watching generally ranks as one of the coldest forms of inactivity, not to be recommended to anyone inclined to restlessness or impatience. November dusks were full of the sweet wheezing and chuckling of Fieldfares and the sharp calls of Redwings. Then, too, we listened for the calls of approaching flights of geese, or heard the clear bugling of Whooper Swans as they flew, silhouetted against the sky, towards a distant loch among the hills. Beyond the tall heads of withered grasses, Goldeneye patrolled the open water in bunches of five or six; later in the winter we heard the whistle of their wings long into the dusk as flight followed flight, to roost in company on a loch. Goosanders fished the stream or sped overhead, signalling alarm at sighting us by their guttural barking. Scanning a distant skyline for incoming harriers might result instead in a glimpse of a Golden Eagle planing slowly to a distant roosting place, or even of a Kestrel still hovering above the moor. I have already mentioned the predators most often seen, in addition to the harriers; strangely, although Buzzards had at least two territories quite near, and regularly roosted in the forest, they scarcely ever appeared over the harriers' roosting ground and we never saw any conflicts between the two species. Once, on a November morning, a Great Grey Shrike obligingly chose the only willow bush in view as a hunting perch.

For several winters, a Green Woodpecker could almost be relied upon to give a short burst of its laughing cry before it retired for the night in one of the old birch trees in the forest. In the earlier years, otters were seen with some regularity; once we were greeted by one in full view on a mid-stream boulder. At all times we were aware of the small resident birds of the spruce forest—Goldcrests, Coal Tits and Wrens—from their calls and rustlings among the needles, or the whirring of their tiny wings close beside us.

The virtual silence of mid-winter watches began to be broken, from late February or early March, by the songs of birds which returned to breed in the forest or on the flow itself. The coming of spring was marked, above all, by the arrival of the Curlews which soon began to make song-flights over the harriers' roosting ground. There was generally little sign that either resented the other's presence. Among all the sounds which heightened awareness of spring, none were more pleasing to hear than the songs of Blackbirds and Song Thrushes from the forest above. As we trudged back from our stance, with the last glow in the western sky, Tawny Owls hooted and Woodcock, lisping and croaking, almost clipped the tops of the conifers on their roding flights.

Reasons for communal roosting in the Hen Harrier

The habit of roosting communally occurs in a large variety of birds. Some of the most spectacular examples, cited by Wynne-Edwards (1962), are found in such differing groups as Cormorants, ducks (Goldeneye), parakeets, Swifts and Swallows, gulls, waders, birds of prey and passerines. In some birds such as Starlings, gulls and many waders, the habit is one of the most arresting features of their winter behaviour, while in others it can easily be overlooked. The usually solitary-roosting Robin, for instance, has been shown by Swann (1975) to be a communal winter rooster in some districts, while Birkhead (1973) regards the diurnal 'standing grounds' of Grey Herons as an example of communal roosting. Although the habit appears to be commonest in species which also feed gregariously, it occurs in a number of birds which are usually solitary feeders. Among these are Wrens, Tree Creepers and Grey Herons, as well as raptors such as the Californian Condor, Turkey Vulture, Rough-legged Buzzard and the harriers.

Differing theories have been offered to explain the function of communal roosting. Lack (1968) regarded the main purpose as protection from predators. Wynne-Edwards (1962), on the other hand, concluded that 'the primary function of the habit was to bring members of a population-unit together so that they could hold epideictic demonstrations resulting in adjustments of population density through emigration'. Ward and Zahavi (1973) argued that the roosts provided a centre at which information on the location of food within the area served by the roost might be obtained; for solitary feeders this could apply 'to the position of good feeding places in relation to the roost, not to the position of the food itself'. Zahavi (1971), however, had differentiated birds, such as Wrens and Tree Creepers, which evidently form temporary crowded roosts for warmth in cold weather. Among harriers, the habit was associated with preparation for migration, by Meinertzhagen (1956) and also by Gurr (1968); but in his study of Australasian Harrier roosts in New Zealand, where this harrier is not migratory, Gurr concluded that communal roosts could facilitate pairing, and might also be a means of providing information for population adjustments, in the manner suggested by Wynne-Edwards.

How far, then, do my own observations in south-west Scotland support any of the above, or different, explanations? Certainly there was evidence that the close proximity of roosting birds enabled them to respond rapidly and communally to suspected danger. Although, in historically recent times, communal roosting has undoubtedly increased the birds' vulnerability to man, the habit must be considered in relation to an earlier situation when the chief danger must have come from other mammals. It can hardly be doubted that solitary roosting would increase the danger in this context. The preference for boggy locations (not universal in Hen Harriers) is no doubt a response to the need for safety against predators, but it might be associated with communal or solitary roosting. It may be argued that the perching and soaring in groups, which often took place before roosting, is consistent with Wynne-Edwards' theory; yet the virtual absence of such behaviour on days when hunting conditions seemed to be worst, must be noted. I find it difficult to understand how even the maximum amount of social flying or perching which was seen, could be regarded in the same light as the elaborate pre-roosting evolutions of birds such as Starlings. Certainly, the open nature of the roosting grounds and, sometimes, the high flights and conspicuous perching of the harriers give good mutual observation, and there are many indications that some birds (females and older birds) have precedence over others (males and younger birds) at the roost. Birds of 'inferior' status might then be kept out of the best sites and come under pressure to move elsewhere. It seems very likely that by noting the flight lines of birds arriving with full crops, other harriers, which might include new arrivals in the district, could learn the whereabouts of good hunting areas. Observations of one bird following another, either to or from the roost, also support the idea of the roost as an information centre.

The communal roosts of finches, Starlings and other passerine birds certainly attract numbers of predators, such as Sparrowhawks and Merlins, and it is difficult to believe that they have a safety advantage. If dangers from modern man are discounted, ground roosting harriers could well be most secure in company, but this may not be the basic reason for roosting together. It seems to me very likely that this behaviour has a primary social function. Roosts may provide staging points in an essentially nomadic winter existence, enabling contact to be made between birds which are experienced and those which are inexperienced in utilising the food resources of a region. Additionally, the roosts appear to give opportunities for males and females to associate in winter and probably to form pairs. There is some evidence that Hen Harriers from widely separated natal regions may interbreed (Chapter 7) and it seems reasonable to suppose that this mingling of populations may arise partly, at least, from association in communal winter roosts. The occurrence of a marked bird from Kincardineshire in one, and very possibly both, roosting areas in south-west Scotland is of interest. Now that an increased number of Orkney Hen Harriers have been colour marked by Nick Picozzi, in 1976, there must be a real chance that some of these birds may be recognised at roosts[1], or as breeding birds, as far afield as south-west Scotland, or even much further.

---

[1] See chapter 7. On 24 October 1976, a ringtail, which must have been wing-tagged on Orkney in 1975, was recognised at Roost 2 by R. C. Dickson.

CHAPTER NINETEEN

THE HEN HARRIER: A CONTROVERSIAL BIRD

Whether or not Hen Harriers continue to inhabit this world is a matter of indifference to the great majority of mankind. When, in 1544, Dr William Turner said that among our countrymen it gets its name from butchering their fowls, it may be supposed that Hen Harriers were commonly disliked by a predominantly rural population. Nobody now knows to what extent they preyed on free ranging poultry, but very little has been heard of this habit in modern times.

The general reduction in suitable habitats for harriers must prevent any likelihood that they will ever compete with man's essential food requirements in the future. Yet, in countries such as Britain, where a small but influential section of the population is intensely keen on game shooting, birds of prey are often still treated as vermin, and the Hen Harrier is apt to be placed in the forefront of this category. The precise meaning of the word, 'vermin', so beloved of writers and advertisers in shooting periodicals, is hardly ever defined. No doubt it will be argued that it ought to refer only to those animals which have been proscribed by law as pests, but any country dweller knows that within the comparative privacy of some shooting preserves the fate of protected species depends on the opinions of landowners, sportsmen and gamekeepers. I have many good friends who enjoy shooting, and I do not for a moment suggest that the majority kill protected species, but what happens to a Buzzard on a Pheasant shoot, or a Hen

Harrier on a grouse moor, is undoubtedly more likely to be decided by personal opinions of the damage or disturbance it might cause to game, than by a consideration of its status under the law. I recall, for instance, speaking to a friendly gamekeeper when Hen Harriers had begun to re-establish themselves in my own district. His reaction was that he would have to see 'what they did', with the implication that if he found any evidence of grouse killing he would take what he considered appropriate action.

Every year I hear that Hen Harriers have been 'taken care of' on grouse moors in south Scotland and I have already described how I found pole traps (illegal since 1904) set on one of these a few years ago. I mention these examples only to corroborate that the decision whether or not to destroy such birds is often made irrespective of the law. I am not, at this point, making any judgement on the effect which Hen Harriers may or may not have on grouse stocks or on the conduct of a grouse shoot. It is, I think, essential to spell out the meaning of the Protection of Birds Acts, in regard to the Hen Harrier and other First Schedule species,[1] as it does not always seem to be fully understood.—I cannot do better than to refer to the booklet *Predatory Birds in Britain* prepared by a working party which included leading representatives of the Game Conservancy, the British Field Sports Society and the Gamekeepers' Association, as well as the National Farmers Union and major fauna preservation and protection bodies. I quote from this: 'The Protection of Birds Act, 1954, contained no provisions under which First Schedule birds (all rare or relatively rare) might be legally killed as pests, but section 8 (1) of the Act of 1967 provides for the issuing of licences to kill First Schedule species where necessary "for the purpose of preventing serious damage to crops, vegetables, fruit, growing timber or any other form of property or to fisheries". It is necessary to emphasise, however, that farmers, game preservers and landowners are not allowed to take direct personal action under this provision. The intention is that those who experience damage to crops, stocks or property by First Schedule birds should report this to the Secretary of State, and that the claim should be investigated before any decision is taken as to whether control measures are necessary. (*Game species in the wild are not regarded in law as property*).' It is therefore quite clear that the killing of wild game birds, such as grouse, by a Hen Harrier could provide no legal grounds for its destruction.

There are some among those who shoot who so dislike the Hen Harrier that they advocate a tacit disregard of the law which protects it. This was made very clear in an article, a few years ago, by a regular contributor in the *Shooting Times*. His interesting and revealing argument is summed up in a final paragraph, as follows: 'Let us take a case which is not as hypothetical as it may seem. An intelligent moorland keeper goes out of his way to protect nesting Peregrines on the border of his beat and is delighted to have Merlins nesting on his moor to the extent that he once came to fisticuffs with

[1] See Appendix 4 for a list showing degrees of protection given to predatory birds.

an egg-collector who tried to bribe him to obtain a fresh clutch of Merlin's eggs. But this same keeper does not welcome Hen Harriers. What would happen if I could catch him shooting a Hen Harrier and a successful prosecution resulted? In the first place, the keeper would not be ostracised by the local population: *he would be regarded as an unlucky martyr.* Secondly, *I should find myself ostracised locally and not one keeper in that district would ever confide in me again.* Thirdly, *it is more than probable that Peregrines and Merlins would never again nest on that moor.* So that if anyone *makes so bold* as to tell me that I must *never* be reluctant in reporting any breach of the law I could, as *a practical conservationist,* only answer him *really adequately* by resorting to the use of a succinct but very vulgar five-letter word'. (Author's italics.)

In other words it seems that the keeper should decide for himself which parts of the law he will obey, and the above writer evidently considers that most people living in the neighbourhood of moorland shooting preserves regard prosecution for killing Hen Harriers as a form of victimisation. I am not sure whether he means to imply that as a result of such a prosecution the keeper would also destroy the Peregrines and Merlins, or that he would allow others to rob their nests or otherwise prevent them from breeding. Either way, it credits the keeper with a strangely vindictive attitude. To my mind, the most disturbing feature of the article is the implication that the law is somehow an impertinence on the moorlands of Britain. A different attitude certainly holds in Holland, where Mr Schipper informs me that there is no persecution of harriers. There, in a region where Hen, Marsh and Montagu's Harriers all thrive, he writes that the protection of these birds of prey is commonly accepted, in spite of some complaints from hunters. Evidently there is no need to fear being ostracised for upholding the protection laws! If anyone says 'but of course harriers do not kill grouse in Holland', my answer would be that the killing of young Pheasants by harriers there *could* easily be regarded as sufficient reason for their destruction.

There are other voices which are even more strongly opposed to the Hen Harrier than the writer in the *Shooting Times.* They would like to see a change in the law so that the species could be legally killed for at least part of the year. Suppose it is proved that predation by Hen Harriers can, even slightly, reduce the numbers of young grouse surviving until the start of the shooting season; there might then be increasing pressure from the shooting lobby to outlaw the Hen Harrier. Yet to conceal the facts of harrier predation on game birds is clearly wrong, and there is no doubt that, in the past, mutual distrust between gamekeepers and ornithologists has been fermented by dogmatic statements, from both sides, based on quite inadequate evidence. I have shown, in this book, that the food of Hen Harriers varies greatly in different localities, often covers a wide spectrum and, even where game birds are commonly taken, it is only too easy to exaggerate their importance as prey. Since game birds are comparatively large their skeletal remains are conspicuous when left at or near nests, while smaller prey may disappear without trace.

In Britain, at any rate, the only game bird which is numerous enough, on some breeding grounds of the Hen Harrier, ever to form an important part of its prey, is the Red Grouse. It is likely that adult, territory-holding Red Grouse can nearly always escape from a harrier and those which are killed are weaklings, mainly doomed to die in winter anyway. It is possible that harrier predation on adults reduces competition for winter food and helps the survival of the stronger birds. The grouse preservers' complaint against Hen Harriers, then, is aimed mainly at predation on chicks when young harriers are being reared, and at the disturbance caused by harriers hunting over a moor immediately before or during a grouse drive. Either of these factors might result in some diminution in the numbers of grouse flying over the guns. It is probable that grouse shooters are, generally, most annoyed by the disturbance factor. As long as the economic value of grouse moors is dictated by the numbers of grouse shot, any predation is bound to tempt gamekeepers to destroy them. A day's shooting for eight guns recently cost £2,000 on a moor in south Scotland and there is clearly no shortage of people, some of them from abroad, who are willing to pay this amount, or perhaps more. There are certainly some people who argue that if grouse moors are so economically valuable, the least suspicion of harm caused by predatory birds should be enough to justify the latter's destruction. After all, they say, what 'use' is a harrier or an eagle; just as some North Sea fishermen ask what 'use' is a seal?

One rather curious reason for the unpopularity of harriers as a group, among some game shooters, is their stealthy low-level method of hunting, which does not arouse the same admiration as the stoop of the Peregrine or the dashing chase of a Merlin. The tendency to judge bird behaviour as courageous or cowardly (or is it sporting or unsporting?) dies hard.

Reluctance to accept the protected status of the Hen Harrier evidently stems from an odd mixture of reasons. It is fair, however, to consider the implications of a possible situation in which colonial breeding of Hen Harriers might reach a very high density on moors where grouse shooting was an important part of the land use. In such an event, the most ardent supporter of Hen Harriers should be prepared to listen carefully to the arguments.

My case for the defence of the Hen Harrier must rest principally on how successfully I have told the story of its life in this book. I hope that I have done enough to show that it is a beautiful and exciting bird. A pair of Hen Harriers in that wonderful manoeuvre of the food pass, or circling high in a spring sky—surely these are visual delights which must be measured far above any statistic of possible game losses? I am certain that in the years to come, as the wilderness retreats further, such experiences are going to be beyond price for more and more people. It is surely inexcusable, when so many of the world's most splendid birds are rapidly becoming rare, that the destruction of birds such as harriers and eagles should still be tolerated. Great numbers of people, in this country, must have shared my excitement as I watched a recent, superbly photographed film of the wildlife of the Spanish forests. The sad implication of the commentary was that little of this would survive for much longer. I look forward to seeing the film which David Scott tells me is being made on the Hen Harrier in Ireland. I hope this reaches a large audience and helps to convince them that here is a bird worthy of conservation.

Some will say that in the light of the recent increase of the Hen Harrier in Britain, Ireland and Holland, I need not be so concerned for its conservation. Yet complacency should be prevented by reference to Bijleveld's (1974) book, in which he showed that in many European countries the breeding population of Hen Harriers has decreased sharply in recent years, most notably in France where Terasse (1964) said that it had dropped by 50% between 1930 and 1964. Such decreases are partly due to reductions in suitable breeding habitat, and there is some evidence that agricultural pesticides have had an adverse effect on breeding success in France, but the devastating toll of birds of prey taken by hunters throughout most of Europe has included great numbers of harriers; as recently as 1969, 328 were named among 8,242 raptors killed in Lower Austria; while in 1959, 1,500 harriers were reported destroyed in the La Vêndée district of France alone.

At the World Conference on Birds of Prey held in Vienna in October 1975, it was unanimously urged by conservationists, hunters and falconers that steps should be taken to give total protection to all birds of prey. There was also agreement on the need for conservation of habitats, the control of pollutants, especially in tropical areas, and for more research into the causes of declining numbers of predatory birds.

One recent example, very close to my own home, must suffice to show that the protection of even our rarest birds of prey is still far from effective. In 1975, only 24 young Red Kites were reared in the British Isles, all in Wales (Lovegrove, 1976). One of these wandered in its first autumn to Kirkcudbrightshire and was shot during a Pheasant shoot. The shooter identified it as a peculiar Buzzard and promptly buried the carcase. The true identification only came to light as a result of a remarkable piece of detection by a local bird photographer who traced and dug up the remains. For reasons which are all too familiar in such circumstances, no prosecution followed. I learned, later, from a neighbouring farmer that no Buzzard (and probably no bird of prey) was safe on that shoot.

It is more than 20 years since a pair of Montagu's Harriers attempted to nest in the same district and, then, the female was gin-trapped on the nest. The Montagu's Harrier is an even rarer bird in Britain than the Red Kite, and its survival over much of Europe is thought to be precarious. When Hen Harriers are still commonly killed, in spite of much publicised protection laws, would the Montagu's be spared? It is not always easy for an expert ornithologist to distinguish between the two species and it can hardly be expected that every gamekeeper would do so.

Many people will say that I unduly stress the risks to rare birds of prey from hunters and game preservers. It can be argued that pesticides, destruction of breeding or hunting habitat and disturbance by all kinds of people, including bird-watchers, may present even greater threats. The importance of all these factors varies for different species but it cannot be denied that direct human destruction has been, and regrettably still is, a major hazard as far as harriers are concerned.

APPENDIX 1

LOCAL NAMES OF THE HEN HARRIER

All the names I have found for the Hen Harrier, in an extensive search of the literature, are given in the following list; some names referred to either Hen or Montagu's harriers, or both.

An t eun fionn Gaelic: The White Bird.

Ash-coloured Buzzard
Ash-coloured Falcon
Ash-coloured Harrier
Ash-coloured Hawk } Ash-coloured Buzzard appears in John Clare's *List of Northamptonshire Birds*, but may refer to Montagu's Harrier. Pennant gave Ash-coloured falcon as a name for Montagu's Harrier. Later references to Ash-coloured Hawks, Falcons or Harriers certainly referred, sometimes, to Hen Harriers. For example, the large total of Ash-coloured Hawks said to have been killed in Ayrshire, 1850–54, could not have been Montagu's. Even St John's statement (1849) that *Falco cineraceous,* the Ash-coloured Harrier, 'breeds near Bonar Bridge', Easter Ross, seems geographically much more likely to refer to the Hen Harrier, and may derive from the rather distinct appearance of 1–2 year old males showing a good deal of dusky colour in their grey plumage, thus looking not unlike male Montagu's.

Blue Furze Hawk Used in Devonshire for adult males.

Blue Gled Widely used for adult males.

Blue Hawk Especially in the Midlands and North of England for adult males. John Clare (1823) clearly distinguishes between Large Blue Hawks (harriers) and Small Blue Hawks (male Sparrowhawks or, in the North of England, male Merlins).

Blue Kite Adult male (Muirhead, Berwickshire, 1889).

Blue Sleeves Adult male, Perth/Angus district, Scotland.

Bod glas Welsh: Blue Kite.

Bod Llwydlas Welsh: Blue-grey Kite.

Bod tinwyn Welsh: White-tailed Kite.

Breid-air-toin Gaelic: white (rag) on rump.

Brown Gled Ringtail harrier, according to Muirhead (1889).

Clamhan Luch Gaelic name, especially in Hebrides, meaning Mouse Hawk.

Dove-coloured Falcon A. H. Evans quotes Wallis' *History of Northumberland,*
1769: 'The Dove-coloured Falcon breeds annually on Cheviot . . .
among Ericae.' Although Evans evidently considered this a reference to
the Hen Harrier (adult male) it may perhaps have referred to a male
Merlin.

Flapper A Caithness name: Harvie-Brown and Buckley (1887).

Furze Hawk Devonshire: D'Urban and Matthew (1895).

Gled Often used for harriers as well as kites.

Grey Gled Commonly used, particularly in south Scotland and the Borders, for
adult males.

Grey-blue Hawk North Wales: mentioned by Forrest (1907).

Hebog Llwydlas Welsh name = blue-grey hawk; Forrest (1907).

Hen Harrier ⎫ Turner, 1544, gives the name as Hen Harroer and says 'it gets its
Hen Harroer ⎭ name among our countrymen from butchering their fowls'. He is
referring to adult males, and considered the Ringtail as a different bird,
though he says it catches its prey in the same manner.

Miller Given by Yarrell, 1874. Evidently refers to adult males, as grey birds, like the
'dusty miller' in colour.

Mittane Dunbar (c 1500) did not include Ringtails in his extensive nomenclature of
Birds of Prey and the Mittane, certainly a hawk, may have been a brown
harrier, which he might be expected to have named.
In 'Forsett is ay the Falconis kynd
    but ever the Mittane is hard in mynd';
the Mittane might be a Goshawk, but Dunbar elsewhere refers to
'Goshalks'.

Moor Hawk Mentioned by D. Nethersole-Thompson. Note that the Marsh Harrier
was called the Moor Buzzard, formerly nesting on moorland bogs in
similar situations to Hen Harriers.

Mouse Hawk English translation of Gaelic name Clamhan Luch.

Rag on Rump Probably English translation of Gaelic Breid-air-toin.

Ringtail ⎫ General name for female or brown-plumaged (young) males.
Ringteale ⎬ Described by Turner, 1544, as follows: 'the Subbuteo I think to be that
Ringtayle ⎭ Hawk which Englishmen call the Ringtail, from the ring of white that
reaches round the tail.' Sibbald gave a list of Hawks and Falcons in his *Scotia
Illustrata* (1684) including the following reference to Hen Harriers: 'Subbuteo, quibusdam Butea albus, the Ring-tail.' This suggests that he
recognised the relationship between Buteo albus (the White Hawk) and the
Ringtail. Various spellings of Ringtail occur in old 'vermin' lists, back to the
17th century.

Saint Julian's Bird (Saint Silin) South Wales; Forrest (1907).

Sanct Martynis Fowle ⎫ The modern French name is Le Busard Saint Martin,
St Martin's Fowl   ⎭ from the arrival of migrants in France about 11
November, St Martin's Day. Sanct Martynis fowle is the form used by the
Scots poet Dunbar, c 1500. It may refer only to the adult male. Dunbar
travelled to Picardy as an emissary of James IV of Scotland.

Seagull Hawk Given by Thompson (Connemara, 1849) and by Muirhead
(Berwickshire, 1889). An attractive and descriptive name for the adult male.

Vuzz Kite Colloquial name in Devonshire, cf Furze Kite.

White aboon Gled A common name in Scotland *Old Statistical Account*, Muirhead, presumably for the adult male, unless 'white aboon' refers to the Ringtail's white rump.

White Hawk Used in Scotland and Ireland for the adult male; Graham, 1852–70; Thompson (1849).

White Kite Used in Marquis of Bute's circular to lairds in Argyll (1808), which specified a reward of five shillings for a White Kite's nest with four eggs. It seems he did not know that the Ringtail was the female Hen Harrier.

I am indebted to Dr K. W. Brewster for drawing my attention to the following piece of harrier lore, in Lloyds' *Bird Facts and Fiction* c 1933: 'We find in falconry sixteen kinds of Hawks or fowls that prey. Of which the Circos (Harrier)—which is lame and limpeth of one leg—was held in ancient time for the luckiest augury in case of weddings and of cattle.'

Pliny says it is 'of lucky omen in nuptial affairs and money business'.

In the Hebrides, should anyone have an unusually lucky day, it is said he must have seen the 'Clamhan Luch' or Hen Harrier.

It used to be said in Wiltshire that these birds alighted in numbers on the ground before rain.

APPENDIX 2

AVIAN SPECIES MENTIONED IN THE TEXT

Bittern *Botaurus stellaris.*
Bittern, American *Botaurus lentiginosus*
Blackbird *Turdus merula*
Bobwhite *Colinus virginianus*
Bullfinch *Pyrrhula pyrrhula*
Bunting, Cirl *Emberiza cirlus*
Bunting, Corn *Emberiza calandra*
Bunting, Reed *Emberiza schoeniclus*
Bunting, Snow *Plectrophenax nivalis*
Buzzard, Common *Buteo buteo*
Buzzard, Rough-legged *Buteo lagopus*
Chaffinch *Fringilla coelebs*
Chiffchaff *Phylloscopus trochilus*
Condor, Californian
   Gymnogyps californianus
Cormorant *Phalacrocorax carbo*
Corncrake *Crex crex*
Crossbill, Continental *Loxia curvirostra*
Crow, Carrion *Corvus corone*
Crow, Hooded *Corvus corone*
Cuckoo *Cuculus canorus*
Curlew *Numenius arquata*

Dipper *Cinclus cinclus*
Diver, Red-throated *Gavia stellata*
Dove, Turtle *Streptopelia turtur*
Dunlin *Calidris alpina*
Dunnock *Prunella modularis*
Eagle, Golden *Aquila chrysaetos*
Eagle, Sea *Haliaeëtus albicilla*
Eagle, Serpent *Spilornis* sp
Falcon, Greenland *Falco rusticolus*
Fieldfare *Turdus pilaris*
Flicker *Colaptes auratus*
Flycatcher, Spotted *Muscicapa striata*
Goldcrest *Regulus regulus*
Goldeneye *Bucephala clangula*
Goldfinch *Carduelis carduelis*
Goosander *Mergus merganser*
Goose, Greylag *Anser anser*
Goshawk *Accipiter gentilis*
Grebe, Little *Tachybaptus ruficollis*
Greenfinch *Chloris chloris*
Grouse, Black *Lyrurus tetrix*
Grouse, Red *Lagopus lagopus*

Gull, Great Black-backed *Larus marinus*
Gull, Black-headed
   Larus ridibundus
Gull, Common *Larus canus*
Gull, Herring *Larus argentatus*
Gull, Lesser Black-backed
   Larus fuscus
Harrier, African Marsh
   Circus ranivorus
Harrier, Australasian
   Circus aeruginosus approximans
Harrier, Black *Circus maurus*
Harrier, Cinereous *Circus cinereus*
Harrier, Hen *Circus cyaneus*
Harrier, Long-winged *Circus buffoni*
Harrier, Marsh *Circus aeruginosus*
Harrier, Montagu's *Circus pygargus*
Harrier, Pallid *Circus macrourus*
Harrier, Pied *Circus melanoleucus*
Harrier, Spotted *Circus assimilis*
Hawk, Marsh (North American Hen
   Harrier) *Circus cyaneus hudsonius*
Heron, Grey *Ardea cinerea*
Hobby *Falco subbuteo*
Hoopoe *Upupa epops*
Jay *Garrulus glanarius*
Kestrel *Falco tinnunculus*
Kingfisher *Alcedo atthis*
Kite, Red *Milvus milvus*
Lapwing *Vanellus vanellus*
Lark, Crested *Galerida cristata*
Lark, Horned *Eremophila alpestris*
Linnet *Acanthis cannabina*
Mallard *Anas platyrhynchus*
Martin, Purple *Progne subis*
Merlin *Falco columbarius*
Moorhen *Gallinula chloropus*
Osprey *Pandion haliaetus*
Ouzel, Ring *Turdus torquatus*
Owl, Barn *Tyto alba*
Owl, Eagle *Bubo bubo*
Owl, Short-eared *Asio flammeus*
Owl, Tawny *Strix aluco*
Oystercatcher *Haematopus ostralogus*
Partridge *Perdix perdix*
Peregrine *Falco peregrinus*
Pheasant *Phasianus colchicus*

Pigeon, Wood *Columba palumbus*
Pipit, Meadow *Anthus pratensis*
Pipit, Tree *Anthus trivialis*
Plover, Golden *Pluvialis apricaria*
Plover, Ringed *Charadrius hiaticula*
Prairie chicken *Tympanuchus cupido*
Ptarmigan *Lagopus mutus*
Raven *Corvus corax*
Redpoll *Acanthis flammea*
Redshank *Tringa totanus*
Redwing *Turdus iliacus*
Robin *Erithacus rubecula*
Rook *Corvus frugilegus*
Sandpiper, Common *Tringa hypoleucus*
Sandpiper, Wood *Tringa glareola*
Shag *Phalacrocorax aristotelis*
Shrike, Great Grey *Lanius excubitor*
Shrike, Woodchat *Lanius senator*
Siskin *Carduelis spinus*
Skylark *Alauda arvensis*
Snipe *Gallinago gallinago*
Sparrowhawk *Accipiter nisus*
Sparrow, House *Passer domesticus*
Starling *Sturnus vulgaris*
Stonechat *Saxicola torquata*
Swallow *Hirundo rusticus*
Swan, Whooper *Cygnus cygnus*
Swift *Apus apus*
Teal *Anas crecca*
Thrush, Mistle *Turdus viscivorus*
Thrush, Song *Turdus philomelus*
Tit, Coal *Parus ater*
Tree Creeper *Certhia familiaris*
Twite *Acanthis flavirostris*
Vulture, Turkey *Cathartes aura*
Wagtail, Pied *Motacilla alba*
Warbler, Grasshopper *Locustella naevia*
Warbler, Willow *Phylloscopus trochilus*
Water Rail *Rallus aquaticus*
Wheatear *Oenanthe oenanthe*
Whinchat *Saxicola rubetra*
Whitethroat *Sylvia communis*
Wigeon *Anas penelope*
Woodcock *Scolopax rusticola*
Woodpecker, Green *Picus viridis*
Wren *Troglodytes troglodytes*
Yellowhammer *Emberiza citrinella*

LIST OF NON-AVIAN SPECIES MENTIONED IN THE TEXT

Adder (Viper) *Vipera berus*
Beetles, Click (Elaterids)
  Campylus lineatus
  Colymbites cupreus:
Beetles, Dor *Geotrupes sylvaticus:*
      geotrupes stercorarius
Beetle, Great Water *Dytiscus marginalis*
Beetles, Ground *Carabus catenulatus:*
      Carabus pterostichus
Beetles, Weevils *Otiorrhynchus*
Birch *Salix sp.*
Bog Cotton, Cotton Grass
  Eriophorum angustifolium
Bog Myrtle *Myrica gale*
Bog-rush *Schoenus nigricans*
Bracken *Pteridium aquilinum*
Broom *Sarothamnus scoparius*
Butterfly, Peacock *Nymphalis io*
Butterfly, Scotch Argus *Erebia aethiops*
Crayfish *Nephrops sp.*
Deer Grass *Scirpus cespitosus*
Deer, Red *Cervus elaphus*
Deer, Roe *Capreolus capreolus*
Flying Fish *Exocoetus volitans*
Fox *Vulpes vulpes*
Foxglove *Digitalis purpurea*
Frog *Rana temporaria*
Hare, Brown *Lepus europaeus*
Hare, Mountain *Lepus timidus*
Hare, Leveret (young Hare) *Lepus sp.*
Hawthorn *Crataegus monogyna*
Heather sp. *Calluna vulgaris:*
      Erica sp.
Hedgehog *Erinaceus europaeus*
Juniper *Juniperus communis*
Larch *Larix sp.*

Lemming (Norway) *Lemnus lemnus*
Lizard *Lacerta sp.*
Marram Grass *Ammophila arenaria*
Meadow Sweet *Filipendula ulmaria*
Mole *Talpa europaea*
Moss, Sphagnum *Sphagnum sp.*
Moth, Emperor *Saturnia pavonia*
Mouse, Meadow *Microtus pennsylvanicus*
Mouse, Wood *Apodemus sylvaticus*
Pine, Lodgepole *Pinus contorta*
Purple Moorgrass *Molinia caerulea*
Rabbit *Oryctolagus cuniculus*
Rat, Brown *Rattus norvegicus*
Rhododendron sp. *Rhododendron sp.*
Rowan *Sorbus aucuparia*
Sea Buckthorn *Hippophaë rhamnoides*
Shrew, Pygmy *Sorex minutus*
Shrew, sp *Sorex sp.*
Skunk *Mephitis sp.*
Slow-worm *Auguis fragilis*
Spruce *Picea sp.*
Squirrel, Ground *Citellus sp.*
Stoat *Mustula erminea*
Thistle sp. *Carduus sp.*
Vole, Mountain or Northern *Microtus*
  oeconomus or *Microtus ratticeps*
Vole, Orkney *Microtus*
  arvalis orcadensis
Vole, Short-tailed Field
  Microtus agrestis
Vole, Water *Arvicola amphibius*
Whin, Gorse *Ulex europaeus*
Willow, Creeping *Salix repens*
Willow *Salix sp.*
Woodrush *Luzula sp.*

PROTECTION UNDER THE ACTS OF 1954 AND 1967

Degrees of Protection afforded to Predatory Birds (dealt with in the booklet *Predatory Birds in Britain*), by the Protection of Birds Acts 1954 and 1967 and subsequent amending orders: see S.I. 1970 No. 678 and No. 716 (S.53).

Ordinary Protection	*Special Protection First Schedule of Act*	*Not Protected* (may be killed or taken only by authorised persons): *Second Schedule of Act*
Buzzard	Bittern	Cormorant
Goosander (England and Wales only)	Buzzard, Honey	Crow, Carrion
	Diver (all species)	Crow, Hooded
Great Crested Grebe	Eagle, Golden	Goosander (Scotland only)
Gull, Black-headed	Goshawk	Gull, Great Black-backed
Gull, Common	Harrier (all species)	Gull, Lesser Black-backed
Heron	Hobby	
Kestrel	Kingfisher	Gull, Herring
Merganser (Red-breasted) (England and Wales only)	Kite	Jackdaw
	Merlin	Jay
Owl, Little	Osprey	Magpie
Owl, Long-eared	Owl, Barn	Merganser, Red-breasted (Scotland only)
Owl, Short-eared	Peregrine	
Owl, Tawny	Sparrowhawk	Rook
Raven (except in Argyll and Skye where it is on Schedule 2)		Shag
Skua, Arctic		
Skua, Great		
Tern, Common		

BIBLIOGRAPHY

Ali, S. and Ripley, D. *Handbook of the Birds of India and Pakistan. Vol. 1.* 1968
Andris, K. Beobachturgen an Schlafplatzen der Kornweihe (*Circus cyaneus*) in der Oberrheinebene. (Sleeping places of the Hen Harrier in the Upper Rhine valley.) *Vogelwelt 91.* 1970
Audubon, J. J. *The Original Water Colour Paintings for the Birds of America.* Introduction by Michael B. Davidson. 1966
Bahr, P. H. Note on nest of Hen Harrier and protection in the Outer Hebrides. *Annals of Scottish Natural History.* 1907
Balfour, E. The Hen Harrier in Orkney. *Bird Notes 27 and 30.* 1959, 1962–63
———— *pers. comm.* (On the Hen Harrier in Orkney, etc.)
———— Iris Colour in the Hen Harrier. *Bird Study 17.* 1970
———— and Cadbury, C. J. A Population Study of the Hen Harrier *Circus cyaneus* in Orkney, in Goodier, R. (ed.). The natural environment of Orkney: Nature Conservancy Council. 1975
———— and Macdonald, M. A. Food and feeding behaviour of the Hen Harrier in Orkney. *Scottish Birds 6.* 1970
Bannerman, D. A. and Lodge, G. E. *The Birds of the British Isles* 1953–63
Baron Geyr. Uber Geselligkeit von Weihen (Circus) auf dem Zug und am Schlafplatz. *Vogelwarte 19*
Bartlett, K. W. W. *pers. comm.* (Five males associating in daytime.)
Bates, D. *pers. comm.* (Association of hunting Merlin and Hen Harrier.)
———— and Raines, R. J. Hunting association of two Birds of Prey. *Cheshire Bird Report.* 1972
Baxter, E. V. and Rintoul, L. J. *A Vertebrate Fauna of Forth.* 1935
———— *The Birds of Scotland.* 1953
Beebe, Frank L. *Field Studies of the Falconiformes of British Columbia.* British Columbia Provincial Museum. 1974
Bell, A. A. *pers. comm.* Results of analyses for organo-Schlorine chemicals. Institute of Terrestrial Ecology.
Bent, A. C. *Life Histories of North American Birds of Prey.* Part 1. 1937
Bergman, S. *In Korean Wilds and Villages.* 1938
Bernis, F. *Aves Migradornis Ibericas.* 1966
Beveridge, F. S. Birds of North Uist. *Scottish Naturalist.* 1918
Bijleveld, M. *Birds of Prey in Europe.* 1974
Birkhead, T. R. A Winter Roost of Grey Herons. *British Birds 66.* 1973
Blake, E. The Hen Harrier—it fears nobody. *Scots Magazine* Dec. 1956
———— Return of the Hen Harrier. *Scottish Field.* Feb. 1961

Blezard, E. *pers. comm.* (Pellet analyses etc.)

Bolam, G. *Birds of Northumberland and the Eastern Borders.* 1912

———— *Wild Life in Wales.* 1913

Booth, E. T. *Rough Notes on the birds observed during 25 years shooting and collecting in the British Isles.* 1881–87

Booth, Graham. *Birds in Islay.* 1975

Breckenridge, W. J. An Ecological Study of some Minnesota Marsh Hawks. *Condor. 37*

Bremner, D. M. and Macdonald, D. Early Fledging of Hen Harrier brood. *Scottish Birds 6.* 1970–71

Brewster, K. W. *pers. comm.* (On many subjects.)

British Birds. Editorial: Birds of Prey—Time for action. 68 Dec. 1975

British Field Sports Society and Council for Nature. *Predatory Birds in Britain*

British Trust for Ornithology and Irish Wildbird Conservancy. *The Atlas of Breeding Birds in Britain and Ireland.* 1976

British Trust for Ornithology. Unpublished Ringing Recoveries of Hen Harriers

Brown, L. and Amadon, D. *Eagles, Hawks and Falcons of the World.* 1968

Brown, L. *British Birds of Prey.* 1976

Bruce, Murray D. *pers. comm.* (per Dr K. W. Brewster). (On the Spotted Harrier.)

Bryant, D. M. *pers. comm.* (Winter records of Hen Harriers in Norfolk.)

Buerschaper, P. Illustrated Catalogue, *Animals in Art*, International Exhibition of Wildlife Art. Royal Ontario Museum, Canada. 1975

Buxton, A. *Fisherman Naturalist.* 1946

Campbell, B. Early Birdmen. *Wildlife and the Countryside.* 1970

Campbell, C. *pers. comm.* (Hen Harrier records at Caerlaverock.)

Campbell, J. W. The Rarer Birds of Prey: their present status in the British Isles. *British Birds. 50.4.* 1957

Chapman, Alfred. Notes and observations on the Birds of North Uist in May 1883. *Scottish Naturalist 73.* 1918

Clare, John. *The Shepherd's Calendar.* (1823) 1964 ed.

Clark Kennedy. *The Birds of Berkshire and Buckinghamshire.* 1868

———— game books, Knockgray, Kirkcudbrightshire. c. 1870–80

Clugston, D. L. *pers. comm.* (Melanistic young Hen Harrier in Wales.)

Colley, L. *pers. comm.* (Hen Harrier records at Caerlaverock.)

Collier, The Birds of the island of Raasay. *Ibis.* 1904

Cox, C. J. *Churchwardens' Accounts.* 1913

Coxon, P. *pers. comm.* (On the Hen Harrier in the Outer Hebrides and south-west Scotland.)

Craighead, J. J. and F. C. *Hawks, Owls and Wildlife.* 1956

Daniel, Rev. W. B. *Rural Sports.* 1807

Delacour, J. *The Living Air.* 1966

Delamain, J. *Why Birds Sing.* trans R. and A. Sarason. 1932

Dickson, R. C. *pers. comm.* (On the Hen Harrier in south-west Scotland.)

———— Prey taken by Hen Harriers in Winter. *Scottish Birds 6.* 1970.

———— Interaction of Short-eared Owl, Kestrel and Hen Harrier over pipit prey. *British Birds 64.* 1971

———— Hen Harriers' hunting behaviour in South-west Scotland. *British Birds 67.* 1974

Dixon, C. *Lost and Vanishing Birds.* 1898

Donnachie, I. L. and MacLeod, Innes. *Old Galloway.* 1974

Doran, G. Some observations on General Nesting Behaviour of the Hen Harrier in Ireland. *Irish Naturalists' Journal. 18–9.* 1976

Dresser, H. E. *Birds of Europe.* 1878

Dunbar, W. (The Fenyeit Friar of Tungland and other poems, c 1500.) in *Collected Poems*

D'Urban, W. S. M. and Matthew, Rev. M. A. *Birds of Devon.* 1895

Durman, R. *Bird Observatories in Britain and Ireland.* 1976

Ennion, E. A. R. *Adventurer's Fen.* 1942

Errington, Paul L. Territory Disputes of three pairs of nesting Marsh Hawks. *Wilson Bulletin 42.* 1930

———— and Breckenridge, W. J. Food Habits of Marsh Hawks in the Glaciated Prairie Regions of North central U.S.A. *American Midland Naturalist 17.* 1936

Evans, A. H. *Fauna of Tweed.* 1911

Fisher, J. *The Shell Bird Book.* 1966

Flint, R. F. *Glacial and Quaternary Geology.* 1971

Forrest, H. E. *The Vertebrate Fauna of North Wales.* 1907

Galushin, V. M. Synchronous fluctuations in populations of raptors and their prey. *Ibis 116.* 1974

Geroudet, P. *Les Rapaces d'Europe.* 1965

Gibson, J. A. Birds of the Island of Arran. *Transactions of the Buteshire Natural History Society 14.* 1955

Gladstone, H. S. *The Birds of Dumfriesshire.* 1910

———— *Notes on the Birds of Dumfriesshire.* 1923

Glegg, W. E. *A History of the Birds of Essex*

Goodin, A. W. *pers. comm.* (Hen Harriers in the Inner Hebrides.)

Gordon, Seton. *Hebridean Memories.* 1923

Graham, H. D. (ed. Harvie-Brown) *Birds of Iona and Mull.* 1890

Gray, R. *Birds of the West of Scotland.* 1871

———— and Anderson, T. *Birds of Ayrshire and Wigtownshire.* 1869

Green, S. *pers. comm.* (Hen Harriers in Orkney.)

Guest, R. *pers. comm.* (On the Australasian Harrier.) (per Dr K. W. Brewster.)

Gurr, L. Communal Roosting of the Australasian Harrier in New Zealand. *Ibis 110.* 1968

Guthrie, D. Some Bird Notes from South Uist. *Scottish Naturalist.* 1919–20

Gwent Bird Report. 1975

Haas. Beobachtungen an Schlafplatz von drei Weihen-arten. *Vogelwarte 19*

Hagen, Y. The Hen Harrier as a breeding bird in Norway. *British Birds 50.4.* 1957

Hamerstrom, F. A Harrier Population Study: in *Peregrine Falcon Populations; their biology and decline.* ed. Hickey, J. J. 1969

———— *pers. comm.* (per Dr K. W. Brewster.)

Hamilton, M. K. *pers. comm.* (Heron attempting to attack Hen Harrier.)

Hammond, Merrill C. and Henry, C. J. Success of Marsh Hawk nests in N. Dakota. *Auk 66.* 1949

Harrison, J. M. *The Birds of Kent.* 1953

Harvie-Brown, J. A. and Buckley, T. E. *A Vertebrate Fauna of Sutherland, Caithness and West Cromarty.* 1887

Harvie Brown, J. A. and Buckley, T. E. *A Vertebrate Fauna of the Moray Basin.* 1895

———— and MacPherson, H. A. *A Vertebrate Fauna of the North-west Highlands and Skye.* 1904

———— *Fauna of the Tay Basin and Strathmore.* 1906

Hiraldo, Fernando. *pers. comm.* (per Dr K. W. Brewster.) (Hen Harrier habitat in Spain.)

Hogg, R. H. *pers. comm.* (Hen Harriers in the Hebrides and South-west Scotland.)

Holloway, Laurence G. *pers. comm.* (melanism in Montagu's Harrier.)

Hope Jones, P. *Birds of Merioneth.* 1972

Hopkin, Nicol. On the Hen Harrier in Arran. *Scottish Naturalist.* 1917

Hopkins, Dr P. *pers. comm.* (Outer Hebrides.)

Hoskins, W. G. *The Making of the English Landscape.* 1955

Ingram, C. The importance of juvenile cannabalism in the breeding of certain birds of prey. *Auk 76.* 1959

Irving, D. L. *pers. comm.* (Counts at Winter roost in South-west Scotland.)

Jakobs, B. Zum überwinter der Kornweihe, *Circus cyaneus* in der südlichen Eifel. *Regulus* 10. 1971

Jardine, Sir W. *Natural History of the Birds of Great Britain and Ireland.* 1834–38

Jenkins, D., Watson, A. and Miller, G. R. Predation and Red Grouse Populations. *Journal of Applied Ecology* 1. 1964

Jones, Ewart. *pers. comm.* (per D. Scott). (Hen Harrier nests and breeding habitat in Ireland.)

Kennedy, P., Ruttledge, R. F. and Scroope, C. F. *The Birds of Ireland.* 1954

King, F. *pers. comm.* (The Hen Harrier in Co. Kerry, Ireland.)

Kinnear, N. B. Note on the Hen Harrier in the Outer Hebrides. *Annals of Scottish Natural History.* 1907

Kirkman, F. B. and Jourdain, F. C. R. *British Birds.* 1932

Lack, D. Ecological Adaptations for Breeding in Birds. 1968

Lawrence, R. D. Wildlife in America (Birds) 1975

Leach, E. P. Montagu's Harrier nesting in South-west Scotland. *Scottish Naturalist* 66. 1954

Lilford, Lord. *The Birds of Northamptonshire and neighbourhood.* 1895

Liljefors, B. *Ute I Markerna.* 1912. (A book of colour plates.)

Lockie, J. D. The Breeding Habits and Food of Short-eared Owls after a vole plague. *Bird Study* 2. 1955

Lockley, R. M. *pers. comm.* (On the Australasian Harrier in New Zealand.)

Lovegrove, Roger. Death on the Welsh Hills. *Wildlife.* August 1976

Lucca, C. de. Bird Migration through Malta. *Ibis 111.* 1969

MacCaskill, D. and B. *Wild Endeavour.* 1975

Macdonald, D. *pers. comm.* (The Hen Harrier in Sutherland.)

———— Further early fledging of Hen Harriers. *Scottish Birds 7.* 1972–73

MacGillivray, D. H. *pers. comm.* (On the Hen Harrier in Arran.) (per L. A. Urquhart)

MacGillivray, W. Description of the Rapacious Birds of Great Britain. 1836

———— *History of British Birds.* 1837–52

Macintyre, D. *Wildlife in the Highlands.* 1936

———— Highland Naturalist Again. 1947

Mackenzie, J. M. D. Montagu's Harrier in Perthshire. *Scottish Naturalist 63.* 1951

Macpherson, H. A. and Duckworth, W. *Birds of Cumberland.* 1886

Macpherson, H. A. *A Vertebrate Fauna of Lakeland.* 1895

McKeand, J. *pers. comm.* (The Hen Harrier in Kintyre.)

McWilliam, Rev J. M. *Birds of the Firth of Clyde.* 1936

Mead, C. J. Movements of British Raptors. *Bird Study 20.* 1973

Meinertzhagen, R. Roost of Wintering Harriers. *Ibis 98.* 1956

Milner, W. M. E. Birds of Sutherlandshire and Ross-shire. *Zoologist.* 1848

Moffat, C. B. ed. *Life and Letters of Alexander Goodman More.* 1898

Mois, Ch. Etude d'un dortoir hivernal de Busards Saint-Martin *Circus cyaneus* en Lorraine belge. *Aves* 3;12. 1975

Montagu's Ornithological Dictionary. ed. J. Rennie. 1931

Moore, N. W. The Past and Present Status of the Buzzard in the British Isles. *British Birds 50.* 1957

Moore, R. *Birds of Devon.* 1969

More, A. G. On the Distribution of Birds in Great Britain during the nesting season. *Ibis. New Series 1.*1865

Moreau, R. E. Ecological changes in the Palearctic Region since the Pliocene. *Proc. Zoological Society, London.* 1955

Muirhead, G. *Birds of Berwickshire.* 1889

Mumford, R. E. *pers. comm.* (Winter Roosts of Marsh Hawks in Indiana.) (per Dr K. W. Brewster)

Nethersole-Thompson, B. *pers. comm.* (Notes on Hen Harriers breeding in East Ross-shire.)

Nethersole-Thompson, D. *pers. comm.* (Notes on Collectors and Hen Harriers in 19th and 20th centuries.)

———— Observations on Nesting Hen Harriers. *Oologist Record 13.* 1933

———— and Watson, A. *The Cairngorms.* 1974

Neufeldt, I. A. Notes on the Nidification of the Pied Harrier *Circus melanoleucus* in Amurland, U.S.S.R. *Journal of Bombay Natural History Society 64.* 1967

New Statistical Account of Scotland. 1845

Nieboer, E. Geographical and Ecological Differentiation in the Genus Circus. Dissertation. Amsterdam. 1973

Oakes, Clifford. *The Birds of Lancashire.* 1953

Ogilvie, F. M. *Field Observations on Britsh Birds.* 1920

Old Statistical Account of Scotland. 1791–97

Ootheca Wolleyana. ed. Newton. 1964

Orton, D. A. *pers. comm.* (The Hen Harrier in Mull and Hunting behaviour.)

Ouston, H. *pers. comm.* (Research on Scotia Illustrata.)

Palmar, C. E. and Greig, J. Montagu's Harrier in Renfrewshire. *Scottish Naturalist 64.* 1942

Palmer, E. M. and Ballance, D. K. *The Birds of Somerset.* 1968

Parslow, J. *Breeding Birds of Britain and Ireland.* 1973

Paterson, J. and Mackeith, T. Pair of Hen Harriers in Renfrewshire. *Scottish Naturalist.* 1915

Paton, E. R. and Pike, O. G. *The Birds of Ayrshire.* 1929

Payn, W. H. *The Birds of Suffolk.* 1962

Peel, C. V. A. *Wild Sport in the Outer Hebrides.* 1901

Pennant, T. *Caledonian Zoology.* 1812 ed.

Pennie, I. D. Birdwatching in Sutherland. *Scottish Birds 2.* 1962–63

Picozzi, N. *pers. comm.* (Hen Harriers in Scotland.)

Porter, R. F., Willis, Ian, Christensen, S. and Nielsen, B. P. *Flight Identification of European Raptors.* 1974

Preston, K. *pers. comm.* (Hen Harriers in Ireland.) per D. Scott

Raines, R. J. Hunting association of two Birds of Prey. *Cheshire Bird Report.* 1972

Ramsay, A. D. K. *pers. comm.* (Hen Harrier records in the Outer Hebrides.)

Randall, Pierce E. Seasonal Food Habits of the Marsh Hawk in Pennsylvania. *Wilson Bulletin 52.* 1940

Ratcliffe, D. A. *pers. comm.* (Hen Harrier in south Scotland etc.)

———— The Peregrine Population in Great Britain in 1971. *Bird Study* 1972

Reading Ornithological Club reports

Renssen, T. A. Social Roosting of Long-winged Harriers (*Circus buffoni*) in Surinam. *Ardea* 1973

Richards, G. A. *Check List of the Birds of Ayrshire.* 1960

Richmond, W. K. *British Birds of Prey.* 1959

Ritchie, J. *The Influence of Man on Animal Life in Scotland.* 1920

Rouwenhorst, J. *pers. comm.* (Hen Harriers in the Netherlands.)

Roxburgh, R. *pers. comm.* (Hen Harriers in Ayrshire.)

Rudebeck, G. Studies on bird-migration based on field studies in southern Sweden. *Var Fagelvärld* suppl. 1. 1950

Russow, K. E. *Bruno Liljefors: an Appreciation.* 1929

Ruttledge, R. F. *A List of the Birds of the Counties of Galway and Mayo.* 1950

———— *Ireland's Birds.* 1966

Ryves, B. H. *Bird Life in Cornwall.* 1948

Sage, B. L. Albinism and Melanism in Birds. *British Birds 55.* 1962

St John, C. *A Tour in Sutherlandshire. 1849.* (1884 ed.)

———— *Wild Sports and Natural History in the Highlands.* 1893

Saunders, Aretes A. A Study of the Nesting of the Marsh Hawk. *Condor 15.* 1913

Saunders' *Manual of British Birds.* ed. Eagle Clarke. 1927

Saxby, H. L. *The Birds of Shetland.* 1874

Scharf, W. C. and Balfour, E. Growth and Development of Nestling Hen Harriers. *Ibis 113.* 1971

Schipper, W. J. A. A Comparative study of prey selection in Sympatric Harriers, *Circus*, in Western Europe. *Le Gerfaut 63.* 1973

———— Over het Voorkomen van Kiekendieven in Flevoland in 1971 en 1972. *Limosa 46.* 1973

———— *pers. comm.* (On the Hen Harrier in the Netherlands.)

———— , Buurma, L. S. and Bossenbroek, P. H. A Comparative Study of Hunting Behaviour of Wintering Hen Harriers *Circus cyaneus* and Marsh Harriers *Circus aeruginosus. Ardea 63.* 1975

Schnell, Gary D. Communal Roosts of Wintering Rough-legged Hawks. (*Buteo lagopus*) *Auk 86.* 1969

Schofield, P. *pers. comm.* (On the Hen Harrier in Wales.)

Scott, D. *pers. comm.* (On the Hen Harrier in Ireland.)

Seago, M. J. *pers. comm.* (On a Hen Harrier breeding record in Norfolk.)

Seebohm, H. *Coloured Figures of the Eggs of British Birds.* 1896

Seigne, J. W. *A Birdwatcher's Notebook.* 1930

Selby, P. J. *Illustrations of British Ornithology.* 1825–33

Service, R. The Diurnal and Nocturnal Raptorial Birds of the Solway Area. *Transactions of the Dumfries and Galloway Natural History and Antiquarian Society 17. 4.* 1903

Shaw, G. *pers. comm.* (On the Hen Harrier in Central Scotland.)

Sibbald, Sir R. *Scotica Illustrata.* 1684

Sim, G. *A Vertebrate Fauna of Dee.* 1903

Smith, R. W. J. *pers. comm.* (Records of Hen Harriers in the Outer Hebrides.)

Smythies, B. E. *The Birds of Burma.* 2nd ed. 1953

Southern, H. N. ed. *Handbook of British Mammals.* 1963

Spencer, R. and Hudson, R. Report on Bird Ringing for 1973. Special Supplement to *Bird Study 22.* 1975

Stanford, J. K. *A Bewilderment of Birds.* 1954

Stephen, D. Article on the breeding and food of Hen Harriers in a Scottish forest. *The Scotsman,* 29.7.1967

Steyn, P. Some Black Harrier records. *Ostrich 43.* 1972

——— *pers. comm.* (On the Black Harrier.) (per Dr K. W. Brewster)

Stirling, W. T. Hen Harrier in Mull in summer. *Scottish Naturalist 63.* 1951

Stoddard, H. L. *The Bob-White Quail, its habits, preservation and increase.* 1931

Strang, P. *pers. comm.* (On the Hen Harrier in Kintyre.)

Svensson, L. Stäpphök C. Macrounus och ängshök C. pygargus—problemet att skilja dem åt. *Var Fågelvärld 30.* 1971

Swann, H. K. *A Dictionary of English and Folklore names of British Birds*

Swann, R. L. Communal Roosting of Robins in Aberdeenshire. *Bird Study 22.2.* 1975

Talbot Kelly, R. B. *Bird Life and the Painter.* 1955

Temperley, G. W. The Natural History of Raasay. *Scottish Naturalist 63.* 1951

Terasse, J. H. *Report on Working Conference on Birds of Prey.* Caen. 1964

Thompson, W. *The Natural History of Ireland.* 1849

Thompson, Sir A. Landsborough. The migration of Birds of Prey as shown by ringing results. *British Birds 51. 1958*

Tibble, J. W. and A. *John Clare,* A Life, 1932.

——— *The prose of John Clare.* 1951

Ticehurst, N. F. Churchwardens' Accounts of Tenterden. *British Birds.* 14.4.1920

Tubbs, C. R. *The Buzzard.* 1974

Tulloch, R. J. *pers. comm.* (Hen Harrier in Shetland.)

Turnbull, W. P. *The Birds of East Lothian and a portion of the surrounding counties.* 1867

Turner, B. S. *pers. comm.* (On the Hen Harrier in Kintyre.)

Turner, Dr W. *Avium Praecipuarum* (1544). trans. A. H. Evans, 1903

Urner, Charles A. Notes on two Ground-nesting Birds of Prey. (Short-eared Owl and Marsh Hawk.) *Auk 42.* 1925

Urquhart, L. A. *pers. comm.* (On the Hen Harrier in Galloway and Arran.)

Usher, R. J. and Warren, R. *The Birds of Ireland.* 1900

Uttendorfer, O. *Neue Ergebnisse über die Ernähung der Greifvögel und Eulen.* 1952

Vaurie, C. *The Birds of the Palearctic Fauna.* 1965

Venables, L. S. V. and U. M. *The Birds and Mammals of Shetland.* 1955

Voous, K. H. *Atlas of European Birds.* 1960

Walker, A. F. G. *pers. comm.* (On the Hen Harrier in Yorkshire.)

Walker, F. J. Roost of Hen Harriers in Walland Marsh. *Kent Bird Report. 2.15.* 1953

Wallace, D. I. M. American Marsh Hawk in Norfolk. *British Birds 64:12.* 1971

Walpole-Bond, J. *Field Studies of Some Rarer British Birds.* 1914

Ward, P. and Zahavi, A. The importance of certain assemblages of birds as information centres for food hunting. *Ibis 115.* 1973

Wassenich, V. Durchzug und Uberwinterung der Kornweihe. *Regulus 9.* 1968

Watson, A. and Jenkins, D. Notes on the Behaviour of the Red Grouse. *British Birds. 57:4.* 1964

Watson, A. Hill Birds of the Cairngorms. *Scottish Birds. 4.* 1966

Watson, (A). Donald. A Raptorial Mystery. *Scottish Birds. 5.* 1969

——— *Birds of Moor and Mountain.* 1972

Watson, A. D. and Dickson, R. C. Communal Roosting of Hen Harriers in Southwest Scotland. *Scottish Birds. 7.* 1972

Watson, A. J. Feeding Ecology of Breeding Merlins, *Falco Columbarius,* in Southwest Scotland. (1973). Unpublished.

——— *pers. comm.* (On the Hen Harrier in Orkney etc.)

Weir, D. N. Insh Marshes. *Birds 4:10.* 1973

Weis, Henning. *Life of the Harrier in Denmark.* 1923

Weller, M. W., Adams, I. C. and Rose, B. J. Winter Roosts of Marsh Hawks and Short-eared Owls in Central Missouri. *Wilson Bulletin, 67.* 1955

Whitaker, D. *pers. comm.* (Note on breeding behaviour.)

White, Clayton M. *pers. comm.* (On the Marsh Hawk's feeding habits in Utah.) (per Dr K. W. Brewster.)

White, Gilbert. *The Natural History of Selborne* (1788). 1924 ed.

Wilhelm, Eugene J. Jr. Marsh Hawk breeding in North-west Arkansas. *Wilson Bulletin. 72.* 1960

Williams, Graham. *pers. comm.* (On the Hen Harrier in Wales.)

Wilson's American Ornithology. ed. Sir W. Jardine. 1876

Witherby, H. F. et al. *The Handbook of British Birds.* 1938–41

Wynne Edwards, V. C. *Animal Dispersal in relation to Social Behaviour.* 1962

Yarrell's British Birds. ed. Newton. Vol. 1. 1874

Young, J. G. *pers. comm.* (On the Hen Harrier in Dumfriesshire.)

Zahavi, A. The Functions of Pre-Roost Gatherings and Communal Roosts. *Ibis 113.* 1971

TABLES

TABLE 1

Harriers of the World: Wing Lengths and Weights*

	Wing length mm		Weight gm	
	male	female	male	female
Spotted Harrier *Circus assimilis*	393	440	400	440
Long-winged Harrier *C. buffoni* (Southern S. America)	413	448		
Long-winged Harrier *C. buffoni* (Guiana)	395	415	391/403	580/645
Hen Harrier *C. cyaneus cyaneus* (West Europe)	338	376	340	500
Hen Harrier *C. cyaneus cyaneus* (East Asia)	348	385		
Marsh Hawk *C. cyaneus hudsonius*	346	390	472	530
Cinereous Harrier *C. cinereous*	329	358		
Pallid Harrier *C. macrourus*	340	371	310	440
Montagu's Harrier *C. pygargus*	365	372	265	345
Pied Harrier *C. melanoleucus*	353	369	290	390
Black Harrier *C. maurus*	344	371		
Marsh Harrier *C. aeruginosus aeruginosus* (West Europe)	393	414	530	720
Marsh Harrier *C. aeruginosus approximans* (New Zealand)	408	425		
African Marsh Harrier *C. ranivorus* (South Africa)	367	383		
African Marsh Harrier *C. ranivorus* (East Africa)	356	365	423	606?

* Wing lengths are from Nieboer (1973), weights are from Brown and Amadon (1968).

TABLE 2
Hen Harrier Prey Identified in Britain and Ireland

MAMMALS
Mole *Talpa europea*
Pygmy Shrew *Sorex minutus*
Rabbit *Oryctogalus cuniculus*
Brown Hare *Lepus europaeus*
Mountain Hare *Lepus timidus*
Orkney Vole *Microtus arvalis orcadensis*
Short-tailed Vole *Microtus agrestis*
Water Vole *Arvicola amphibius*
Wood Mouse *Apodemus sylvaticus*
House Mouse *Mus musculus*
Brown Rat *Rattus norvegicus*
Hedgehog *Erinaeus europaeus*

REPTILES
Lizard *Lacerta sp*
Slow-worm *Angius fragilis*
Adder *Vipera berus*

AMPHIBIANS (*Batrachia*)
Common Frog

FISH Species not identified

BIRDS
Mallard *Anas platyrhynchos*
Teal *Anas crecca*
[Wigeon *Anas penelope*: identification probable (possibly Mallard), full-grown bird attacked, lifted and dropped]
Hen Harrier *Circus cyaneus* (young)
Merlin *Falco columbarius* (young)
Kestrel *Falco tinnunculus* (young)
Red Grouse *Lagopus lagopus*
Ptarmigan *Lagopus mutus*
Black Grouse *Lyrurus tetrix* (young)
Partridge *Perdix perdix*
Pheasant *Phasianus colchicus*
Water Rail *Rallus aquaticus*
Corncrake *Crex crex*
Moorhen *Gallinula chloropus*
Oystercatcher *Haematopus ostralegus*
Lapwing *Vanellus vanellus*
Golden Plover *Pluvialis apricaria*
Snipe *Gallinago gallinago*
Woodcock *Scolopax rusticola* (young)
Curlew *Numenius arquata* (young)
Redshank *Tringa totanus*
Dunlin *Calidris alpina*
Wood Pigeon *Columba palumbus* (young)
Short-eared Owl *Asio flammeus* (young)
Skylark *Alauda arvensis*

Wren *Troglodytes troglodytes*
Fieldfare *Turdus pilaris*
Song Thrush *Turdus philomelos*
Blackbird *Turdus merula*
Wheatear *Oenanthe oenanthe*
Stonechat *Saxicola torquata*
Whinchat *Saxicola rubetra*
Robin *Erithacus rubecula* (young)
Grasshopper Warbler *Locustella naevia* (young)
Whitethroat *Sylvia communis* (young)
Willow Warbler *Phylloscopus trochilus* or Chiffchaff *Phylloscopus collybita* (young)
[Dunnock *Prunella modularis* identification probable]
Meadow Pipit *Anthus pratensis*
Starling *Sturnus vulgaris*
Greenfinch *Carduelis chloris*
Linnet *Acanthis cannabina*
Twite *Acanthis flavirostris*
Redpoll *Acanthis flammea*
Bullfinch *Pyrrhula pyrrhula*
Crossbill *Loxia curvirostra*
Chaffinch *Fringilla coelebs*
Corn Bunting *Emberiza calandra*
Yellowhammer *Emberiza citrinella*
Reed Bunting *Emberiza schoeniclus*
Snow Bunting *Plectophenax nivalis*
House Sparrow *Passer domesticus*

Domestic Fowl (young)
Domestic Duck (young)

Eggs of ground-nesting birds

BEETLES
Dor beetles:
    Geotrupes sylvaticus
    Geotrupes sterconarius
Ground beetles:
    Carabus catenulatus
    [*Carabus pterostichus* (Identification probable)]
Click beetles (*Elaterids*):
    Corymbites cupreus
    Campylus lineatus
Great Diving Beetle *Dytiscus marginalis*
Weevils *Otiorrhynchus sp*

MOTHS
Emperor *Saturnia pavonia* (cocoon)

TABLE 3

(see overleaf, pages 284–85)

TABLE 4

Aggression of Adults in relation to Nesting Success

(1) ALL NESTS (34)

	Number of nests	Successful	Failed
Aggressive (♀ or ♂)	13 (38%)	11 (85%)	2 (15%)
Mild (♀ and ♂)	21 (62%)	13 (62%)	8 (38%)

(2) MOORLAND NESTS

	Number of nests	Successful	Failed
Aggressive (♀)	7 (54%)	5 (71%)	2 (27%)
Mild (♀ and ♂)	6 (46%)	2 (33%)	4 (67%)

(3) FOREST NESTS

	Number of nests	Successful	Failed
Aggressive (♀ or ♂)	6 (29%)	6 (100%)	0 (0%)
Mild (♀ and ♂)	15 (71%)	11 (73%)	4 (27%)

TABLE 5

First year and Older Birds recovered distantly

	Recoveries	Recovered more than 80 km from where ringed
First year	72	29 (40%)
Older	57	21 (37%)

TABLE 6

First year and Older Birds recovered distantly Sept–April

	Recoveries Sept–April	Recovered more than 80 km from where ringed Sept–April
First year	63	24 (38%)
Older	34	18 (53%)

TABLE 3

Analyses for Organo-chlorine Residues

Results expressed in parts per million net weight. (T = Trace)

Monks Wood Ref. No.	Date	County	Circumstances	Sex	Autopsy	DDE
LIVERS						
247	9/63	Argyll	Dead in hills (in heather)	♀	?	5.1
347	1/64	Perth	Dead in turnip field	♂ imm.	Negative	12.3
582	8/64	Orkney	?	♀	Erysipelas	0.2
617	10/64	Wilts.	Shot	♀	Shot	1.2
939	8/65	Orkney	?	?	Nephritis	0.6
1083	3/66	Kincardine	?	♀	Enteritis?	2.5
1534	3/67	Norfolk	Found dead	♀	Negative	6.3
2024	2/69	Lancs.	In convulsions	Ad ♀	Negative ?Lungs	0.9
EGGS						
213	1963	Caithness	?(Egg broken)			3.3
405	1963	Orkney	'Addled' C/4			3.1
482	1964	Merioneth	?			0.5
552	1964	Argyll	'Addled' some young flew			1.7
536	1964	Kirkcudbright	C/6, all failed			1.5
622	1964	Perthshire	?			4.1
772	1965	N. Wales	C/5, all failed			2.0
1049	1964	Northumberland	C/5, 1 fledged			3.1
1053	1964	Northumberland	C/4, 2 fledged			3.7

TDE	DDT	Dieldrin	Heptachlor Epoxide	γ BHC	α BHC	β BHC	HCB	PCB	DME
		0.6			T	T			
(—1.5—)		27.0	0.2	T	T	0.4			0.4
T		T	T	T					
0.3									
		0.2							
		0.2							
0.4		32.0	0.5						
0.2		0.1							
0.1	0.1	0.2	0.1		T	0.1			
—1.3—		0.3	T	T	T	0.2			Average of 4 eggs
—T—		0.1	T	T	T				
—0.08—		0.3	0.1	T	T	T			Average of 5 eggs
		0.6	0.03	T	T	T			Average of 3 eggs
—0.45—		0.5	0.5			0.1			Average of 2 eggs
0.2	0.1		T			T			4 broken only 1 analysed
0.3	0.3	0.5							
0.3	0.3	0.6							

(per A. A. Bell, The Institute of Terrestrial Ecology, Abbots Ripton, Huntingdon)

For tables 4, 5 and 6 see page 283

TABLE 7

First Year and Older Birds recovered distantly May–August

	Recoveries (May to August)	Recovered more than 80 km from where ringed as chicks (May to August)
First year	9	5 (56%)
Older	22	3 (14%)

TABLE 8

Mortality of Hen Harriers after Fledging (from Ringing Recoveries)

age in years	sex unknown	male	female	total	%
0– 1	58	14	13	85	62
1– 2	5	3	7	15	11
2– 3	3	5	5	13	9
3– 4	7	0	1	8	6
4– 5	2	2	0	4	3
5– 6	4	0	0	4	3
6– 7	0	1	2	3	2
7– 8	1	0	0	1	0.7
8– 9	0	0	0	0	0
9–10	1	0	1	2	1.3
10–11	0	0	0	0	0
11–12	2	0	0	2	1.3
12–13	1	0	0	1	0.7

TABLE 9

Prey identified at Nest from a Hide

Prey	Age not known	Juvenile	Total	Percentage
Meadow Pipit	5	1	6	18
Skylark	2	1	3	9
Robin	–	1	1	3
Unidentified small passerine birds	6	5	11	33
Wren?	1	–	1	3
Snipe	1	–	1	3
Red Grouse	–	3	3	9
Pheasant	–	2	2	6
Pheasant or grouse sp.	–	1	1	3
Wood Pigeon	1	3	4	12
	16	17	33	

TABLE 10

Details of Eggs and Young at Hen Harrier Nests on Moorland and
Forest study area in S.W. Scotland from 1959 to 1975

MOORLAND A

Year	Eggs	Hatched	Fledged
1959	5	4	4
1960	5	3	3
1961	(2+)	0	0
1961	7	5	3
1962	5	0	0
1962	2	2	2
1962	5	4	0
1964	6	3	0
1964	6	0	0
1964	(4+)	3	3
1965	(5+)	5	5
1966	(1+)	0	0
1966	(2+)	0	0

MOORLAND B

Year	Eggs	Hatched	Fledged
1968	?	?	3
1969	4	4	2
1970	?	4	0
1971	4	3	0
1972	5	4	0
1973	5	4	0
1973	5	4	0
1974	3	?	0
1974	?	3	3
1975	5	0	0

MOORLAND F

Year	Eggs	Hatched	Fledged
1963	9	0	0

MOORLAND G

Year	Eggs	Hatched	Fledged
1960	5	?	3

FOREST H

Year	Eggs	Hatched	Fledged
1972	4	(2+)	0

FOREST C and E

Year	Eggs	Hatched	Fledged
1962*	5	3	3
1965	2	0	0
1966	?	?	3
1968	5	?	4
1968	?	4	3
1968	?	3	3
1969	?	?	2
1969	?	?	(2+)
1970	?	?	2
1970	(3+)	1	1
1970	?	?	(1+)
1970	?	?	(1+)
1971	4	3	3
1971	4	0	0
1971	?	?	3
1972	2	2	2
1973	?	4	4
1973	?	?	3
1974	5	4	4
1974	5	(2+)	0
1975	5	5	4
1975	5	3	1
1975	?	3	3

FOREST J

Year	Eggs	Hatched	Fledged
1971	?	?	(2+)

FOREST K

Year	Eggs	Hatched	Fledged
1972	?	4	0

* This nest was in unplanted ground within forest and is taken as a 'forest' nest.

TABLE 11
Average Number of Young Fledged per Nest with Eggs in
Moorland and Forest Sites

Locality	Total No. of nests	No. of young	Av. young per nest	No. of successful nests	Av. young per suc- cessful nest
Moorland A	13	20	1.5	6	3.3
Moorland B	10	8	0.8	3	2.7
Moorland (Total)	25	31	1.2	10	3.1
Forest (C.E.)	23	52+	2.3+	20	2.6+
Forest (total)	26	54+	2.1+	21*	2.6*+

* A total of 48 young were known to have fledged from 17 nests, giving an average of 2.8 young per successful nest.

TABLE 12
Number and Percentage of Nests in which Eggs Hatched and young Fledged

Locality	No. of nests	No. (%) nests, young hatched	No. (%) nests, young fledged
Moorland A	13	8(62)	6 (46)
Moorland B	10	8+ (80+)	3 (30)
Moorland Total	25	17 (68)	10 (40)
Forest (C.E.)	23	21 (91)	19 (83)
Forest total	26	24 (92)	20 (77)

TABLE 13
Number and Percentage of Young Hatched and Fledged at Nests from
which Complete Data available

Locality	No. nests	No. eggs	No. (%) young hatched	No. (%) per egg laid	young fledged per young hatched
Moorland A	8	41	21 (51)	12 (29)	12 (57)
Moorland B	6	28	19 (68)	2 (7)	2 (11)
Moorland Total	15	78	40 (51)	14 (18)	14 (35)
Forest Total	8	32	20 (63)	17 (53)	17 (85)

TABLE 14
Failed Nests (with eggs or young)

Locality	No. nests	No. failed	Percentage failed
Moorland A	13	7	54
Moorland B	10	7	70
Moorland Total	25	15	60
Forest (C. E)	25	3	13
Forest Total	26	5	19
All Areas	51	20	39

TABLE 15

Details of Failed Nests with Eggs or Young, with some Reason for Failure

	Nest contents	*Reasons for failure*
MOORLAND A		
1. 1961	2 or more eggs	Probably deserted; eggs found sucked by crows
2. 1962	5 eggs	Unknown; probably crows
3. 1962	4 chicks	Unknown; chicks found dead in nest
4. 1964	6 eggs	Unknown; eggs did not hatch
5. 1964	3 chicks	Unknown; chicks found dead outside nest
6. 1966	1 or more eggs	? deserted; egg found sucked by crow
7. 1966	2 or more eggs	? deserted; eggs found sucked by crow
MOORLAND B		
8. 1970	4 chicks	Probably man
9. 1971	3 chicks	Probably man (poisoned food found at nest)
10. 1972	4 chicks	Probably man
11. 1973	4 chicks	Probably man
12. 1973	4 chicks	Probably man
13. 1974	3 eggs or chicks	Probably man
14. 1975	5 eggs	Unknown; possibly man
MOORLAND G		
15. 1963	9 eggs	Unknown (shepherd blamed Blacked-backed Gulls)
FOREST (C, E)		
16. 1965	2 eggs	Eggs did not hatch
17. 1971	4 eggs	Eggs did not hatch; at least two broken
18. 1974	2 or more chicks	Predation; fox?
FOREST H		
19. 1972	2 or more chicks	Predation; man? (chicks found dead outside nest)
FOREST K		
20. 1972	4 chicks	Unknown

TABLE 16

Analysis of Eggs from Nest No. 4

	Weight	pp'-DDE(ppm)	pp'-TDE(ppm)- pp'-DDT(ppm)	Dieldrin(ppm)	Heptachlor epoxide(ppm)
1.	6.5 g	1.7	——0.2——	0.7	0.1
2.	11 g	1.5	0	0.6	trace
3.	13 g	1.3	trace	0.5	trace

Total Chlorinated residues c. 2.7, 2.1 and 1.8.

(per A. A. Bell, The Institute of Terrestrial Ecology,
Abbots Ripton, Huntingdon)

Tables 17–23 summarise prey identifications made in the breeding season in Areas A, B, C and E. Because the findings from prey remains and pellets are subject to different biases they have been treated separately.

TABLE 17

Prey at Moorland and Forest Breeding Sites (Areas A, B, C and E)

| | | | | Totals | |
| | | | Age | Kills or | In |
Birds	Adult	Juv.	unknown	remains	pellets
Red Grouse	6	24	15	45	5
Meadow Pipit	1	13	16	30	15
Skylark	0	5	8	13	6
Snipe	0	0	4	4	2
Wood Pigeon	0	4	0	4	0
Black Grouse	0	2	1	3	0
		(inc.			
		1 chick)			
Grouse sp?	0	0	2	2	1
Whinchat	0	2	1	3	0
		(incl. 1			
		nestling)			
Reed Bunting or					
Meadow Pipit	0	0	0	0	2
Curlew	0	2	0	2	0
Hen Harrier	0	2	0	2	0
		(nestlings)			
Pheasant	0	2	0	2	0
Pheasant or					
Grouse sp?	0	0	1	1	0
Lapwing?	0	0	0	0	1
Wren?	0	0	1	1	0
Thrush?	0	0	0	0	1
Wheatear?	0	1	0	1	0
Stonechat?	0	0	0	0	1
Robin	0	1	0	1	1?
Grasshopper Warbler	0	1	0	1	0
Whitethroat	0	1	0	1	0
Willow Warbler	0	1	0	1	0
or Chiffchaff		(nestling)			
Starling	0	2	0	2	0
Redpoll or Linnet	0	0	1	1	0
Bullfinch	0	0	0	0	1
Crossbill	1	0	0	1	0

| | | | | *Totals* | |
Birds	Adult	Juv.	Age unknown	Kills or remains	In pellets
Chaffinch	0	1	0	1	0
Chaffinch or					
Reed Bunting	0	0	1	1	0
Yellowhammer	0	0	1	1	0
Reed Bunting	0	0	1	1	0
House Sparrow	0	0	0	0	1
Unidentified					
Passerine birds	0	0	0	0	16
Unidentified birds	0	0	0	0	3
Totals:	8	64	53	125	56

| | | | | *Totals* | |
Mammals	Adult	Juv.	Age unknown	Kills or remains	In pellets
Field Vole	0	0	4	4	5
Shrew?	0	0	0	0	1
Totals:	0	0	4	4	6

Invertebrates
Beetles:

Carabid	3 in 3 pellets	⎫	
Elaterid	4 in 3 pellets	⎬	18 in pellets
Otiorrhynchus (Weevils)	11 in 4 pellets	⎭	

Total Items:

Kills or Remains:	129
in Pellets:	80
	209

TABLE 18
Prey Identified from:

(1) Fresh kills or remains, mainly from nests or feeding places used by well-grown young near nests

	No.	%
Birds	92	96
Mammals	4	4

(a) *Birds*		% of birds
Passerines	38	41
Grouse sp.	47	51
Other medium-sized birds	7	8

(b) *Mammals*		% of mammals
Field Voles	4	100

(2) Observations from a hide at one nest, July–Aug. 1975

	No.	%
Birds	33	100
Mammals	0	0

(a) *Birds*		% of birds
Passerines	22	67
Grouse sp. and Pheasant	6	18
Other medium-sized birds	5	15

(3) In pellets found at or near nests (invertebrates excluded)

	No.	%
Birds	56	90
Mammals	6	10

(a) *Birds* (excluding 3 unidentified birds)

	No.	% of birds
Passerines	44	83
Grouse sp.	6	11
Other medium-sized birds	3	6

(b) *Mammals*		% of mammals
Field Voles	5	83
Shrew?	1	17

TABLE 19
Prey Identified at Breeding Sites on Moorland Area A

				Totals	
			Age	*Kills or*	*In*
Birds	*Adult*	*Juv.*	*unknown*	*remains*	*pellets*
Meadow Pipit	0	4	4	8	0
Skylark	0	3	5	8	0
Red Grouse	1	3	3	7	0
Whinchat	0	2	1	3	0
		(1 nestling)			
Snipe	0	0	1	1	0
Starling	0	1	0	1	0
Total birds:	1	13	14	28	0
Mammals					
Field Vole	0	0	0	0	1

TABLE 20
Prey at Breeding Sites on Moorland Area B (R. C. Dickson)

				Totals	
			Age	*Kills or*	*In*
Birds	*Adult*	*Juv.*	*unknown*	*remains*	*pellets*
Red Grouse	0	1	0	1	0
Hen Harrier	0	1	0	1	0
		(chick)			
Curlew	0	2	0	2	0
Meadow Pipit	0	0	2	2	0
Total birds:	0	4	2	6	0
Mammals					
Field Voles	0	0	4	4	0

TABLE 21
Prey at Forest Breeding Sites, Areas C and E

| | | | | Totals | |
| | | | | Kills or | In |
Birds	Adult	Juv.	Age unknown	remains	pellets
Red Grouse	5	19	13	37	5
Meadow Pipit	1	9	10	20	15
Skylark	0	2	3	5	6
Snipe	0	0	3	3	2
Wood Pigeon	0	4	0	4	0
Black Grouse	0	2	1	3	0
Grouse sp?	0	0	2	2	1
Reed Bunting or					
Meadow Pipit	0	0	0	0	2
Pheasant	0	2	0	2	0
Hen Harrier	0	1	0	1	0
Pheasant or					
Grouse sp?	0	0	1	1	0
Lapwing?	0	0	0	0	1
Wren?	0	0	1	1	0
Thrush?	0	0	0	0	1
Stonechat?	0	0	0	0	1
Wheatear?	0	1	0	1	0
Robin	0	1	0	1	1?
Grasshopper Warbler	0	1	0	1	0
Whitethroat	0	1	0	1	0
Willow Warbler or Chiffchaff	0	1 (nestling)	0	1	0
Starling	0	1	0	1	0
Redpoll or Linnet	0	0	1	1	0
Bullfinch	0	0	0	0	1
Crossbill	1	0	0	1	0
Chaffinch	0	1	0	1	0
Chaffinch or					
Reed Bunting	0	0	1	1	0
Yellowhammer	0	0	1	1	0
Reed Bunting	0	0	1	1	0
House Sparrow	0	0	0	0	1
Unidentified					
Passerine birds	0	0	0	0	16
Unidentified birds	0	0	0	0	3
Total birds:	7	46	38	91	56

Mammals

Field Vole	4 in 4 pellets
Shrew?	1 in 1 pellet

Total mammals:

Invertebrates

Beetles

Carabids	3 in 3 pellets
Elaterids	4 in 3 pellets
Otiorrhynchus (Weevils)	11 in 4 pellets

TABLE 22
Analyses of Pellets Collected from Hen Harrier Nests

The following analyses of 22 pellets from forest nests were carried out by the late Ernest Blezard and are given in full, as examples of detailed investigation by an expert in this field.

1. Field Vole fur and bones.
2. Pipit, Red Grouse feathers, bone scraps. Carabid beetle—? Pterostichus. 2 weevils—Otiorrhynchus, bound molinia.
3. Red Grouse (? juv), feathers, bone scraps. Heather tips and grit from victim, bound with molinia.
4. Feathers and other remains including lower mandible of a Red Grouse chick. Elaterid beetle—Corymbites cupreus Fabr. Small carabid beetle (? sp.). Small quartz grit: large amount Molinia binding.
5. Meadow Pipit including entire leg. 2 Elaterid beetles—Campylus lineatus L. Grass and heather scraps.
6. Pipit remains: scraps of heather.
7. Pipit remains: grass.
8. Small pellet, simply soil with merest pulped feather remains.
9.⎫
10.⎪
11.⎬ Not separable. Red Grouse, Skylark, ? Meadow Pipit. 2 weevils—Otiorrhynchus.
12.⎪ Grass in two.
13.⎭
14. Meadow Pipit feathers. Field vole fur. Beetle fragments.
15. Mostly field vole fur with Meadow Pipit and Snipe feathers and beetle fragments.
16. Meadow Pipit feathers. Beetle remains ? spp. Bulked with Molinia or 'Flying Bent'.
17. Field vole fur, bones and teeth.
18. Pipit and Snipe feathers. Beetle fragments including Elaterids and Otiorrhynchus. Bound with grass.
19. Pipit feathers. Beetle fragments including a Carabid. Shreds of grass.
20. Pipit feathers and bones including part of skull. Peaty soil.
21. Pipit feathers and bones. Minute fragments of beetle. Bits of heather and rush, bound with grass shreds.
22. Feathers of Redpoll or Linnet, scraps of bone. Remains of 6 weevils —Otiorrhynchus—comprising one body and six heads with other bits. Shreds of grass.

TABLE 23
Prey almost certainly Caught in Forest

Black Grouse	3
Pheasant	2
Wood Pigeon	4
Wren?	1
Thrush?	1
Robin	1 (1?)
Grasshopper Warbler	1
Whitethroat	1
Willow Warbler or Chiffchaff	1
Redpoll or Linnet	1
Bullfinch	1
Crossbill	1
Chaffinch	1
Total:	19 (20?)

TABLE 24
Most Numerous Birds of Moorland A in Breeding Season, in Approximate Order of Abundance

1. Meadow Pipit.
2. Skylark.
3. Red Grouse, Curlew.
4. Golden Plover, Snipe, Wheatear, Whinchat, Wren.
5. *Black Grouse, Lapwing, Common Gull, Black-headed Gull, Cuckoo, Carrion Crow, *Rook, *Mistle Thrush, *Song Thrush, Stonechat, *Starling, Pied Wagtail, Linnet, Reed Bunting.
6. Mallard, Kestrel, Pheasant, Oystercatcher, Short-eared Owl, Swallow, Ring Ouzel, Blackbird, Whitethroat, Willow Warbler.

  * Species which, generally, use the area for feeding, etc, only, and do not nest there.

TABLE 25
Nesting Birds on Moorland B
(listed by R. C. Dickson, *not* in order of abundance)

Mallard	Lapwing	Dunlin	Carrion Crow
Teal	Ringed Plover	Common Gull	Wheatear
Greylag Goose	Golden Plover	Black-headed Gull	Stonechat
Kestrel	Snipe	Cuckoo	Whinchat
Red Grouse	Curlew	Short-eared Owl	Meadow Pipit
Pheasant	Common Sandpiper	Skylark	Pied Wagtail
Moorhen	Redshank	Swallow	Reed Bunting
Oystercatcher			

TABLE 26
Most Numerous Birds of 5–15 year old Forest, in Areas C, D and E,
*in Breeding Season in Approximate Order of Abundance**

1. { Chaffinch.
   { Wren, Robin, Goldcrest, Willow Warbler.
2. Wood Pigeon, Coal Tit, Song Thrush, Meadow Pipit, Redpoll.
3. Red Grouse, Black Grouse, Pheasant, Black-headed Gull, Blackbird, Mistle Thrush, Stonechat, Whinchat, Grasshopper Warbler, Bullfinch.
4. Common Gull, Short-eared Owl, Dunnock, Whitethroat, Tree Pipit, Siskin, Reed Bunting.
5. Sparrowhawk, Kestrel, Jay, Chiffchaff, Crossbill.

* The comparative numbers of different species change greatly during the 5–15 year period. Some, such as Meadow Pipit and Red Grouse disappear after the early years while others, such as Wood Pigeon, Sparrowhawk, Jay, Siskin and Crossbill, only appear towards the end of the period. According to D. Moss, Sparrowhawks do not usually nest in the forests until the trees are about 20 years old, but they were quite often seen in summer in 14–15 year old blocks of trees.

TABLE 27
Prey Identified in Pellets collected from the Winter Roost (Roost 1) adjacent to Area C,
in April 1968, February 1971, and February 1975

1. April 1968: 23 pellets

		No. of pellets
Red Grouse	in	5
Unidentified birds	in	9
Field vole	in	4
Mountain hare	in	2
Hare	in	4
Water vole	in	1
Beetles:		
Carabus catenulatus	in	1 ⎫
Geotrupes sylvaticus	in	4 ⎪
Geotrupes stercorarius	in	1 ⎬ 10
Geotrupes sp. ?	in at least	2 ⎪
Dytiscus marginalis	in	2 ⎭
Emperor Moth cocoon	in	1

Note: Additional remains of Red Grouse, field vole, hare, water vole and beetles were found in broken up pellets.

(*Table 27 continued*)

2. *February 1971: 30 pellets*

		No. of pellets
Red Grouse	in	2
Unidentified birds, not larger than Starlings, including 1 Finch sp.	in	22
Unidentified birds of uncertain size	in	2
Field vole	in	2
Pigmy shrew	in	1
Beetles sp. ?	in	2
Moth sp. ? cocoon	in	1

3. *February 1975: 50 pellets*

		No. of pellets				No. of pellets
Red Grouse	in	1	Bullfinch	in	2
? Woodcock	in	1	'Finch-sized bird'	in	3
Skylark	in	3	'Thrush-sized bird'	in	2
? Skylark	in	3	'Bigger than Starling smaller than Grouse'	in	1
Meadow Pipit	in	8	Unidentified bird	in	1
? Meadow Pipit	in	1	Rabbit or Hare	in	11
? Reed Bunting	in	1	Field Vole	in	1
? Dunnock	in	1	Fur, unidentified sp.	in	6
? Chaffinch	in	1			
? Greenfinch	in	3			

TABLE 28

Prey Analysis from Pellets at Winter Roost 1 near Area C,
Collected April 1968, February 1971 and February 1975

	No. of pellets	%
Birds	72	70
Mammals	32	30

(In addition, Beetles were found in at least 12 pellets and moth cocoons in 2)

Birds and Mammals in Pellets (above)

Birds	No. of pellets	% of birds
Red Grouse	8	11
Smaller birds mainly passerines	52	72
Birds, no size identification	12	17

Mammals	No. of pellets	% of mammals	
Mountain Hare	2	6	
Hare	4	12	52
Rabbit or Hare	11	34	
Water Vole	1	3	
Field Vole	7	23	29
Pigmy Shrew	1	3	
Unidentified	6	19	

(In addition remains of Field Vole, Water Vole and Hare were found in an unspecified number of broken up pellets.)

TABLE 29
Numbers of Diurnal Sightings of Adult Males and Ringtails within 24 kilometres of Roost 1 in 3 Winters (Sept.–March)

Year	No. of adult ♂	No. of ringtails	Total
1973/74	16 (76%)	5 (24%)	21
1974/75	20 (47%)	23 (53%)	43
1975/76	13 (30%)	31 (70%)	44

TABLE 30(a)
Monthly Totals of Hunting Hen Harriers sighted within 24 kilometres of Roost 1, Sept.–March (1953–1976)

	S	O	N	D	J	F	M
Ad. ♂'s	8 (40%)	19 (45%)	17 (38%)	21 (47%)	20 (49%)	23 (56%)	6 (32%)
Ringtails	12 (60%)	23 (55%)	28 (62%)	24 (53%)	21 (51%)	18 (44%)	13 (68%)
Total	20	42	45	45	41	41	19

TABLE 30(b)

All sightings, as above

Ad. ♂'s	114	45%
Ringtails	139	55%
Total	253	

INDEX

Abernethy Forest, 66
Adder (Viper) *Vipera berus*, 98
Africa, 28, 34
Alexander, Edwin, 162
Ali, Salim, 27, 149
Andalusia, 46
Andris, K., 237
Angus, 79, 81
Antrim, Co., 64, 84
Argyll, 63, 66, 80, 83, 139, 152
Arkansas, 97
Arran, 63, 68, 80, 83, 87, 103
Arthur, George, 76
Asia, 35, 149
Atlas of Breeding Birds in Britain and Ireland, 65, 83
Audubon, J. J., 148, 151, 162
Austin, W., 180
Australia, 20, 28
Austria, 265
Auvergne, 14, 36, 110
Avium Praecipuarium, 50
Ayrshire, 59, 66, 68, 81, 84

Bahr, P. H., 71, 122
Balfour, E., 17, 40–43, 74, 80, 93, 99, 100, 101, 109, 113, 115–117, 120–122, 124, 127–129, 131, 132, 136–138, 140–143, 145, 148, 152, 156, 179, 181, 186, 193, 210, 237, 250
Balmoral, 59
Bannerman, D. A., 88, 89, 97, 110, 124, 210
Bartlett, K. W., 92
Bates, D. J., 43, 93
Baxter, E. V. and Rintoul, L. J., 58, 68, 72, 79
Beebe, Frank L., 116
Beetle, Great Water *Dytiscus marginalis*, 233, 249

Belgium, 153
Bell, A. A., 104, 139, 155, 285
Bent, A. C., 112, 113, 129, 142
Bernis, F., 154
Berwickshire, 55, 58, 60
Beveridge, F. S., 72
Bijleveld, M., 139
Billie Mire, 55
Birds of Ayrshire and Wigtownshire, 61
Birds of Berwickshire, 55
Birds of Europe and North Africa, 14
Birds of Iona and Mull, 60
Birkhead, T. R., 258
Bittern *Botaurus stellaris*, 55
  American *Botaurus lentiginosus*, 97
Blackbird *Turdus merula*, 258
Blair, H.M.S., 88, 140
Blake, E., 79, 80, 121, 123, 128, 137, 237
Blezard, Ernest, 68, 237
Bobwhite *Colinus virginianus*, 96
Bolam, G., 54, 58, 60, 64, 70, 122
Booth, E. T., 62–63
Booth, Graham, 82
Bournemouth, 54
Breckenridge, W. J., 89, 96, 105, 106, 115, 125, 134
Bremner, D. M., 128
Brewster, K. W., 105, 144, 196
British Birds, 39, 55, 79, 236
British Trust for Ornithology, 65, 150
Broun, Maurice, 150
Brown, Leslie, 116, 126, 128, 129
Brown, Leslie and Amadon, D., 27, 28, 91, 107, 125, 128,

149, 150, 156, 237
Buerschaper, Peter, 164
Bulgaria, 237
Bullfinch *Pyrrhula pyrrhula*, 52, 233
Bunting, Cirl *Emberiza cirlus*, 14
  Corn *Emberiza calandra*, 16
  Reed *Emberiza schoeniclus*, 178, 248
Burma, 15, 26, 28, 149
Bute, Marquess of, 59
Buxton, Anthony, 28, 37, 40, 46, 97, 132, 137
Buzard Saint Martin, 50
Buzzard, Common *Buteo buteo*, 14, 29, 36, 50, 52, 59, 90, 91, 144, 171, 185, 188, 190, 192, 198, 224, 233, 261, 265
  Rough-legged *Buteo lagopus*, 29, 59, 90, 258

Cadbury, James, 100, 126–127, 138, 140, 156
Caernarvon, 69
Cairngorms, 80–81
Caithness, 63, 66, 79, 83, 105, 155
Calf of Man, 150
Campbell, Bruce, 62
Campbell, C. A. B., 86
Campbell, J. W., 43, 70, 72, 78, 101, 176
Cape Province, 20, 23
Chaffinch *Fringilla coelebs*, 99, 116, 185, 226
Chance, Edgar P., 73–74
Chapman, Abel, 71
Chapman, Alfred, 71
Cheshire, 52, 93
China, 28

Churchwardens' Accounts, 52
Clamhan Luch, 61, 70, 72
Clare, John, 53, 54
Clark, Hugh, 170
Clark Kennedy, Capt., 98
Clugston, David L., 44
Coke of Holkham, T., 53
Col de Bertolet, 150
Collett, Pam, 82
Condor, Californian *Gymnogyps californianus*, 258
Connemara, 57
Copeland Island, 150
Cork, Co., 78, 82
Cormorant *Phalacrocorax carbo*, 52, 258
Corncrake *Crex crex*, 99
Cornwall, 69
Cox, J. C., 52
Coxon, P., 251
Craighead, J. J. and F. C., 91, 95, 236, 241, 243, 256
Crawhall, Joseph, 161
Crayfish *Nephrops sp.*, 97
Crichton, A. W., 62
Crossbill, Continental *Loxia curvirostra*, 198, 224
Crow *Corvus corone*, 143, 144, 175, 187, 188, 249
Cuckoo *Cuculus canorus*, 178, 197
Curlew *Numenius arquata*, 92, 100, 101, 102, 106, 174–175, 192, 225, 228, 258

Daeman, B. A. P. J. and Lorig, T. P. J., 143
Dalziel, Frank, 171
Daniel, Rev. W. B., 90
Dartmoor, 55
Deer Red, *Cervus elaphus*, 197
  Roe *Capreolus capreolus*, 198
Deeside, 53, 66, 80, 81, 83, 98
Delacour, J., 23
Delamain, Jacques, 29, 46, 88, 114, 116, 119, 123, 124, 131
Denmark, 46, 122, 149, 152
Denney, Sir Maurice, 74
Descriptions of Rapacious Birds of Great Britain, 57
Devonshire, 55, 69–70, 98
Dickson, R. C., 89, 91, 92, 94, 104, 117, 121, 122, 125, 127, 148, 150, 167, 168, 175, 192, 204, 225, 230, 231, 239, 240, 242, 249,

250, 254, 255, 260
Dipper *Cinclus cinclus*, 52
Diver, Red-throated *Gavia stellata*, 62
Dixon, Charles, 66, 122, 143
Donnachie, I. L. and Macleod, Innes, 54
Donside, 66, 81
Doran, Garry, 120
Douglas, C. E., 125
Douglas, John, 74–76, 100, 124, 126, 129, 140
Dove, Turtle *Streptopelia turtur*, 87
Down, Co., 150
Dresser, H. E., 23
Dumfriesshire, 68, 82, 84
Duncan, Sir Arthur, 171, 173, 176
Dunbar, William, 49
D'Urban, W. S. M. and Matthew, M. A., 105

Eagle *Aquila sp.*, 52, 59, 61, 81
Eagle, Golden *Aquila chrysaetos*, 15, 50, 120, 144, 148, 155, 171, 191, 192, 193, 198, 257
Eagle, Sea *Haliaeëtus albicilla*, 50
Eagle, Serpent *Spilornis sp.*, 28
East Anglia, 33
Edward VII, King, 186
Egg collectors, 72–76
Ennion, Eric, 86, 159
Errington, Paul L., 96, 106
Evans, A. H., 50
Exmoor, 70

Falcon, Greenland *Falco rusticolus*, 90
Falsterbo, 150
Fauna of Lakeland, 55
Fieldfare *Turdus pilarus*, 97, 105, 232, 257
Finland, 97, 153
Fisher, James, 50, 54
Flicker *Colaptes auratus*, 97
Flycatcher, Spotted *Muscicapa striata*, 160, 162
Forestry Commission, 80, 193
Forrest, H. E., 56, 64
Fox *Vulpes vulpes*, 143, 144, 148, 155, 193, 199, 249
France, 14, 23, 36–37, 85, 97, 98, 110, 139, 150, 154, 254, 265
Frog *Rana temporaria*, 104

Galloway, 17, 44, 54, 68, 84,

92, 95, 104, 105, 139, 150, 155, 170–260
Galway, Co., 57
Germany, 34, 98, 152, 154, 237, 238, 254
Geroudet, P., 86, 88, 98, 110, 129, 133
Gibraltar Point, 150, 152
Gibson, J. A., 80
Gilroy, Norman, 73–74
Gladstone, Sir Hugh, 68
Goldcrest *Regulus regulus*, 258
Goldfinch *Carduelis carduelis*, 14
Goldeneye *Bucephala clangula*, 257, 258
Goodin, Alan, 2 7
Goosander *Mergus merganser*, 17, 257
Goose, Greylag *Anser anser*, 89, 128
Gordon, Seton, 92, 101
Goshawk *Accipiter gentilis*, 14, 36, 50, 51, 59, 90
Graham, H. D., 60
Gray, Robert, 41, 60, 70, 71, 101
Gray, Robert and Anderson, T., 59, 61
Grebe, Little *Tachybaptus ruficollis*, 116
Green, Sunniva, 100, 152
Greyhen *Lyrurus tetrix*, 63
Grouse, Black *Lyrurus tetrix*, 63, 98, 197, 207, 226, 248, 249
Grouse, Red *Lagopus lagopus*, 57, 78, 88, 98, 99, 100, 101, 102, 104, 105, 106, 107, 167, 176, 194, 207, 210, 223, 224, 226, 228, 229, 248, 249, 263
Grouse shooting, 59, 261–266
Guinea Fowl, 96
Gull, Black-headed *Larus ridibundus*, 198
Gull, Great Black-backed *Larus marinus*, 171
Gull, Herring *Larus argentatus*, 143
Gunn, J. R., 74
Guthrie, Donald, 101, 103
Gurr, L., 23, 246, 259
Gwent Bird Report, 150

Hagen, Y., 97
Hamerstrom, F., 96, 109, 112, 113, 114, 115, 119, 140, 143

Hamilton, M. K., 194
Hampshire, 69
Handbook of British Birds, 15, 39, 129, 176
Handbook of British Mammals, 100
Hare *Lepus eureopaeus*, 104, 229
Hare, Mountain *Lepus timidus*, 104, 229
Harrier, African Marsh *Circus ranivorus*, 20, 28
Harrier, Black *Circus maurus*, 20, 23, 28, 32, 34
Harrier, Cinereous *Circus cinereus*, 27, 34
Harrier, Hen *Circus cyaneus* (see also Hawk, Marsh)
   age, 140, 156, 186, 221
   aggression, 16, 141–143, 173, 179, 181, 186, 201, 249–250, 283
   albinism, 41–43, 140
   artists view, 158–164
   breeding success, 85, 104–105, 138, 221, 287–288; failure, 138–140, 192–193, 194–195, 201, 288–289
   cannibalism, 136–137
   captive birds, 54–55
   chicks, 130–138, 178, 182; brooding, 207; feeding, 132–134, 207–208, 211; fledging period, 137, 215; growth and behaviour, 209–217; hatching dates, 220; sexing and ageing, 38, 41, 45; sex ratios, 221–222
   clutch size, 138, 190, 287
   conflicts, 126
   copulation, 119, 193
   destruction of, 15, 53, 59, 62, 192, 265–266
   display and courtship, 16, 114–116, 189, 193, 200, 201
   eggs, 128–129
   egg-laying, 128, 179, 188, 220
   encounter with Golden Eagle, 194; with Heron, 194
   first description of, 50
   flight, 87–88, 91
   food, 27, 67–68, 70, 72, 76, 87–89, 91, 95–108, 176, 189, 198, 207–217, 223, 282, 286, 290–298;

carrion feeding, 24, 96, 104–105
food pass, 16, 117, 202
forest nesting habitat, description of, 197–198
game preservation and, 52, 57, 58–60, 61, 63–64, 66, 78, 80–82, 103, 107, 176, 186, 193, 261–266
heather burning and, 194
hearing, 90
history and distribution; in Britain and Ireland, 49–85; maps, 65, 67, 69, 71, 73, 75, 77; world distribution maps, 24, 25; of Marsh Hawk, 26
hunting activity and rhythm, 134
hunting behaviour, 24, 32, 86–94, 226–228
hunting encounters, with kestrels, 93–94
hunting encounters with Merlins, 92–93
hunting encounters with Peregrine, 94
hunting encounters with Short-eared Owls, 93–94
hunting habitats, 35, 94–95; in South-west Scotland, 223–234
hunting at roost, 248
identification, 36–41; of juveniles, 38; of second year males, 40
incubation period, 129
inn sign featuring, 70
juveniles, 38, 147–148, 150, 225
land improvement affecting, 52, 58
local names, 267–268
melanism, 44–46
migration, 149–157
moult, 37, 39–41, 145–146, 186, 211
mortality and causes of death, 156, 285
nests, 120–121, 178; "cock-nests", 121, 122; nest predation, 144, 188, 189
nest building, 119–120, 187, 189, 193
nest finding, 197, 202
nest hunters, 72–76
nest sanitation, 132, 209
nest-sites, 122, 123, 192, 193, 200, 218, 219

nesting neighbours, 94, 175, 187, 192
nesting sociably, 124–125
nest spacing, 125, 191, 202
numbers in Britain and Ireland, 84
pair fidelity, 113
parasites on, 145
pesticides and, 85, 139, 155, 191, 284–285, 289
photographing, 205–206
polygyny, 16, 75, 125–127, 191, 203, 221
pre-nesting behaviour, 113, 184, 189, 202
prey identified in Britain and Ireland, 282; *see also* food
prey selection, 105–107
prey weights, 107, 224
protection of, 70, 72–76, 80, 81, 107, 265
return to breeding grounds, 113, 183, 202
ringing recoveries, 79, 150 et seq., 185, 187, 190, 192, 199, 222, 283, 286; maps 153–154
ringtail, 49 et. seq.
roosting, 114, 202, 225
roosts, communal, 16, 17, 92, 152, 182, 235–260, 299; pairing at, 246–247
sex differences in colour and size, 36
sheep farming and, 59
'skydancing', 114–116
study areas in south-west Scotland, 167–168
territory, 125
voice, 116, 147, 178, 180, 184, 185, 189
weights, 107, 281
wing length, 281
wing-tagged, 256, 260
in winter, 69, 95, 229–260
Harrier, Long-winged *Circus buffoni*, 20, 23, 27, 32, 34
Harrier, Marsh *Circus aerugi-nosus*, 15, 16, 19, 20, 23, 27, 28, 29, 31, 33, 34, 35, 41, 87, 89, 97, 126, 132, 134, 137, 144, 145, 187, 208, 246, 263
Harrier, Montagu's *Circus pygargus*, 14, 16, 17, 19, 20, 23, 24, 26, 27, 28, 29, 30, 32, 33, 34, 36–38, 41, 44–46, 55, 59, 64, 86–89,

Harrier, Montagu's *cont.*
91, 97, 111, 114, 119,
122–126, 129, 131, 134,
137, 141, 144–145, 148,
158, 170, 177–178, 181,
183, 186, 208, 244, 263,
265–266
Harrier, Pallid *Circus macro-*
urus, 15, 16, 20, 23, 27, 29,
32, 34, 37–38, 177
Harrier, Pied *Circus melano-*
leucas, 15, 20, 26, 27, 32,
34, 35, 90, 119, 129, 132,
145, 158
Harrier, Spotted *Circus*
assimilis, 20, 23, 28, 34
Harriers *Circus sp.*
albinism, 41–43
colour, 29–32; and climate,
32
display, 29
distribution maps, 22–26, 30
flight, 19, 20, 28
food, 23–25
food pass, 23
habitats, 20
hunting, 30–31
hybrids, 35
melanism, 32, 43–46
morphology, 31
mortality, 155, 286
origins, 34–35
roosts, communal, 20, 23
sex differences in size, 35
sexual dimorphism, 24
soaring flight, 19
structure, 35
weights, 281
wing lengths, 281
wing loading, 19
Harrison, J. C., 158
Harrison, J. M., 64
Harvie-Brown, J. A., 67
Harvie-Brown, J. A. and
Buckley, T. E., 43, 58, 60,
66, 72, 105, 140
Harvie-Brown, J. A. and
Macpherson, H. A., 64, 66
Hawk, Marsh (North American
Hen Harrier) *Circus*
cyaneus hudsonius, 34, 37,
39, 91, 95, 96, 106, 112,
116, 122, 125, 128, 129,
134, 136, 137, 141, 144,
147, 148, 162, 235, 236,
237, 241, 243, 256
Heron, Grey *Ardea cinerea*, 15,
52, 66, 194, 258
Heysham, John, 54–55, 98, 132

Hiraldo, Fernando, 94
Hobby *Falco subbuteo*, 14
Hogg, R. H., 82, 237, 240
Hollands, F. G., 131
Holloway, Lawrence G., 46
Hoopoe *Upupa epops*, 14
Hopkins, Nicol, 68
Hopkins, Peter G., 82, 102
Hoskins, W. G., 51, 53
Hughes-Onslow, Sir Geoffrey,
171
Humphreys, G. R., 77
Hungary, 98

Ibis, 63
Ingram, C., 137
Inner Hebrides, 63, 82
Invernesshire, 59, 60
Iowa, 96
Ireland, 32, 33, 35, 43, 56–57,
64, 70, 76–78, 82, 84–85,
105, 112, 122, 123, 125,
126, 128, 139, 150, 152,
251, 265
Irish Bird Report, 82, 150
Irish Wildbird Conservancy, 65
Irving, David L., 240
Isle of May, 150

Jakobs, B., 237
Jardine, Sir William, 57, 58,
105, 171, 235
Jay *Garrulus glanarius*, 144
Jenkins, David, 88, 106
Jones, Ewart, 78, 82, 112
Jourdain, Rev. F. C. R., 70

Kearton, Richard, 74
Kent Bird Report, 236
Kent, 52, 63
Kenya, 23
Kerry, 57, 64, 78, 93, 128, 152,
237
Kestrel *Falco tinunculus*, 14,
50, 58, 60, 90, 91, 112,
134, 155, 175, 187, 198,
233, 257
Kincardineshire, 79, 80, 104,
105, 139, 150, 256, 260
King, Frank, 35, 43, 77–78, 82,
93, 112, 123, 127, 128,
152, 237, 251
Kinnear, N. B., (Sir Norman),
71
Kintyre, 66, 80, 83, 84, 102,
103, 110, 128, 141, 150,
187, 197
Kirkcudbrightshire, 32, 49, 81,
84, 98
Kite, *Milvus sp.*, 50, 52, 54, 70

Kite, Red *Milvus milvus*, 14,
265
Knights, Chris, 125

La Brenne, 110
Lack, David, 258
Lakeland, 52
Lammermuirs, 50, 63, 82
Lancashire, 70
Lapwing *Vanellus vanellus*, 57,
89, 99, 100, 105, 115
Lark, 98
Lark, Crested *Galerida cristata*,
88
Lark, Horned *Eremophila*
alpestris, 96
La Rochelle, 14
Latham, John, 54
Lawrence, R. D., 129
Lemming *Lemnus lemnus*, 97
Leveret, 98, 99
Liljefors, Bruno, 159, 160
Limerick, Co., 78
Lincolnshire, 39, 152
Linnet, 189
Lizard *Lacerta sp.*, 97
Lockie, J. D., 107
Lockley, Ronald, 25
Lodge, G. E., 13, 158
Louth, C., 150
Lorraine, 98, 152, 237, 238,
246, 248
Lovegrove, Roger, 265
Lowe, Willoughby P., 27
Lundy Island, 105
Luxembourg, 152, 238, 254

McCann, R. J., 43–44
MacCaskill, D., 93, 126, 145
Macdonald, D., 16, 128
Macdonald, M. A., 99, 100,
131, 132, 137
Macgillivray, D. H., 88, 103
Macgillivray, W., 57, 70, 89, 99
Macintyre, Dugald, 67, 89, 102,
236
McKeand, John, 80
Mackeith, Thornton, 68
Macpherson, H. A., 52, 55, 64,
236
McWilliam, Rev. J. M., 68
Majorca (Mallorca), 46
Mallard *Anas platyrhyncus*, 98,
127, 257
Martin, Purple *Progne subis*, 96
Marquiss, M., 196
Mayo, Co., 57
Mead, C. J., 149, 152, 153
Mearns, R., 196, 203
Meinertzhagen, R., 23, 259

Merlin *Falco columbarius*, 50, 58, 60, 61, 66, 92–93, 127, 134, 138, 155, 176, 198, 209, 249, 259, 264
Mice, 101
Michigan, 91
Mills, Alan (A.W.F.), 81, 172, 178
Milner, Sir William, 62
Minnesota, 96
Mois, Ch., 98, 150, 152, 237, 238, 248, 254
Moffat, C. B., 57
Mole *Talpa europaea*, 98
Montagu, G., 40, 54–55
Moorfoot Hills, 187
More, A. G., 63–64
Morocco, 46
Moss, D., 228
Mouse, Meadow *Microtus pennsylvanicus*, 95
Muirhead, G., 55, 63
Mullins, J. R., 43–44
Mumford, R. E., 236
Munro, Ian (J.H.B.), 143

Naturalist's ramble to the Orcades, 62
Neale, Edward, 63
Netherlands, The, 32, 79, 95, 97, 111, 128, 132, 152, 153, 154, 232, 237, 263, 265
Nethersole-Thompson, Bruin, 104
Nethersole-Thompson, D., 54, 62–63, 66, 69–70, 72–76, 78, 81, 110, 126–127, 128, 129, 140
Neufeldt, I. A., 26, 90, 119, 129, 132, 145
Newcastle Town Moor, 54
Newton Common, Carlisle, 54, 98
New Zealand, 25, 259
Nicholson, E. M., 32
Nieboer, E., 24, 27, 28, 31, 34, 35, 39, 143
Nisber, F., 43
Norfolk, 39, 46, 53, 97, 99, 155
North America, 20, 91, 95–96, 112, 113, 122, 139, 143, 145, 149, 150, 236
North Korea, 28
North Uist, 60, 122
Northumberland, 54, 58, 84, 111
Norway, 79, 87, 94, 97, 105, 124, 143, 152, 154

Oakes, Clifford, 64, 70
Ogilvie, F. M., 72, 99, 150
Oologists' Record, 70
Ootheca Wolleyana, 56
Orkney, 43, 51, 58, 61, 62, 66, 70, 72–76, 79–80, 82, 99–103, 109–110, 113, 122, 126, 136, 140, 141, 148, 155, 260
Orton, Dick, 87, 100, 209
Osprey *Pandion haliaetus*, 52, 61
Otter, *Lutra lutra*, 249
Outer Hebrides, 51, 58, 60, 67, 70–72, 76, 82, 87, 92, 101–103, 110, 122
Owl, Barn *Tyto alba*, 198, 249
Owl, Eagle *Bubo bubo*, 50
Owl, Short-eared *Asio flammeus*, 90, 107, 111, 112, 127, 137, 144, 173, 175, 176, 185, 187, 188, 190, 198, 203, 233, 244, 249
Owl, Tawny *Stvix aluco*, 258

Palmer, E. M. and Ballance, D. K., 64, 70
Parslow, J., 84
Partridge *Perdix perdix*, 61, 90, 98, 99
Paterson, Alan, 238
Paterson, John, 68
Paton, Richmond, 68
Payn, W. H., 70
Peacock butterfly *Nymphalis io*, 212
Peel, C. V. A., 70
Pennie, Ian (I.D.), 66, 78, 81
Pennsylvania, 96, 151
Peregrine *Falco peregrinus*, 18, 50, 51, 61, 66, 74, 81, 94, 127, 148, 171, 198, 209, 249, 264
Perthshire, 14, 63, 66, 78–79, 80, 81, 83, 104, 155, 185
Peterborough, 53–54
Peterson, R. T., 162
Pheasant *Phasianus colchicus*, 92, 96, 97, 102, 105, 106, 208, 213, 226, 261, 263, 265
Picozzi, N., 43, 80, 82, 89, 90, 99, 104, 126, 127, 139, 150, 209, 256, 260
Pigeon, Wood *Columba palumbus*, 92, 203, 209, 212, 214, 215, 216, 224
Pipit, Meadow *Anthus pratensis*, 87, 89, 91, 99, 100, 101, 102, 104, 107, 108, 174, 176, 179, 189, 209, 216, 217, 223, 224, 232, 248
Plover, Golden *Pluvialis apricaria*, 57, 97, 99, 101, 175, 186, 192, 225, 228
Pole traps, 192
Poortvliet, Rien, 164
Portal, Maurice, 170
Prairie Chicken *Tympanuchus cupido*, 128
Preston, Ken, 82
Prestt, Ian, 194
Protection of Birds Acts, 81, 262, 272
Ptarmigan *Lagopus mutus*, 99
Pyrenees, 19

Quail *Coturnix coturnix*, 74
Queen's County, 64

Raasay, 66
Rabbit *Oryctolagus cuniculus*, 70, 76, 96, 97, 99, 100, 101, 102, 104, 105, 106, 226, 229
Rail, Water *Rallus aquaticus*, 105
Raines, R. J., 44, 93
Randall, Pierce E., 96, 236
Rat, Brown *Rattus norvegicus*, 98, 101, 207
Ratcliffe, D. A., 68, 107, 139, 170
Raven *Corvus corax*, 52, 54, 59, 175, 198
Redpoll *Acanthis flammea*, 197
Redshank *Tringa totanus*, 230
Redwing *Turdus iliacus*, 232, 257
Renfrewshire, 68
Richardson, Bernard, 14
Richmond, W. K., 59, 129, 134, 141
Ring Ouzel *Turdus torquatus*, 127, 185, 187
Ripley, Dillon, 27, 149
Ritchie, James, 59
Roberts, E. Langley, 185, 190, 196, 200
Robertson, Duncan J., 76
Robertson, William, 60
Robin *Erithacus rubecula*, 91, 197, 217, 258
Roche, Peter, 82
Rook *Corvus frugilegus*, 66
Ross-shire, 41, 66
Roxburgh, R. (Dick), 196

Rumania, 34
Russow, K. E., 159
Ruttledge, R. F., 57, 77, 82, 122
Ryves, B. H., 16, 46, 70, 178, 181, 183

Sage, Brian L., 41, 43–44
Sahara, 19
St John, Charles, 61, 98
Sandpiper, Common *Tringa hypoleucus*, 207
Sandpiper, Wood *Tringa glareola*, 97
Saxby, H. L., 99, 105
Scharf, W. C., 136, 137, 144, 210
Schipper, W., 23, 27, 32, 35, 87, 88, 91, 95, 97, 98, 106, 111, 126, 132, 134, 181, 227, 232, 237, 263
Scandinavia, 85, 110
Scotia Illustrata, 51
Scotch Argus *Erebia aethiops*, 212
Scott, David, 43, 65, 77–78, 82, 84, 105, 112, 122, 125, 128, 143, 265
Scottish Birds, 192
Seago, Michael, 84
Selby, P. J., 57–58, 62, 235
Selwyn, J. G., 196
Shag *Phalacrocorax aristotelis*, 52
Sharrock, J. T. R., 33, 65
Shaw, Geoffrey, 82
Shelley, Lewis O., 147
Shepherd's Calendar, The, 53
Shetlands, 63, 72, 99, 102
Shooting Times, The, 262–263
Shrew *Sorex sp.*, 230
Shrew, Pygmy *Sorex minutus*, 282
Shrike, Great grey *Lanius excubitor*, 160, 257
Shrike, Woodchat *Lanius senator*, 14
Sibbald, Sir Robert, 51
Sim, G. A., 66
Simpson, Charles, 159
Skirving, Scott, 68
Skunk *Mephitis sp.*, 143
Skye, 63, 64, 66
Skylark *Alauda arvensis*, 89, 99, 102, 104, 107, 174, 176, 179, 182, 189, 201, 211, 224, 230, 231, 232, 248
Slieve Bloom, 77, 82
Smith, Lionel, 68

Smith, Bobby (R.T.), 181
Smythies, B. E., 149
Snipe *Gallinago gallinago*, 57, 88, 102, 175, 194, 207, 236, 248
South America, 20, 34, 149
Southern, H. N., 72, 100
South Uist, 87, 102, 122
Spain, 94, 154, 265
Sparrow, House *Passer domesticus*, 53, 59, 98
Sparrowhawk *Accipiter nisus*, 50, 51, 139, 213, 249, 259
Spencer, R., 140
Speyside, 66
Squirrel, Ground *Citellus sp.*, 96
Sri Lanka, 20
Starling *Sturnus vulgaris*, 88, 99, 102, 104, 107, 174, 176, 179, 182, 189, 201, 224, 230, 231, 232, 248
Statistical Accounts of Scotland, 58
Stephen, David, 103
Stewart, Jimmy, 189, 193, 224, 226
Steyn, Peter, 23
Stoddard, H. L., 236
Stonechat *Saxicola torquata*, 105, 248
Strang, Peter, 80, 102, 125, 126, 128, 141, 150
Suffolk, 33, 70, 99
Surrey, 69–70
Sutherland, 66, 78, 79, 82, 83, 98, 128, 140
Svensson, Lars, 37, 181
Swallow *Hirundo rusticus*, 257
Swan, Whooper *Cygnus cygnus*, 257
Swann, R. L., 258
Sweden, 34, 154
Swift *Apus apus*, 258

Talbot Kelly, R. B., 159
Teal *Anas crecca*, 128, 257
Temperley, George W., 66
Terasse, J. H., 110, 265
Thomson, J. Murray, 78
Thompson, W., 56–57, 64, 88
Thorburn, Archibald, 13, 158
Thrush, Mistle *Turdus viscivorus*, 185
Thrush, Song *Turdus philomelus*, 178, 197, 258
Ticehurst, N. F., 52
Tinbergen, N., 134

Tipperary, Co., 43, 57, 64, 77
Tit, Coal *Parus ater*, 258
Tour of Sutherlandshire, 61
Tree Creeper *Certhia familiaris*, 258, 259
Tubbs, C. R., 52, 224
Tulloch, Bobby, 102
Tunnicliffe, C. F., 158
Turnbull, W. P., 53
Turner, Brian S., 82, 139, 206
Turner, William, 50, 51, 261

Urner, Charles A., 97, 122
Urquhart, Louis (L.A.), 87, 91, 92, 105, 168, 170, 190, 196, 209, 212, 229, 239, 256
Ussher, R. J., 64
U.S.S.R., 26, 98
Uttendorfer, O., 98

Vaurie, C., 34
Vietnam, 23
Viper, *see* Adder
Vole, *Microtus sp.*, 70, 72, 76, 87, 92, 97, 98, 101–106, 187, 190, 223, 226, 230
Vole, Orkney *Microtus arvalis orcadensis*, 99, 100, 105, 107, 108
Vole, Water *Arvicola amphibius*, 99, 248
Voous, K. H., 34
Vulture, Turkey *Cathartes aura*, 258

Wagtail, Pied *Motacilla alba*, 257
Wales, 43, 44, 56, 64, 70, 84, 85, 87, 105, 112, 150
Walker, F. J., 236
Wallace, D. I. M., 39
Walney Island, 150
Walpole-Bond, J., 72–74, 120, 236
Warbler, Grasshopper *Locustella naevia*, 197
Warbler, Willow *Phyllostopus trochilus*, 127, 185, 187
Ward, P., 258
Wassenich, V., 237
Waterford, Co., 57, 64, 77, 82
Waterston, George, 76, 187
Watson, Adam, 80–81, 88, 106
Watson, Jeffrey, 19, 107, 134, 196, 225, 239
Weir, Hon. D. N., 160, 237
Weis, Henning, 17, 23, 46, 122, 137, 143, 145, 181, 208, 244

Weller, M. W., 236
Wexford, 82
Wheatear *Oenanthe oenanthe*, 176, 189
Whinchat *Saxicola rubetra*, 57, 176, 178, 182, 189
Whitaker, Arthur, 74
Whitaker, David, 121, 131
White, Clayton M., 96
White, Gilbert, 53, 55
Whitethroat *Sylvia communis*, 178
Wicklow, Co., 57, 82
Wigeon *Anas penelope*, 89
Wigtownshire, 59, 82, 84

Wilhelm, Eugene J., 97, 129
Williams, Graham, 70, 81, 84, 88, 105, 112
Williams, Michael, 196
Wisconsin, 96, 109, 112, 113, 136, 139–140
Woodcock *Scolopax rusticola*, 104
Woodpecker, Green *Picus viridis*, 52, 258
World Conference on Birds of Prey, 33, 265
Wren *Troglodytes troglodytes*, 127, 197, 207, 230, 248, 258, 259

Wynne-Edwards, V. C., 258, 259

Yellowhammer *Emberiza citrinella*, 98
Yorkshire, 64
Young, Jim (J.F.), 186, 205, 206
Young, John (J.G.), 193
Yugoslavia, 98

Zahara, 46
Zahavi, A., 258, 259